FROM SPECIFICATION TO EMBEDDED SYSTEMS APPLICATION

IFIP – The International Federation for Information Processing

IFIP was founded in 1960 under the auspices of UNESCO, following the First World Computer Congress held in Paris the previous year. An umbrella organization for societies working in information processing, IFIP's aim is two-fold: to support information processing within its member countries and to encourage technology transfer to developing nations. As its mission statement clearly states,

> IFIP's mission is to be the leading, truly international, apolitical organization which encourages and assists in the development, exploitation and application of information technology for the benefit of all people.

IFIP is a non-profitmaking organization, run almost solely by 2500 volunteers. It operates through a number of technical committees, which organize events and publications. IFIP's events range from an international congress to local seminars, but the most important are:

• The IFIP World Computer Congress, held every second year;
• Open conferences;
• Working conferences.

The flagship event is the IFIP World Computer Congress, at which both invited and contributed papers are presented. Contributed papers are rigorously refereed and the rejection rate is high.

As with the Congress, participation in the open conferences is open to all and papers may be invited or submitted. Again, submitted papers are stringently refereed.

The working conferences are structured differently. They are usually run by a working group and attendance is small and by invitation only. Their purpose is to create an atmosphere conducive to innovation and development. Refereeing is less rigorous and papers are subjected to extensive group discussion.

Publications arising from IFIP events vary. The papers presented at the IFIP World Computer Congress and at open conferences are published as conference proceedings, while the results of the working conferences are often published as collections of selected and edited papers.

Any national society whose primary activity is in information may apply to become a full member of IFIP, although full membership is restricted to one society per country. Full members are entitled to vote at the annual General Assembly. National societies preferring a less committed involvement may apply for associate or corresponding membership. Associate members enjoy the same benefits as full members, but without voting rights. Corresponding members are not represented in IFIP bodies. Affiliated membership is open to non-national societies, and individual and honorary membership schemes are also offered.

FROM SPECIFICATION TO EMBEDDED SYSTEMS APPLICATION

IFIP TC10 Working Conference:
International Embedded Systems Symposium (IESS),
August 15-17, 2005, Manaus, Brazil

Edited by

Achim Rettberg
Paderborn University/ C-LAB
Germany

Mauro C. Zanella
ZF Lemförder Fahrwerktechnik GmbH & Co. KG
Germany

Franz J. Rammig
Paderborn University
Germany

Library of Congress Cataloging-in-Publication Data

A C.I.P. Catalogue record for this book is available from the Library of Congress.

From Specification to Embedded Systems Application, Edited by Achim Rettberg, Mauro C. Zanella and Franz J. Rammig

   p.cm. (The International Federation for Information Processing)

ISBN 978-1-4419-3899-2   eISBN 978-0-387-27559-8

   Printed on acid-free paper.

9 8 7 6 5 4 3 2 1
springeronline.com

Contents

3   Software Synthesis and Power Management

4   Formal Verification and Testing

5   Special Aspects in System Design

Preface

The International Embedded Systems Symposium (IESS) is an IFIP TC-10 Working Conference that brings together experts from industry and academia to create through presentations and discussions an atmosphere conductive to innovation and development. The discrepancy between the venue conference, Amazon forest in Manaus (Brazil), and the technological research provides an harmonic atmosphere for the technology transfer within the participants.

As almost no other technology, embedded systems is an essential element of many innovations in automotive engineering. New functions and improvements of already existing functions, as well as the compliance with traffic regulations and customer requirements, have only become possible by the increasing use of electronic systems, especially in the fields of driving, safety, reliability, and functionality. Along with the functionalities that increase in number and have to cooperate, the complexity of the entire system will increase.

Synergy effects resulting from distributed application functionalities via several electronic control devices, exchanging information through the network bring about more complex system architectures with many different sub-networks, operating with different velocities and different protocol implementations.

To manage the increasing complexity of these systems a deterministic behaviour of the control units and the communication network must be provided for, in particular when dealing with a distributed functionality, resource management or redundant realization.

The topics which have been chosen for this working conference are very timely: design methodology, modeling, specification, software synthesis, power management, formal verification, testing, network, communication systems, distributed control systems, resource management and special aspects in system design.

We all hope that this working conference in this beautiful part of the world will be a memorable event to all involved.

Achim Rettberg, Mauro C. Zanella and Franz J. Rammig

IFIP TC10 Working Conference: International Embedded Systems Symposium (IESS), August 15-17, 2005, Manaus, Brazil

General Chairs
Achim Rettberg
Mauro C. Zanella

Co-Chairs
Franz J. Rammig

Program Committee
Jürgen Becker, University Karlsruhe (Germany)
Michael Becker, Dr. Ing. h.c. F. Porsche (Germany)
Brandon Blodget, Xilinx Research Labs (USA)
Rainer Dömer, University of Irvine (USA)
Nikil Dutt, University of Irvine (USA)
Rolf Ernst, Technical University Braunschweig (Germany)
Uwe Honekamp, Vector Informatik (Germany)
Ricardo Jacobi, UNB (Brazil)
Kane Kim, University of Irvine (USA)
Bernd Kleinjohann, C-LAB (Germany)
Hermann Kopetz, Technical University Vienna (Austria)
Horst Krimmel, ZF Friedrichshafen (Germany)
Jean-Claude Laprie, LAAS (France)
Thomas Lehmann, Philips (Germany)
Joachim Lückel, University Paderborn (Germany)
Carlos Pereira, UFRGS (Brazil)
Franz Rammig, University Paderborn (Co-Chair, Germany)
Achim Rettberg, C-LAB (Chair, Germany)
Stefan Schimpf, Robert Bosch Ltda. (Brazil)
Joachim Stroop, dSPACE (Germany)
Flavio R. Wagner, UFRGS (Brazil)
Mauro Zanella, ZF Lemförder Fahrwerktechnik (Chair, Germany)

Organizing Committee
Achim Rettberg and Mauro C. Zanella

Sponsoring and Co-Organizing Institution
    IFIP TC 10, WG 10.5 and SIG-ES
    ZF Lemförder Fahrwerktechnik GmbH & Co. KG

Acknowledgement

    Special thanks to the authors for their contributions, and for the Program Committee members for their time reviewing the contributions. Last but not least, we would like to thanks the IFIP organization and ZF Lemförder for the support and sponsoring this event.

DOMAIN-CROSSING SOFTWARE PRODUCT LINES IN EMBEDDED, AUTOMOTIVE SYSTEMS

Stefan Kubica
Audi Electronics Venture GmbH
stefan.kubica@audi.de

Wolfgang Friess
AUDI AG
wolfgang.friess@audi.de

Christian Allmann
Audi Electronics Venture GmbH
christian.allmann@audi.de

Thorsten Koelzow
Audi Electronics Venture GmbH
thorsten.koelzow@audi.de

Abstract: The development of software-functions in the automotive domain is subject to multiple conditions. These conditions are for example the rising number of various functions in the car, the simultaneously increasing cost pressure and shortened development cycles. To come up with these conditions, an improvement of reuse is very promising. In this paper the point of view is that a software-function is separable in two domains, the application-domain and the standard-software-domain. Looking at the reuse activities of both domains together provides more generality and synergy-effects. A reuse approach that fits both domains is the approach of domain-crossing software product lines. This paper reports about an ongoing research project about adapting of software product lines in the specific domains and describes a concept for bringing them together. For proving the concept an accompanying tool was implemented and is introduced afterwards.

Keywords: Software Product Lines, Standard-Software, Application-Software, Reuse, Cross-Domain

1.   INTRODUCTION

The demand of customers for new innovative functions in cars keeps on rising. Therefore, the car manufacturers equip their new types with a lot of new software functions. Figure 1 points out the raising complexity of functions e.g. in the infotainment sector. The manufacturer has to deal with multiple factors influencing the development of functions. On the one hand there is increasing cost pressure and shortened development cycles and on the other hand there is a demand for more quality and personalisation of the functions by customers.

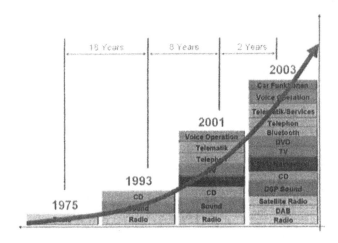

Figure 1.   Increasing complexity, e.g. in the infotainment domain [Schleuter, 2002]

As described in [Endres and Rombach, 2003], reuse of software reduces cycle time and increases productivity and quality. Therefore, getting the possibility of a more efficient reuse of software-functions could solve the described problems. In this paper software reuse means, using parts of a function more than once. The challenge is to decide the kind of reuse and what is required to achieve it. A short introduction in the automotive development of functions is given. By examination the whole domain more precisely it occurs that one possible point of view is to share the whole domain of function development into two domains to handle with, the application-domain and the standard-software-domain. Figure 2 shows the two prevalent domains.
The application-domain contains the process of developing the functionality. There are activities in the automotive domain to implement a model-based development process. As described in [Langenwalter and Erkkinen, 2004] the model-based development of functions has several advantages like e.g. iterative development steps, early tests, the possibility of reuse and the generation of production code from models.

The standard-software-domain contains the system-components needed for the ECU (Electronic Control Unit). These components are e.g. the operating system, drivers and the network management. Figure 2 shows an overview of the included components. The configuration of this components depends on the requirements of the functions and on the given hardware-architecture.

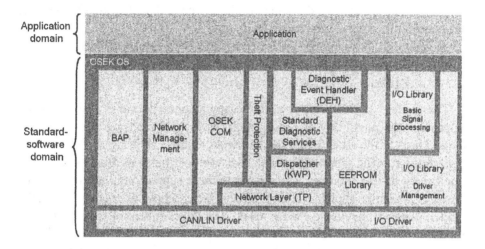

Figure 2. Standard Software Core of the Volkswagen-Group

To come up with the mentioned more effective reuse, it is necessary to support the development-process with additional software development techniques. We propose not only a separate solution for each domain, but a cross-domain solution. By combining reuse-techniques of each domain, it is possible to reach more generality and to benfit from synergy-effects. The method of software product lines offers some answers to the given problems. As described in [Northrop, 1998] software product lines help to reach goals as for example high quality, quick time to market, low cost production and low cost maintenance. To reach these goals would give the development process the improved efficiency and productivity demanded and also an instrument to handle the raising variability. The literature offers several methods for implementing a software product line, like FODA (Feature-Oriented Domain Analyse [Kang et al., 1990]), FeatuRSEB (Feature Reuse-Driven Software Engineering Business [Boellert, 2002]) and FAST (Family-Oriented Abstraction, Specification, and Translation [Weiss and Lai, 1999]). The challenge is to develop an adequate method useable for both described domains. In this paper, a concept of a software product line-framework which combines the software product lines of the application-domain with using model-parts and the standard-software-domain with the possibility to configure the standard-software components. Furthermore, the first ready steps and the resulting tool-chain are described.

2.   PRECONDITIONS FOR DOMAIN-CROSSING PRODUCT LINES

For combining the two domains of application and standard-software, first we consider the specific aspects of both.

2.1   Application Development with Software Product Lines

The model-based development in the application-domain is a first step for improving the possibility of reuse. Reasons for this are for example the independence of the model from the hardware because of using a generator for getting the specific production code. Also the possibility of distributed development by having modules and clear interfaces support reuseability. But to develop the entire application as a model, for example as Matlab/Simulink-model, does not inevitable ensure reuse. The development of various models for various variants of an application contains several disadvantages. These disadvantages are for example the number of possible model-variants of an application is increasing very fast. The problem is, that basic changes of the functionality of the application have to be made in all existing model-variants. The introduction of an additionally functionality in the application can double the number of possible variants and being able to reuse one of the existing model-variants requires expert-knowledge to get the model that fits best.

As described in [Hein et al., 2000] the software product line-approach offers some answers to the given problems. To split the functionality of an application into separate features gives the possibility to generate different variants from one common base. For getting an useable general approach, multiple steps have to be defined. In Figure 3 these steps are shown. In [Böckle et al., 2004] is described, that in general there are two parts inside the process of a software product line development.

Domain engineering includes all activities connected with the development of the software product line. These activities are:

1 Domain scoping: In this step the possible variants of the application were traced.

2 Define features: Extraction of the features and decision if a feature is a common or a variable one.

3 Deposit features with logic: The dependencies between the features were deposit with a mathematical logic. This logic is implemented with an adapted feature-tree notation.

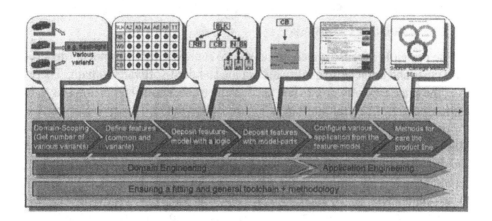

Figure 3.   Concept for introducing the software product line for application-development

> 4 Depositing the features with model-parts. These model-parts have to represent the requirements of the respective feature.

The first two steps are realised with an adapted approach of the Fraunhofer IESE (Institut Experimentelles Software Engineering) called CaVE (Common and Variable Extraction [John and Dörr, 2003]). Within a common project the CaVE-approach was adapted and gives methods for extracting features from function-specifications methodology. The realisation of the third step, the common feature-notation for both domains, is described in a following section. Step 4 is subject to future work.

Application engineering includes all activities connected with the use of the developed software product line. These activities are:

1 • Configurator: Giving the possibility of choose features of the software product line to match the several requirements of a new application demanded.

   • Composing-algorithm: Put together the model-parts connected with the selected features to an entire model.

2 Test and Care: Methods for testing the chosen combinations and for carrying the product line (e.g. adding new features to the product line)

The configurator is part of the tool-chain described in one of the following sections. The composing-algorithm is connected to the depositing of the features with model-parts and is also future work.

2.2   Standard-Software Configuration with Software Product Lines

The principle of reuse is a common way to shorten the development time, reduce costs and to increase quality also in the standard-software domain. Therefore, the standard-software, as it is used in electronic control units nowadays, is composed out of several moduls as Figure 2 shows. Only the modules needed for the specific control unit are integrated into the standard-software system. This adaption is necessary to reduce the memory consumption of the software and therefore to reduce costs.

To increase the reusabiltiy of the standard-software modules, it is necessary to set parameters of the moduls to the specific usage of the module. With this mechanism of parametrisation it is possible to reuse standard-software modules in several electronic control units. The challenge in the domain of standard-software is not to enable different variants of the system, but to manage the complexity of the whole standard-software system and the dependencies between the parameters of the modules.

The concept of modelling commonalities and variabilities of many, similar software products with feature models can help to face this challenge. The usability of a feature model-based configuration of an OSEK-conform operating system is already shown in [Czarnecki et al., 2002]. OSEK is the german abbreviation for 'Open Systems and the Corresponding Interfaces for Automotive Electronics' and stand for a joint project in the German automotive industry aiming at an industry standard for an open-ended architecture for distributed control units in vehicles.

One result is the standard for automotive operating systems. Czarnecki and collegues showed that the parameters of an OSEK operating system can represented with feature models and a configuration file can be generated with techniques of template-based code generation. The usage of product line approaches in the embedded domain is also shown by [Beuche, 2003]. He introduced an approach for composing embedded systems with feature models to represent variabilities of similar systems.

To enable a feature model-based configuration for standard-software the given concepts have to be extended to model not only the operating system, but all standard-software modules. Beside the necessity of realizing a generation for different configuration files another challenge has to be solved. By extending the concept to several moduls the importance of considering relations and dependencies between different parameters is increasing. The possibilities of current feature model notations to describe relations are rather limited and have to be extended. An approach to formalize relations in feature models is shown in [Streitferdt et al., 2003]. There, an adaption of OCL (Object Constraint Language [OMG, 2003]) is used to describe relations and dependencies. The application of such concepts to the standard-software domain is still missing and one aim of our ongoing research.

3.   REALISATION

A common feature model notation, fitting the requirements of both domains is the first step to bring them together. A concept for a common notation and a tool are introduced in the following.

3.1   Concept

The previous sections have shown, that the two domains have many commonalities but also many differences. These commonalities and differences must be addressed by a common feature model notation to enable a common modelling of the two domains. For the application domain there are three main specialities. Because of the model-based development in this domain, it must be possible to establish a link between features and the corresponding model fractal which implements the feature. Beside that, it must be possible to define unique interfaces of the model. One way to realize this, is to model the interface signals themselves as features. To integrate a model-based product line for applications in a real world development process, it must furthermore be possible to link process documents like requirements or test cases to the features. The link of requirements is necessary to enable the automatic creation of a product concept catalogue for the generated application.

As shown in section 2.2, the purpose of feature modelling in the standard-software domain is to model the parameters of the different moduls. These parameters often have to be defined as values. An example will illustrate this problem. One parameter of a CAN driver modul could be the size of the communication buffer. So to configure this modul, the parameter *CAN-BUFFERSIZE* has to be defined with a value within a given range. Beside that, there could be a higher level modul, for example a transport protocol, which communicates with the can driver. Then the *TP-BUFFERSIZE* of the second module has to have the same value as the first parameter for compatibility reasons. This short example shows, that in the standard-software domain, there are parameters and relations between parameters. This has to be addressed by a feature model notation.

To enable a common modelling we combined several aspects of existing feature model notations and extended them:

- The basis for our notation is the orignial FODA notation. Feature modeling was proposed as part of the Feature-Oriented Domain Analysis method (FODA). The idea of the FODA notation is to model optional and mandatory features of a system in a hierarchical tree.

- The possibility of modelling feature parameters was added by Czarnecki with the introduction of attributes [Czarnecki et al., 2002]. These attributes are a way to represent a choice of values belonging to a feature. For our notation, it is also possible to add parameters to the features.

- We also added the principle of feature cardinalities from Czarnecki [Czarnecki et al., 2004]. With cardinalities it is possible to model how many instances of a feature must be implemented in the system.

- A possibility, which is not given by existing notations is to add references to all kinds of files to a feature. This is necessary to add documents from the development process to the features, like mentioned before. Also for feature relations it is possible to add references to files in which the relation is described in a formal way.

This proposal of a common notation is integrated in an experimental tool described in the following section. A common editor for feature modelling of both domains and a common output file to store the selected features is also part of a common method for a product-line based development of applications and standard-software.

3.2   Cross-Domain SPL-Tool

An important point to ensure the usability of a product line-based approach for the development of electronic control units is an adequate tool support. On this account we have developed a tool to support the requirements of a common notation for several domains like they are shown in the previous section. Such a cross domain software product line tool (CDS-Tool) is introduced in this section. An overview of the tool structure is shown in Figure 4.

The CPS-Tool has several features differentiating it from other tools, like Consul [Beuche, 2003] or the FeaturePlugin for Eclipse [Antkiewicz and Czarnecki, 2004]. First of all, the tool is integrated in the company software process. This means, the tool is part of the development work flow. To avoid isolated application relevant artefacts like specification documents, model files or code fragments are included in the software product line approach. The tool makes allowance for this requirement by applying such artefacts to each single feature. During feature specification in the domain engineering for each specified relation between single features (e.g require, exclude relation) the basic development artefacts can be deposit. This preparation has the advantage that feature dependencies and constraints can be verified by the deposit specification documents. These documents are stored in the project database. Any change in these documents is directly observable.

The deposit artefacts advise the engineer if his reached decisions are conform

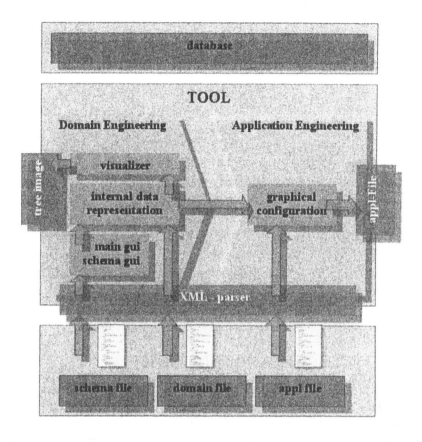

Figure 4.   Overview of the structure of the CDS-Tool

to the specification documents. Currently this step must be executed by hand; in the future a constraint checker will automate this step. Beneath the deposit conditions for feature relations it is possible to supplement feature parameters with documents (as file references or simple logical terms). All these additional feature specifications (condition, implementation, description files) help to ensure traceability in the software development process. Figure 5 shows the editor to add references to several files in the tool. They help to facilitate project version management and support product maintainability. To increase the acceptance of the tool from developers, it is moreover possible to view a feature model in a graphical tree-view. With all of this, the requirements from section 3.1 are addressed by the CDS-Tool.

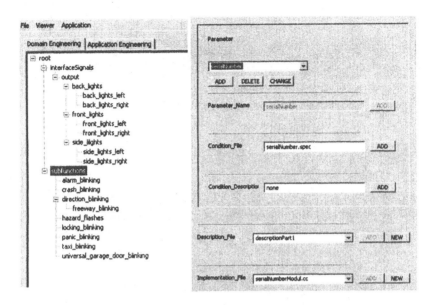

Figure 5.   Treeview and Dialog of the Domain-Engineering-Part of the CDS-Tool

4.   CONCLUSION AND OUTLOOK

This paper presented an ongoing research out of the field of adapting soft-ware product lines to the automotive domain. After an introduction to the different domains in this area, we showed that a common feature model nota-tion is the first step to bring different domains together and gave a proposal for such a notation.

The next step of our work is to complete the tool chain for the whole genera-tion process. For this, we have to solve the problem of composing model fractals of a model-based application family to different family-members. In the do-main of standard-software, we have to generate configuration files out of the feature model to use existing standard-software.

In parallel we will go on with case studies to gain more experience in com-bining models of different domains. Especially interactions between the two domains are of special importance to get the biggest benefit of the synergy effects mentioned in the introduction. The standard-software offers its fea-tures, modelled in the feature model, to the application. So on the other side, the application features have to express their requirements to the features of the standard-software to enable a semi-automatic preselection of standard-software features. Beside that, there must be a mapping of these requirements to the features of the standard-software. The concept of such a cross-domain middleware will be part of our future work.

REFERENCES

Antkiewicz, Michal and Czarnecki, Krzysztof (2004). FeaturePlugin: Feature Modeling Plug-In for Eclipse. http://www.swen.uwaterloo.ca/ kczarnec/etx04.pdf.

Böckle, G., Knauber, P., Pohl, K., and Schmied, K. (2004). *Software Produktlinien - Methoden, Einführung und Praxis.* dpunkt.verlag GmbH, Heidelberg.

Beuche, Danilo (2003). *Composition and Construction of Embedded Software Families.* PhD thesis, Otto-von-Guericke Universität Magdeburg.

Boellert, K. (2002). *Objektorientierte Entwicklung von Software-Produktlinien zur Serienferti-gung von Software-Systemen.* Technical University of Illmenau, Illmenau.

Czarnecki, Krzysztof, Bednasch, Thomas, Unger, Peter, and Eisenecker, Ulrich W. (2002). Gen-erative Programming for Embedded Software: An Industrial Experience Report. In *GPCE*, pages 156–172.

Czarnecki, Krzysztof, Helsen, Simon, and Eisenecker, Ulrich W. (2004). Staged Configuration Using Feature Models. In *SPLC*, pages 266–283.

Endres, A. and Rombach, D. (2003). *A Handbook of Software and System Engineering.* Pearson Addison Wesley, England, Harlow.

Hein, A., Schlick, M., and Vinga-Martins, R. (2000). *Applying Feature Models in Industrial Settings.* P. Donohoe, Software Product Lines - Experience and Research Directions, Kluwer Academic Publishers.

John, I. and Dörr, J. (06/2003). *Elicitation of Requirements from User Documentation.* Proceed-ings of REFSQ'03, Klagenfurt.

Kang, Kyo C., Cohen, Sholom G., Hess, James A., Novak, William E., and Peterson, A. Spencer (1990). Feature-Oriented Domain Analysis (FODA) Feasibility Study. Technical report, Carnegie Mellon University, Software Engineering Institute.

Langenwalter, J. and Erkkinen, T. (02/2004). *Entwicklung von Embedded Systemen fuer Auto-mobile.* auto & elektronik, Heidelberg.

Northrop, L. (1998). *Essentials of successful product line practise.* Ground System Architecture Workshop, California.

OMG (2003). UML 2.0 OCL Specification. http://www.omg.org/docs/ptc/03-10-14.pdf.

Schleuter, W. (01/2002). *Herausforderungen der Automobil-Elektronik.* Köln: IKB Un-ternehmerforum, Köln.

Streitferdt, Detlef, Riebisch, Matthias, and Philippow, Ilka (2003). Details of Formalized Rela-tions in Feature Models Using OCL. In *ECBS*, pages 297–304.

Weiss, D. M. and Lai, C. T. R. (12/1999). *Software Product-Line Engineering: A FamilyBased Software Development Process.* Addison-Wesley Pub Co.

MECHATRONICS DESIGN AND VERIFICATION
Using VHDL-AMS to Bridge the Gap

Thomas Heurung
Mentor Graphics

Abstract: Mechanical parts that are controlled by electronic circuitry and software are commonly referred to as mechatronic components and systems. The design of such systems is classically divided into the design of the mechanical hardware, the electronic circuitry and the software - with little communication going on between the different engineering domains. This separation often results in communication problems based on incomplete or incorrect specifications and an inability to optimize the complete system instead of just certain aspects. Part of the reason for this failure is that although tools and methodologies are available that address the domain specific tasks, few tools are available that cross domain borders. This paper illustrates a VHDL-AMS simulation-based design methodology for software controlled, electro-mechanical components using an autonomous robot as an example. Starting with considerations for the overall architecture the design is successively augmented with implementation details that allow the verification of software control algorithms, the design and layout the electronics circuitry as well as the specification of parameters for the mechanical and electro-mechanical hardware. The example used is the design of a TekBot™, which is part of the platforms for learning™ concept created by the Oregon State University to teach students about digital logic and analog circuitry. VHDL-AMS based simulation is used to facilitate this task by making good decisions about the required components as well as designing and verifying the implementation. The same design is used for both PCB layout and as a testbench for the software for debugging the software algorithms. The final simulated design includes models of mechanical and electro-mechanical hardware, digital and analog electronic circuitry at behavioral and component levels as well as software executed on an instruction set model.

Keywords: Mechatronic Design, VHDL-AMS

1.   INTRODUCTION

The TekBot™ is part of the platforms for learning™ concept created by Oregon State University to teach students about digital logic and analog circuitry. This paper uses the Tekbot (figure 1) design to illustrate a design and verification methodology for a mechatronic system – an autonomous automotive robot. VHDL-AMS, the Analog-Mixed-Signal extension (IEEE 1076.1) of the digital hardware description language VDHL, was used as the main modeling language. Starting with the drivetrain, the complete system was modeled and simulated with VHDL-AMS, moving from abstract, behavioral level to SPICE transistor level. The goals of simulating on different abstraction levels vary from estimating the power consumption to verifying the software control algorithm. The participating students modeled some of the components directly in VHDL-AMS, some by using a macro modeling approach and some by using SPICE components.

Figure 1. The Tekbot

Some of the requirements for the Tekbot are:
- Act autonomously
- Sort randomly distributed balls (black and orange) into color-coded corners of a 3m by 3m arena
- A blue diagonal between the colored corners is available for navigation

2. ARCHITECTURE

Based on the requirements, the design of the general architecture is straightforward. Sensors provide data about the environment to the control system that controls the movement of the Tekbot and activates the ball capturing system. At this stage of the design, the engineer needs to make decisions such as the kind of sensors to use for the color detection, how to find out the direction and color of the ball that's closest to the current position, and what propulsion system offers enough speed and control at the lowest cost. Design variants and their impact on cost, power consumption and performance need to be analyzed.

Budget constraints led to a sensor system consisting of an ultra-sonic rangefinder and three-color LEDs with photo-sensors. Using the LEDs to emit different colored light pulses and measuring the reflected light intensity allows identifying the color of an object. In the case of the Tekbot this is used to detect the color of a captured ball and the color of the current location in the arena.

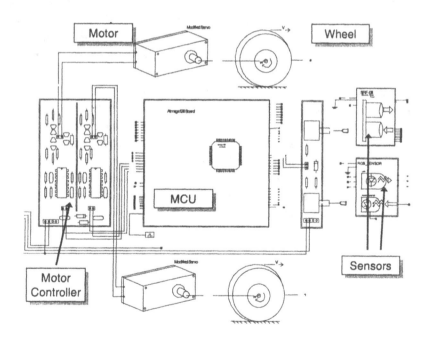

Figure 2. Tekbot Architecture

For this level of analysis, the simulation needs to be fast and not very detailed. The models need to work with fairly abstract parameters, such as energy consumption and delivered torque or the range of sonic sensors. This can be handled in VHDL-AMS with ideal, highly abstract models for the power supply, color sensors and range finder, control unit, motor controller, motor and wheel.

As the verification of the software algorithm for the control of the Tekbot is a central part of the simulation a realistic testbench is required. In this case the testbench is a model of the arena, including the distributed balls. Based on the current position and orientation of the Tekbot, the arena model returns the signal run-times of the range finder signals as well as the amount of reflected light for the optical sensors.

An inexpensive and fast way to find the best architecture is to simulate different configurations and design variants and automatically test them against the specification – this is virtually impossible with hardware prototypes.

3.   COMPONENT DESIGN

Two motors for the "drivetrain" are part of the basic Tekbot chassis. Using different rotational velocities for the wheels control the direction of the movement and opposite turning directions allow for tight turns and turning on the spot. The simulation models serve as part of a meaningful testbench for the H-Bridge driver design as well as the verification of the software algorithm. If the motor is not already specified, this kind of simulation allows to identify the required motor parameters and to qualify a suitable motor. A model of an ideal motor (figure 3) is based on electrical and mechanical differential equations that can be found in standard literature. Together with a simple model for the wheels the electrical signals are translated into rotational movement of the motor shaft and then into a position of the wheels within the arena. This also provides an estimate about system properties such as speed, turning radius and power consumption.

```
architecture ideal of motor is
    quantity v across i through p to n;
    quantity   w_shaft   across   torq_shaft   through   shaft   to
rotational_velocity_ref;
    quantity w : real;
    quantity torq : real;
begin
            torq == -1.0*kt*i + d*w + j*w'dot;
            v  == kt*w + i*r_int + l*i'dot;
            w_shaft == w/kg;
            torq_shaft == torq/kg;
end architecture ideal;
```

Figure 3. Motor Model

Using this multi-technology simulation provides the designer with a view onto the complete system with the right physical units and parameter values right from the datasheet of components. A simple behavioral model of the motor controller with the H-bridge driver (figure 4), the motors and the wheels is sufficient for early verification of the control software.

```
architecture ideal of motor_controller is
    quantity L_motor_v across L_motor_i through L_motor_p to
L_motor_n;
    quantity Vcc_c across Vcc to ref;
begin
    if L_en = '0' and L_dir = '1' use
       L_motor_v == motor_voltage;
    elsif L_en = '0' and L_dir = '0' use
       L_motor_v == -motor_voltage;
    else
       L_motor_v == 0.0;
    end use;
end architecture ideal;
```

Figure 4. Abstract Model of H-Bridge

VHDL-AMS supports moving from a high-level, abstract model to a more realistic implementation by using different model descriptions, so called architectures, for the same model. After the engineer has made decisions about the configuration and components for the actual implementation of the H-Bridge, it could look like the transistor design in figure 5.

Correct tuning of the H-bridges requires detailed device behavior. Therefore it becomes important at this stage to be able to use SPICE models for simulation, as many manufacturers provide detailed and characterized SPICE models on their websites. With the use of a suitable tool, such as SystemVision, the schematic from figure 5 can then be used to layout a PCB board and get the data required for manufacturing the actual board.

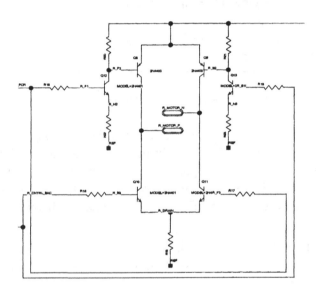

Figure 5. Transistor-level H-Bridge

4.   SOFTWARE VERIFICATION

Using different architectures in VHDL-AMS can be used to facilitate not only the hardware design, but also the software design. With all the hardware models on an abstract level, the implementation of the algorithm as C-code or as a state-chart is sufficient to validate the control strategy. With the strong digital capabilities of VHDL-AMS it is possible to move closer towards implementation than with usual signal-flow based tools. This adds an additional level of reality to the simulation that is helpful when used at the right stage in the design flow.

The digital brain of the robot is a board produced by the Oregon State University with an Atmel Atmega128 microcontroller (MCU) plus peripheral hardware such as extended SRAM. An open source VHDL model of an Atmega103 was modified to model the Atmega128, including peripherals such as multiple interface ports and an analog-to-digital converter (ADC). This allows using target compiled code in the simulation in order to get very detailed information on how the software interacts with the MCU hardware, giving the benefits of:

- obtaining the correct connectivity of the individual components
- easier design and debug of the low level software drivers
- validation of correct control algorithm before hardware is available
- automatic regression testing of the complete system

For software designers the simulation approach offers the possibility of starting the debugging earlier in the design flow, with realistic stimuli and responses. Knowing all the conditions of the physical system at every time-step by analyzing the simulation results (figure 6) enables the software developer to correlate the actual behavior of the system with the execution of the software in the debugger. This effectively leads to more confidence in the code when trying to run the first prototype and less painstaking debugging on the hardware.

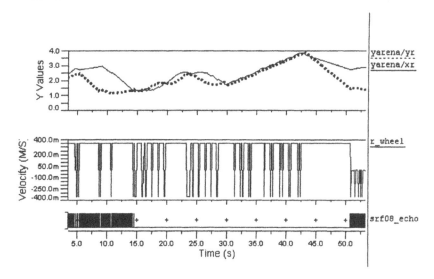

Figure 6. Simulation Results in EZWave

The Tekbot software designers for example were required to know the position of the Tekbot in the arena for the design and debugging of the line-following algorithm. Important analog waveforms therefore are the x and y coordinates of the left and right wheel, the speed of the wheels and the feedback from the sensors. Figure 6 shows the corresponding waveforms for the right wheel. Displaying the coordinates over time doesn't result in an easily understandable spatial representation, but displaying the x over the y coordinate does. Exporting the simulated waveforms and importing them into Microsoft Excel allowed a representation of the simulation results that is easy to relate with the function of the control algorithm (figure 7 and figure 8).

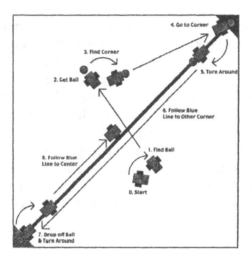

Figure 7. Implemented Algorithm

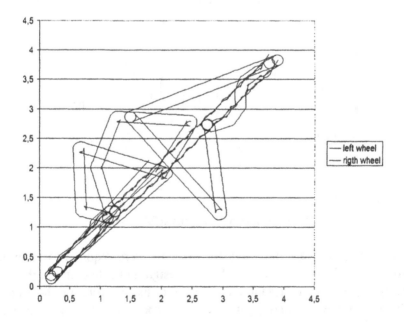

Figure 8. Intended Algorithm vs. Implemented Algorithm

5.   VERIFICATION AND OPTIMIZATION

Setting up the simulation of the full system or just parts of it is often time-consuming, but it enables automatic regression testing. Changes in the software or the hardware can be simulated and the results automatically verified against the specification or previous results – using exactly the same, reproducible tests repeatedly and saving engineer's time. While this is nothing new for IC designers, this methodology represents a fundamental improvement for the mechatronic design flow.

The ability to view the whole mechatronic system, including mechanical as well as electrical effects, means it is easier to find ways to optimize cost and robustness of the design. It enables engineers to move a problem into a design domain where it can be addressed more efficiently. The drivetrain, for example, has mechanical tolerances that make it behave less than ideal. Instead of purchasing a more expensive motor with fewer tolerances, the motor controller, or even cheaper – the software, can be designed to compensate for the tolerance, leading to the same system behavior at a lower cost.

6.   OUTLOOK

Time constraints left a couple of aspects un-addressed in this project. One aspect is the analysis of different options for the control system implementation. A software implementation on a MCU is not necessarily the most efficient way to control the hardware. Other alternatives, such as FPGA or ASIC designs could be better options for some designs. With modern tools it is possible to use C code to drive hardware design flows for these technologies, possibly helping to identify the best implementation solution quicker and easier.

Another aspect is the use of more advanced analyses. For example engineers often use sensitivity or statistical analyses, such as Monte-Carlo analysis, as part of a structured process to identify areas for optimization. VHDL-AMS language constructs allow parameter variations, but libraries with statistical analyses are not part of the language definition. Such libraries currently become available as part of efforts of standardization committees.

7.   CONCLUSION

The Tekbot design team used this VHDL-AMS based design methodology. According to the team, this project would not have been completed without the ability to simulate electrical and mechanical hardware and software together. The simulations uncovered many flaws in the algorithms used for ball detection and line following. The ability to use a waveform viewer to pinpoint the cause of a bug greatly aided in the process of optimizing the ball detection and line following routines.

One of the biggest benefits experienced was the ability to model and simulate the design very early in the process. The design team was able to find problems prior to hardware prototyping. Changes could be made and re-simulated quickly. This enabled more time to be spent on making the design right before testing it on physical hardware and to stay within the very limited budget.

REFERENCES

Dan Block, Tekbot technical paper, 2004, Tekbot design team member; http://www.mentor.com/system/tech_pubs/

Mike Loudenback et. al., 2004, Tekbot technical manual; http://classes.engr.oregonstate.edu/eecs/fall2003/ece441/groups/g20

Scott Cooper, 2004, "Design Team Collaboration within a Modeling and Analysis Environment", Mentor Graphics; http://www.mentor.com/system/tech_pubs/

IEEE 1076.1 (VHDL-AMS) Working Group; http://www.eda.org/vhdl-ams/

ENSURING HIGH QUALITY IN SPECIFICATIONS FOR AUTOMOTIVE EMBEDDED CONTROL SYSTEMS

Eva Rakotomalala,[1] Jean-Pierre Elloy,[2] Pierre Molinaro, [2] Bernard Bavoux,[1] and Didier Jampi[1]

[1]*PSA Peugeot Citroen, 2 route de Gisy 78943 Velizy-Villacoublay cedex, France;*
[2]*IRCCYN Ecole Centrale Nantes, 1, rue de la Noe 44000 Nantes, France*

Abstract: Achieving confidence in safety, and robustness of complex systems is a key issue for an automotive manufacturer. Specifications are the first and crucial stage of the engineering process. The aim is to provide a high level of quality assurance for the specifications of systems incorporing several reused parts. This paper presents a method using an external modeling of the function supervision. We propose a framework based on modes analysis and a formal operation which allows to combine automaton descriptions of modes by adding logic commutations between modes.

Keywords: Formal specification, Embedded Systems, Safety, Verification

1. INTRODUCTION AND CONTRIBUTIONS

The automotive industry is quickly increasing the complexity of its new vehicle designs. Adding functionality or coupling between existing functions makes it more difficult to have high confidence in specifications definition and completeness, then in implementation correctness. The dysfunctionning of an electronic functionality which can occur during operational use of vehicle, can have 3 off-line origins and 3 in operation origins. Off-line, errors which cause dysfunctionning can be due to: 1- incomplete specifications which do not describe all the properties of safety and liveness, 2- incomplete checks which do not test the specification in every situation, 3- implementation errors. In operation, the dysfunctionning can be due to: 4- errors caused by failures in the device (operating system, protocol, hardware), 5- the reception by the functionality of sequences of incoherent signal data or events (generally emitted by other inconsistent or failing functionalities) , 6- the reception by the functionality of sequences of data or events, of which occurrences were not considered in the specifications.

- The treatment of dysfunctionning due to situation 1 is related to system engineering, which steps establish all the requirements that the functionality to be developed must meet. These requirements are built according to the sequences of signals which the functionality can receive from its environment. These sequences are supposed all known. If the environment changes, if the functionality is reused in another environment or if other functions (inter-system) generate sequences of additional input signals, the requirements can be incomplete.

- The treatment of dysfunctionning due to situations 2 and 3 is related to techniques which principles are from now on well-known: model based engineering, validation of these models by model checking (Alur et al., 1993) or theorem proving (Boyer and Moore, 1984), and finally automatic generation of code from this validated model. One limit of these techniques is their complexity in term of algorithmic, consequently, these techniques are currently especially applied to the critical cores of applications. Complete application can thus present incoherence of functioning which are not detected (non-exhaustive checking).

- The situations of type 4 are the subject of currently academic work (wrappers) which aim is to detect and to confine the errors of the device by the installation of observers which, on line, check the coherence of the sequences of signals emitted by the device. The detected errors are transmitted to the application programs.

- The object of this paper is to propose a method which identifies from design phases of conception, all the situations which can produce dysfunctionning of type 5 and 6. The method solicits the designer then so that it proposes alternatives of reaction to these situations which are not considered in the specifications. The treatment of the cases of dysfunctionning 5 and 6 are of importance in automotive application, because they can occur either because of residual defects at the end of dysfunctionnings 1, 2 or 3, or because of the incompletely controlled re-use of functionalities in different versions of vehicles, or during the construction of new inter-systems services which emit new sequences of signals to the functionalities they are associated with.

The proposed method is intended to be applied upstream of the design phase of new functionality or during the analysis of the re-use, in a new environment, as illustrated in the figure 1.

It is about a formal method because:

- it is based on a modeling of the inputs and outputs of the functionality. In this modeling, the inputs and outputs are coded by Boolean signals.

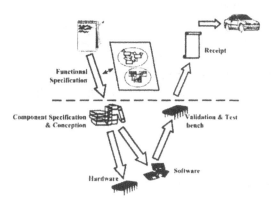

Figure 1.   Domain of applicability of the method.

Coding depends on the studied case: either these signals are real if they are logical sizes (frequent case of the functionalities cockpit), or coding models the presence (the update) and the absence of data, or coding is the binary conversion of enumerated data, etc...

- it is based on a model of the specifications of the studied functionality. This model, of Finite State Machine (FSM) type, is a graph of states which describes only the dependences between the Boolean values of the inputs and the outputs of the functionality without describing how these output signals are calculated. In our approach, a finite state machine is modeling the entity connected to sensors and actuators. The input of the sensors (signal processing) and the control command of the actuators (automation algorithms) are not directly involved in this study. They are associated to the inputs from sensor and to the outputs towards the actuators

- it analyzes and fulfills the properties of completeness (Leveson, 1995) and consistency (Heimdahl and Leveson, 1996) of the model, which are two key properties of automaton specification with high level of quality, independently of the checking of the requirements of the functionality.

A specification is "complete" if there is a state transition or behavior specified for any input or set of inputs that may occur. Consistency requires that there is no more than one state transition for any input or set of inputs that may occur. In this context, the proposed method is not in competition with the techniques of model checking or theorem proving. Applied in upstream phases of these techniques, the proposed method ensure that these techniques will carry out an exhaustive validation of the function. In addition, the model built by the method is independent of that of the model checking. Our model describes what the function must carry out whereas the model checking is based on a model which describes how it is carried. In this paper, we propose an approach based on the notion of modal decomposition, upon which the global behavior of the control system is described. A formal operation is then introduced to combine and to define legal modes commutations with respect of properties of consistency and completeness of the resulting automaton. Perspectives to increase robustness of the system against inconsistent inputs are finally proposed.

2.   BASIC CONCEPT

The detailed study of real cases showed us that it is very useful to obtain the external model of a functionality to be developed by following a modal step. This step consists in breaking up the behavior of each component implied in the functionality into its various operating modes, each mode is representative of the activity of the component under specific operating conditions. The question of modal decomposition is not recent, it was already the subject of many scientific as well as technical works (Degani and Kirlik, 1995) (Jonhson, 1990). Modes differ between them by their functional components and the services which they provide (Elloy, 2002). The mode term designs nominal mode as well as failure mode or downgraded mode. In the literature, there is no general method for decomposing the system in its modes. At most, some guides exist, which are often limited to an applied domain (Moreno and Peulot, 1997). The method we propose is not based on any particular technique of decomposition of modes: all are applicable provided that modes define a mutually exclusive set of system behaviors. It is essential however that the initial system is broken up into the greatest number of elementary components as possible and that the behavior of each one of these components is broken up into the greatest number of possible modes. These two conditions make the method we propose the most efficient: i) it reduces the initial problem, which can be of a great complexity, to a set of independent subproblems, each one of reasonable complexity, ii) it automatically builds the relations between all the elementary models, in order to guarantee the coherence and the consistency of the operation of the total system.

3.   METHOD STEPS

The proposed approach consists of the following major steps, as illustrated on the figure 2.

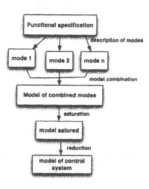

Figure 2.   Method steps

3.1   Description of modes

During this first step, modes are identified and described independently from the specification requirements. The proposed approach use a formal modeling language for describing each mode. The formalism of modeling used is based on the general model of Finite State Machine (FSM). It is well recognized in both the research literature and in practice, that state machine model is a convenient way for describing the behavior of model-based system (Sherry and Cuard, 1995). A machine modeling a system can be thought of as having a set of states. The behavior of the system can be described by the possible transitions from one state to one another (Arnold, 1992) (Gill, 1962). This type of modeling is particularly adapted to the specification of control logic system (Harel, 1987). There are two basic types of state machines: Moore state machines (Moore, 1956) and Mealy state machines (Mealy, 1955). They differ only in how they compute their output signals. For our approach, we use an extension of Moore machine so that the state of the machine is defined by the current values of inputs and the current values of outputs

Formally, « a machine M » with n inputs and p outputs, in our approach is defined as:

$M = (E, S, Q, I, F, T)$ where:

E	:	$\{e_1, \dots e_n\}$ set of n boolean inputs ($n \geq 1$),
S	:	$\{s_1, \dots s_n\}$ set of p boolean outputs ($p \geq 1$),
Q	:	set of possible states, $card(Q_A) \leq 2^{n+p}$,
I	:	set of initial states ($I \subseteq 2^{n+p}$)
F	:	set of terminal states ($F \subseteq 2^{n+p}$)
T	:	set of transitions ($T \subseteq 2^{n+p} \times 2^{n+p}$)

A state (e, s) is defined by the combination of inputs e and outputs s. An initial state, represented by a circle with an arrow, defines state whereby mode can be entered. Terminal state, represented by the underlined circle, defines state whereby mode can be left.

   Figure 3. Initial state   *Figure 4.* Terminal state

A transition $(e,\ s,\ e',\ s')$, is illustrated on the figure 5.

Figure 5. Transition

  The formalism of modeling uses a graphic reduction for the representation of states. The notation illustrated on the left of the figure is a graphic reduction of the automaton at the right of the figure 6.

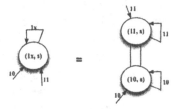

Figure 6. Representation of state

  The advantages of this graphic reduction which does not distort the semantics is the possibility to perform complex computation on automaton and the use of tools based on BDD (Binary decision diagram) to verify proprieties, by avoiding exponential growth of states. Checking the resulting system for properties of reachability is possible with almost no limitation due to the use of BDD instead of an explicit automaton.

3.2 Modal combination

This step consists in combination of the modes independently described in order to build the machine representing the complete behavior of the system.

To guarantee determinism of specification, the modal combination of two machines $M_1 = (E_1, S_1, Q_1, I_1, F_1, T_1)$ and $M_2 = (E_2, S_2, Q_2, I_2, F_2, T_2)$ must be preformed under some conditions. First, the modes to be combined must present the same Boolean inputs ($E_1 = E_2$) and outputs ($S_1 = S_2$). Then, the set of modes must be disjoined ($reachable(M_1) \cap reachable(M_2) = \varnothing$).

Formally, *the modal combination* of two machines $M_1 = (E_1, S_1, Q_1, I_1, F_1, T_1)$ and $M_2 = (E_2, S_2, Q_2, I_2, F_2, T_2)$ builds a machine $M = (E, S, Q, I, F, T)$ where:

- $E = E_1 = E_2, \quad S = S_1 = S_2, \quad Q = Q_1 \cup Q_2$

- $I = I_1 \cup I_2, \quad F = F_1 \cup F_2, \quad T = T_1 \cup T_2,$

According to the way in which the designers have identified the modes, two situations can be met:

- All the modes identified are exclusive of other modes. The machines modeling modes do not share any common state, including the initial states.

- Modes are not disjoined. Their accessible parts share common states. A preliminary fusion operation of modes is possible if the common states to the modes present the same properties in terms of states and transitions. If not, a supplementary Boolean output is introduced to differentiate identical states of modes.

To guarantee completeness of specifications, any possible and impossible evolutions of the global system must be considered. The impossible evolutions are those of the occurrence in a given state of a certain combination of inputs which are physically impossible. During the modal combination, the designer will have to introduce additional modes which correspond to the occurring of these events of *impossible* evolution. These additional modes are often called *Default mode or Reply mode*. This step constraints the designer to think explicitly of the occurrences of all the combination inputs and to evaluate their incidence. This constraint is an important factor for the safety of the system.

3.3 Saturation

The saturation is the operation which follows upon the modal combination. Its purpose is to complete the model from modal combination by setting connections between modes, so that the automaton resulting is deterministic, complete and reachable.

The saturation operation of a machine $M = (E, S, Q, I, F, T)$ with n inputs and p outputs from combination modal consists in computing a machine $M' = (E', S', Q', I', F', T')$, so that:

- from each reachable terminal state of M, the complementary transitions of set of transitions starting from this state is computed. According to the hypothesis that mode is always entered via its initial states, these complementary transitions are added towards each initial states of M.

- for each transition added, an action is associated so that, this action is disjoined of these starting from the state and this action is stable towards the target state. The stability of a transition towards a target state implies the coherence between the input transition and the condition to stay in the state.

Formally, $M' = (E', S', Q', I', F', T')$ where:

- $E' = E,\ S' = S,\ Q' = Q,\ F' = F,\ I' = I,$

- $T' = T \cup \left\{ \begin{array}{l} \forall\,(e,\,s) \in reachable(M) \\ \text{and } \forall\,(e,\,s) \in F \\ \text{and } \forall\,(e',\,s') \in I \\ \text{and } \forall\,s''\,(e,\,s,\,e',\,s'') \notin T \\ \text{and } e \neq e' \ : \ (e,\,s,\,e',\,s') \end{array} \right\}.$

Due to this definition of saturation, the determinism and the completeness of the machine resulting from saturation is ensured by construction under these conditions:

- modes are disjoined other them. The intersection of their reachable states is empty.

- the set of initial states inputs forms a *partition* of the set of possible combination values of inputs. That means, they are mutually exclusive and the set of them is collectively exhaustive.

- all the states are terminal. If not, completeness is ensured only for terminal states, for the non - terminal states, the object of the approach is to detect these incompleteness and to inform the designer, so that he proposes alternative strategies for the treatment of these incompletenesses.

An example of construction by saturation is illustrated on the figure 7, which consists of a a manual basic wiper system. It is comprised of the wiper switch, the sensor for detecting the position of the wiper arms and the actuator.

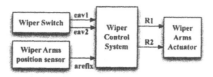

Figure 7. Manual Wiper Function

The boolean inputs of the Wiper Control System are eav1, eav2 and arefix, which combinations correspond to the selected mode. The boolean outputs are R1 and R2, which correspond to the command emitted by actuator to the the wiper arms . From the specification of the function, 5 modes are displayed : mode "stop", mode"speed1", mode"speed2", mode"wait stop", mode "Default switch". The description of each mode using moore machine is given on the figure 8.

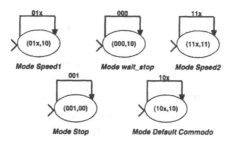

Figure 8. Wiper System modes

The external model of the wiper system after saturation is illustrated on the figure 9. TThe resulting automaton respects properties of completeness and consistency by construction.

4. ROBUSTNESS TO INCONSISTENT INPUTS

A goal for the proposed approach is to assist in writing complete and consistent functional specifications. Safe functional specifications imply that the global system must design to cope with all possible fault conditions. We are focused on fault conditions resulting from input component failures. The obvious solution, is to increase the reliability of the components and to build fault tolerance into system design to take in account these failures. This can be considered a priori in several ways:

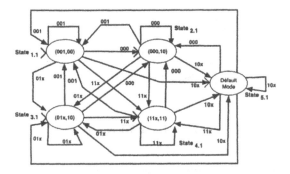

Figure 9.   External model after saturation

4.1   Perspective 1: failures are treated by the control system.

A first perspective consists in considering these components failures as an integral part of the operating modes of control system. The automaton modeling the control system after saturation takes into account all possible circumstances, including those resulting from the anomalies of components. Then, the failed transitions are identified and a specific default mode is defined as an additional state of the control system. These failed transitions are then redirect towards this state. This perspective is illustrated on the figure 10.

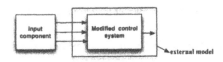

Figure 10.   Failures are treated by control system

4.2   Perspective 2: failures are treated by a filter.

In this case, the control system does not have to face the occurrence of these failures and to treat them. The failures are filtered at the output of components, as illustrated on the Figure 11.

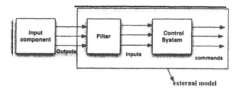

Figure 11. Failures are treated by a filter

4.3 Perspective 3: failures are supervised by parallel monitoring.

A third perspective considers that the failures are detected by a specific monitoring module which relays the control system when failure occurs. The role of this monitoring box is to force the signal command in case of undesired behavior. In absence of failures from input components, the command from the control system is applied. In the opposite case, specific command which is previously established to treat this circumstance is applied.

The role of the monitoring box is that of a detector of failure and a selector. This configuration is illustrated on the figure 12.

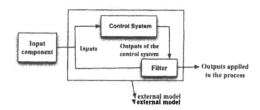

Figure 12. Failures are supervised by parallel monitoring

These three possibilities can be considered. It is up to the designer to choose the one which is suitable for his application.

5. CONCLUSION AND FUTURE WORK

We have outlined an approach for the design of a safe control system by reducing potential specification errors. The system is described according to its "operating mode" and the formal operation of "saturation" creates transitions for commutation between modes with respect of properties of consistency and completeness of the automaton resulting. This work is still in evolution steps. For the future, we plan to investigate the formalization of the whole steps of the design process. This can be used as a starting point for the definition of formal tools based on BDD representation.

REFERENCES

Alur, R., Courcoibetis, C., and Dill, D. (1993). Model checking in dense real-time. *Information and computation*, 104:2–34.

Arnold, A. (1992). *Systemes de Transitions Finis et Semantique des Processus Communiquants*. Masson.

Boyer, R. and Moore, J. (1984). Proof checking, theorem proving, and program verification. In *Contemporary Mathematics, Automated Theorem Proving : after 25 years*, pages 119–132, Rhode Island. American mathematical society.

Degani, A. and Kirlik, A. (1995). Modes in human-automation interaction : initial observations about modeling approach. In *Proceeding of the IEE International Conference on Systems, Man, and Cybernetics*, pages 3443–3450, Vancouver, Canada. IEE.

Elloy, J.-P. (2002). Modelisation des modes de fonctionnement dans une architecture vehicule en ail. Technical report, AEE.

Gill, A. (1962). *Introduction to the Theory of Finite-State Machines*. Mc Graw-Hill, New York.

Harel, D. (1987). *Statecharts : a visual formalism of complex systems*. Science of Computer programming 8:231-274.

Heimdahl, M. and Leveson, N. G. (1996). Completeness and consistency analysis of state-based requirements. *IEEE Transactions on Software Engineering*.

Jonhson, J. (1990). Modes in non computer devices. *International Journal of Man-Machines Studies*, 32:423–438.

Leveson, N. G. (1995). *Safeware: System Safety and Computers*. Addison Wesley, Reading, Massachusetts.

Mealy, G. H. (1955). Method for synthesizing sequential circuits. *Bell System Tech.*, 34:1045–1079.

Moore, E. F. (1956). Experiments on sequential machines. In *Automata Studies*, pages 129–156, C.E. Shannon and J. McCarthy, editors. Princeton University Press, New Jersey.

Moreno, S. and Peulot, E. (1997). *Le GEMMA : Mode de Marche et d'arrêt*. Educalivre-Collcetion A. Capliez.

Sherry, L. and Cuard, J. (1995). A formalism for the specification of operationally embedded reactive systems. In *14th digital avionics systems conference*, Cambridge MA. AIAA/IEEE.

FROM MODEL TO REQUIREMENTS: PATTERN-BASED ANALYSIS IN DISTRIBUTED DEVELOPMENT OF EMBEDDED SYSTEMS

Clive Thomsen, Judita Kruse, Rolf Ernst
Institute of Computer and Communication Network Engineering,
Technical University of Braunschweig
thomsen|kruse|ernst@ida.ing.tu-bs.de

Abstract: As design complexity of embedded systems raises with each new technology generation, development becomes a more and more challenging task for a single manufacturer or system house. To counter this, we see a continuing trend to spread development over several companies with differing core competencies. This is either done by purchasing ready made IP blocks or by setting up a distributed design process. For both approaches, the system designer has to designate a sufficient specification for the components externally supplied, to ensure proper functionality after system integration.

To support the designer in this task, we propose pattern-based analysis of a central structural system model. We present an approach to derive inter-system dependencies of design properties by model transformation, which allows the efficient use of analysis and verification tools in early design stages. This enables easy specification validation.

Keywords: Requirements, Model Transformation, Pattern-based Analysis, Embedded Systems

1.   INTRODUCTION

Embedded systems are getting more and more complex. In a single car, a dozen of microprocessors can be found today, spread over several control units, communicating over a variety of networks and field buses. With the increasing use of MpSoCs we expect a dramatic boost in complexity, as more and more service functions and features can be added to the systems while additionally allowing lower production cost through higher integration level.

This poses a high challenge on the development process. Often, the development is still based on text documents and manual data exchange. New ways and tools are needed to face the complexity explosion.

Let's have a look at the following setting: A *customer* gives a *system house* the assignment to develop an embedded system. The customer poses a wide set of functional requirements on the unit, specifying unit operation and protocol of external interfaces. Solutions for generally dealing with these requirements can be found in [3],[4].

Additionally there will be a set of requirements not directly coupled with the unit's function. These non-functional requirements can be roughly grouped into four categories:

Development effort: The development may not cost more or take longer than the customer admits.

Resource usage: How many resources like power or memory are used by the unit.

Unit performance: The rating of the unit. Often given as throughput, response time or real-time requirements.

Operating conditions: The unit must be compliant with environmental influences like radiation or extreme temperatures.

At the system house a *system architect* will try to find a *system structure* which provides the requested functionality and is suitable in terms of the non-functional requirements. If very high performance or low power consumption is needed, the architect may choose an implementation in specialized hardware. If the architect focuses on platform reuse, he will favor a co-design approach, where the functionality is implemented as software, running on a ready-made embedded processor.

Next, the architect will specify sets of requirements for each sub-system. These sub-requirements must fulfill two prerequisites:

- *Assertability:* The requirements must be assertable by the sub-system suppliers. This can be a problem if the requirements are technically challenging, as the supplier may refuse to guarantee meeting those on a contractual basis. We have suggested flexible contracting schemes as a solution to this issue in [5],[6].

- *Validity:* The requirements on the sub-systems must be valid in the overall system context. The architect must ensure, that meeting all sub-requirements is sufficient for meeting the overall requirements.

To do so, the system architect needs knowledge about the dependencies between different system properties. As shown in figure 1 each property of the overall system is dependent on the properties of the sub-systems. The actual characteristics of these dependencies D_1 to D_4 is determined by the system structure the architect has defined.

The system architect has two choices to deal with these dependencies. She may rely on her design experience to roughly estimate them and to determine sub-requirements which will lead – to her best knowledge – to satisfactory

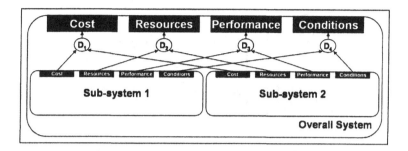

Figure 1.   Dependencies between sub and overall system

results. However, in complex systems , there is an imminent risk of missing important dependencies. Additionally, when only estimating dependencies, the designer tends to be conservative, to lower her risk of missing overall requirements, leading to an over-sized design.

For very challenging or tight requirements, she may want to use a corresponding analysis tool kit. Especially in the area of real-time and throughput many promising approaches are currently under development or becoming available [7],[8],[9]. These tools have in common, that the architect has to provide the system structure as a specific input model for the tool. For complex systems this modeling may be a time-consuming, cumbersome and thus error-prone task.

Both approaches are insufficient for today's complex embedded systems. As a solution we want to suggest pattern-based analysis of a structural design model. This approach is based on the observation, that the architecture of complex systems can be decomposed into a limited set of simpler structural entities, so called "patterns". A pattern is the encapsulation of a well approved design scheme [1],[2]. Based on this observation, we want to achieve an automated transformation of the system architecture into models suitable for analysis tools: The system architecture is scanned for known design patterns, these are transformed into the corresponding analysis patterns and composed into an overall analysis model.

We will introduce our approach of pattern-based analysis for embedded systems in the next section. After presenting an example in section 3 we will conclude in 4.

2.   PATTERN-BASED ANALYSIS

This section introduces to pattern-based analysis and how it supports design processes.

Figure 2 shows the major building blocks of our suggested system:

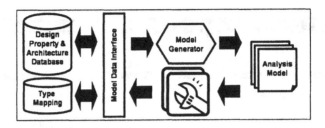

Figure 2.   Data-flow for pattern-based analysis

The central *design property and architecture database* contains a *structure model* capturing the system architecture and properties of the different system components.

The database is accessed via the *model data interface* (MDI). This interface provides a generic view on the design structure, decoupled from the modeling language used in the database. Further details con be found in section 2.1.

The *model generator* uses the MDI to transform the structure model found in the database into an analysis model targted for a certain anlysis. This model is augmented with all needed input values from the property database and processed by the analysis tool. The obtained results are back annotated into the database, using the MDI again.

Often, one analysis depends on results obatined by other tools. We monitor the property database and re-execute tools, if their input values have changed. This builds up a network of tools and ensures concistency within the database.

The system architect can now enter different the cornercases scenarios of her specification into the property database, to test if these will lead to satisfactory overall system behaviour. Of course, this procedure could be automated, allowing convenient specification validation.

For conducting the model transformations, we have developed the *model traverse language* (MTL), an XML-based script language described in section 2.2.

Often the design architecture is composed of user-defined components unknown to the model generator. The *type mapping* provides equivalence relations between user-defined types and those known to the model generator.

2.1   The Model Data Interface

In this section we will have a closer look on MDI, a generic interface to access a system architecture model.

To automatically derive dependencies from a system model, we need information about the internal communication paths and the mapping of functionality onto implementation resources. Communication is especially important for performance requirements like throughput or response time. To calculate these properties we need knowledge of all components of a communication path and their behavior. The mapping determines how resources are shared between different system components. To calculate to load of a CPU for example, we need to know which tasks should run on it.

In today's requirement management tools, hierarchical models are used, similar to the AP233 data model [10]. These simple models are insufficient for an automated dependency analysis, as they neither provide information about communication nor about mapping. A new, upcoming modeling standard dealing with these issues is SysML, an UML extension [11]. But SysML is still in the standardization phase and no modeling tools are available yet.

To overcome this situation, we have defined the model data interface, a generic representation of structure models. Figure 3 shows an UML diagram

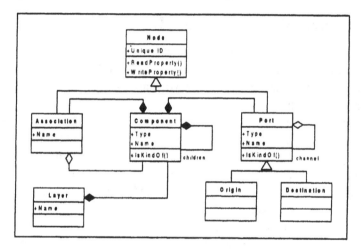

Figure 3.   UML description of MDI

of the interface.

The core class of the interface is the *component*. A component represents an entity in the design to be modeled. An arbitrary name can be assigned to each component. As todays designs are mostly organized hierarchically, component can be the composition of further child components, allowing the modeling of a component tree.

To model communication, a component provides a set of *ports*, which can be interconnected to form channels. We distinguish *origin* and *destination* port classes to reflect the flow of the modeled communication. For example, origin ports correspond to bus masters, destination ports to bus slaves.

To capture mappings, the modeling language provides *associations*, a labeled and directed relation between components.

Components, associations and ports share the super class *Node*. Each node owns an ID to uniquely identify the modeled entity in the system. Additionally a node allows storage and retrieval of properties using textual key values. As data format for properties XML DOM elements are used [12].

Ports and components carry a "type" attribute to denote the characteristics of the underlying entity. In system models, very precise and specialized types are used, like "ARM" or "CAN", while analysis models often use more generalized types, like "CPU resource" or "bus". The "IsKindOf" evaluates the type mapping to check, if the port or component is the specialization of a generalized type.

The structure model can be separated into different *layers*. A layer is a sub-model presenting a certain view on the system. For example, typical layers for embedded systems would be "hardware architecture", "software architecture" or "data flow".

2.2   Analytical Patterns in MTL

This section features a brief discussion of the model traverse language (MTL). A MTL script describes how to generate an input model for a certain analysis tool targeted by the script. MTL is an XML-based script language, interpreted in a two stage process.

In the first stage, a *pattern processor* interprets the MTL script to traverse the structure model, inspecting the different components encountered to find known design patterns. When a pattern has been recognized, the corresponding analytical model is generated in an *intermediate* output format.

This intermediate contains the generated model encoded as XML and a description of its property dependencies. The dependency description is used to re-invoke the corresponding analytical tool, when component properties change, to ensure database consistency. An example of an intermediate output can be found in figure 8.

The second stage is responsible for tool invocation. First all needed component properties are fetched from the database and annotated in the intermediate. Next a wrapper script is called to invoke the analytical tool and to extract the newly calculated component properties from the tool output.

The pattern processor construes the structure model as *model graph*, using components, ports and association classes as node set and their relations as edge set. MTL statements operate on the model graph and can be grouped in three categories.

Traverse statements allow to navigate along specified edges of the model graph. These statements can have child-statements and a *filter expression*. A filter expression allows to select on which nodes the child-statement shall be executed, based on node properties like its type.

Control-flow statements are sub-function calls or repeat loops, for example. A special tag statement and a corresponding filter expression allow setting and testing of arbitrary flags on model nodes. Thus algorithms depending on graph search can be implemented.

Generate statements construct the intermediate representation. A node statement inserts specified XML elements into the intermediate representation. Data statements indicate that a property should be accessed for all members of the node set. This is done by inserting special markers denoting the identifier of the model node and the name of the accessed property.

3. EXAMPLE

In this section we look at a small design to exemplify our approach.

The system to develop is a position controller. The unit must keep track of its position and can make corrections through a PWM controlled motor. The unit shall exchange target and actual position value over a network interface with an external system. Additionally, the unit should control the motor's temperature. As platform, a microprocessor with CAN Interface is used, The data exchange and the regulator itself shall be implemented in software, while for temperature control a threshold switch is used

After modeling the system, a SymTA/S [9]analysis shall be performed to evaluate real-time performance, followed by a simple power estimation.

We will separate our example into three layers: A functional layer, containing all functional units and their data-flow, a software and a hardware layer. Figure 4 shows the functional layer. As the complexity of the design is very

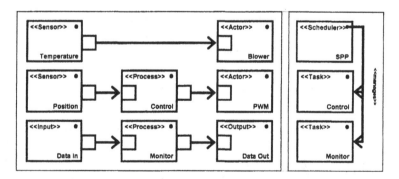

Figure 4.   Functional view and software arcitecture of example system

low, we get along with a limited set of types: "Sensors" and "actors" as standard components of controllers, "processes" providing the functionality, as well as "input" and "output" ports to communicate with the environment.

The software uses a "scheduler" to manage two "tasks", which implement the functionality of the processes found in the functional model (also 4).

In figure 5 we see the hardware layer of the structure model. All communication is handled by a central "packet bus". We find the implementations

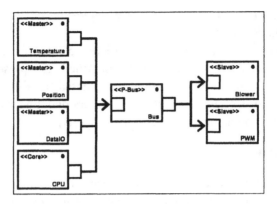

Figure 5.   View on example platform

of the sensors and the external interface acting as bus masters, as well as the CPU-core. The actors are connected as slaves devices.

Figure 6 shows the type mapping used for the hardware layer. For the power

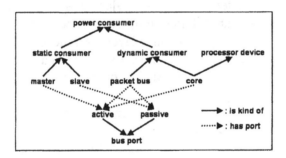

Figure 6.   Graph of types in hardware layer

analysis model knows about "static consumer" and "dynamic consumer" type. A static consumer shows a nearly constant power usage, while the dynamic consumer's power usage is linearly dependent on its utilization. During model generation, bus and CPU will be mapped to a dynamic consumer, while for all other elements static power usage is assumed.

Not shown explicitly shown in figures 4 and 5 is a "schedules" association connecting scheduler and CPU, as well as "implemented-by" associations between layers, which are indicated by name equality of components. Also, as the bus is the only communication device in the system, we can spare the mapping of communication channels.

To generate the SymTA/S model, a corresponding analysis pattern is applied on the functional view. The pattern generates appropriate nodes for all found components and special communication nodes to map the channels. The

the software layer will be evaluated to associate the two nodes created for the Control and the Monitor process with a CPU resources.

Now the needed input data can be fetched from the database, like execution times of the tasks, length of messages, communication behavior of the sensors, or clock rate of bus and processor, etc.. A wrapper script now feeds model and data into SymTA/S. Figure 7 shows a screen-shot of the resulting SymTA/S

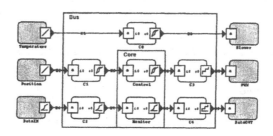

Figure 7. SymTA/S model of system

model.

Figure 8 is an excerpt of the intermediate model generated from the power analysis pattern. For better readability, reference identifiers have been replaced by the name of the corresponding model component. The headline denotes how the file was produced. The "dataout" tag declares that this intermediate will provide the property "power". For static power consumer, it will just fetch the power values from the property database. For dynamic power con-

```
<intermediate pattern="power" target=overall system>
    <dataout ID=overall system property="power"/>
    <static>
        <datain ID=position sensor property="power"/>
    </static>
    <static> [ ... ] </static>
    <dynamic>
        <datain ID=CPU property="idle power"/>
        <datain ID=CPU property="load power"/>
        <datain ID=CPU property="utilization" />
        <dataout ID=CPU property="power" />
    </dynamic>
    <dynamic> [ ... ] </dynamic>
</intermediate>
```

Figure 8. Output of power pattern applied to overall system

sumers, idle power, load power and utilization are fetched to compute the components consumption. When the required properties have been fetched from the database, the file can easily be evaluated directly by a corresponding script, which calculates the dynamic powers and the overall power consumption.

4. CONCLUSION

Early design validation becomes a more and more important issue in embedded system design processes. Pattern-based analysis is applied on a central model capturing the design architecture. It can be used to invoke multiple analysis tools and to track down inter-dependencies in the design. We have introduced the model data interface for accessing a user supplied structure model and MTL as a language to express pattern-based model transformations.

Our further work will be on interfacing our approach with standards for requirement handling and system modeling like AP233 and SysML. Additionally base of available patterns and supported analysis tools should be extended.

In the long run we want to study the aspect of data quality in the property database and how our system can be used for risk management in later design stages.

REFERENCES

[1] E. Gamma, R. Helm, R. Johnson, J. Vlissides. *Design Patterns*. Addison-Wesley Publishing Group (1995).

[2] C. Alexander, S. Ishikawa, M. Silverstein, M. Jacobson, I. Fiksdahl-King, S. Angel. *A Pattern Language*. Oxford University Press, New York (1977)

[3] Mueller, D. *demanda II, A prototype for Requirement Capture & Formalization*.In *IMW - Institutsmitteilung Nr. 26*, Germany, Clausthal (2001), ISSN 0947-2274.

[4] DOORS. http://www.telelogic.com/products/doorsers/doors/.

[5] J. Kruse, T. Volling, C. Thomsen, R. Ernst, T. Spengler. *Towards flexible Systems Engineering by Using Flexible Quantity Contracts*. In Proc. *Automation, Assistance and Embedded Real Time Platforms for Transportation* (AAET'05), Braunschweig, Germany, 2005.

[6] J. Kruse, T. Volling, C. Thomsen, R. Ernst, T. Spengler. *Introducing Flexible quantity contracts into distributed SoC and embedded system design processes*. In Proc. *Design, Automation, and Test in Europe (DATE'05)*, Munich, Germany, 2005.

[7] S. K. S. Chakraborty, L. Thiehle.*A general framework for analyzing system properties in platform-based embedded system designs*. In Proc. *Design, Automation and Test in Europe (DATE'03)*. Germany, Munich, Mar. 2003.

[8] AADL. http://www.aadl.info/

[9] SymTA/S. http://www.symta.org

[10] AP233, http://ap233.eurostep.com/.

[11] SysML, http://www.sysml.org/.

[12] *Document Object Core Model*, http://www.w3.org/TR/DOM-Level-2-Core/core.html.

AN EMBEDDED SW DESIGN EXPLORATION APPROACH BASED ON UML ESTIMATION TOOLS

Marcio F. da S. Oliveira[1], Lisane B. de Brisolara[1], Luigi Carro[1,2], Flávio R. Wagner[1]

[1]*Computer Science Institute - Federal University of Rio Grande do Sul, PO Box 15064, Porto Alegre, Brazil;*
[2]*Electrical Engineering Department - Federal University of Rio Grande do Sul, Av. Osvaldo Aranha, 103, Porto Alegre, Brazil*

Abstract: Software engineers, when modeling an application using object-oriented concepts and the UML language, do not have an idea of the impact of their modeling decisions on issues such as performance, energy, and memory footprint for a given embedded platform. However, these are critical characteristics for embedded systems and should be taken into account in early design stages. In our approach, estimation of data and program memory, performance and energy are obtained from an initial UML specification. It allows the designer to evaluate and compare different modeling solutions, thus supporting design space exploration at a very high abstraction level. A case study is used to demonstrate our approach, in which an application is modeled in different ways and the alternative solutions are compared using the high-level estimations. Experimental results are presented and demonstrate the effectiveness of the estimates in an early design space exploration.

Keywords: Embedded Software, UML, Estimation, Design Space Exploration

1.   INTRODUCTION

Advances in technology increase the functionality in an embedded system. At the same time, the life cycle of embedded products becomes increasingly tighter. In this scenario, productivity and quality are simultaneously required in embedded systems design in order to deliver competitive products. Selic [1] emphasizes that the use of techniques starting from higher abstraction levels is crucial to the design success.

In this context, the Unified Modeling Language (UML) has gained in popularity as a tool for specification and design of embedded systems. In [2], one can find several efforts that describe the use of UML during the different phases of an embedded system design process.

Beyond the rising of abstraction level, platform-based design is required to improve the design productivity [3]. In platform-based design, design derivatives are mainly configured by software, and software development is where most of the design time is spent. But the quality of the software development also directly impacts the system properties (performance, energy consumption, memory footprint, etc.).

Nowadays, the software designer writes the application code and relies on a compiler to optimize it. Compiler code optimizations have been traditionally oriented to improve performance. However, the optimization goals for embedded systems are dominated not only by performance, but memory accesses and energy consumption are equally important [4].

It is widely known that design decisions taken at higher abstraction levels can lead to substantially superior improvements. This context suggests the support to a fast design space exploration in the early design steps. However, software engineers, when developing an application using UML, do not have a concrete measure of the impact of their modeling decisions on issues such as performance and energy for a specific embedded platform.

This paper proposes an approach that allows a better evaluation of modeling solutions, through the estimation of the final system physical characteristics directly from UML models, thus supporting a very early design space exploration. Our approach provides the estimation of memory, performance, and energy consumption for a system modeling solution.

An experiment demonstrates that different UML modeling solutions for the same application result in different performance, energy consumption and memory footprint. It also shows that, by using our estimation tool from UML, the designer can really explore the system software architecture, by exploring different solutions at early stages, already at the UML level. The experiment shows that the designer can obtain a reasonable amount of certitude on the best direction to be followed in order to optimize the design and meet system requirements, when comparing different modeling approaches.

This paper is organized as follows. Section 2 gives an overview of related work. Section 3 introduces our proposal for embedded software design exploration, including the adopted modeling approach and the proposed estimation methodology. Section 4 presents the experiment that consists of an example of design space exploration scenario, comparing alternative solutions. Section 5 draws main conclusions and discusses future work.

2. RELATED WORK

Bernardi et al. [5] propose the automatic translation of state and sequence diagrams into a generalized stochastic Petri net and a composition of the resulting net models in order to reach an analysis goal. This proposal allows the analysis of the system execution time, but the operation times have to be manually included in the model.

Theelen et al. [6] propose an UML profile and a methodology for performance modeling of UML-based systems. The UML models are translated into an executable model specified in POOSL (Parallel Object-Oriented Specification Language). Some behavioral aspects and time delays can be specified in a probabilistic way, through provided libraries. However, the designer needs to go down the abstraction level from UML to POOSL to estimate system properties.

Petriu and Woodside [7] present an approach that uses the UML-SPT profile, where desired values for performance measures are manually added to the model. A performance model is then derived, from which the performance analyses are computed by simulation or by analytical techniques.

Chen et al. [8] proposed a design methodology that uses an UML Platform profile to model both application and platform. In this methodology, the analysis and synthesis tools available in the Metropolis framework are used to support design space exploration. This work, however, presents a very intrusive methodology, forcing the designer to use a very particular modeling approach. It also relies on simulation to obtain performance estimations.

All previous works lack an efficient estimation method to obtain information related to performance, such as number of instructions or execution time, and usually this information must be manually specified in the models. Moreover, these approaches do not consider important costs for embedded systems, such as memory and energy consumption. This work proposes a multi-variable methodology, where energy and memory footprint can also be estimated, not only performance. Moreover, our approach is not based on simulation, thus requiring less time to provide estimates and less detail about the system implementation, when compared to other approaches.

3. OUR PROPOSAL FOR EMBEDDED SOFTWARE DESIGN EXPLORATION

We propose an UML-based estimation approach, which allows the estimation of the system properties by mapping the application model into a given pre-characterized platform. It can be used to support design space exploration at a very high abstraction level. An estimation tool called SPEU has been developed to implement this approach. In order to support the estimation process, rules for modeling the application and a way to represent information about a given platform have been defined. Both the modeling and estimation approaches are described in this section.

3.1 Modeling approach

We chose UML as the modeling language for several reasons: (i) UML is a recognized standard that is becoming very popular, especially in industry; (ii) UML offers extension mechanisms; and (iii) UML does not depend on any particular methodology, so that one can define his/her own methodology for modeling and design space exploration.

Simple rules are imposed to the designer in order to allow automatic estimation of models. Basically, Class and Sequence diagrams are used in the application model. Structural information can be specified in the class diagram, such as multiplicity for vectors. The behavioral information is captured from the Sequence diagrams, in which we can specify interaction, conditional execution, and dependences between execution scenarios.

Access methods and delegations of these methods are usually employed in the object-oriented programming approach. In order to identify these methods, some restrictions are imposed to the designer: (i) the "get" or "set" prefix must precede the class field name that has its method invoked; (ii) if the class does not have a field specified in its method name, this means that the method delegates an access to another class; (iii) the suffix "Content" should be used, indicating that the method is accessing the structure contents, like vector or matrix positions. A distinction between these methods is important because they have different costs.

The platform model could contain information about processor architecture, API, operating system, application components, and device drivers. Currently, we use only architectural aspects, such as data types and instruction set (sizes and number of execution cycles). Also program and data memory allocation aspects are considered, including allocation rules of dynamic frame and reserved memory.

3.2   Estimation approach

Our approach allows the estimation of performance, energy consumption, and data and program memory size. These system properties are the basis for other requirement analyses, like quality of service (QoS) assessment about the application in communication, schedulability, and resource usage. The approach is based on the mapping of the application model into a platform model.

The estimation process starts with a static analysis of the application model, which does not require simulation. From the Class Diagrams, structural and static information, like memory required by classes, including attributes and methods, are extracted. Moreover, access methods and number and types of parameters are also identified. Furthermore, behavioral information is extracted from the Sequence Diagrams, including the number of method calls, conditional and loop operations. A pseudo-trace is generated that contains symbolic instructions like "getField", "getMatrixContent", "interactionExecution", and "loadParameterByValue".

The result is mapped into the platform, in order to obtain the estimates of system properties. The information provided by the platform memory model is used to determine the required memory size. Information about fields in classes, together with their multiplicity, is used to compute the data memory. Moreover, the worst-case scenario of nested invocation methods is identified, and the memory volume of allocated methods is computed. The sizes of instructions and method declarations are added to estimate the program memory size, using the information about the instruction set and program memory allocation model specified in the platform. Then, this result is added to the data memory to determine the total memory size.

From the pseudo-trace and from the performance and energy costs associated with the symbolic instructions, the performance and energy estimates can be computed. As there is no knowledge about the algorithms executed by the objects, just collaborations between objects and information on conditional and iteration executions are used. However, it is important to highlight that the behaviors that are most relevant to the performance estimation are captured by this methodology.

4.   EXPERIMENT

In order to illustrate a design space exploration scenario, alternative solutions for Sokoban, a popular logic game, were developed. For each solution, the application model was mapped into the femtoJava platform [9], based on a Java microcontroller. Afterwards, these solutions are compared using the SPEU estimations as a guide.

4.1   Alternative application models

Two alternative solutions have been modeled. However, the second one was designed to improve performance. The scenarios of the second solution use the same algorithms as the first one. Therefore, only design decisions that impact the collaborations between objects are evaluated, thus enhancing the design space exploration at this level. Figure 2 illustrates the Class Diagrams for the first solution.

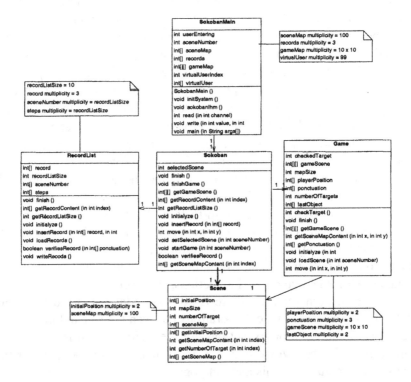

Figure 1. First solution's Class Diagram.

The second solution was designed to improve performance, through the removal of the encapsulation and union of the classes *Sokoban* and *Game*. With this modification, the objects can interact directly with each other, while in the first solution the *Sokoban* class concentrated the interactions in order to encapsulate the classes like components. Therefore, the second solution has less nested invocation methods than the first one and does not have delegation methods, thus requiring less memory and fewer cycles to be executed. Figures 2 and 3 illustrate the sequence diagrams for the *Move Player* scenario for the first and second solutions, respectively.

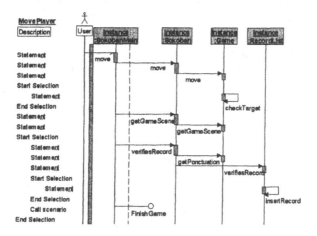

Figure 2. First solution's Move Player scenario.

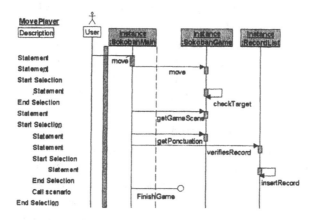

Figure 3. Second solution's Move Player scenario.

4.2 System design exploration results

The SPEU estimates for the two models are compared against the results obtained through a cycle-accurate simulation of the system implementation using the CACO-PS power and performance simulator [10]. The hardware system and the Java byte codes of the application are obtained using

Marcio F. da S. Oliveira, Lisane B. de Brisolara, Luigi Carro,
                                                            Flávio R. Wagner

SASHIMI [9], the femtoJava platform synthesis tool. Results for the first and second solutions are depicted in Table 1.

The femtoJava platform does not have dynamic object allocation. Therefore, the data memory allocated only for class fields is the same in the estimated and in the exact values. However, the frames of method executions are dynamically allocated, thus causing a small error in the total data memory estimation. The estimated value represents the minimum data memory required for the application execution. The larger errors for the program memory were already expected, since information about the implementation of the methods is not available.

Table 1. Design exploration results for the alternative solutions.

Property	First Solution			Second Solution		
	SPEU	**Exact**	**Error**	**SPEU**	**Exact**	**Error**
Data memory	657	663	-0.90	645	648	-0.46
Program Memory	383	1,094	-61.86	141	1,044	-86.5
Performance best-case	42,784	113,999	-62.47	35,673	107,207	-66.73
Energy best-case	38,145,635	89,343,862	-57.31	32,354,787	83,744,347	-61.37

In the same way, the performance and energy estimated by SPEU present errors of 62,47% and 57,31% respectively, with regard to the exact values for the first solution. The SPEU estimates for the second solution present approximately the same error as the estimates for the first model. The resulting errors can be easily explained, since at the UML level there is a lack of concrete information about the actual implementation of the algorithms. However, this absolute error result does not preclude a design exploration, where a relative trend in the cost of alternative modeling solutions is more important than absolute estimates.

We can observe in Table 1 that the second solution has an estimated improvement of 16.63% in its performance. The minimum data memory required to execute the application is smaller in the second solution than in the first one. Also the estimated energy consumption was reduced in 15.18% when compared to the first solution. The program memory size was also reduced, since classes and delegation methods were removed in the second solution.

When the final implementations are compared, the second modeling solution presents an improvement of 6.06% in its performance. This smaller value, when compared to the estimated one (16.63%), is due to the error resulting from estimations at such high level of abstraction. Whenever static information is the only one available, like in [11], relatively large errors in the performance analysis of embedded software might be expected.

Nevertheless, using the relative errors one can still explore the design space in an effective manner.

However, the errors compared in Table 2 show that the estimations follow the same tendency as the exact values. The experiment showed that the second solution is really more efficient than the first one, as the estimation had indicated.

Table 2. Relative errors of the solutions (%).

Property	Gain (%)	
	SPEU	Exact
Data memory	-0.90	-0.46
Program Memory	-61.86	-86.5
Performance best-case	-62.47	-66.73
Energy best-case	-57.31	-61.37

These results demonstrate that at a very high abstraction level it is already possible to explore the design space according to the system requirements, since alternative modeling solutions present different estimated results that are correlated to the results obtained in the final implementation. Therefore, the designer can explore alternative UML modeling solutions in such a way that the final synthesized application obtains improvements in performance, energy consumption, or memory footprint, or is more amenable to fulfill given system requirements.

5. CONCLUSIONS AND FUTURE WORK

In this paper, we have presented an approach for embedded software design exploration based on UML estimation tools. To support this approach, an estimation methodology has been also proposed, which allows the evaluation of models while exploring the design space, in order to find a model that better fulfills the application requirements.

Experimental results have confirmed the hypothesis that it is possible to explore the design space based on modeling decisions taken at very high levels of abstraction. Selecting the best modeling approach already at the UML level might result in gains in terms of physical characteristics like memory footprint, performance, and energy consumption.

These facts reinforce the need for a design space exploration environment, as shown in this paper, where the designer can explore the models to obtain object-oriented applications that are as optimized as possible for embedded systems.

Future work will address the improvement of the estimations by adding information extracted from other UML diagrams and from the UML SPT profile. Moreover, by having more detailed information about the platforms, for instance about its communication mechanisms and scheduling algorithm, we hope to increase the absolute precision of the method.

REFERENCES

1. B. Selic, Models, Software Models and UML. In: UML for Real: Design of Embedded Real-Time Systems, ch. 1, Kluwer Academic Publishers, Dordrecht, Netherlands, 2003.
2. L. Lavagno, G. Martin, B. Selic, UML for Real: Design of Embedded Real-Time Systems. Kluwer Academic Publishers, 2003.
3. D. Verkest, J. Kunkel, F. Schirrmeister, System Level Design Using C++. In: Design, Automation and Test in Europe, Paris, France, March, 2000.
4. M. Leeman et al, Automated Dynamic Memory Data Type Implentation Exploration and Optimization. In: IEEE Computer Society Annual Symposium on VLSI. Florida, February, 2003.
5. S. Bernardi, S. Donatelli, J. Merseguer, From UML Sequence Diagrams and StateCharts to Analysable Petri Net models. In: 3rd ACM International Workshop on Software and Performance, Rome, Italy, July, 2002.
6. B. D. Theelen, P.H.A. van der Putten, J.P.M. Voeten, Using the SHE Method for UML-based Performance Modeling. In: System Specification and Design Languages, ch. 12, Kluwer Academic Publishers, Dordrecht, Netherlands, 2003.
7. D.C. Petriu, C. M. Woodside, Performance analysis with UML: layered queueing models from the performance profile. In: UML for Real: Design of Embedded Real-Time Systems, ch 11 . Kluwer Academic Publishers, Dordrecht, Netherlands, 2003.
8. R. Chen, M. Sgroi, G. Martin, L. Lavagno, A. Sangiovanni-Vicentelli, J. Rabaey, Embedded System Design Using UML and Platforms. In: Forum on Specification and Design Languages, September, 2002.
9. S. Ito, L. Carro, R. Jacobi, Making Java Work for Microcontroller Applications. In: IEEE Design & Test of Computers. v. 18, n. 5, September-October, 2001.
10. A. C. Beck, J. C. B. Mattos, F. R. Wagner, L. Carro, CACO-PS: A General Purpose Cycle-Accurate Configurable Power Simulator. In: 16th Symposium on Integrated Circuits and Systems Design. São Paulo, Brazil, September, 2003.
11. S. Y. Li, S. Malik, Performance Analysis of Embedded Software Using Implicit Path Enumeration. In: IEEE Transactions on Computer-Aided Design of Integrated Circuits and Systems, v. 16, n. 12, December, 1997.

AN APPLICATION-ORIENTED APPROACH FOR THE GENERATION OF SOC-BASED EMBEDDED SYSTEMS

Fauze V. Polpeta and Antônio A. Fröhlich
Federal University of Santa Catarina, Brazil
{fauze,guto}@lisha.ufsc.br

Abstract: This paper outlines a strategy for automating the design of embedded systems including their hardware and software components. We focus in the *Hardware Mediator* construct, a portability artifact that was originally proposed to enable the port of component-based operating systems to very distinct architectures. Besides giving rise to a highly adaptable system-hardware interface, these mediators are approached as a new co-design artifact that can be used to enable the generation of customized *system-on-a-chip* instances and the associated run-time support systems considering the requirements of target applications.

Keywords: Application-Oriented System Design, Embedded Systems, Hardware Mediators, Operating Systems, System-on-a-Chip

1. INTRODUCTION

Embedded systems are becoming more and more complex, yet, there is no room for development strategies that incur in extended time-to-market in this extremely competitive sector. In this context, the *System-on-a-Chip* (SoC) define a compromise between system complexity and development costs [2]. Furthermore, the advances in programmable logic devices (PLD) are enabling developers to instantiate and to evaluate complex SoC designs in a short period of time. This can drastically decreases the time-to-market and turns PLDs an important technologic alternative in the development of embedded systems.

Indeed, some *embedded systems* can be completely implemented in hardware using the SoC approach. However, the more complex the application, the greater is the probability it will need some kind of *run-time support system* and an *application program*. This is, after all, the reason why so many groups are concentrating efforts to develop processor soft cores such as Leon2 and OpenRisc [11]. Nevertheless, run-time support systems are often neglected by currently available SoC development methodologies and tools, being mostly restricted to simple processor scheduling routines and the definition of a hardware abstraction layer. The gap between software and hardware gets even bigger when we recall that one of the primary goals of an operating system is to grant the portability of applications, since ordinary operating systems cannot go with the dynamism of SoCs.

In this paper we discuss the use of *Hardware Mediators* [16] to enable the automatic generation of SoC-based embedded systems. The deployment of *Application-Oriented System Design* (AOSD) [4] on the context where hardware mediators were originally proposed—*software-hardware interfacing*—fosters this portability artifact to a new perspective on the design of embedded systems. Mediators are figured as pointers for generating a "machine description" that matches, in association with a run-time support system, the requirements of dedicated applications. The following sections describe the basics of the AOSD method, the concepts of hardware mediators and how these mediators can be deployed on the generation of SoC-based embedded systems. Subsequently, in a experimental case study, we consider the EPOS system [5], an application-oriented operating system that relies on hardware mediators to foster portability and also to enable automatic hardware generation. The paper is closed with a discussion of related works and the author's perspectives.

2.   APPLICATION-ORIENTED SYSTEM DESIGN

Application-Oriented System Design (AOSD) [4] proposes some alternatives to proceed the engineering of a domain towards software components. In principle, an application-oriented decomposition of the problem domain can be obtained following the guidelines of *Object-Oriented Decomposition* [3]. However, some subtle yet important differences must be considered. First, object-oriented decomposition gathers objects with similar behavior in class hierarchies by applying variability analysis to identify how one entity specializes the other. Besides leading to the famous "fragile base class" problem [12], this policy assumes that specializations of an abstraction (i.e. *subclasses*) are only deployed in presence of their more generic versions (i.e. *superclasses*).

Applying variability analysis in the sense of *Family-Based Design* [15] to produce independently deployable abstractions, modeled as members of a family, can avoid this restriction and improve on application-orientation. Certainly, some family members will still be modeled as specializations of others, as in *Incremental System Design* [7], but this is no longer an imperative rule. For example, instead of modeling connection-oriented as a specialization of connectionless communication (or vice-versa), what would misuse a network that natively operates in the opposite mode, one could model both as autonomous members of a family.

A second important difference between application-oriented and object- oriented decomposition concerns environmental dependencies. Variability analysis, as carried out in object-oriented decomposition, does not emphasizes the differentiation of variations that belong to the essence of an abstraction from those that emanate from the execution scenarios being considered for it. Abstractions that incorporate environmental dependencies have a smaller chance of being reused in new scenarios, and, given that an application-oriented operating system will be confronted with a new scenario virtually every time a new application is defined, allowing such dependencies could severely hamper the system.

Nevertheless, one can reduce such dependencies by applying the key concept of *Aspect-Oriented Programming* [8], i.e. aspect separation, to the decomposition process. By doing so, one can tell variations that will shape new family members from those that will yield scenario aspects. For example, instead of modeling a new member for a family of communication mechanisms that is able to operate in the presence of multiple threads, one could model multithreading as a scenario aspect that, when activated, would lock the communication mechanism (or some of its operations) in a critical section.

Based on these premises, Application-Oriented Systems Design guides a domain engineering procedure (see Figure 1) that models software components with the aid of three major constructs: families of scenario-independent abstractions, scenario adapters and inflated interfaces.

2.1   Families of scenario independent abstractions

During domain decomposition, abstractions are identified from domain entities and grouped in families according to their commonalities. Yet during this phase, aspect separation is used to shape scenario-independent abstractions, thus enabling them to be reused in a variety of scenarios. These abstractions are subsequently implemented to give rise to the actual software components.

2.2   Scenario adapters

As explained earlier, AOSD dictates that scenario dependencies must be factored out as *aspects*, thus keeping abstractions scenario-independent. However, for this strategy to work, means must be provided to apply factored aspects to abstractions in a transparent way. The traditional approach to do this would be deploying an *aspect weaver*, though the *scenario adapter* construct [6] has the same potentialities without requiring an external tool. A scenario adapter wraps an abstraction, intermediating its communication with scenario-dependent clients to perform the necessary scenario adaptations.

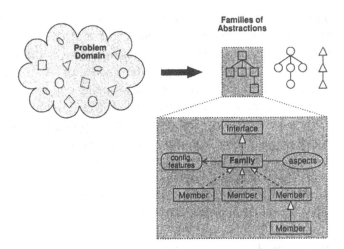

Figure 1.   Overview of application-oriented domain decomposition.

2.3   Inflated interfaces

Inflated interfaces summarize the features of all members of a family, creating a unique view of the family as a "super component". It allows application programmers to write their applications based on well-know, comprehensive interfaces, postponing the decision about which member of the family shall be used until enough configuration knowledge is acquired. The binding of an inflated interface to one of the members of a family can thus be made by automatic configuration tools that identify which features of the family were used in order to choose the simplest realization that implements the requested interface subset at compile-time.

3.   HARDWARE MEDIATORS

An operating system designed according to the premises of Application-Oriented System Design can be summarily viewed as sets of software components that can be configured, adapted and integrated in order to give rise to highly customized and scenario-specific instances of run-time support systems. However, besides all the benefits claimed by software component engineering, such a class of run-time support systems is prone to the same need for portability as their more conventional relatives.

Traditional portability strategies, mainly focused in hardware abstraction layers (HAL) and virtual machines (VM), are not concerned with the AOSD's purposes. Being a product of a system engineering process (instead of a domain engineering process), these strategies usually build a monolithic abstraction layer that encapsulates all the resources available in the hardware platform without properly regarding the application needs. Such modeling may be a problem when the platforms to be interfaced are based on SoCs. The diversity of architectures and devices in these platforms lead us to diagnose that the traditional specification techniques for sw-hw interfacing are still far from the ideal "plug-and-play" [14]. In addition, whenever SoCs are built on *Programmable Logic Devices* such as FPGAs, the hardware specifications can be modified in a short period of time [17], and thus compromising much more the portability of the system.

In order to deal with this dynamism and to foster the portability of system abstractions to virtually any architecture, a system designed according to the concepts of AOSD relies on the hardware mediator construct. As discussed in *Hardware Mediators: a Portability Artifact for Component-Based Systems* [16], the main idea behind this portability artifact is not to build an universal hardware abstraction layer or virtual machine, but sustaining an *interface contract* between the operating system and the hardware. Each hardware component is mediated via its own mediator, thus granting the portability of abstractions that use it without creating unnecessary dependencies. Indeed, hardware mediators are intended to be mostly static-metaprograms and thus "dissolve" themselves in the system abstractions as soon as the interface contract is met. In other words, a hardware mediator delivers the functionality of the corresponding hardware component through a system-oriented interface.

An important element of hardware mediators are *configurable features*, which designate features of mediators that can be switched on and off according to the requirements dictated by abstractions. A configurable feature is not restricted to a flag indicating whether a preexisting hardware feature must be activated or not. Usually, it also incorporates a *Generic Programmed* [13] implementation of the algorithms and data structures that are necessary to implement that feature when the hardware itself does not provide it. An example of configurable feature is the generation of CRC codes in mediators that abstract communication devices.

Likewise abstractions in AOSD (Figure 1), hardware mediators are organized in families whose members represent significant entities in the hardware domain. Such modeling enables the generation of object-code only for those mediators that are necessary to support the application. Non-functional aspects and cross-cutting properties are factored out as *scenario aspects* that can be applied to family members as required. For instance, families like UART and NIC (*Network Interface Card*) must often operate in exclusive-access mode. This could be achieved by applying a share-control aspect to the families.

4.   CO-DESIGNING WITH HARDWARE MEDIATORS

Although originally devised to give rise to highly adaptable system- hardware interface, hardware mediators can be also used for generating application-oriented hardware instances. More specifically, in the context of programmable logic, where hardware components, namely soft-IPs, are described using hardware description languages (e.g. VHDL, VERILOG) in order to implement the elements of the underling hardware technology. Hence, by associating hardware mediators with those descriptions one can infer which hardware components are necessary to support the application.

A component-based system can thus rely on hardware mediators not only to interface its system abstractions to the hardware, but also to dictate which components will build-up the target hardware. As soon as a hardware mediator is selected to interface a hardware component, the associated IP is selected from a repository in order to integrate a hardware description that will be synthesized in a PLD device. Such a description in the form of a SoC would embed only the hardware components necessary to support the run-time system and, in turn, the application.

For instance, consider a family of NIC mediators and a family of NIC hardware components whose members are associated to the members of the mediator's family. From a given application that uses a system abstraction to implement an Ethernet network one can infer that a member of the family NIC will be instantiated. However, the decision of which specific member will be instantiated, since all members are functionally equivalent, is up to the application's programmer. This situation characterizes what we named a *combined IP-selection*. The hardware devices are inferred considering an application requirement and a specific decision of the application's programmer.

Another scenario, named *discreet IP-selection*, is related to the selection of hardware components considering only the application's requirements — no explicit programmer decision must be taken. A good example for this scenario is related to the memory management scheme that will be implemented by the run-time support system. Once the application programmer uses system abstractions that rely on a *paging* scheme (e.g. *multitasking*), the MMU mediator is automatically inferred and, consequently, a memory management unit will be selected for synthesis. Conversely, when a *flat* memory scheme is adopted no memory management unit is synthesized.

A third scenario, named *explicit IP-selection*, represents the chance of the programmer to choose the hardware components that will be instantiated in the system. Even if the respective mediators are "hidden" by system abstractions, the programmer explicitly selects the hardware components that he is intending to embed in the SoC. Indeed, this selection strategy is always taken when the programmer initially specifies which architecture model (e.g. SPARCV8, OR32) the system will follow.

Furthermore, the approach is not restricted to the specification of which IPs will be instantiated in a PLD device. The element *configurable feature* explained earlier can be also deployed on hardware components. They can be used to configure IPs in order to properly support the application and also to switch on and off some functionalities that can be implemented in hardware or in software. As exemplified earlier with CRC codes, a configurable feature can be used to enable the generation of these codes in a UART mediator for data transmitted over a serial communication line. Such codes, otherwise, could be generated by the hardware itself instead of the software. In this case, since the IP that implements the UART device supports generation of CRC codes, a hardware configurable feature would be activated in order to enable the synthesis of these functionalities in the SoC.

5. CASE STUDY: SOCS IN EPOS

The Embedded Parallel Operating System (EPOS) aims at delivering adequate run-time support for dedicated computing applications. Relying on the *Application-Oriented System Design* method, EPOS consists of families of software components that can be adapted to fulfill the requirements of particular applications. In order to maintain the portability of its systems abstractions and to enable the generation of application-oriented SoCs, the EPOS system relies on the hardware mediator construct.

An application written on EPOS can be submitted to a tool that scans it searching for references to the *inflated interfaces*, thus rendering the features of each family that are necessary to support the application at run-time. This task is accomplished by a tool, the analyzer, that outputs an specification of requirements in the form of partial component interface declarations, including methods, types and constants that were used by the application.

The primary specification produced by the analyzer is subsequently fed into a second tool, the configurator, that consults a build-up database to create the description of the system's configuration. This database holds information about each component in the repository, as well as dependencies and composition rules that are used by the configurator to build a dependency three. The output of the configurator consists of a set of keys that define the binding of inflated interfaces to abstractions and activate the scenario aspects eventually identified as necessary to satisfy the constraints dictated by the target application or by the configured execution scenario. On the side of the hardware components, the configurator produces a list of instantiated mediators and specifies which of these mediators promote IP synthesis.

The last step in the generation process is accomplished by the generator. This tool translates the keys produced by the configurator into parameters for a statically metaprogramed component framework and causes the compilation of a tailored operating system instance. In addition, whenever a SoC needs to be tailored, the `generator`, based on the IP configurable features, produces a synthesis configuration file. This file, as well as the selected IPs, are passed to

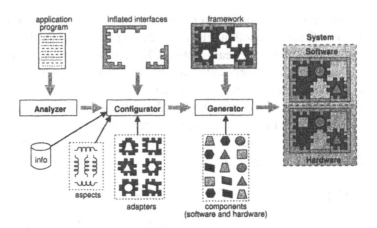

Figure 2. An overview of the tools involved in the automatic generation of run-time support and hardware instances.

a third-party tool, which in turn performs the synthesis of a SoC. An overview of the whole procedure is depicted in Figure 2.

5.1   Sample Instance: Leon SoCs in EPOS

In order to evaluate our approach for automating the design of SoC-based embedded systems we used the *Leon2 Processor*. This "processor" was created in order to enable the development of customized SoCs based on the SPARCV8 CPU core. The "modular" design of LEON2 enable us to specify which of its IPs will be synthesized in the SoC. The logic necessary to glue the IPs is implicitly defined in the source-code through a set of programming asserts, which are, in turn, used to properly configure and plug-in the IPs in a AMBA bus framework [1]. The Figure 3(a) shows the block diagram of LEON2. Besides the CPU core, LEON2 includes a set of peripherals that can be plugged in as soon as the user selects them.

The experiments were performed on a Xilinx Virtex2 FPGA development kit and consisted of evaluating an application for which a run-time support system and a SoC should be generated. The application implemented two threads, *TX* and *RX*, which were executed in a cooperative environment in order to send and receive data through an UART. Aiming at signaling the *RX* thread to deal with new data in the UART buffer the mechanism of *interrupts* was used. Consequently, the mediator and the IP of the interrupt controller (IC) were selected to be instantiated. As regards the memory management scheme, it was based on a *flat* address-space and therefore, no MMU components were instantiated in the system. The Figure 3(b) depicts the block diagram of the SoC that was generated after submit the application to the sequence of tools presented in section 5.

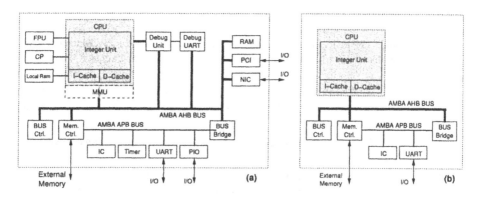

Figure 3. Block diagram of Leon2 (a) and the SoC that was experimentally customized (b).

Aiming at clarifying the expressiveness of this sample instance, it is important to compare the obtained results to the numbers of ordinary operating system that were ported to the LEON2 platform. Usually these systems are generated to compromise all the features that the SoC is able to provide. The absence of a component-based engineering and the lack of modern software engineering techniques affects not only the size and performance of the final system, but also effectively increase NRE costs and time-to-market. For instance, the EPOS instance generated to support the experimental application was 2.94 Kbytes and the associated SoC (Figure 3(b)) took 29% of the Virtex2 FPGA area. Traditional ports of UCLINUX [9] and ECOS [10] to the Leon2 platform have, respectively, 2,740 and 432.94 Kbytes each and the both were ported to a SoC instance with 13,261 LUTs (*Look-up-Table*), which represents 60% of the Virtex2 area.

6. CONCLUSION AND FUTURE WORK

In this article we conjectured about the the use of *hardware mediators* as a new co-design artifact. The deployment of AOSD in the context where mediators were originally proposed leaded us to use this portability artifact for the automatic generation of SoC-based embedded systems. The presented results are quite simple and just showed the viability of generating run-time support systems and system-on-chip instances considering the application's requirements. However, as exemplified in the section 4, we are not only able to identify which devices shall be instantiated in the SoC but, in fact, to configure each system component in order to better fits the application's requirements. In this sense a large gamma of new experiments started to be evaluated, such as processor scalability, memory hierarchy exploration and power management. The results obtained so far are encouraging and we hope present them soon.

REFERENCES

[1] ARM (2003). *The de facto Standard for On-Chip Bus.* Advanced RISC Machines Limited, online document edition. http://www.arm.com/ products/ solutions/ AMBAHomePage.html.

[2] Bergamaschi, R. A., Bhattacharya, S., Wagner, R., Fellenz, C., Muhlada, M., Lee, W. R., White, F., and Daveau, J.-M. (2001). Automating the Design of SoCs Using Cores. *IEEE Des. Test*, 18(5):32–45.

[3] Booch, G. (1994). *Object-Oriented Analysis and Design with Applications.* Addison-Wesley, 2nd edition.

[4] Fröhlich, A. A. (2001). *Application-Oriented Operating Systems.* Number 17 in GMD Research Series. GMD - Forschungszentrum Informationstechnik, Sankt Augustin.

[5] Fröhlich, A. A. and Schröder-Preikschat, W. (1999). High Performance Application-Oriented Operating Systems – The EPOS Approach. In *Proceedings of the 11th Symposium on Computer Architecture and High Performance Computing*, pages 3–9, Natal, Brazil.

[6] Fröhlich, A. A. and Schröder-Preikschat, W. (2000). Scenario adapters: Efficiently Adapting Components. In *Proceedings of the 4th World Multiconference on Systemics, Cybernetics and Informatics*, Orlando, U.S.A.

[7] Habermann, A. N., Flon, L., and Cooprider, L. (1976). Modularization and Hierarchy in a Family of Operating Systems. *Commun. ACM*, 19(5):266–272.

[8] Kiczales, G., Lamping, J., Mendhekar, A., Maeda, C., Lopes, C. V., Loingtier, J.-M., and Irwin, J. (1997). Aspect-Oriented Programming. In *Proceedings of the European Conference on Object-oriented Programming'97*, volume 1241 of *Lecture Notes in Computer Science*, pages 220–242, Jyv skyl, Finland. Springer.

[9] Wurm, M. (2003). uClinux for Sparc-mmuless with Ethernet MAC. Technical report, Graz University of Technology.

[10] Massa, A. (2002). *Embedded SW. Development with eCos.* Prentice Hall, 1st edition.

[11] Mattsson, D. and Christensson, M. (2004). Evaluation of Synthesizable CPU Cores. Technical report, Chalmers University Of Technology.

[12] Mikhajlov, L. and Sekerinski, E. (1998). A Study of the Fragile Base Class Problem. In *Proceedings of the 12th European Conference on Object-Oriented Programming*, pages 355–382. Springer-Verlag.

[13] Musser, D. R. and Stepanov, A. A. (1989). Generic Programming. In *Proceedings of the First International Joint' Conference of ISSAC and AAECC*, number 358 in Lecture Notes in Computer Science, pages 13–25, Rome, Italy. Springer.

[14] Neville-Neil, G. and Whitney, T. (2003). SoC: Software, Hardware, Nightmare, Bliss. *ACM Queue*, 1(2):24.

[15] Parnas, D. L. (1976). On the Design and Development of Program Families. *IEEE Transactions on Software Engineering*, SE-2(1):1–9.

[16] Polpeta, F. V. and Fröhlich, A. A. (2004). Hardware Mediators: A Portability Artifact for Component-based Systems. In *Proceeding of the International Conference on Embedded and Ubiquitous Computing*, volume 3207 of *LNCS*, pages 271–280, Aizu,Japan. Springer.

[17] Rutenbar, R. A., Baron, M., Daniel, T., Jayaraman, R., Or-Bach, Z., Rose, J., and Sechen, C. (2001). (When) Will FPGAs kill ASICs? In *Proceedings of the 38th conference on Design automation*, pages 321–322. ACM Press.

SOFTWARE AND DRIVER SYNTHESIS FROM TRANSACTION LEVEL MODELS

Haobo Yu, Rainer Dömer, Daniel D. Gajski
Center of Embedded Computer Systems
University of California, Irvine

Abstract: This work presents a method of automatically generating embedded software including bus driver code from a transaction level model (TLM). For the application software, a real time operating system (RTOS) adapter is introduced to model scheduling and synchronization at C level. ANSI-C code is generated targeting this RTOS adapter. Bus drivers are also automatically created for HW/SW communication. Finally, the software image file is created from the C code, bus driver code, RTOS adapter and RTOS library code.

   As a result, efficient embedded software is synthesized from abstract, target CPU independent source code, eliminating the need for manual RTOS targeting, I/O driver coding and system integration.

1.   INTRODUCTION

The rapid development of semiconductor process technology and the increasing use of RISC/DSP cores contribute to an increased importance of embedded software in SoC. A typical SoC design today includes one or more processors, memory, dedicated hardware, and a complex communication architecture. To drive the hardware, target specific SoC software is needed which contains real time operating systems and bus drivers, along with the specific application software. The increasing complexity of software in such SoC designs requires that a large period of the design time will actually be used for software development.

Transaction level models (TLM) are widely used in SoC modeling for early design space exploration. After the SoC architecture is fixed, separate HW/SW models are created from the TLM. Usually, the TLM is written in a system level description language (SLDL) (e.g. SystemC [9] or SpecC [6]). Today however, the TLM is mostly used only as a reference model for software engineers. Most of the embedded software is still written manually from scratch. This is a slow and error-prone

process. Moreover, to validate the manually written software, designers
have to simulate the compiled binary through either a hardware prototype or slow instruction set simulators (ISS). Both approaches hinder
the SoC development process significantly since the prototype is usually only available in the later stages of the design process and the ISS
simulation is extremely slow.

To tackle this problem, it is desirable that we can derive SoC software directly from the TLM and the generated software can be validated and tested before any platform prototype is available. This paper
solves these problems by introducing software synthesis which automatically generates application as well as bus driver code from the TLM.
Rather than binary code simulation, the generated software can be directly re-imported into the original TLM and simulated with the rest of
the system at C level. As a result, simulation speed increases by orders
of magnitude, while cycle and pin accurate I/O is still available at the
bus level.

The rest of this paper is organized as follows: After a brief overview
of related work, Section 2 describes the overall design flow of our software synthesis process. Section 3 through Section 6 then address RTOS
targeting, application code generation, bus driver synthesis, and binary
image generation in detail. Finally, experimental results are listed in
Section 7, and Section 8 concludes this work.

1.1   Related Work

A lot of work has been spent on software synthesis. There are approaches to code generation from UML [1], from graphical finite state
machine design environments (e.g. StateCharts [10]), from DSP graphical programming environments (e.g. Ptolemy [13]), or from synchronous
programming languages (e.g. Esterel [2]). In POLIS [5], a way of generating C code from co-design finite state machines is described. However,
this work targets mainly reactive real-time systems and cannot be easily
applied to more general applications. There are also works on software
scheduling, including quasi-static scheduling in Petri-Nets [12], and a
combination of static and dynamic task scheduling [3]. Operating system based software synthesis can be found in [4] and [7].

The focus in this paper is similar to the approaches [11] and [9]. [11]
presents software generation from SystemC based on the redefinition and
overloading of SystemC class library elements. In [9], a software-software
communication synthesis approach by substituting SystemC modules
with an equivalent C structure is proposed. However, the code generated
by these two approaches can not be validated through insertion into

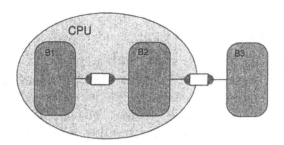

(a) Specification model

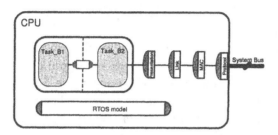

(b) TLM

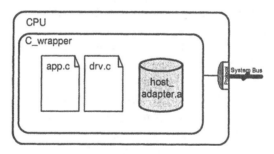

(c) C model

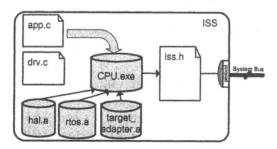

(d) Implementation model

Figure 1.   Software synthesis flow.

the original system model and the I/O drivers of the system are not addressed.

2.   DESIGN FLOW

The system design process starts with a specification model written by the designer to specify the desired system functionality, as shown in Fig. 1(a). Then, a system architecture model is derived through system partitioning and system bus selection. During this process, the system functionality is partitioned onto multiple processing elements (PEs) and a communication architecture consisting of abstract communication channels is inserted to represent the refined communication between PEs [14]. The resulting model, shown in Fig. 1(b), serves as the input for the software code generation.

During system partitioning, RTOS scheduling is inserted for the processor PEs that require dynamic scheduling support [8]. Software tasks are created from behaviors mapped to the same PE and an abstract RTOS model is inserted to manage the generated software tasks so that the software can be simulated at the fast transaction level.

Next, from the TLM, software C code is generated, as shown in Fig. 1(c). Application code (*app.c*) is generated for the software tasks and bus drivers (*drv.c*) are created for the abstract communication adapter channels. For validation, the generated C code is re-imported into the system model through a wrapper. Designers can use this C model for fast co-simulation of the system, avoiding the time consuming instruction set simulator (ISS) co-simulation for many cases.

Finally the generated C code is compiled into the processors instruction set and linked against the target RTOS to produce the final binary image. For final timing analysis, the binary code can also be simulated by use of an ISS, as shown in Fig. 1(d).

3.   RTOS ADAPTER

To support multitasking, a RTOS kernel is usually needed for the generated C code. However, there exists a large variety of RTOS providing different interfaces. One solution is to create specific software code for each target RTOS. An alternative solution is to use a general interface which abstracts away the underlining target specific RTOS implementations. In other words, a middleware layer can be used to adapt the specific RTOS to a general API. Our approach follows the second solution, using a RTOS adapter which provides a common interface to specific RTOS services. The RTOS adapter is essentially a middleware layer between the specific RTOS and the generated application software.

```
    void   OSStart(void);
    void   OSInit(void);
    void   OSWaitfor(sim_time);
    /*Task Management*/
 5  task_t TaskCreate(task_f *f,task_a arg,int pri);
    void   TaskDelete(task_t t);
    void   TaskJoin(task_t t);
    void   TaskRun(task_t t1, task_t t2);
    void   TaskSuspend(task_t t);
10  void   TaskResume(task_t t);
    /*Inter Task Synchronization*/
    void   SemRelease(sem_t  *sem);
    void   SemAquire(sem_t  *sem);
    void   EventNotify(evt_t e);
15  void   EventWait(evt_t e);
    /*Channels*/
    void   MutexAquire(mtx_t m);
    void   MutexRelease(mtx_t m);
    void   QueueSend(const void *d, unsigned long l);
20  void   QueueReceive(void *d, unsigned long l);
    ...
```

Figure 2.   RTOS adapter interface

3.1   Adapter Procedural Interface

The interface of our RTOS adapter is defined in Fig. 2. *OSInit* initializes the relevant kernel data structures while *OSStart* starts the task scheduling. In addition, *OSWaitfor* is provided to enable time modeling in the simulation. That is, the software tasks can call *OSWaitfor* to advance the system simulation time. This is used only for simulation and it will be ignored later in the real code.

Task management is the most important part of the RTOS adapter. This includes standard functions for task creation (*TaskCreate*), task completion (*TaskJoin*), task termination (*TaskDelete*), and temporary task suspension (*TaskSuspend, TaskResume*).

The RTOS adapter also provides two kinds of task synchronization services: semaphore and event. Inter-task communication is provided by abstract channels. Together, these functions support resource sharing, connection oriented data exchange, and any combination of these services. Note that the RTOS adapter provides a similar interface as the standard SLDL channel library. Thus, during code generation, most standard SLDL synchronization methods can be directly converted to this interface.

3.2   Host Adapter Library

In our approach, two RTOS adapter libraries are created for the interface defined above, one for the host and one for the target platform. The host adapter library is linked against the SLDL simulation engine

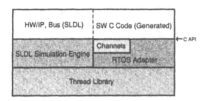
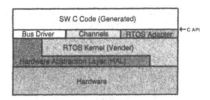

(a) Software modeling using SLDL　　　(b) Target software implementation

Figure 3.　Software implementation layers

so that the C code can co-simulate with the rest of the system code in SLDL. As shown in Fig. 3(a), the lowest layer of the host software stack is the thread library. This can be any host library supporting thread management (e.g POSIX thread library, Win32 thread library, or QuickThreads). On top of the thread management layer, both the SLDL simulation engine and the host RTOS library are implemented. The SLDL simulation engine provides standard system level constructs (channels, behaviors, interfaces etc.) for modeling custom hardware, IP cores and system busses, while the host RTOS adapter provides the C API for the OS related functions.

For host simulation, the highest layer is a TLM for the application including the hardware, software and the communication channels. The software (*app.c*, *drv.c*) for each processor is encapsulated in a SLDL wrapper. The RTOS adapter provides the generated C code with standard OS services. Communication between software C code and the rest of the system is performed through the ports of the wrapper.

3.3　Target Adapter Library

Fig. 3(b) shows the target software implementation. This is based upon the processor's hardware including its instruction set architecture (ISA), its I/O interfaces and its interrupt handling mechanisms. The hardware abstraction layer (HAL) is then implemented in software on top of this layer. It provides an abstraction of the processor hardware and is used as an interface for higher software layers. The next layer is the RTOS kernel for the target processor, which can be a commercial or a custom RTOS. The RTOS kernel implements basic multitasking and synchronization functionality corresponding to the services provided by the RTOS adapter. On top of the RTOS kernel is the target RTOS adapter which resembles a middleware layer translating task management APIs of the RTOS adapter into the corresponding APIs of the target RTOS kernel. Furthermore, the inter-task communication functionality of the RTOS adapter is directly implemented by using inter-process communication (IPC) mechanisms that are part of the target RTOS kernel. Note that bus drivers are implemented on top of both HAL library and RTOS kernel.

4.   APPLICATION CODE GENERATION

In the code generation process, C code is generated for all the parts of the system mapped to a processor. Specifically, SLDL constructs, including behaviors, channels and interfaces, are converted into C code. Essentially, this step synthesizes the hierarchy and port mapping elements contained in the SLDL description into ANSI C code.

For details on this code generation process, please refer to [15].

4.1   OS Targeting for Task Management

Generally, computation within the TLM is described through hierarchical and parallel composition of behaviors. This can be implemented in software using hierarchical C structures. For concurrent behaviors, however, multiple software tasks are needed to implement the specification.

This process is illustrated in Fig. 4. In the specification model (Fig. 4(a)), two behaviors *B*1 and *B*2 are running in parallel inside behavior *CPU*. After the RTOS scheduling step, two software tasks (*Task_B1* and *Task_B2*) are created dynamically and scheduled by the abstract RTOS model, as shown in Fig. 4(b) [16]. Next, C code is generated for these tasks, as shown in Fig. 4(c) [15].

```
behavior B1()
{void main(void)
...}
behavior B2()
5 {void main(void)
...}
behavior CPU()
{B1 b1();
 B2 b2();
10 void main(void)
{


15  par
  { b1.main();
    b2.main();
  }

20 }
```

```
behavior Task_B1()
{void main(void)
...}
behavior Task_B2()
5 {void main(void)
...}
behavior Task_CPU(RTOS os)
{Task_B1 task_b1(os);
 Task_B2 task_b2(os);
10 void main(void) {
 Task me;
 task_b1.os_task_create();
 task_b2.os_task_create();
 me = os.fork();
15 par {
    b1.main();
    b2.main();
  }
  os.join(me);}
20 }
```

```
struct Task_B1 {...};
void  Task_B1_main(struct
           Task_B1 *This)
{...}
5 struct Task_B2 {...};
void  Task_B2_main(struct
           Task_B2 *This)
{...}
struct Task_CPU        {
 struct Task_B1 task_b1;
 struct Task_B2 task_b2 }
10 void Task_CPU_main(struct
         Task_B1B2 *This)
{
TaskCreate(&Task_B1_main,
         &This->task_b1, 1);
TaskCreate(&Task_B2_main,
         &This->task_b2, 2);
15 TaskJoin(NULL);
}
```

(a) Spec. model   (b) Multi task TLM   (c) C code

Figure 4.   C code generation for task management

4.2   OS Targeting for Task Communication

Channels in the TLM can be divided into two categories: intra- and inter-PE channels. For the software implementation, the former are converted into task communication, while the latter are implemented as bus drivers.

The intra-PE channels can be further divided into two categories, SLDL standard channels and user defined channels. During the code generation process, methods of SLDL standard channels can be directly converted into the corresponding channel APIs of the RTOS adapter. User defined channels, on the other hand, are implemented the same way as the behaviors.

5.   BUS DRIVER GENERATION

In the partitioned system specification, communication between different PEs is performed through message passing channels with different semantics (blocked vs. non-blocked) and different data types. Then, the bus driver synthesis step refines the system communication architecture from an abstract message-passing down to an actual implementation over pins and wires.

Channel refinement is performed before the bus driver code can be created. This includes the definition of the overall network topology and generation of point-to-point communication links. The point-to-point links are then grouped into physical links and packet transfers for each link are implemented. Note that four layers of communication channels are inserted to drive the low layer communication media interfaces of each PE, as illustrated in Fig. 1(b) earlier.

Table 1 summarizes the communication channels, which refine the message passing channel to protocol word/frame transactions. The highest layer is the presentation channel which provides services to send and receive messages of arbitrary, abstract data type between different PEs. The next layer is the link channel which provides services to exchange data packets in the form of uninterpreted byte blocks. Typically, in a bus-based master/slave arrangement, each logical link is split into a data stream under the control of the master and a handshake (interrupt) from slave to master. So, in the implementation, the master side waits for a semaphore (which will be released by a client interrupt) before initiating a write or read transfer.

The media access (MAC) channel implements external interfaces of the HAL library for a processor PE. It is responsible for slicing blocks of bytes into unit transfers available at the bus interface. Finally, the

Name	C code

Presentation
• Typed, named messages
• Data formatting
	`App_send(struct App *This, struct S *buf)`
	`{`
	  `Link_send(This->link,(void *)&buf, sizeof(buf));`
	`}`

Link
• Point-to-Point logical links
• Synchronization
• Addressing
	`Link_send(struct Link *This,void *d, unsigned l)`
	`{`
	  `SemAquire(This->sem);`
	  `MAC_write(This->mac, This->addr,d,l);`
	`}`

Media Access
• Shared medium streams
• Data slicing
	`MAC_write(struct Mac *This,unsigned addr,`
	        `void *d,unsigned l){`
	  `for(...)`
	    `word = ...;`
	    `Protocol_writeWord(addr,word);`
	`}`

Protocol
• Word/frame transmission
• Protocol timing
	`Protocol_writeWord(U32 addr, WORD data)`
	`{`
	  `*addr = data; /*memory mapped IO*/`
	`}`

Table 1. C code generation for communication adapter channels.

protocol channel provides services to transfer words or frames over the physical medium.

In our implementation, the MAC and protocol channels are taken out of the processor database, while the presentation and link channels are created automatically. As we can see from Table 1, the bus driver (*drv.c*) is created by converting the four communication adapter channels into C and assembly code. This is then used by the application to drive the protocol channel. Note that the protocol channel implementation varies depending on how the processor is connected to the system bus. Usually, in a typical memory mapped I/O arrangement, the protocol layer send/receive primitives correspond to load and store instructions in the processor.

6. TARGET SPECIFIC BINARY CREATION

As the final step of software synthesis, the output C code is then compiled into the target processor's instruction set using the C compiler available for the processor. During this process, a HAL library is needed to provide target specific initialization and run time environment routines. It also provides the implementation for the MAC and protocol channels used during the bus driver synthesis.

Finally, the compiled object code is linked against the RTOS kernel, the target RTOS adapter library and the processor HAL library to generate executable code for the processor. A final simulation model can be created by replacing the component model of the processor with the ISS wrapper behavior of the target processor.

7.　EXPERIMENTAL RESULTS

We have implemented the proposed software synthesis tool and applied it to a set of design examples: a GSM voice codec, a JPEG encoder, a motor control system, and a MP3 decoder. For each example application, we have created a set of architectures varying in the number of hardware units that accellerate some part of the computation.

Using our software synthesis tool, we were able to generate the entire embedded software for each target architecture automatically. Moreover, code generation took less than a second in every case.

Design (loc), architecture		CPU, num. of co-proc.	Scheduling policy	Bhvrs./ Chnls.	SW Tasks	C code (loc)	Time (sec)
Vocoder 9,191	arch1	DSP56600, 1	RR	109/3	2	8,297	0.34
	arch2	DSP56600, 2	RR	104/4	2	8,098	0.35
	arch3	Coldfire, 3	priority	109/5	2	8,334	0.44
	arch4	Coldfire, 4	priority	111/6	2	8,537	0.50
JPEG 2,251	arch1	DSP56600, 1	static	26/3	1	1,119	0.11
	arch2	DSP56600, 2	static	37/4	1	1,553	0.10
	arch3	Coldfire, 3	static	39/5	1	1,636	0.09
	arch4	Coldfire, 4	static	39/6	1	1,679	0.11
Motor 2,049	arch1	TX-49, 1	RR	28/9	34	1,931	0.07
	arch2	TX-49, 2	RR	27/10	6	1,916	0.06
	arch3	TX-49, 3	priority	25/8	4	1,720	0.05
	arch4	TX-49, 4	priority	25/9	4	1,745	0.08
MP3 8,592	arch1	Coldfire, 1	RR	148/6	7	27,191	0.76
	arch2	Coldfire, 5	RR	147/7	16	25,524	0.85

Table 2.　Software synthesis results.

Details of our experimental results are summarized in Table 2. We have targeted three different CPUs, the Motorola DSP 56600, the Motorola Coldfire processor, and the Toshiba TX-49 processor. Each CPU is assisted by a number of hardware accelleration units, as listed in the table. Also listed are the scheduling policy (round-robin, priority-based, or static), the number of behaviors and channels in the SLDL model, the number of parallel software tasks, the number of lines of code (loc) of generated C code, and the run-time of our software synthesis tool (on a 2.4 GHz AMD Opteron PC).

As discussed in Section 6, MAC and protocol layer channels are inserted from the HAL library during the bus driver synthesis. Based on these channels, our synthesis tool creates the bus drivers for the different target processors. Then, to create the final executable image, the C code is compiled into binary code for the target RTOS. For our experiments, we have used the μC/OS-II RTOS which requires only a few lines of interface code for each function in the adapter API.

It could be argued that there is little or no productivity gain if our software synthesis flow is applied to just a single target architecture, because the amount of work in writing the specification TLM is about the same when writing the target C code directly. However, this argument does not hold if the target architecture changes or multiple architectures are analyzed during system design exploration. Then, the specification model is written only once, but many target architecture models can be generated automatically within seconds. Thus, the productivity gain is tremendous and true design space exploration becomes possible.

8. CONCLUSIONS

In this work, we have proposed steps to synthesize embedded software code and bus drivers from a TLM. A RTOS adapter library is introduced to facilitate the OS targeting process as well as to enable the generated C code to co-simulate with the rest of the system model. C code is automatically synthesized from the SLDL description of the input TLM. Parallel behaviors are converted into concurrent software tasks. Intra-PE channels are converted into inter-process synchronization and communication primitives, whereas inter-PE channels are converted into software bus drivers.

The automation of the SoC software generation process frees the designer from the tedious and error-prone tasks of creating software manually after SW/HW partitioning. Since the final software is directly derived from the TLM, validation of the software code becomes significantly easier than for manually written code.

In summary, we have developed a software synthesis tool that supports the automatic generation of efficient embedded software from an abstract TLM. Our experiments clearly demonstrate the applicability and benefits of the software synthesis approach in a system design environment.

Currently, our synthesis tool is written for the SpecC SLDL because of its simplicity and easy availability. Future work includes the extension of this methodology for SystemC SLDL, as well as the optimization of the generated code and support for more target RTOS and processors.

REFERENCES

[1] Rational. http://www.rational.com/uml/index.html.

[2] F. Boussinot and R. de Simone. The ESTEREL Language. In *Proceedings of the IEEE*, September 1991.

[3] J. Cortadella. Task Generation and Compile Time Scheduling for Mixed Data-Control Embedded Software. In *Proceedings of the Design Automation Conference*, pages 489–494, June 2000.

[4] D. Desmet, D. Verkest, and H. Man. Operating System Based Software Generation for System-on-Chip. In *Proceedings of the Design Automation Conference*, pages 396–401, June 2000.

[5] F.Balarin, P.Giusto, A.Jurecska, C.Passerone, E.Sentovich, B.Tabbara, M.Chiodo, H.Hsieh, L.Lavagno, A.Sangiovanni-Vincentelli, and K.Suzuki. *Hardware-Software Co-design of Embedded Systems – The POLIS approach*. Kluwer Academic Publishers, 1997.

[6] D. Gajski, J. Zhu, R. Dömer, A. Gerstlauer, and S. Zhao. *SpecC: Specification Language and Methodology*. Kluwer Academic Publishers, March 2000.

[7] L. Gauthier, S. Yoo, and A. Jerraya. Automatic Generation and Targeting of Application-Specific Operating Systems and Embedded Systems Software. *IEEE Trans. on Computer-Aided Design of Integrated Circuits and Systems*, Nov 2001.

[8] A. Gerstlauer, H. Yu, and D. Gajski. RTOS Modeling in System Level Design. *Proceedings of Design Automation and Test in Europe (DATE)*, 2002.

[9] T. Grötker, S. Liao, G. Martin, and S. Swan. *System Design with SystemC*. Kluwer Academic Publishers, 2002.

[10] D. Harel, H. Lachover, A. Naamad, A. Pnueli, M. Politi, R. Sherman, A. Shtull-Trauring, and M. Trachtenbrot. STATEMATE: A Working Environment for the Development of Complex Reactive Systems. *IEEE Transactions on Software Engineering*, April 1990.

[11] F. Herrera, H. Posadas, P. Sanchez, and E. Villar. Systematic Embedded Software Generation from SystemC. *Proceedings of Design Automation and Test in Europe (DATE)*, 2003.

[12] B. Lin. Software Synthesis of Process-Based Concurrent Programs. In *Proceedings of the Design Automation Conference*, 1998.

[13] J. L. Pino, S. Ha, E. A. Lee, and J. T. Buck. Software Synthesis for DSP using Ptolemy. *Journal of VLSI Signal Processing*, 1995.

[14] D. Shin, S. Abdi, and D. Gajski. Automatic Generation of Bus Functional Models from Transaction Level Models. In *Proceedings of the Asia and South Pacific Design Automation Conference*, 2004.

[15] H. Yu, R. Dömer, and D. D. Gajski. Embedded Software Generation from System Level Design Languages. In *Proceedings of the Asia and South Pacific Design Automation Conference*, Jan 2004.

[16] H. Yu, A. Gerstlauer, and D. D. Gajski. RTOS Scheduling in Transaction Level Models. In *Proceedings of the International Symposium on System Synthesis*, 2003.

EMBEDDED HARD REAL-TIME SOFTWARE SYNTHESIS CONSIDERING DISPATCHER OVERHEADS

Raimundo Barreto
DCC-UFAM. Manaus-AM-Brazil

Eduardo Tavares, Paulo Maciel, Marília Neves, Meuse Oliveira Jr,
Leonardo Amorim
CIn - UFPE. Recife-PE-Brazil.

Arthur Bessa
Fundação Centro de Análises, Pesquisas e Inovação Tecnológica. Manaus-AM-Brazil

Ricardo Lima
DSC - UPE. Recife-PE-Brazil
{ rsb, eagt, prmm, mln2, mnoj, lab2 } @cin.ufpe.br, arthur.bessa@fucapi.br, ricardo@dsc.upe.br

Abstract: Due to the increasing complexity and diversity of requirements, embedded software has become much harder to design. For instance, since several applications demand safety properties, the correctness and timeliness verification is an issue to be concerned. Usually, complex embedded real-time systems rely on specialized operating system kernels. However, operating systems may introduce significant overheads in execution time as well as in memory requirement. Software synthesis might be an alternative approach to operating systems usage, since it can generate tailored code for satisfying functional, performance, and resource constraints, and automatically generate runtime support (scheduling, resource management, communication, etc) customized for each particular specification. An often neglected situation in software synthesis research is the dispatcher and timer interrupt handler overheads. This paper provides a formal approach, based on time Petri nets, for synthesizing a timely and predictable scheduled code considering dispatcher overheads.

1.   INTRODUCTION

Our lives have become more dependent on embedded systems. Due to the increasing complexity and diversity of requirements, embedded software has become much harder to design. Since several applications demand safety properties, the correctness and timeliness verification is an important issue. Usually, complex embedded real-time systems rely on specialized operating system kernels. However, operating systems may introduce significant overheads in execution time as well as in memory requirement. Software synthesis might be an alternative approach to operating systems usage, since it can generate tailored code for satisfying functional, performance, and resource constraints, and automatically generate runtime support (scheduling, resource management, communication, etc) customized for each specification.

In order to reduce overheads in the execution of tasks, the code generation includes a small dispatcher to perform this activity. However, an often neglected situation in software synthesis research is the dispatcher and timer interrupt handler overheads. The solution adopted in this work explicitly models the WCET (worst-case execution time) of the dispatcher and timer interrupt handler. In this case, the overhead is considered during the schedule generation, leading to a more realistic estimation of system behavior.

Taking into account such needs, the main contribution of this paper is to provide an approach based on time Petri nets for synthesizing a timely and predictable scheduled code considering dispatcher overheads. This paper is an extension of our previous work [4], which presented how to reach feasible schedules by using a time Petri net model on single and/or multi-processor architectures.

2.   RELATED WORK

Xu and Parnas [9] present a branch-and-bound algorithm that finds an optimal pre-runtime schedule on a single processor for real-time process segments with release, deadline, and arbitrary exclusion and precedence relations. Despite the importance of their work, real-world experimental results are not presented. Abdelzaher and Shin [1] extended Xu and Parnas' work in order to deal with distributed real-time systems. This algorithm takes into account delays, precedence relations imposed by interprocess communications, and considers many possibilities for improving the scheduling lateness at the cost of complexity. Sgroi et al. [8] propose a software synthesis method based on quasi-static scheduling using free-choice Petri nets. After obtaining a feasible schedule, C code is generated by traversing a set of conflict-free Petri nets. That work does not deal with real-time constraints, which are left to a real-time operating system. Amnell et al. [2] present a framework for development of real-time embedded systems based on timed automata with annotated code.

They describe how to compile the design model to executable programs with predictable behavior. However, their solution is well suited for independent tasks, since it relies on a fixed-priority scheduling, where it may not reach feasible schedules when considering arbitrary intertask relations.

This paper proposes a time Petri net formalism for tasks modeling in order to find a feasible pre-runtime schedule, and for synthesizing predictable and timely scheduled code. This work brings an effective contribution since it opens up a new possibility for automatic code generation of real-time systems.

3. COMPUTATIONAL MODEL

Computational model syntax is given by a time Petri net [6], and its semantics by a timed labeled transition system. A time Petri net (TPN) is a bipartite directed graph represented by a tuple $\mathcal{P} = (P, T, F, W, m_0, I)$. P (places) and T (transitions) are non-empty disjoint sets of nodes. The edges are represented by $F \subseteq (P \times T) \cup (T \times P)$. $W : F \to \mathbb{N}$ represents the weight of the edges. A TPN marking m_i is a vector $m_i \in \mathbb{N}^{|P|}$, and m_0 is the initial marking. $I : T \to \mathbb{N} \times \mathbb{N}$ represents the timing constraints, where $I(t) = (EFT(t), LFT(t)) \ \forall t \in T$, $EFT(t) \leq LFT(t)$, $EFT(t)$ is the Earliest Firing Time, and $LFT(t)$ is the Latest Firing Time.

An extended time Petri net with code and priorities is represented by $\mathcal{P}_a = (\mathcal{P}, \mathcal{CS}, \pi)$. $\mathcal{P}$ is the underlying time Petri net, $\mathcal{CS}:T \nrightarrow \mathcal{ST}$ is a partial function that assigns transitions to behavioral source code, where $\mathcal{ST}$ is a set of source tasks codes, and $\pi : T \to \mathbb{N}$ is a priority function.

A set of enabled transitions is denoted by: $ET(m_i) = \{t \in T \mid m_i(p_j) \geq W(p_j, t)\}$, $\forall p_j \in P$. The time elapsed, since the respective transition enabling, is denoted by a clock vector $c_i \in \mathbb{N}^{|ET(m_i)|}$. The dynamic firing interval $(I_D(t))$ is dynamically modified whenever the respective clock variable $c(t)$ is incremented, and t does not fire. $I_D(t)$ is computed as follows: $I_D(t) = (DLB(t), DUB(t))$, where $DLB(t) = max(0, EFT(t) - c(t))$, $DUB(t) = LFT(t) - c(t)$, $DLB(t)$ is the Dynamic Lower Bound, and $DLB(t)$ is the Dynamic Upper Bound.

Let $\mathcal{P}$ be a time Petri net, M be the set of reachable markings of $\mathcal{P}$, and C be the set of clock vectors. The set of states S of $\mathcal{P}$ is given by $S \subseteq (M \times C)$, that is a state is defined by a marking, and the respective clock vector. $FT(s)$ is the set of fireable transitions at state s defined by: $FT_P(s) = \{t_i \in ET(m) \mid \pi(t_i) = min(\pi(t_k)) \wedge DLB(t_i) \leq min(DUB(t_k)), \forall t_k \in ET(m)\}$. The *firing domain* for t at state s, is defined by the interval: $FD_s(t) = [DLB(t), min(DUB(t_k))]$.

A timed labeled transition system (TLTS) is a quadruple $\mathcal{L} = (S, \Sigma, \to, s_0)$, where S is a finite set of states, Σ is an alphabet of labels representing actions, $\to \subseteq S \times \Sigma \times S$ is the transition relation, and $s_0 \in S$ is the initial state.

The semantics of a TPN $\mathcal{P}$ is defined by associating a TLTS $\mathcal{L}_{\mathcal{P}} = (S, \Sigma, \rightarrow, s_0)$: (i) S is the set of states of $\mathcal{P}$; (ii) $\Sigma \subseteq (T \times \mathbb{N})$ is a set of actions labeled with (t, θ) corresponding to the firing of a firable transition (t) at time (θ) in the firing interval $FD_s(t)$, $\forall s \in S$; (iii) $\rightarrow \subseteq S \times \Sigma \times S$ is the transition relation; (iv) s_0 is the initial state of $\mathcal{P}$.

4.   SPECIFICATION MODEL

The specification model is composed by: (i) a set of periodic preemptable tasks with bounded discrete time constraints; and (ii) intertask relations, such as precedence and exclusion relations.

Let $\mathcal{T}$ be the set of tasks in a system. A periodic task is defined by $\tau_i = (ph_i, r_i, c_i, d_i, p_i)$, where ph_i is the initial phase; r_i is the release time; c_i is the worst case computation time required for execution of task τ_i; d_i is the deadline; and p_i is the period. A task is classified as sporadic if it can be randomly activated, but the minimum period between two activations is known. Preruntime scheduling can only schedule periodic tasks. However, Mok [7] has proposed a translation from sporadic to periodic tasks. A task τ_i *precedes* task τ_j, if τ_j can only start executing after τ_i has finished. A task τ_i *excludes* task τ_j, if no execution of τ_j can start while task τ_i is executing. If it is considered a single processor, then task τ_i could not be preempted by task τ_j.

5.   MODELING REAL-TIME SYSTEMS

In this work, the proposed modeling adopts a formal method for describing systems with timing constraints. The proposed modeling applies composition rules on building blocks models. For lacking of space, this section aims to present just an overview. For more details the reader is referred to [3].

5.1   Tasks Modeling

The considered building blocks are: (i) Fork; (ii) Join; (iii) Periodic Task Arrival; (iv) Deadline Checking; (v) Non-preemptive Task Structure; (vi) Preemptive Task Structure; and (vii) Processors. These blocks are summarized below: **a) Fork Block.** Let us suppose that the system has n tasks. The fork block is responsible for starting all tasks in the system. This block models the creation of n concurrent tasks. **b) Join Block.** Usually, concurrent activities need to synchronize with each other. The join block execution states that all tasks in the system have concluded their execution in the schedule period. **c) Periodic Task Arrival Block.** This block models the periodic invocation for all task instances in the schedule period (P_S). **d) Deadline Checking Block.** The proposed modeling method uses elementary net structures to capture deadline missing. The scheduling algorithm (Section 6.1) must eliminate states that represent undesirable situations like this one. **e) Task Structure Block**. The task structure may implement either preemptive or non-preemptive scheduling methods. Considering a non-preemptive method, the processor is just released after the entire computation to be finished. The preemptive method implies that a task are implicitly split into all possible subtasks, where the computation time of each subtask is exactly equal to one task time unit (TTU). **g) Processor Block**. The processor modeling consists of a single place, where its marking states how many processors are available.

Inter-tasks relations are modeled as follows:

a) Modeling Precedence Relations. Precedence relations are defined between pairs of tasks. It models the fact that one task can only start execution after finishing the other one.

b) Modeling Exclusion Relations. Exclusion relations are also defined between pairs of tasks. Let us suppose that τ_i EXCLUDES τ_j is specified. This relation models a situation that two tasks cannot be concurrently executing at the same time. In other words, if task τ_i starts executing, task τ_j have to wait up to task τ_i finishes execution. Usually, this relation is well-suited for tasks that access the same critical region.

5.2   Dispatcher Overhead Modeling

The dispatcher overhead is captured in the grant-processor transition. When the task is non-preemptive, the timing interval of the grant-processor transition corresponds to the WCET of the dispatcher. Since this is a simple solution, in the following presentation, the dispatcher overhead only considers preemptive tasks. When the task is preemptive, the model is slightly more complex. In this case, the proposed modeling adopts the TPN with priorities.

The proposed model considers two grant-processor transitions: grant-processor-with-overhead (t_{gw_i}) and grant-processor-without-overhead (t_{gwo_i}). As it can be seen in Figure 1, the timing interval $([\alpha, \alpha])$ for transition t_{gw_i} models such timing overhead. Place $p_{proc_k T_i}$ states that task τ_i was the last executed task by the processor $proc_k$. The dispatcher overhead is considered in two situations: (1) when the next task to use the processor is different from the task that used the processor before; or (2) when a task instance ends its execution. The first situation is represented by the place $p_{proc_k T_i}$, where if such place is marked, it implies that the processor was lastly allocated to task τ_i. However, the second situation needs an explanation. Supposing that a task instance i of task τ_j ends its execution, and the following task to be executed is the task instance $i + 1$ of the same task τ_j. In this case, although the two instances are from the same task, the dispatcher calling is mandatory. As presented below, for solving this problem the model consider two final transitions, one that removes the marking in place $p_{proc_k T_i}$ and the other that does not.

In spite of this block may seem complicated, it is worth noting that this modeling is performed automatically. In this proposed model, transition t_{gwo_i} has priority equal to zero (the highest) and transition t_{gw_i} has priority equal to one (lower than). In the same way, transitions $t_{c_{i_j}}$, $1 \leq j \leq n_k$ $i \neq j$, for each task τ_i, has highest priority (value equal to zero) related to transitions $t_{c_{i_i}}$. Figure 2 shows the TPN of tasks T_0 and T_1 considering the modeling of the dispatcher overhead.

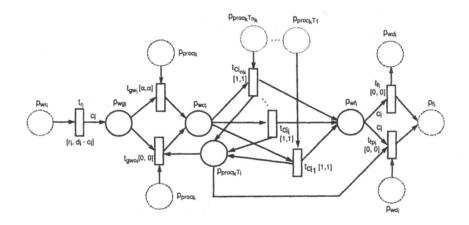

Figure 1.   Building Block Dispatcher Overhead

6.   SOFTWARE SYNTHESIS APPROACH

This section presents the software synthesis approach. It shows methods for scheduling synthesis and code generation phases.

6.1   Pre-Runtime Scheduling Synthesis

This section shows a description of how to minimize the state space size, and the algorithm that implements the proposed method.

Minimizing State Space Size.   The analysis based on the interleaving of actions is the fundamental point to be considered when analyzing state space explosion problem. Thus, the analysis of n concurrent actions has to verify all $n!$ interleaving possibilities, unless there are dependencies between these actions. This work proposes three ways for minimizing the state space size:

Modeling. The proposed method models dependencies between actions explicitly. **Partial-Order.** If actions can be executed in any order, such that the system always reaches the same state, these actions are *independent*. In other words, it does not matter in which order these are executed [5]. Independent

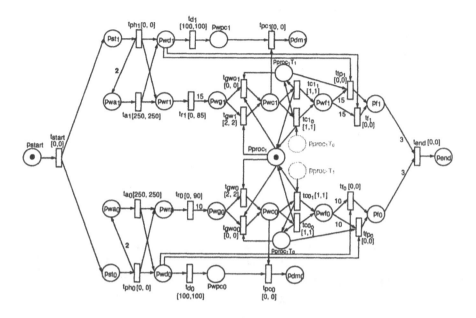

Figure 2. Tasks T_0 and T_1 modeled with dispatcher overhead

actions are those that do not disable any other action, such as: arrival, release, precedence, processor releasing, and so on. This reduction method proposes to give a different *choice-priority* level for each class of independent activities. The dependent activities, like *processor granting*, have lowest choice-priority. Therefore, when changing from one state to another state, it is sufficient to analyze the class with highest choice-priority and pruning the other ones. **Removing Undesirable States.** Section 5.1 presents how to model undesirable error states, for instance, states that represent missed deadlines. The method proposed is of interest for schedules that do not reach any of these undesirable states. When generating the TLTS, transitions leading to undesirable error states have to be discarded.

Pre-Runtime Scheduling Algorithm. The algorithm proposed (Fig. 3) is a depth-first search method on a TLTS. So, the TLTS is partially generated, according to the need. The *stop criterion* is obtained whenever the desirable final marking M^F is reached. For more information about this algorithm the interested reader is referred to [3].

6.2   Scheduled Code Generation

This section aims to present the approach for C-code generation starting from the scheduling found. The code is generated by traversing the TLTS

```
1 scheduling-synthesis(S,M^F,TPN)
2 {
3    if (S.M = M^F) return TRUE;
4    tag(S);
5    PT = pruning(firable(S));
6    if (|PT| = 0) return FALSE;
7    for each (⟨t,θ⟩ ∈ PT) {
8       S'= fire(S, t, θ);
9       if (untagged(S') ∧
10         scheduling-synthesis (S',M^F,TPN)){
11         add-in-trans-system (S,S',t,θ);
12         return TRUE;
13      }
14   }
15   return FALSE;
16 }
```

Figure 3.   Scheduling Synthesis Algorithm

(feasible firing schedule), and detecting the time where the tasks are to be executed. Thus, the generated code executes the tasks in accordance with the previously computed schedule. Figure 4 shows a simplified version of the proposed dispatcher. The data structures include a table containing the respective information: (i) start time; (ii) a flag indicating if either it is a new task instance or a premption resuming; (iii) task id; and (iv) a function pointer. This table is stored in an array of type SchItem. There are some shared variables that stores information about the size of the schedule (SCHEDULE_SIZE), information of the task currently executing (struct SchItem item), a pointer to the task function (taskFunction), and so on. Before calling a task, the dispatcher has to check some situations: (a) it may save the context (line 7); (b) it may restore the context (line 10); and (c) it stores the function pointer (line 13). Additionally, the table representing the feasible schedule is accessed as a circular list (line 15). The timer is automatically programmed using the start time of the next task instance to be called (line 16). After all these activities, the timer is activated to interrupt at the start time of the next task (line 17).

```
1 void dispatcher()
2 {
3    struct SchItem item = sch[schIndex];
4    globalClock = item.starttime;
5
6    if(currentTaskPreempted) {
7       // context saving
8    }
9    if(item.isPreemptionReturn) {
10      // context restoring
11   }
12   else {
13      taskFunction = item.functionPointer;
14   }
15   schIndex = ((++schIndex)%SCHEDULE_SIZE);
16   progrTimer(sch[schIndex].starttime);
17   activateTimer();
18 }
```

Figure 4.   Dispatcher

7. EXPERIMENTAL RESULTS

Table 1 shows the application of the scheduling method to several case studies. In that table, *instances* represent the number of tasks' instances. *state-min* is the minimum number of states to be verified, *found* counts the number of states actually verified for finding a feasible schedule, and *time* expresses the algorithm execution time in seconds. All experiments were performed on a Duron 900 Mhz, 256 MB RAM, OS Linux, and compiler GCC 3.3.2.

Table 1. Experimental results summary

Example	instances	state-min	found	time(s)
Control Application	28	50	50	0.001
Robotic Arm	37	150	150	0.014
Mine Pump	782	3130	3255	0.462
Heated-Humidifier	**1505**	**6022**	**6022**	**0.486**
Unmanned Vehicle	433	4701	14761	2.571

Table 2. Heated-Humidifier Specification

Task	r	c	d	p
A (temp-sensor-start)	0	1	1,500	10,000
B (temp-sensor-handler)	11	1	1,500	10,000
C (PWM)	0	8	1,500	10,000
D (pulse-generator)	0	4	4	50
E (temp-adjust-part1)	0	1	5,000	10,000
F (temp-adjust-part2)	1501	2	5,000	10,000

Intertask Relations
A PRECEDES B
B PRECEDES C
E PRECEDES F

However, one of these examples, a heated-humidifier, is considered in order to depict the practical usability of the software synthesis method in more details. This control system inserts water vapor in the gaseous mixture used in a sort of electro-medical systems. Table 2 shows part of the specification model. Considering the 8051-family architecture, the overhead of the interrupt and dispatcher is equal to $20\mu s$ (2 TTUs). The values are expressed in *task time units* (TTUs), where each TTU is equal to $10\mu s$. A feasible schedule was found in 0.486 seconds, verifying 6022 states, which is the minimum number of states to be verified. Figure 5 shows the heated-humidifier generated code.

8. CONCLUSIONS

This paper proposed an methodology for embedded hard real-time software synthesis based on time Petri nets. Predictability is an important concern when considering time-critical systems. The pre-runtime scheduling approach

```
void taskT1() {...}    void taskT2() {...}
void taskT3() {...}    void taskT4() {...}
void taskT5() {...}    void taskT6() {...}
#define SCHEDULE_SIZE 505
struct SchItem sch[SCHEDULE_SIZE] =
{
  {0,   false, 4, (int *)taskT4},
  {24,  false, 1, (int *)taskT1},
  {50,  false, 4, (int *)taskT4},
  {74,  false, 5, (int *)taskT5},
  {100, false, 4, (int *)taskT4},
  {124, false, 2, (int *)taskT2},
  {150, false, 4, (int *)taskT4},
  {174, false, 3, (int *)taskT3},
  {200, false, 4, (int *)taskT4},
      .
      .
      .
}
```

Figure 5.   Heated-Humidifier Generated Code

is used in order to guarantee that all critical tasks meet their deadlines. In spite of the analysis technique (i.e. state space exploration) is not new, to the best of our present knowledge, there is no similar work reported that uses formal methods for modeling time-critical systems, considers arbitrary precedence/exclusion relations, finds pre-runtime schedules, and generates timely and predictable scheduled code. The code is synthesized by traversing a feasible firing schedule. In order to depict the software synthesis methodology, we presented a heated-humidifier case study. As future work, it is proposed to adopt the code concatenation approach for minimizing the overhead due to tasks calling. Obviously, this solution reduces the amount of dispatcher calls.

REFERENCES

[1] T. Abdelzaher and K. Shin. Combined task and message scheduling in distributed real-time systems. *IEEE Trans. Parallel Distributed Systems*, 10(11):1179–1191, Nov 1999.

[2] T. Amnell, E. Fersman, P. Pettersson, H. Sun, and W. Yi. Code synthesis for timed automata. *Nordic Journal of Computing*, 2003.

[3] R. Barreto. *A Time Petri Net-Based Methodology for Embedded Hard Real-Time Software Synthesis*. PhD Thesis, Centro de Informática - UFPE, April 2005.

[4] R. Barreto, P. Maciel, M. Neves, E. Tavares, and R. Lima. A novel approach for off-line multiprocessor scheduling in embedded hard real-time systems. In *DIPES*, August 2004.

[5] P. Godefroid. *Partial Order Methods for the Verification of Concurrent Systems*. PhD Thesis, University of Liege, Nov. 1994.

[6] P. Merlin and D. J. Faber. Recoverability of communication protocols. *IEEE Trans. Comm.*, 24(9):1036–1043, Sep. 1976.

[7] A. K. Mok. *Fundamental Design Problems of Distributed Systems for the Hard-Real-Time Environment*. PhD Thesis, MIT, May 1983.

[8] M. Sgroi, L. Lavagno, Y. Watanabe, and A. Sangiovanni-Vincentelli. Synthesis of embedded software using free-choice petri nets. *DAC'99*, June 1999.

[9] J. Xu and D. Parnas. Scheduling processes with release times, deadlines, precedence, and exclusion relations. *IEEE Trans. Soft. Engineering*, 16(3):360–369, March 1990.

ENERGY MANAGEMENT FOR THE TELEPRESENCE SYSTEM TSR

R. Brockers, M. Botte, B. Mertsching
{brockers, botte, mertsching}@upb.de
GET Lab, Faculty EIM, University of Paderborn, Germany

Abstract: Mobile robot action planning in telepresence applications is strongly limited by the availability of high-performance power resources. While by definition no manual maintenance to replace discharged accumulators can be provided, adequate energy management becomes highly important for using all present resources with highest efficiency. In this paper we introduce an energy management system, following the Smart-Battery-System[1] standard to implement a multi-accumulator power supply for the telesensory robot TSR. The system provides global composite resource information giving a base for robot action planning under different configurations.

Keywords: Mobile Robot, Energy Management, Smart Battery System, Telepresence, Robotics

1. INTRODUCTION

The operating range of a mobile system is highly influenced by the availability of the internal power supply. Power consumption, together with available power resources like accumulator batteries, limits the operating time in which a system can interact with its environment. This is a crucial point that becomes even more serious when dealing with operator controlled manipulation robots utilized in hazardous areas like in space or in contaminated surroundings where no manual recharging or refreshing of the power supply is possible. Designing electrical power supplies for a mobile robot system has to cope with this problem. The supply has to provide the system with all present power resources while discharging accumulators at the optimal operating state to raise efficiency.

In this paper we introduce a power supply design for a mobile robot for telepresence applications. The special topic of a telepresence system focuses on the explained situation because the robot generally acts as a manipulator in a far-off surrounding, radio controlled via an operator with the help of an adapted human machine interface. Especially, far-off in this formulation does not only mean distant places. A telepresence system is by definition designed to overcome a physical barrier which, generally, cannot be passed by the human operator. This can be the distance, but also scaling, dangerous surroundings or a different medium. In these applications a manual surveillance of the power supply like changing the accumulators or connecting to a power charging station is mostly impossible, which raises the importance of an optimal power management solution.

The presented power supply follows the Smart Battery Standard[1] that was introduced in 1998 by the Smart Battery System Implementers Forum (SBS-IF), a consortium of different companies working in the field of mobile energy supply components. In contrast to standard solutions our design focuses on the telepresence application implementing an on-board energy planning instance to estimate global power resources depending on different activation levels of the mobile system. This gives the possibility of energy dependant action planning with different robot configurations that can be switched by the human operator or, in a later stage, by the semi-autonomous mobile system to maximize operating time.

In this contribution we concentrate on the description of the TSR hardware part of the implemented power manager forming the basic data source and the primary instance for battery surveillance.

In the following we give a short overview of the used telesensory robot for which the energy management system was designed. In the third section we explain the realized Smart Battery System providing some tested results in section four. A short preview of future work completes the paper.

2.   TSR – A MOBILE ROBOT FOR TELEPRESENCE APPLICATIONS

Telepresence together with the associated topics Telesensorics and Teleactorics are recently investigated topics in today's robotics research. In a telepresence system, a manipulator like a mobile robot is controlled by a human operator with the help of an adapted human-machine-interface providing him with as much sensorial information as possible to facilitate a realistic interacting with a remote environment. In the optimal case the operator himself feels totally immersed into the far-off environment and interacts as located on-site.

At GET Lab, a new robot system called TSR was developed for telesensory application to explore telepresence topics[2].

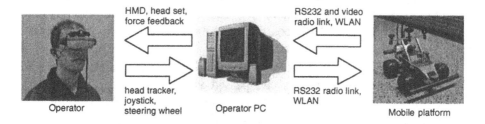

Figure 1. The telesensory robot TSR developed at the GET Lab

The system consists of a 4WD mobile robot that is radio controlled by a human operator via an operator PC, realizing the human-machine interface (figure 1). To achieve an immersion as deep as possible the data acquisition on the robot is adapted to the human perception together with a suitable presentation of the information: For example the most important human sense, visual perception, is realized by a 2 DOF stereo camera head, which is controlled by the head movements of the operator recorded with a head tracker on top of a head mounted display that visualizes the acquired stereo images.

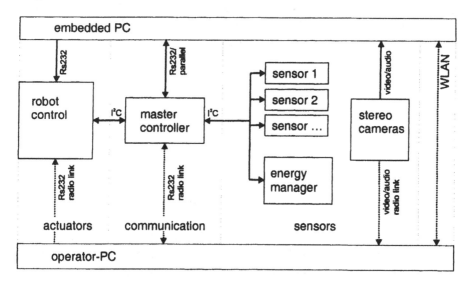

Figure 2. Main components of TSR mobile platform

Other feedback loops take advantage of several sensor information as e.g. vibration, distance to obstacles or pan-and-tilt angles of the robot to implement a haptic interface with the help of force feedback input devices.

The main components of the robot are shown in figure 2. There are four main categories integrated on the mobile platform: the sensors for information acquisition, actuators for robot control, a communication module and an embedded PC board for the execution of semi-autonomous tasks, e.g. realizing a homing process.

All sensory information except the visual and audio information are digitalized by micro controllers and passed via I^2C interface to a Master Controller unit that collects available data and provides it to the operator PC and the internal embedded PC via RS232 links.

The Master Controller is the center of communication. It controls all sensor configurations and the information flow between operator and robot. To provide power supply information to the whole system, the later described power management system has to connect to the Master Controllers I^2C interface, making it possible to easily integrate the new component into the communication system.

3.   ENERGY MANAGEMENT SYSTEM

The mobile platform power supply is divided into a motor supply path, providing energy for the driving engine with its power, and a second power path to supply all other TSR components like the embedded PC, the servo actuators or the sensor and communication components (see fig. 3).

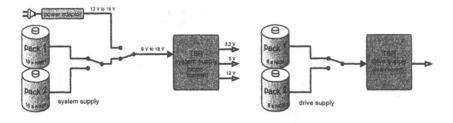

Figure 3. TSR power supplies (schematic): a) system supply, b) drive supply

In this paper the realization of a Smart Battery System for the system supply is described, which is the critical instance limiting the functionality of the mobile platform due to the high energy demand of the controlling hardware.

An energy management has to deal with the following objectives:

- extending accumulator discharge time by implementing simultaneously discharging which reduces power loss
- electronically switching battery packs to guarantee system stability during accumulator change
- charging battery packs with hot plugged AC-adaptor automatically
- providing global run-time-to-empty and remaining-capacity data

To implement the desired functionality a complete Smart Battery System has to be installed.

3.1   Smart Battery System (SBS)

A Smart Battery System (fig. 4) consists of one or more Smart Batteries connected to a Smart Battery Selector and a Smart Battery Charger. The selector chooses the system power supply which can be a connected accumulator or a AC-DC-power adapter plugged to the electricity network. The Smart Battery Charger controls the charging of the Smart Batteries when the power adaptor has been detected.

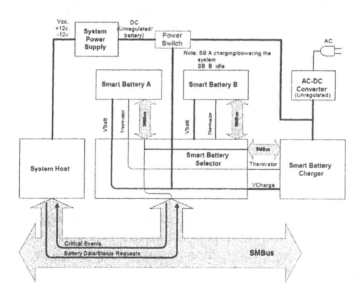

Figure 4. Smart Battery System. Overview [4]

Finally a system host supervises the whole system. It can request the battery data or status via SMBus and reacts to reported critical events.

3.2   Implementation on TSR

The primary objective of the TSR battery management system is to get access to specific battery data for run-time planning and robot configuration. To provide this information system-wide, we have to set up an energy manager following the full SBS standard. First the battery packs have to be extended by supervising ICs that monitor the implicit battery parameters like voltage, current and remaining capacity, turning them into Smart Batteries.

The selector/charger combination is realized with a SBS-Manager connected to two Smart Battery Packs and an additional microcontroller representing the system host.

3.2.1   Smart Battery

According to the Smart Battery System specification every accumulator pack is equipped with a BQ2060A gas gauge IC (Texas Instruments) to measure all accumulator specific data. The IC supports SBS Smart Battery Data Specification v1.1[5]. It monitors and provides all required battery parameters and maintains an accurate record of the available charge. All data, including the battery's remaining capacity, temperature, voltage, current, and remaining run-time predictions, can be addressed via 2-wire SMBus interface. The BQ2060A works with an external EEPROM, which stores all configuration information such as the battery's chemistry, number of cells, self-discharge rate or design voltage and capacity. As an additional feature a 4- or 5-segment LED display can be connected to the BQ2060A for remaining capacity indication. Connected permanently to the battery pack we achieve a Smart Battery, which can be directly connected to any SBS-Manager within a Smart Battery System.

3.2.2   Smart Battery Manager

The SBS is managed by a LTC 1760 Dual Smart Battery System Manager (Linear Technology) which implements a SBS charger/selector for two Smart Batteries. The IC controls both selecting the system power source by a proprietary power path architecture and automatic charging of battery packs when a power adaptor is present. Fast autonomous power source selection ($<10\mu s$) guarantees a stable system power supply even during hot plug events like connecting or disconnecting of batteries or a wall adaptor during operation.

A main advantage of the LTC1760 is the support of simultaneous charging and discharging of both batteries which extends the typical battery run-time up to 10% while charging times are reduced by up to 50%[6].

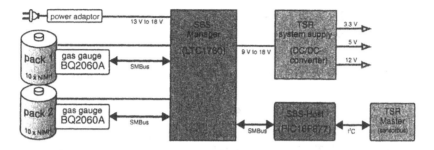

Figure 5. TSR energy management system for the system supply (overview)

The chip implements all elements of a Smart Battery System Manager version 1.1[1] except for the generation of composite battery information. It communicates with the attached Smart Batteries and a connected SBS host via SMBus and manages proper operation with only a few additional components. The power switches are implemented with external FETs while the battery charger is realized with a synchronous buck charger, both directly driven by the chip[6].

3.3 System Host

The SBS-system is controlled and monitored by a PIC16F877 microcontroller (Microchip) to provide battery information to the TSR system and compute composite battery information like global power prognoses. The controller communicates with the SBS-system via SMBus interface and is connected to the TSR system via I²C following the standard sensor protocol on TSR. Doing so, the whole energy management unit appears as a configurable sensor unit, whose information is propagated system-wide on the internal sensor bus making it accessible to a controlling instance on TSR and, via radio link, to the human operator.

Beside monitored single battery information like available charge, current, voltage or error, global power prognoses are reported to the TSR system. Due to the computational limits of the used microcontroller it was focused on approximate values to estimate global power reserves. The following global values are calculated by the SBS-host:

Global-Remaining-Capacity [Wh]
The global remaining capacity appears as the sum of the particular capacities.

$$GRC = C_{rem,BAT1} + C_{rem,BAT2}$$

Global-Relative-State-Of-Charge [%]
The relative value is related to the particular full charge capacity.

$$GRSOC = 100 \cdot GRC / (C_{full,BAT1} + C_{full,BAT1})$$

Global-Measurement-Error [%]
Each Smart battery provides an error measurement to assess its estimation quality that depends on the number of calibration cycles in which the gas gauge IC learns the capacity of the connected accumulator. To simplify error propagation, we take the maximum error of the connected batteries as the global estimation error:

$$GError = \max\{err_{max,BAT1}, err_{max,BAT2}\}$$

Global-Run-Time-To-Empty [min]
The Global-Run-Time-To-Empty is computed on a power basis for several robot configurations with different power consumption (see table 1).

$$GRTTE_{act} = 60 \cdot C_{rem,corrected} / P_{act}$$
$$GRTTE_{55} = 60 \cdot C_{rem,corrected} / 55W$$
$$GRTTE_{30} = 60 \cdot C_{rem,corrected} / 30W$$
$$GRTTE_{17} = 60 \cdot C_{rem,corrected} / 17W$$

The remaining capacity $C_{rem,corrected}$ is the overall value of both batteries corrected with the error estimates to provide the minimum remaining capacity. P_{act} is the momentary required power:

$$C_{rem,min} = C_{rem,BAT1} - err_{max,Bat1}C_{full,BAT1} + C_{rem,BAT2} - err_{max,Bat2}C_{full,BAT2}$$
$$P_{act} = I_{BAT1}U_{BAT1} + I_{BAT2}U_{BAT2}$$

Global-Time-To-Full-Charge [min]
According to the discharge case, the LTC1760 charges the batteries simultaneously with a current proportional to their missing capacity to full charge, so both packs are fully charged at the same time. To provide a global waiting time until full charge is reached, the maximal time-to-full of each battery is used:

$$GTTF = \max\{t_{to\_full,BAT1}, t_{to\_full,BAT2}\}$$

Table 1. Power consumption for different TSR configurations

Configuration	Symbol	Consumed power
Full scale with maximal power (embedded PC, framegrabber, video, all sensors)	P_{55}	55W
Telepresence mode (embedded PC switched off)	P_{30}	30W
Reduced telesensory mode (actuator control via RS232 link, reduced sensors)	P_{17}	17W

4.   RESULTS

To evaluate the intended prolongation of the accumulator run-time we show the measured discharge curves for simultaneous and separate discharging. Figure 6 shows the accumulator voltage during discharge at TSR standby operation. The run-time was extended by about 10% in the dual discharging mode compared to the successive discharging due to lower power loss at the batteries internal resistance.

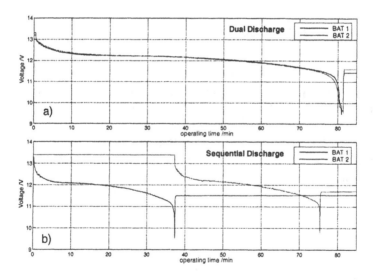

Figure 6. Accumulator voltage during simultaneous (a) and separate (b) discharging of two Smart Battery packs (BAT1 and BAT2)

Figure 7 shows the provided Global-Run-Time-To-Empty prognosis (GRTTE) for different robot configurations (cp. table 1) together with the individual estimation of each battery pack RTTE(BAT1) and RTTE(BAT2) confronted with the values of the true remaining run-time (true RTTE). The robot was driven with full functionality in a stand-by mode.

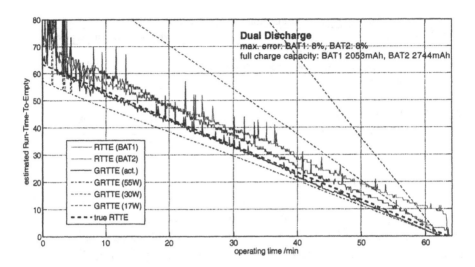

Figure 7. Estimated and effective Run-Time-To-Empty (RTTE) for different robot configurations together with the individual RTTE of each battery pack

5.   FUTURE WORKS

After implementing an energy management system for the TSR system supply the next step is to implement a semi-autonomous planning instance to configure the TSR depending on the momentary energy state. A possible strategy is a stepwise disconnecting of modules in case of low energy reserves up to the extreme case when the robot is only guided via a single serial radio link allowing the return to a charging station during the remaining prolonged operation time.

REFERENCES

1. Smart Battery System Implementers Forum: Smart Battery System Manager Specification. Version 1.0 (Release B), 8/9/1999, http://www.sbs-forum.org
2. R. Stemmer, R. Brockers, S. Drüe, J. Thiem: Comprehensive Data Acquisition for a Telepresence Application. In: International Conference on Systems, Man and Cybernetics, IEEE, 2004, pp. 5344-5349
3. Texas Instruments: bq2060A – SBS v1.1-Compliant Gas Gauge IC. Datasheet # SLUS 500A, May 2002
4. Smart Battery System Implementers Forum: Smart Battery Selector Specification. Revision 1.0, 9/5/1996, http://www.sbs-forum.org
5. Smart Battery System Implementers Forum: Smart Battery Data Specification. Revision 1.1, 11/12/1998, http://www.sbs-forum.org
6. Linear Technology: LTC1760 – Dual Smart Battery System Manager. Datasheet Rev. 1760f, 2003

AN ENERGY-AWARE EXPLORATION APPROACH BASED ON OPEN SOFTWARE ENVIRONMENT

A.G. Silva-Filho, R. Eskinazi, P.S.B. Nascimento, and M.E. Lima
Federal University of Pernambuco[1] and Politechnic School of Engineering[2]
Fone: (+55) 8121268430, Recife-PE, Brazil
{agsf, res, psbn, mel}@cin.ufpe.br

Abstract: In this work it is presented an automated method for tuning memory hierarchy to embedded applications in order to reduce energy consumption. Detailed studies were performed on TCaT heuristic in order to obtain a new exploration approach. Experiments show a reduction of approximately 4 times in the energy consumption by using our heuristic, considering two-level caches. An open software environment, based on SystemC, to explore architectures aiming energy consumption on cache memory hierarchy, has been extended. MediaBench benchmark has been used.

Keywords: Energy Consumption, ADLs, Exploration Heuristics

1. INTRODUCTION

Nowadays, cache memory structure may consume up to 50% of a microprocessor's energy [1]. This situation motivates designers of embedded microprocessor platforms to evaluate the impact of such parameter in their applications regarding to performance, cost and energy usage [3].

Among existing Architecture Description Language (ADLs), ArchC [2] is offered as a promising one based on SystemC, able to model processors, as well as memory hierarchies. Although ArchC does not extract energy consumption results from architecture behavior, its advantage is that it allows a previous analysis of the architecture, before hardware synthesis.

The traditional method to explore the huge solution space of possible configurations for a given memory hierarchy is based on exhaustive searching. However, it is often prohibitive due to the long spent time.

The heuristic developed by Zhang et al. [6] is based on single cache level approach. Two out of three parameters are maintained fixed during analysis in order to study the impact of the third one on the miss rate and energy consumption.

Although the previous heuristic was intended for only one level, Gordon-Ross [7] applied this heuristic and observed that for two cache levels the results were not good. Thus, Gordon-Ross extended this "initial heuristic" and proposed the TcaT heuristic that provides energy savings of 53% when compared with Zhang heuristic.

Summary: In this work we propose two contributions: (i) An ArchC extension to provide energy consumption evaluation, and (ii) A new heuristic for tuning memory hierarchy to embedded applications considering two-levels cache, intended for reducing energy consumption.

2.   ENERGY-AWARE ARCHC MODEL

Currently, the ArchC [2] ADL does not allow the architecture exploration for platform-tuning in terms of energy consumption. Our work extends ArchC to allow the accomplishment of this.

The ArchC pre-processor takes as input the system-level specification, including the instruction set and architecture description, and automatically generates a SystemC behavioral model of the architecture. The SystemC model is compiled with GCC and it generates an executable specification of the architecture. By executing this model, reports about the system behavior are issued.

Some parameters such as: supply operation and technology parameters were incorporated to the ArchC description in order to estimate energy consumption.

A set of classes were integrated to the ArchC language, allowing its use in energy-aware descriptions of memory hierarchies for processor-based architectures. Each instance defined in the AC_ARCH description is monitored through "*read*" and "*write*" behavioral operations. All these accesses are annotated and so the energy consumption is calculated. The outcome from the generated model simulation is the consumed energy for each cache component described.

There are basically two components that establish the amount of energy dissipated in a CMOS circuit: Static and dynamic dissipations. In this work, the two components are modelled. The equations of the eCACTI power analytical model [5] were chosen to model the cache memory energy consumption, since it offers results at a reasonable accuracy for high-level descriptions.

3. PROPOSED HEURISTIC

TECH (Two-level Cache Exploration Heuristic) allows the exploration of the two-level caches and selects the cache parameters in a specific order based on their impact on energy. First, the best cache size is obtained for the level two cache by varying its size decreasingly. That is made varying only the cache sizes of the second level from a maximum to a minimum value, which can't be inferior to the first level cache size. The procedure stops when the energy consumption of the new cache configuration is bigger than a previous configuration. Once found the best configuration for the second cache level (lesser energy consumption), this value is fixed, and the exploration continues varying increasingly the cache size of first level until to find the best configuration. This configuration is found varying only the cache size of the first level from a minimum value to a cache size immediately smaller than the second level. The stop criterion is the same as in the second level. Here, the first and second cache sizes are fixed. Now, in a second stage, the heuristic increases the cache line size of the second level initially, until find a new configuration with energy consumption inferior to previous configuration. The same procedure is carried out with cache of first level. Finally, the same procedure is carried out with cache associativity, for the two cache levels.

4. SPECIFYING THE SYSTEM

In Figure 1, a MIPS memory hierarchy is composed by separate level one instruction (IC1) and data caches (DM1), separate level two instruction (IC2) and data caches (DM2) and main memory (MEM). IC1 is declared as a direct-mapped, 1024 blocks (or lines), 2 words/block, write-through, write-allocate, 1.7V power supply, 500MHz frequency cache and 0.08μm transistor technology. DM1 is declared as a two-way set associative, 2048 lines, 1 words/block, LRU replaced, write-back, write-allocate, 1.7V power supply, 500MHz frequency cache and 0.08μm transistor technology. IC2 and DM2 are declared of a similar manner. In ArchC, the method *bindsTo* defines how the memory hierarchy is established.

```
AC_ARCH(mips1) {
   ac_mem  MEM:5M;
   ac_powercache IC1("dm", 1024, 2, "wt" , "wal" , 1.7, 500, 0.08);
   ac_powercache IC2("dm", 2048, 2, "wt" , "wal" , 1.7, 500, 0.08);
   ac_powercache DM1("2w", 2048, 1, "lru", "wb", "wal", 1.7, 500, 0.08);
   ac_powercache DM2("2w", 4096, 1, "lru", "wb", "wal", 1.7, 500, 0.08);
   ac_regbank RG:8;   ac_regbank RB:256;   ac_reg PSR,Y;
   ARCH_CTOR ( mips1 ) {
      ac_isa("mips1_isa.ac");
      IC1.bindsTo( IC2 );
      DM1.bindsTo( DM2 );
      IC2.bindsTo( MEM );
      DM2.bindsTo( MEM );
   };  };
```

Figure 1. Mips Memory hierarchy

5.   CASE STUDY

Here an example using a representative audio compression algorithm (ADPCM) from MediaBench suite [4] is applied. A Mips core processor with memory hierarchy structure was used. It was considered a power supply of 1.7V, write-back and write-allocate write policy, 500MHz cache frequency and 0.08μm transistor technology.

The proposed heuristic (TECH) can be applied separately for instruction and data caches. In order to demonstrate the heuristic evaluation, only instruction cache is analysed. We apply the proposed heuristic using the proposed environment (ArchC). The cache range parameters in this case was: 2k to 512k bytes for cache size, 8 to 64 bytes for cache line size and 1 to 8 for associativity.

Studies done over this application indicate that the energy consumption contributions by varying of the cache line size and cache associativity are lower than the contributions due the varying of the cache size. Based on this studies, we discover by simulations that to define the cache size of the last cache level, initially, is important to limit the increases of first cache level.

Preliminary studies have shown that our heuristic has reached results as good as TcaT in this case. The results for this application concludes that different order exploration can conduce the cache memory energy consumption for different levels. Figure 2 shows the normalized energy consumption, for level one and two caches considering both heuristics TcaT (case 1) and TECH (case 2).

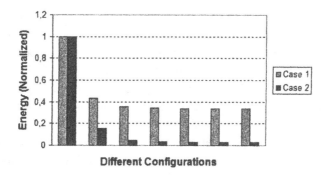

Figure 2. Different energy levels (two cases)

In this case, results can demonstrate that some care must be done when architecture space exploration viewing energy consumption is performed. TCaT [7] uses a configurable cache approach (by using reconfigurable device such as FPGAs) with limmited exploration space due to the fact that cache architecture only supports a certain range of configurations. This aspect can discard importants configurations that consumes lower energy in the space exploration. On the other hand, by using our heuristic approach, we are worried with the cache configuration that provide low energy consumption. Experiments show a reduction of approximately 4 times in the energy consumption. For this case, our results are as good as TCaT [7] results.

6. CONCLUSION

An environment capable to extract cache memory energy consumption from an architecture behavior has been suggested. This extension enables a suitable evaluation at system-level specification. Through energy consumption reporting for each cache memory component, the designer is able to analyze and adjust the efficiency of the architectural parameters that may impact on the overall energy consumption and performance of the system.

A heuristic (TECH) for tuning memory hierarchy to embedded applications in order to reduce energy consumption is presented. The proposed heuristic have presented good results for two-level caches energy analyses, when compared with existing heuristic. Preliminary results, show a reduction of approximately 4 times in the energy consumption.

Additionally, a cycle-accurate power cache model is under development to provide a more detailed power analysis.

REFERENCES

1. H. Chang; L. Code; M. Hunt, G. Martin, A.J. McNelly, and L. Todd, "Surviving the SOC revolution: a guide to platform-based design"; Kluwer A.P., 1 ed., 1999.

2. The ArchC Architecture Description Language, 2004; In: www.archc.org

3. Macii, Enrico; L. Benini; M. Poncino; "Energy-Aware Design of Embedded Memories: A Survey of Technologies, Architectures and Optimization Techniques", *ACM Transactions on Embedded Computing Systems*; Vol. 2, No. 1, pp. 5-32, February 2003.

4. MediaBench.   The   MediaBench   benchmark   suite.   In http://cares.icsl.ucla.edu/MediaBench/, 2004.

5. Dutt, Nikil; Mamidipaka, Mahesh; "eCACTI: An Enhanced Power Estimation Model for On-chip Caches", TR 04-28; set. 2004.

6. Zhang, D., Vahid, F., Cache configuration exploration on prototyping platforms. 14th IEEE International Workshop on Rapid System Prototyping, June 2003.

7. Gordon-Ross, Ann, Vahid, F., Dutt, Nikil, Automatic Tuning of Two-Level Caches to Embedded Applications, DATE, pp.208-213, Feb 2004.

FUNCTIONAL VERIFICATION FOR UML - BASED MODEL DRIVEN DESIGN OF EMBEDDED SYSTEMS

Martin Kardos, Norbert Fristacky
[1]*Heinz Nixdorf Institute, University of Paderborn, Germany;* [2]*Faculty of Informatics and Information Technologies, Slovak University of Technology, Bratislava, Slovakia*

Abstract: Modeling and formal specification in combination with formal verification can substantially contribute to the correctness and quality of design of embedded systems and consequently help reduce the development costs. This paper tackles the problem of providing a fully automated formal verification for UML-based design of embedded systems. For verification it employs the model checking technique. Unlike other approaches, the paper focuses on supporting a consistent subset of UML diagrams that cover all main aspects of an embedded system, i.e. the structure, communication and behavior. The whole approach is evaluated on a case study of a Manufacturing Flow System with distributed control.

Key words: Embedded System Design, UML, AsmL, Formal Verification, Model Checking

1.   INTRODUCTION

The increasing complexity of today's embedded systems imposes new demands on the overall design process and on the used design languages and verification techniques. Specification and modeling techniques, such as UML, offering facilities for structural decomposition, abstraction, refinement, concern separation, etc., can be employed at the *system level* of the design process to cope with the system complexity. However, the employment of these techniques into the design process of embedded systems can not succeed without appropriate support for verification. Therefore, verification techniques are needed that are able to identify the design errors hidden in the abstract and often incomplete models at the earlier stages of the system design.

In this paper we present an approach for automated formal verification of UML-based design of embedded systems that employs for verification the model checking technique. The verification concept is presented in Section 3. Unlike other approaches, the main objective of this work is aimed on supporting a consistent subset of UML diagrams that cover all aspects of an embedded system, i.e. the structure, communication and behavior. The supported UML subset (the *Verifiable UML*) is discussed in Section 2. A prerequisite for employing formal verification into the design process is the presence of a rigorous formal specification of the UML semantics. The formalization of the *Verifiable UML* by means of the AsmL language is the subject of Section 4. The overall verification approach is evaluated on a case study of a *Material Flow System* that is discussed in detail in Section 5. The novelty of the presented verification approach and its relation to other research work is discussed in Section 6. Finally, in Section 7 the conclusion is drawn and the direction of the future work is presented.

2.   VERIFIABLE UML

UML[1] [1] is a large-scale modeling language defining a set of diagrams to capture different aspects of modeled systems at different abstraction levels and under different points of view. It provides diagrams that can be seamlessly applied at the different stages of a system life-cycle like requirements specification and analysis, design, realization and deployment.

The work presented in this paper focuses mainly on the design phase. Therefore diagrams have been considered that are typically used during the design phase for modeling the main aspects of an embedded system. The diagrams considered are the *class* and *component diagram* for modeling system structure (architecture), the *state machine diagram* for modeling system behavior and the *action semantics*[2] for modeling operations inside the classes. We denote this subset of UML as *Verifiable UML*, i.e. a subset for which the formal verification is supported inside our approach. Although we support currently only the mentioned diagrams, in general, the *Verifiable UML* can be further extended with other UML diagrams, e.g. the activity diagram or the sequence diagram[3].

---

[1] We consider the latest UML 2.0.
[2] Here the syntax of the AsmL language has been taken as textual notation.
[3] An additional effort would be required to formalize these diagrams.

3.   VERIFICATION CONCEPT

A concept of the proposed verification approach is shown in Figure 1. The picture contains three different levels covered by the verification approach. The *modeling level* represents an input level for the verification. Here, the UML model of a specific system (the *System model*) is created and the *system properties* to be verified are defined. In addition, the formal specification of the *Verifiable UML* described in Section 2 is considered to be a fixed immutable input for the verification[4].

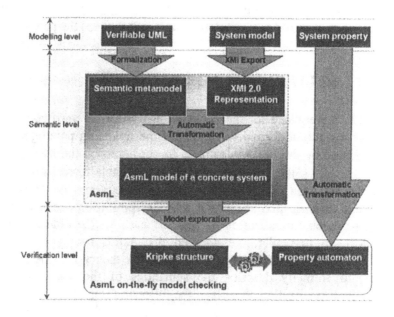

Figure 1. Verification concept for UML-based design

The models and transformations occurring at the *semantic level* form the foundation for the formal verification. At first, the semantics of the *Verifiable UML* is formalized. This step is depicted by the *Formalization* arrow. The formalization is briefly explained in Section 4. It results in a rigorous model of the *Verifiable UML* semantics described in the AsmL language, and in a set of transformation rules applied on the original *system model* to produce the *AsmL model of a concrete system*. The transformation works over an XMI representation of the *system model*. The *XMI export* functionality has to be supported by the selected modeling tool.

---

[4] The Verifiable UML can be further modified or extended but this implies a consequent adaptation of the semantic metamodel and the transformation rules.

The *verification level* represents the defined verification method and its algorithms. The applied verification method is based on the model checking technique and was specifically designed for verification of AsmL specifications [2]. Basically, the verification takes on input an AsmL specification, in our case the *AsmL model of a concrete system*, and the specified *system property* (a CTL* formula). First, the *system property* is transformed to a specific automaton denoted as the *property automaton*. Subsequently, an on-the-fly model checking algorithm is started that tries to prove the soundness of the given property. During the run-time the algorithm drives the *model exploration* and builds a corresponding *Kripke structure*. As verification result the algorithm returns "ok", if the verified property holds, otherwise it provides a counterexample that violates the property.

4.   FORMALIZING UML SEMANTICS

The main prerequisite for the application of a formal verification is the presence of a rigorous formal semantics of the modeling paradigm, in our case represented by the *Verifiable UML*. In our approach the *Abstract State Machines* (ASMs) [3][4] has been chosen as a suitable formalism to define the formal semantics of UML. The ASMs have approved their strong modeling and specification abilities in various application domains [5] also including work on formalization of selected parts of the older version of UML [6][7]. In particular, we adopted the AsmL language [8][9], an executable specification language built upon the theory of Abstract State Machines, to formally describe the semantics of the *Verifiable UML*. Basically, the formalization consists of the following steps:

1. Defining transformation rules to transform a UML class diagram[5] into the corresponding AsmL model.

   The transformation of a UML Class diagram to a corresponding AsmL model consists in defining a mapping of the graphical notation (syntax) used in UML to the textual syntax of AsmL. Such a transformation results in an AsmL model whose structure definition directly reflects the transformed diagram. This approach is widely used by the existing UML tools for the source code generation in the target programming language. However, unlike the usual programming languages, the AsmL expressiveness allows to cover also enhanced modeling concepts incorporated into the UML 2.0 Class diagram, e.g. the pre and postconditions inside the methods, derived attributes, or enhanced association types like sets, bags, sequences, etc.

---

[5]   It includes also the component diagram that is just a specialization of the class diagram

2. Defining a semantic model for the UML state machine in AsmL
   The informal operational semantics of a state machine defined in the UML specification is converted into a precise AsmL specification. The resulting AsmL model covers the whole UML state machine (except the time aspect) including complex and history states, inter-level transitions, deferred events, etc. This work has been partially published in [10].
3. Defining a mapping of the UML action semantics to AsmL constructs
   Since AsmL is a high-level specification language with strong expressivity, it is a good candidate for modeling the class operations (methods) and the actions contained inside the state machine diagram. To show a conformance to the action semantics proposed by UML, a mapping of the action semantics to AsmL should be provided.

5.   MATERIAL FLOW SYSTEM CASE STUDY

This section elaborates the application of the proposed verification approach to the design of embedded control software for the *Material Flow System* (MFS) case study shown in Figure 2.

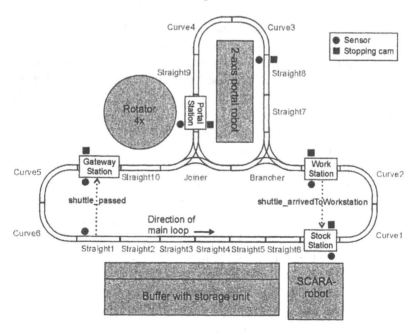

Figure 2. Material flow system - schematic view

The MFS is based on a modern modular material flow technology that allows to build complex transportation topologies by composing standard modules such as straight and curved tracks, switches (joiner and brancher), and stations. In the current configuration the MFS is used for producing bottle openers. Special vehicles called shuttles are employed to transport material pieces over the railway between stations where some processing takes place. While operating, tracks are permanently supplied with current such that shuttles keep moving over the railway in a fixed direction until they are arrested by means of stopping cams placed at certain points along the tracks (see Figure 2). Some tracks are additionally equipped with inductive sensors to detect the arrival or departure of a shuttle. Finally, each shuttle has a built-in device that avoids collisions by enforcing a minimum distance from the foregoing shuttle. The control of the MFS is realized by a network of concurrently operating and asynchronously communicating control devices attached to active tracks (e.g. stations, switches) and robots.

5.1   Architecture

The MFS architecture is modeled using the UML class diagram shown in Figure 3. The topology of the MFS is modeled by a set of interconnected tracks. Therefore, we defined the abstract class *Track* that models a single track. A track must be connected to its neighboring track. This connection is modeled by the *direction* association. The reference to the neighboring track (in the main loop direction) is stored in the attribute *next*. To detect the arrival or departure of a shuttle, a track can own an arriving or leaving sensor respectively, modeled via associations with the *Sensor* class. The signal communication is initiated by the sensor and realized by sending a signal instance to all tracks contained in the *signaledTracks* attribute (the *communicates* association). In some cases a track has to be able to stop the shuttle, e.g. when some processing of the transported material is required. This capability is modeled through the association with the *StartAndStopUnit* class that models a stopping clam. Finally, a track owns the *at* association with the *Shuttle* class used to detect when a shuttle is positioned on a track. In addition, *Track* implements the *ITrack* interface that is used to simulate the movement of a shuttle along the track. The *Track* class is an abstract class. For modeling specific kinds of tracks we further specialize the *Track* class and define the classes *Station*, *TransferGate*, *Straight* and *Curve*. The last two classes are leaf classes that model the straight and curved tracks, respectively. The *Station* class is again an abstract class that models tracks, at which a shuttle has to be stopped and some processing is executed. A station owns a *name* and provides methods for stopping (*setStopper()*) and releasing (*releaseStopper()*) a shuttle. The concrete stations are modeled by following specialized classes: *Stock*, *Workstation*, *Portal* and *Gateway*. The *TransferGate* class models a type of track that can switch its position in order to change the moving direction of a shuttle. There are two allowed directions the straight or the fork direction.

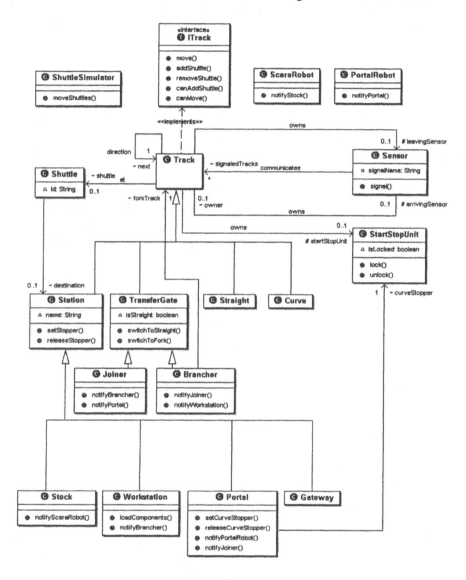

Figure 3. MFS architecture – class diagram

The current position of a *TransferGate* is indicated by the *isStraight* attribute. The methods *switchToStraight()* and *switchToFork()* are used to force the switching. Depending on the usage we recognize two different kinds of a transfer gate: the *Brancher* that forks the direction and the *Joiner* that joins two directions (see Figure 2). Finally, we have to mention the standalone classes *ScaraRobot*, *PortalRobot*, *Shuttle* and *ShuttleSimulator*.

The first two model the robot machines placed along the *Stock* and the *Portal* stations. The *Shuttle* class models a shuttle. A shuttle is identified by its *id* and owns a reference to the *destination* station it has to go to. The *ShuttleSimulator* class is an auxiliary class used to simulate the movement of shuttles.

5.2   Behavior

According to the UML specification a class can have a behavior. Such a class is called an active class. In MFS following classes are active: stations *Stock, Workstation, Portal* and *Gateway*, transfer gates *Brancher* and *Joiner*, robots *ScaraRobot* and *PortalRobot,* and the auxiliary class *ShuttleSimulator*.

The *Stock* station serves for unloading of finished goods (in our case bottle openers) from the shuttle and for storing them in the storage unit. The action of unloading and storing initiated by the *Stock* station is realized by the *ScaraRobot*. Figure 4 shows the state machine modeling the life-cycle of the *Stock* station.

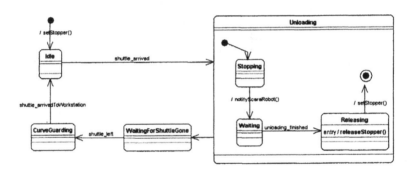

Figure 4. UML Statemachine of the Stock station

At the beginning of the life-cycle the *Stock* station fires the transition from the *initial* state to the *Idle* state and sets the stopping cam. When the *shuttle_arrived* event occurs (sent by the associated arriving sensor) the state machine enters the *Unloading* state and initiates the unloading of the good by notifying the *ScaraRobot*. Then it waits in the *Wait* state until the unloading is confirmed by the *unloading_finished* event sent by the *ScaraRobot*. After the confirmation, the stopping cam is released in the *Releasing* state and the shuttle moves on. Subsequently, the stopping cam is set again to stop a possibly approaching next shuttle. After reaching the state *WaitingForShuttleGone* the state machine waits until the *shuttle_left* event occurs (sent by the leaving sensor) and then moves further to the *CurveGuarding* state. It stays in the *CurveGuarding* state until the shuttle reaches the *Workstation*. Finally, the state machine moves to the *Idle* state.

The *Workstation* serves for loading the material onto the shuttle and for assigning a task to the shuttle (method *LoadComponents()*). The task assignment is realized by setting or resetting the destination attribute of the shuttle instance. If the destination is set to *Portal* then a shuttle has been assigned a task to produce a bottle opener. The behavior of the Workstation class is shown in Figure 5. At the beginning of the life-cycle the *Workstation* moves from the *initial* state to the *Idle* state and sets the stopping cam. After a shuttle has arrived to *Workstation* it is loaded with components and gets assigned a task (the *Loading* state). When a shuttle is loaded the state machine moves to the *SwitchingBrancher* state. In this state the switching of the *Brancher* is initiated with respect to the shuttle's task (action *notifyBrancher()*). If the shuttle is assigned a task the *Brancher* is asked to switch to fork direction otherwise the straight direction is required. After receiving the *brancher_ready* event from the *Brancher*, the stopping cam is released and the shuttle moves on. After the shuttle has left, the state machine moves to the *Idle* state and sets the stopping cam.

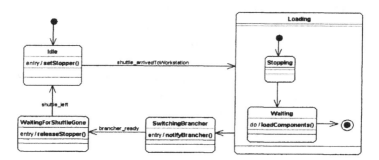

Figure 5. UML Statemachine of the Workstation

Because of space limitations we omit the description of behaviors for the remaining active classes.

5.3   Verification

Before the verification can take place the properties to verify have to be specified. In the MFS case study we wanted to check following two properties: 1) every shuttle has to fulfill its task and reach its starting location, and 2) there must not appear a situation where two shuttles are located within one curve area. The second property represents a safety property in order to avoid a possible collision of shuttles. The collision may happen when two shuttles are located one after another in the same curve area and the front shuttle is out of the reach area of the collision detection sensor of the back shuttle. We write the informal properties formally in form of temporal logic formulas "**AF(AllFinished)**" and "**AG(!CollisionEmergency)**". The *AllFinished* and *CollisionEmergency* represent propositions that are evaluated in every state of the verified system. They are expressed as AsmL expressions shown in Table 1.

Table 1. Proposition expressions in AsmL

AllFinished	**forall** s in Shuttle_Instances **holds** s.cycleCounter >= 1
CollisionEmergency	**exists** c in Curve_Instances **where** c.shuttle <> **null and** c.next **is** Curve **and** c.next.shuttle <> **null**

The *AllFinished* evaluates to true when every shuttle has passed its starting locations, i.e. the counter of shuttle cycles is greater than 1. The *CollisionEmergency* evaluates to true when two curves, such that one is the successor of the other, both contain a shuttle.

At first, we transformed the UML model of the *MFS* to a corresponding AsmL model following the transformations on the *semantic level* as depicted in Figure 1. Subsequently we conducted the verification of the MFS model and discovered several design errors that caused the violation of the given properties. The two most crucial errors are covered by following scenarios:

1. The *setStopper()* action of the *Stock* station behavior (Figure 4) placed at the transition leaving the *Releasing* state was in the old version of the *Stock* station behavior placed as the entry action of state *WaitingForShuttleGone*. In case of three shuttles *Shuttle(1-3)* placed initially at tracks *Straight(6-4)* (Figure 2) a situation happened where *Shuttle1* arrived to the *Workstation* and *Shuttle2* was located at *Curve2* followed by *Shuttle3* moving on *Curve1*. This was a violation of the second property.

2. When a shuttle arrived at a station while the station's state machine was in another state than *Idle,* the occurred *shuttle_arrived* event has been dispatched in wrong state and consequently discarded because it did not fire any transition. The arrived shuttle stayed at the station without being ever served. This violated the first property. The problem was solved by making the *shuttle_arrived* event deferrable.

6.   RELATED WORK

Since UML is a complex modeling language, there exist no verification approaches that would cover the whole UML. Basically, only a very restricted subset of UML is supported. For example, a plethora of approaches towards model checking different variations of statecharts such as *Harel* statecharts [11], *STATEMATE* statecharts [12][13] and *UML* statecharts [14,15,16,17,18,19,20] have been presented in recent years. The basic idea of all these methods is to transform the considered statechart model to the input language of an existing model checking tool, say SMV, SPIN or UPPAAL for example. The semantics of the statechart is reflected through the input language of some model checking tool or through an intermediate representation that is further mapped into the model checker's language. Since the expressiveness of the model checker's input language is very restricted, it imposes strong limitations on the supported semantics.

Unlike these methods, our method presented in this paper uses the ASM-based specification language AsmL to define the semantics of the UML model. The expressive power of AsmL allows us to formalize the UML semantics without imposing any constraints on the supported UML diagrams. Therefore, in our formalization of UML we consider not only the complete semantics of UML state machine but also the whole class diagram for modeling the system structure and the UML action semantics for modeling operations inside the classes. Moreover, this UML subset (the *VerifiableUML*) can be fully executed and tested by the tools coming with AsmL. Further advantage of our approach in comparison to the conventional approaches is the employment of the model checking tool specially developed for the verification of AsmL specifications [2]. This eliminates the necessity of additional model transformations and additionally provides greater capabilities for properties definitions.

7.   CONCLUSION AND FUTURE WORK

In this paper we have presented an approach towards the formal verification of UML-based design of embedded systems. The main ideas consist in using the AsmL specification language to define the formal semantic model of the supported executable part of UML (the *Verifiable UML*) and consequently employing model checking technique specifically designed for AsmL (the novelty of this approach is discussed in the Related Work section). As a future work the main intension is to evaluate the presented verification approach on more complex systems in order to test its scalability and to approve its practical utilization.

REFERENCES

[1]   Object Management Group. UML 2.0 Superstructure Specification. OMG Final Adopted Specification, February 2004. URL: http://www.omg.org/cgi-bin/doc?ptc/2004-10-02.
[2]   M. Kardos: An approach to model checking AsmL specifications, In Proceedings of the 12th International Workshop on Abstract State Machines, ASM2005, Paris, France, March 8-11, 2005

[3] Y. Gurevich: Evolving Algebras 1993: Lipari Guide; E. Börger (Eds.): Specification and Validation Methods, Oxford University Press, 1995.

[4] E. Börger and R. Stärk: Abstract State Machines: A Method for High-Level System Design and Analysis. Springer-Verlag, 2003.

[5] Abstract State Machines web page: http://www.eecs.umich.edu/gasm/

[6] E. Börger, A. Cavarra, and E. Riccobene: An ASM Semantics for UML Activity Diagrams, in Teodor Rus, ed., Algebraic Methodology and Software Technology, 8th International Conference, AMAST 2000, Iowa City, Iowa, USA, May 20-27, 2000, Proceedings, Springer LNCS 1816, 2000, 293--308.

[7] K. Compton, J. K. Huggins, and W. Shen: A Semantic Model for the State Machine in the Unified Modeling Language. In Gianna Reggio, Alexander Knapp, Bernhard Rumpe, Bran Selic, and Roel Wieringa, eds., "Dynamic Behaviour in UML Models: Semantic Questions", Workshop Proceedings, UML 2000 Workshop, Ludwig-Maximilians-Universität München, Institut für Informatik, Bericht 0006, October 2000, 25-31.

[8] Y. Gurevich, B. Rossman and W. Schulte: Semantic Essence of AsmL. To appear in the Journal of Theoretical Computer Science (in special issue dedicated to FMCO 2003), 2005

[9] Y. Gurevich, W. Schulte, C. Campbell, W. Grieskamp. AsmL: The Abstract State Machine Language Version 2.0. http://research.microsoft.com/foundations/AsmL/default.html

[10] M. Kardos, F. Rammig: Model Based Formal Verification of Distributed Production Control Systems. Integration of Software Specification Techniques for Applications in Engineering. Springer Verlag, 2004 LNCS 3147, S. 451-473

[11] W. Chan, R.J. Anderson, P. Beame, S. Burns, F. Modugno, D. Notkin, and J.D. Reese: Model checking large software specifications. IEEE Transactionson Software Engineering, 24(7), 1998.

[12] E. M. Clarke and W. Heinle. Modular translation of statecharts to SMV. Technical Report CMU-CS-00-XXX, Carnegie-Mellon University School of Computer Science, 2000.

[13] E. Mikk, Y. Lakhnech, M. Siegel, and G.J. Holzmann. Implementing statecharts in PROMELA/SPIN. In Proceedings of the 2nd IEEE Workshop on Industrial-Strength Formal Specification Techniques, pages 90–101. IEEE Computer Society, October 1998.

[14] T. Schäfer, A. Knapp, and S. Merz. Model Checking UML State Machines and Collaborations. In *Proc. Wsh. Software Model Checking*, Volume 55(3) of *Elect. Notes Theo. Comp. Sci.*, Paries, 2001.

[15] A. Knapp, S. Merz, and C. Rauh. Model Checking Timed UML State Machines and Collaborations. *Proc. 7th Int. Symp. Formal Techniques in Real-Time and Fault Tolerant Systems*, LNCS 2469, pages 395-416. ©Springer, Berlin, 2002

[16] K. Diethers, U. Goltz and M. Huhn. Model Checking UML Statecharts with Time. In Proc. of the Workshop on Critical Systems Development with UML, 2002.

[17] A. David, M. Möller, and W. Yi. Formal Verification of UML Statecharts with Real-Time Extensions. In Proc. of FASE 2002 (ETAPS 2002). LNCS 2306, p218-232, 2002.

[18] S. Gnesi and D. Latella. Model Checking UML Statechart Diagrams using JACK. In *Proc. Fourth IEEE International Symposium on High Assuarance Systems Engineering*, IEEE Press, 1999.

[19] D. Latella, I. Majzik, and M. Massink. Automatic verification of a behavioural subset of UML statechart diagrams using the SPIN model-checker. Formal Aspects of Computing, 11(6):637–664, 1999.

[20] I. Paltor and J. Lilius. vUML: A tool for verifying UML models. In R.J. Hall and E. Tyugu, editors, Proc. of the 14th IEEE International Conference on Automated Software Engineering, ASE'99. IEEE, 1999.

SPECIFICATION-BASED TESTING OF REAL-TIME EMBEDDED SYSTEMS*

Manuel Núñez and Ismael Rodríguez
Departamento Sistemas Informáticos y Programación, Facultad de Informática
Universidad Complutense de Madrid, 28040 Madrid, Spain
{mn,isrodrig}@sip.ucm.es

Abstract: In this paper we present a formal framework to test real-time embedded systems where temporal requirements play a relevant role. First, we introduce our formal model to specify this kind of systems. It is a modification of the classical EFSM formalism where actions will be attached with a temporal constraint. This constraint expresses the maximal and/or minimal time this action should take during its execution in the current configuration. Then, we use this formalism to construct models that represent the set of temporal requirements in a system. In turn, they are automatically obtained from the temporal requirements defined for each component in the system. Tests for checking these requirements are defined and a formal mechanism to apply them to real systems is described.

1.   INTRODUCTION

Embedded systems that are constructed nowadays have reached a high level of complexity. They may consist of a huge amount of components that interact with each other and may have been designed by different teams or companies. In this context, guaranteeing the reliability of each component and/or the integration of all of them is a great challenge. In particular, the integration of components yields an explosion of relevant configurations to be considered and checked, and selecting the most critical ones by hand is not feasible. The systematic testing of systems has been a topic of research and application of formal methods for years. Formal methods provide systematic testing mechanisms where systems are faced to some selected foreseen situations. Then, the correctness of the system is assessed by comparing its behavior with the one provided by a set of requirements or a specification. Due to the high cost of

*Research partially supported by the Spanish MCYT project TIC2003-07848-C02-01, the Junta de Castilla-La Mancha project PAC-03-001, and the Marie Curie project MRTN-CT-2003-505121/TAROT.

testing in any development project, the use of systematic and formal methods for testing has attracted the attention of several manufacturers.

In the beginning, specification languages proposed to create models of systems by considering only its functional characteristics. That is, models expressed constraints as *"after an action A is produced, an action B should/must be produced as well."* Thus, formal testing was constrained to check functional properties (see e.g. [Lee and Yannakakis, 1996] for a good survey on testing finite state machines). Besides, there were also some proposals to specifically deal with embedded and/or component-based systems (see e.g. [Petrenko et al., 1996; Lima and Cavalli, 1997]). Nevertheless, this kind of properties turned out to be insufficient for representing other critical features of systems. To cope with this problem, new models were developed to deal with additional characteristics such as the time consumed by actions, the probability of taking an action, the resources consumed to perform an action, or the probability that an action takes a given time to be performed. However, the inclusion of temporal issues in specification languages did not have a great impact on the development of new testing methodologies.

In this paper we present a formalism based on classical EFSMs (*extended finite state machines*) whose aim is to facilitate the specification of embedded systems where temporal aspects play a relevant role. In addition, we will present the basic concepts of a testing framework for these systems. The application of tests to check temporal issues and the obtention of diagnosis results concerning their correctness is defined. Our language will provide us with the possibility of separately describing the behavior of each component of a system. An automatic transformation mechanism that allows to create a single model from the models of some interacting components will be provided as well. This mechanism will not consider any possible combination of configurations of components. On the contrary, only *reachable* situations will be considered, which will diminish the usual state explosion problem.

Our formalism allows to express constraints about the time consumed by each action. Variables will affect the behavior of components and systems as well as the time consumed by actions. In particular, variables will have the capability to enable/disable actions. Every action in the model will be equipped with a temporal constraint expressing the (required) behavior for that action. For example, temporal constraints on actions could require than an action a takes *less* than 2 seconds, next action b takes *more* than 3 seconds and *less* than 5 seconds, and, finally, action c takes *exactly* 7 seconds. Let us suppose that the sequence of actions a, b, c is a possible communication sequence inside the system and that this sequence is observed from the outside of the system as the observable action d. If an external observer tries to check the temporal correctness of a system according to that requirement, then she should observe that the action d never takes less than 10 seconds nor more than

14 seconds. Let us note that the accomplishment of that requirement does not imply that each individual action in the sequence a, b, c accomplishes its own specific requirement. That is, if the temporal constraint for d is fulfilled, an external observer can only claim that the temporal correctness of actions a, b, c is *possible*. Let us note that if a *black box* testing approach is considered (see e.g. [Myers, 1979]) then it is irrelevant whether the temporal constraints on a, b, and c are fulfilled as long as the temporal behavior of the only observable action (d) is correct. Let us suppose now that there is no upper bound for the time consumed by b. Then, the only temporal constraint for d would require that it does not take less than 10 seconds. Our testing methodology will allow tests to analyze the temporal aspects of systems.

The concepts that we introduce in this paper can be useful for testing other models of timed systems. For example, the definitions can be easily adapted to timed automata [Alur and Dill, 1994]. Other definitions of timed I/O automata (e.g. [Higashino et al., 1999; Springintveld et al., 2001]) are restricted to deterministic behavior, while we are more expressive since we allow non-determinism in specifications and (partially) in implementations. Regarding testing for timed systems, some proposals have already appeared in the literature (e.g. [Clarke and Lee, 1997; Higashino et al., 1999; Springintveld et al., 2001]). Our proposal is inspired in [Núñez and Rodríguez, 2003] and differs from the previous ones in several points, mainly because the treatment of time is different. We do not have a notion of clock(s) together with time constraints; we associate time to the execution of actions (the time that it takes for a system to perform and action).

The rest of the paper is organized as follows. In Section 2 we define our language in terms of processes and systems. In Section 3 we show how test cases are defined and describe how to apply them to implementations. Finally, in Section 4 we present our conclusions and some directions for further research.

2. FORMAL SPECIFICATION MODEL: TIMED EFSM

In this section we introduce our timed model for specifying systems where temporal constraints play a relevant role. The main difference with respect to usual EFSMs consists in the addition of *time*. Constraints on the time consumed by actions will be given by means of *intervals*. If the action a is attached with the temporal requirement (t_1, t_2) then the execution of a should take at least t_1 units of time and at most t_2 units. Intervals like $(0, t_2)$, (t_1, ∞), or $(0, \infty)$ denote the absence of any temporal lower/upper bound and the absence of any bound, respectively. Variables will be introduced as a way to add some expressivity to classical finite state machines and as communication mechanism between components of the system. For instance, a variable x can be used as a counter that is incremented every time the action b is performed. Then, if b is enabled only if x is less than or equal to 5, then b will be executed at most

5 times. In our model, variables affect temporal requirements as well. For example, we can specify that the time consumed by b is given by a value that is double than that of variable x. Then, the first execution of b must take 2 units of time, the next one 4 units, and so on. Next we introduce the definition of Timed EFSM. We suppose that the number of different variables is equal to m.

DEFINITION 1 A *Timed Extended Finite State Machine*, in short TEFSM, is a tuple $M = (S, I, O, Tr, s_{in}, \bar{y})$ where S is a finite set of states, I is the set of input actions, O is the set of output actions, Tr is the set of transitions, s_{in} is the initial state, and $\bar{y} \in \mathbf{R}^m$ is a tuple of variables.

Each transition $\delta \in Tr$ is a tuple $\delta = (s, s', i, o, Q, Z, C)$ where $s, s' \in S$ are the initial and final states of the transition, $i \in I$ and $o \in O$ are the input and output actions, respectively, associated with the transition, $Q : \mathbf{R}^m \longrightarrow$ Bool is a predicate on the set of variables, $Z : \mathbf{R}^m \longrightarrow \mathbf{R}^m$ is a transformation over the current variables, and $C : \mathbf{R}^m \longrightarrow (\mathbf{R}_+ \cup \{\infty\}) \times (\mathbf{R}_+ \cup \{\infty\})$ returns, for a given value of the variables, a time interval. Intervals of the form (t, t) where the lower and upper bounds coincide will be written just as t.

A *configuration* in M is a pair $(s, \bar{x})$ where $s \in S$ is the current state and $\bar{x}$ is the current tuple of variable values.

We say that $\sigma = (s, s', (i_1/o_1, \ldots, i_r/o_r), Q, Z, C)$ is a timed *trace* of M if there exist transitions $\delta_1, \ldots, \delta_r \in Tr$ such that $\delta_1 = (s, s_1, i_1, o_1, Q_1, Z_1, C_1)$, $\ldots, \delta_r = (s_{r-1}, s', i_r, o_r, Q_r, Z_r, C_r)$, the predicate Q is defined such that it holds $Q(\bar{x}) = (Q_1(\bar{x}) \wedge Q_2(Z_1(\bar{x})) \wedge \ldots \wedge Q_r(Z_{r-1}(\ldots (Z_1(\bar{x})) \ldots)))$, the transformation Z is defined as $Z(\bar{x}) = Z_r(Z_{r-1}(\ldots (Z_1(\bar{x})) \ldots))$, and C is defined as $C(\bar{x}) = C_1(\bar{x}) + C_2(Z_1(\bar{x})) + \cdots + C_r(Z_{r-1}(\ldots (Z_1(\bar{x})) \ldots))$. Finally, the addition over intervals is defined as follows: $(a_1, a_2) + (b_1, b_2) = (a_1 + b_1, a_2 + b_2)$. ☐

Intuitively, for a configuration $(s, \bar{x})$, a transition $\delta = (s, s', i, o, Q, Z, C)$ indicates that if the machine is in state s, receives the input i, and the predicate Q holds for $\bar{x}$, then after a time belonging to the interval $(t_1, t_2) = C(\bar{x})$ (assuming $t_2 \geq t_1$ and $t_1 \neq \infty$) the machine emits the output o and the values of the variables are transformed according to Z. Let us note that (the value of) variables may disable the execution of actions not only by the effect of the function Q but also by the function C. Traces are defined as a sequence of transitions. In this case, the predicate, the transformation function, and the time associated with the trace are computed from the corresponding to each transition belonging to the sequence. Finally, we suppose that addition in real numbers is extended in the following way: $\infty + r = \infty$.

2.1   Composition of components to specify systems

A system is made of several components. Some of the actions performed by these components will be hidden indicating that they are not visible, that is, they can be neither controlled nor observed. In order to facilitate the understanding, we do not define a *compressed* version of systems where internal communications are omitted yet. So, we generate the whole graph (including both internal and external actions) and then we *delete* internal communications (getting what we call a *simplified system*). Alternatively, we will also present a method to *directly* create the corresponding simplified system.

DEFINITION 2 Let $M_1, \ldots, M_n$ be TEFSMs where for all $1 \leq i \leq n$ we have $M_i = (S_i, I_i, O_i, Tr_i, s_{in_i}, \bar{y}_i)$. Let $I \subseteq \bigcup_i I_i$ and $O \subseteq \bigcup_i O_i$, such that $I \cap O = \emptyset$. The *system* created by the composition of $M_1, \ldots, M_n$ with respect to the actions sets I and O, denoted by $\text{Sys}(M_1, \ldots, M_n, I, O)$, is defined as the TEFSM $M = (S, I, O, Tr, s_{in}, \bar{y})$ where:

- The initial state s_{in} is defined as $s_{in} = (s_{in_1}, \ldots, s_{in_n})$.

- The initial tuple of (tuples of) variable values is $\bar{y} = (\bar{y}_1, \ldots, \bar{y}_n)$.

- $S = S_1 \times \cdots \times S_n$. Actually, it is enough to consider those states reachable from s_{in} by sequences of transitions belonging to Tr.

- Let $s = (s_1, \ldots, s_j, \ldots, s_n)$ and $s' = (s_1, \ldots, s'_j, \ldots, s_n)$ be two states. Then, $(s_j, s'_j, i, o, Q_j, Z_j, C_j) \in Tr_j$ implies $(s, s', i, o, Q, Z, C) \in Tr$, where $Q(\bar{x}_1, \ldots, \bar{x}_n) \equiv Q_j(\bar{x}_j)$, $C(\bar{x}_1, \ldots, \bar{x}_n) = C_j(\bar{x}_j)$ and we have $Z(\bar{x}_1, \ldots, \bar{x}_n) = (\bar{x}_1, \ldots, Z_j(\bar{x}_j), \ldots, \bar{x}_n)$.

Let $\delta = (s, s', (i_1/o_1, \ldots, i_r/o_r), Q, Z, C)$ be a trace for the TEFSM previously defined. We say that δ is a *chained trace* if $o_r \in O$, $i_1 \in I$, and for all $2 \leq l \leq r$ we have $i_l \notin I \cup O$ and $i_l = o_{l-1}$. $\qquad\square$

Let us note that actions not belonging to $I \cup O$ are considered as internal. A chained trace consists of an external input action, a consecutive sequence of paired output/input actions, and finally an external output action. Chained traces are the basis to define our simplified systems. In order to abstract internal computations, systems are transformed into *simplified systems*. The idea is that transitions of a simplified systems are those chained traces belonging to the original system.

DEFINITION 3 Let $Comp = (S, I, O, Tr, s_{in}, \bar{y})$ be a system. We say that $M' = (S', I, O, Tr', s_{in}, \bar{y})$ is the *simplified system* associated with $Comp$, denoted by $\text{Simp}(Comp)$, if S' and Tr' fulfill the following recursive definition:

- $s_{in} \in S'$, and

- If $s \in S'$ and $\delta = (s, s', (i_1/o_1, \ldots, i_r/o_r), Q, Z, C)$ is a chained trace of $Comp$ then $s' \in S'$ and $(s, s', i_1, o_r, Q, Z, C) \in Tr'$.

We say that $i_1/o_1, \ldots, i_r/o_r$ is a *non-timed evolution*, or simply *evolution*, of M' if there exists a trace $(s_{in}, s', (i_1/o_1, \ldots, i_r/o_r), Q, Z, C)$ of M' such that $Q(\bar{y})$ holds. Given a simplified system $Scomp$, $\texttt{NTEvol}(Scomp)$ denotes the set of non-timed evolutions of $Scomp$.

We say that $((i_1/o_1, \ldots, i_r/o_r), (t_1, t_2))$ is a *timed evolution* of M' if there exists a trace $(s_{in}, s', (i_1/o_1, \ldots, i_r/o_r), Q, Z, C)$ of M' such that $Q(\bar{y})$ holds and $(t_1, t_2) = C(\bar{y})$. Given a simplified system $Scomp$, $\texttt{TEvol}(Scomp)$ denotes the set of timed evolutions of $Scomp$.   □

As we said before, a chained trace is converted into a single transition. Then, an evolution is a trace from the initial state of the simplified system. Let us note that all the actions appearing in evolutions are visible (as internal actions are removed by considering transitions formed from chained traces).

2.2   Alternative definition of simplified systems

In this section we present a direct way to define simplified systems without computing the corresponding auxiliary systems. Intuitively, we compute the states of the composition only when they are needed to define the rest of the composite system. In fact, if we are interested only in a part of the whole systems, we could use this method to generate *on the fly* only that portion of the system. For example, one may be interested in the system reachable from a given state s such that all the possible sequences of transitions have labels belonging to some certain sets of inputs and outputs.

DEFINITION 4 Let $M_1, \ldots, M_n$ be TEFSMs with $M_i = (S_i, I_i, O_i, T_i, s_{in_i}, \bar{y}_i)$. We write $(s_1, \ldots, s_j, \ldots, s_n) \xrightarrow{j, \delta, i, o} (s_1, \ldots, s'_j, \ldots, s_n)$ if there exists j such that $\delta = (s_j, s'_j, i, o, Q, Z, C) \in T_j$.

Let $I \subseteq \bigcup_i I_i$ and $O \subseteq \bigcup_i O_i$ be set of actions such that $I \cap O = \emptyset$. The *simplified system* created by the composition of the systems $M_1, \ldots, M_n$ with respect to the set of actions I and O, denoted by $\texttt{SimpSys}(M_1, \ldots, M_n, I, O)$, is given by the tuple $(S, I, O, T, s_{in}, \bar{y})$, where:

- The initial state s_{in} is defined as $s_{in} = (s_{in_1}, \ldots, s_{in_n})$.

- The initial tuple of (tuples of) variable values is $\bar{y} = (\bar{y}_1, \ldots, \bar{y}_n)$.

- $S \subseteq S_1 \times \cdots \times S_n$ is defined as the set of states belonging to T and reachable from s_{in}.

- A transition (v, w, i, o, Q, Z, C) between the states $v = (v_1, \ldots, v_n)$ and $w = (w_1, \ldots, w_n)$ belongs to T if there exist $i_1 \ldots, i_r, o_1, \ldots, o_r$ such that:

    - $o = o_r \in O$,

- $i = i_1 \in I$,
- for all $2 \le l \le r$ we have $i_l \notin I \cup O$ and $i_l = o_{l-1}$,
- there exist $\delta_1, \ldots, \delta_r$, $j_1, \ldots, j_r$ and $s_1, \ldots, s_{r-1}$, where for all $1 \le l \le r-1$, $s_l = (s_{l1}, \ldots, s_{ln})$, such that

$$v \xrightarrow{j_1, \delta_1, i_1, o_1} s_1 \xrightarrow{j_2, \delta_2, i_2, o_2} \ldots s_{r-1} \xrightarrow{j_r, \delta_r, i_r, o_r} w$$

where for all $1 \le l \le r$, $\delta_l = (s_{lj_l}, s_{l+1j_l}, i_l, o_l, \check{Q}_l, \check{Z}_l, \check{C}_l)$,

- $Q(\bar{x}) \equiv (Q_1(\bar{x}) \wedge Q_2(Z_1(\bar{x})) \wedge \ldots \wedge Q_n(Z_{n-1}(\ldots(Z_1(\bar{x}))\ldots)))$.
- $Z(\bar{x}) = Z_n(Z_{n-1}(\ldots(Z_1(\bar{x}))\ldots))$.
- $C(\bar{x}) = C_1(\bar{x}) + C_2(Z_1(\bar{x})) + \ldots + C_n(Z_{n-1}(\ldots(Z_1(\bar{x}))\ldots))$.

In the previous three items, for all $1 \le l \le r$ we have:

$$\begin{aligned} Q_l(\bar{x}_1, \ldots, \bar{x}_n) &\equiv (\check{Q}_l(\bar{x}_{j_l})) \\ Z_l(\bar{x}_1, \ldots, \bar{x}_n) &= (\bar{x}_1, \ldots, \check{Z}_l(\bar{x}_{j_l}), \ldots, \bar{x}_n) \\ C_l(\bar{x}_1, \ldots, \bar{x}_n) &= \check{C}_l(\bar{x}_{j_l}) \end{aligned}$$

□

The next result states that simplified systems defined by applying either the Definitions 2 and 3, or the previous definition coincide. The proof of the result follows by taking into account that the way transitions are defined in both Definitions 3 and 4 generate the corresponding states of the system as well as the transitions between them in the same way. Specifically, in both cases the states of the simplified system consist of the tuple of initial states of all TEFSMs as well as any tuple of states that can be reached by chained traces or sequences of chained traces from the initial state.

LEMMA 5 Let $M_1, \ldots, M_n$ be TEFSMs where each M_i is given by $M_i = (S_i, I_i, O_i, Tr_i, s_{in_i}, \bar{y}_i)$, and let $I \subseteq \bigcup_i I_i$ and $O \subseteq \bigcup_i O_i$ be such that $I \cap O = \emptyset$. Then, we have that

$$\mathrm{Simp}(\mathrm{Sys}(P_1, \ldots, P_n, I, O)) = \mathrm{SimpSys}(P_1, \ldots, P_n, I, O)$$

□

3. DEFINITION AND APPLICATION OF TEST CASES

A test represents a sequence of inputs applied to the implementation. Once an output is received, we check whether it is the expected one or not. In the latter case, a fail signal is produced. In the former case, either a pass signal is emitted (indicating successful termination) or the testing process continues by applying another input. If we are testing an implementation with input and

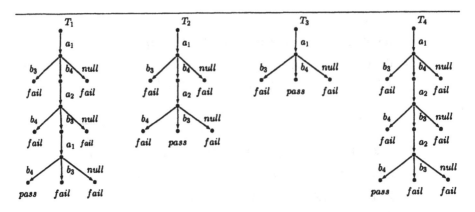

Figure 1.   Examples of Test Cases.

output sets I and O, respectively, tests are deterministic acyclic I/O labelled transition systems (i.e. trees) with a strict alternation between an input action and the set of output actions. After an output action we may find either a leaf or another input action. Leaves can be labelled either by *pass* or by *fail*. In the first case we add a *time stamp*, an interval that will be contrasted with the time that the implementation took to arrive to that point. We also add a time stamp in input states to record the time that the performance of the preceding output action took.

DEFINITION 6   A *test case* is a tuple $T = (S, I, O, Tr, s_0, S_I, S_O, S_F, S_P, C)$ where S is the set of states, I and O are disjoint sets of input and output actions, respectively, $Tr \subseteq S \times I \cup O \times S$ is the transition relation, $s_0 \in S$ is the initial state, and the sets $S_I, S_O, S_F, S_P \subseteq S$ are a partition of S. The transition relation and the sets of states fulfill the following conditions:

- S_I is the set of *input* states. We have that $s_0 \in S_I$. For any input state $s \in S_I$ there exists a unique outgoing transition $(s, a, s') \in Tr$. For this transition we have that $a \in I$ and $s' \in S_O$.

- S_O is the set of *output* states. For any output state $s \in S_O$ we have that for any $o \in O$ there exists a unique state s' such that $(s, o, s') \in Tr$. In this case, $s' \notin S_O$. Moreover, there do not exist $i \in I, s' \in S$ such that $(s, i, s') \in Tr$.

- S_F and S_P are the sets of *fail* and *pass* states, respectively. We say that these states are *terminal*. Besides, for any state $s \in S_F \cup S_P$ we have that there do not exist $a \in I \cup O$ and $s' \in S$ such that $(s, a, s') \in Tr$.

Finally, $C : S_P \cup S_I \longrightarrow (\mathbf{R}_+ \cup \{\infty\}) \times (\mathbf{R}_+ \cup \{\infty\})$ is a function associating time interval stamps with passing and input states.

Let $\sigma = i_1/o_1, \ldots, i_r/o_r$. We write $T \overset{\sigma}{\Longrightarrow} s$ if $s \in S_F \cup S_P$ and there exist states $s_{12}, s_{21}, s_{22}, \ldots s_{r1}, s_{r2} \in S$ such that $\{(s_0, i_1, s_{12}), (s_{r2}, o_r, s)\} \subseteq Tr$, for all $2 \leq j \leq r$ we have $(s_{j1}, i_j, s_{j2}) \in Tr$, and for all $1 \leq j \leq r-1$ we have $(s_{j2}, o_j, s_{(j+1)1}) \in Tr$.

We say that a test case T is an *instance* of the test case T' if they only differ in the associated function C assigning time intervals.

We say that a test case T is *valid* if the graph induced by T is a tree with root at the initial state s_0. □

In Figure 1 we present some examples of test cases (time stamps are omitted). Next we define the application of a tests suite (i.e. a set of tests) to an implementation. We say that the tests suite $\mathcal{T}$ is *passed* if for any test the terminal states reached by the composition of implementation and test belong to the set of *passing* states. Besides, we give timing conditions according to the temporal constraints included in tests.

DEFINITION 7 Let I be a simplified system and T be a valid test. We write $I \parallel T \overset{\sigma}{\Longrightarrow}_t s^T$ if $T \overset{\sigma}{\Longrightarrow} s^T$ and $(\sigma, t) \in \text{TEvol}(I)$.

We say that I *passes* the set of tests $\mathcal{T}$, denoted by $\text{pass}(I, \mathcal{T})$, if for all test $T = (S, I, O, Tr, s, S_I, S_O, S_F, S_P, C) \in \mathcal{T}$ and $\sigma \in \text{NTEvol}(I)$ there do not exist s^T and t such that $I \parallel T \overset{\sigma}{\Longrightarrow}_t s^T$ and $s^T \in S_F$.

We say that I *passes temporally* the set of tests $\mathcal{T}$ if $\text{pass}(I, \mathcal{T})$ and for all $(\sigma, t) \in \text{TEvol}(I)$ such that $T' \overset{\sigma}{\Longrightarrow} s^{T'}$ for some $T' \in \mathcal{T}$, we have that for all $T = (S, I, O, Tr, s, S_I, S_O, S_F, S_P, C) \in \mathcal{T}$ such that $I \parallel T \overset{\sigma}{\Longrightarrow}_t s^T$ with $s^T \in S_P \cap S_I$ it holds that $t \in C(s^T)$. □

That is, for passing a test suite we require that (a) no functional behavior that is forbidden by any test is produced by the system and (b) any temporal behavior produced by the system is accepted by all the tests belonging to the test suite.

4. CONCLUSIONS AND FUTURE WORK

In this paper we have presented a model that is suitable for defining the temporal requirements to specify embedded systems. Besides, we have defined how to test an embedded system to find out whether these requirements are fulfilled. The formalism proposed is an extension of the classical EFSMs where actions are provided with the possibility of expressing temporal constraints. These constraints allow to impose maximal and/or minimal bounds for the time consumed by an action as well as strict temporal requirements. The temporal behavior of a system is automatically inferred from the temporal behavior of each component of the system. In particular, temporal constraints on external actions are computed from the temporal constraints on the internal actions participating in the execution of that external action. Tests are sequences of input actions that stimulate the system and record the outputs produced in response. After each output is received, the test checks whether the time consumed by the trace produced so far fits into the constraint defined by the test.

We are developing temporal implementation relations for embedded systems that define the conditions required for an implementation to *conform* to a specification. In this line, we will take as starting point our previous work in [Núñez and Rodríguez, 2002]. Besides, we are constructing a test derivation algorithm to produce *sound* and *complete* test suites according to these relations, that is, the implementation conforms to the specification if and only if the implementation passes all the tests belonging to the test suite derived from the specification. In this case, we will try to use our recent work on testing probabilistic systems [López et al., 2005] where such a derivation algorithm, although for a probabilistic model, is presented.

REFERENCES

Alur, R. and Dill, D. (1994). A theory of timed automata. *Theoretical Computer Science*, 126:183–235.

Clarke, D. and Lee, I. (1997). Automatic generation of tests for timing constraints from requirements. In *3rd Workshop on Object-Oriented Real-Time Dependable Systems*.

Higashino, T., Nakata, A., Taniguchi, K., and Cavalli, A. (1999). Generating test cases for a timed I/O automaton model. In *12th Workshop on Testing of Communicating Systems*, pages 197–214. Kluwer Academic Publishers.

Lee, D. and Yannakakis, M. (1996). Principles and methods of testing finite state machines: A survey. *Proceedings of the IEEE*, 84(8):1090–1123.

Lima, L. and Cavalli, A. (1997). A pragmatic approach to generating tests sequences for embedded systems. In *10th Workshop on Testing of Communicating Systems*, pages 288–307. Chapman & Hall.

López, N., Núñez, M., and Rodríguez, I. (2005). Testing of symbolic-probabilistic systems. In *4th Int. Workshop on Formal Approaches to Testing of Software (FATES 2004), LNCS 3395*, pages 49–63. Springer.

Myers, G. (1979). *The Art of Software Testing*. John Wiley and Sons.

Núñez, M. and Rodríguez, I. (2002). Encoding PAMR into (timed) EFSMs. In *FORTE 2002, LNCS 2529*, pages 1–16. Springer.

Núñez, M. and Rodríguez, I. (2003). Towards testing stochastic timed systems. In *FORTE 2003, LNCS 2767*, pages 335–350. Springer.

Petrenko, A., Yevtushenko, N., and Bochmann, G. v. (1996). Fault models for testing in context. In *Formal Description Techniques for Distributed Systems and Communication Protocols (IX), and Protocol Specification, Testing, and Verification (XVI)*, pages 163–178. Chapman & Hall.

Springintveld, J., Vaandrager, F., and D'Argenio, P. (2001). Testing timed automata. *Theoretical Computer Science*, 254(1-2):225–257.

A FORMAL METHODOLOGY TO TEST COMPLEX EMBEDDED SYSTEMS: APPLICATION TO INTERACTIVE DRIVING SYSTEM *

Manuel Núñez,[1] Fernando L. Pelayo[2] and Ismael Rodríguez[1]

[1]*Departamento Sistemas Informáticos y Programación, Facultad de Informática*
Universidad Complutense de Madrid, 28040 Madrid, Spain
{mn,isrodrig}@sip.ucm.es

[2]*Departamento de Informática, Facultad de Informática*
Universidad Castilla-La Mancha, 02071 Albacete, Spain
fpelayo@info-ab.uclm.es

Abstract: Complex embedded systems may integrate heterogeneous components. Each component can be defined by using a different specification formalism, or in terms of other components. In order to test the conformance of an implementation with respect to a specification we can use a different testing methodology for each of the (different group of) components. Still, this approach might overlook details regarding the relation among the units of the system under test. In our framework, a *unit* is a set of functionalities of interaction of the system with the environment. These functionalities can be possibly defined in terms of the ones appearing in *lower* units. Essentially, in order to test the functionalities corresponding to a unit, tests may use capabilities described in lower units. These capabilities will be provided by the system under test once they have been previously tested by using some lower-level tests. In order to illustrate our framework we present a running example where the *Interactive Driving System* developed by ADAM Opel A.G. [Opel, 2005] is described.

1. INTRODUCTION

In order to ensure a greater reliability of critical systems, design languages must be based on a (semi-)formal framework. Actually, in order to build complex systems, it is very important to provide a formal design to contrast the capabilities provided by the system with the expected ones. Depending on the system to be designed, very different specification formalisms can be used.

*Research partially supported by the Spanish MCYT project TIC2003-07848-C02, the Junta de Castilla-La Mancha project PAC-03-001, and the Marie Curie project MRTN-CT-2003-505121/TAROT.

Embedded systems are nowadays so complex that to completely specify their behavior is a very difficult task. In particular, these systems are very heterogeneous and include a big amount of components with different natures. Thus, instead of using a unique specification framework to formally define the behavior of systems, it is more adequate to define distinguished parts of the system by using different formalisms. For each of the parts we may choose the most suitable formalism. Let us remark that the use of different notations is not restricted to the description of different components: It can be used to provide different *views* or interpretations of the same component. This approach has being used in several programming methodologies such as *functional programming* (e.g. [Bird and Wadler, 1988]), *aspect oriented programming* (e.g. [Kiczales et al., 1997]) and *component software* (e.g. [Szyperski, 1998]). In this paper, however, we consider different formalisms only as a means to define different components, not the same component in different ways.

In addition to be composed by several parts, embedded systems often present a *hierarchical* structure. Thus, its definition can be decomposed into different levels of abstraction, consisting each of these levels of several units. In this case, the behavior of each unit will be formally specified by using a (possibly) different formalism. Before we begin to describe how our testing approach is implemented, we will introduce a running example of a *multi-level* specification in the automotive industry: the *Interactive Driving System*, in short IDS, developed by Opel/Vauxhall is the brain of some new models of GM-Europe like Vectra and Astra. What makes this system revolutionary is that it enables the suspension, brake, engine, and steering systems to *talk* to each other in order to provide the best response for different driving scenarios. It senses the driving condition and synchronizes the performance of every component of the chassis and engine to adapt and respond. This behavior results in one of the best coordinated driving dynamics in their respective classes. Simply put, the IDS consists of the following three entities:

- *Electro-Hydraulic Power Steering*, in short EHPS,

- *Electronic Stability Program*, in short ESP, and

- *Shock absorbers Control*, in short CDC.

In turn, we can distinguish the following components in the ESP:

- *Anti-lock Braking System*, in short ABS,

- *Brake Assist System*, in short BAS,

- *Cornering Brake Control*, in short CBC,

- *Electronic Brake-force Distribution*, in short EBD, and

- *Traction Control*, in short TC.

These entities can be seen as *agents* whose behavior consist in performing their work on their particular domains fulfilling the requirements under which they where designed. In order to specify these agents we may consider three different levels of abstraction. The lowest level controls that the hardware components both capture the physical magnitudes and execute the physical orders properly. In order to formally specify the behavior at this level we can use formalisms such as LOTOS [LOTOS, 1988] or SDL [ITU92, 1992]. The intermediate level must guarantee that the real behavior of the vehicle verifies its main objective, that is, anti-lock braking systems guarantee the lock-freeness of the wheels for speeds over 5 *Km/h*. The behavior in this level can be best defined by using a generic language for the description of agents such as AgentSpeak(L) [Rao, 1996] or 3APL [Hindriks et al., 1998]. The highest level of abstraction is devoted to satisfy the intentions of the driver. Therefore, a general purpose specification language such as UML [Booch et al., 1998] could be an adequate formalism to specify the behavior of agents to control the *speed*, *trajectory*, and *angular moment* of the automobile.

The previous running example shows that the formal specification of complex heterogeneous embedded systems represents an important challenge for traditional testing methodologies. First, specifications are not described by using a unique language. In fact, several languages can be used to specify different (sets of) functionalities, that is, different units. Our notion of unit differs from the concept of *component* where functionalities may be for internal use and do not have to interact with the environment. Systems have a hierarchical structure (different levels). The first level contains those units that do not depend on other units. For any $i > 1$, the i-th level contains those units that depend only on units belonging to lower levels. Let us remark that our approach contains, as a particular case, standard approaches for the specification and testing of component-based systems.

Even though the specification of multi-level systems is a stand-alone goal, in this paper we will go one step further. Our goal is to test the conformance of an implementation under test, in short IUT, with respect to a specification. Obviously, even if a system is specified in different stages, we will have a unique integrated implementation, not one implementation for each of the units/levels. In fact, this implementation will be often given in terms of a *black box*, where the internal structure is not observable. Thus, we need tests that can stimulate the IUT by means of basic low level operations that can be understood by it. For example, in our running example we need to fix which basic messages have to be exchanged between the different units to communicate the current trajectory of the automobile.

An obvious alternative to our approach can be taken if each unit of the IUT can be *disconnected* from those units it depends on. If this is possible then we could test different parts of the IUT in an *isolated* way. Unfortunately, it is not always feasible to disconnect parts of the IUT from other parts they depend on directly. In particular, this process could require some knowledge of the IUT that is not available if it is a black box. Besides, we lose the capability to check the correctness of the *integration* and *assembling* of the parts of the IUT.

The rest of the paper is structured as follows. The next section represents the bulk of the paper. First, we informally present the main features of our testing approach. Next, we introduce the main definitions that will be used during this paper. Finally, we formally define our testing methodology. In Section 3 we introduce how our model is applied to the framework of *Interactive Dynamical Behavior of Automobiles*. Finally, in Section 4 we present our conclusions.

2.   THE MULTI-LEVEL TESTING METHODOLOGY

In this section we present our multi-level testing approach. We begin by informally introducing the main characteristics of our approach. We will also review how traditional formal testing works and we will show how these techniques can be adapted/modified/discarded in the case of multi-level testing.

2.1   Informal presentation

In formal testing we usually extract some tests from the considered specification and apply them to the implementation under test (IUT). By comparing the obtained results with the ones expected by the specification we can generate a *diagnosis* about the correctness (usually, the incorrectness) of the IUT. These tests usually represent *stimulation plans* of the IUT by providing sequences of events (called *inputs*) that can be interpreted by the IUT. The IUT replies, for each input, with another event (called *outputs*). If the specification language specializes in defining simple communication events then these events can be straightforwardly reproduced and identified. In this case, it will be easy to apply the tests to the IUT, since the events clearly define how to stimulate the IUT. On the contrary, if the specification language deals with a higher level of abstraction then it will be more complex to decide how the test will apply the foreseen inputs to the IUT.

Coming back to our running example, let us suppose that we specify the Interactive Dynamical Behavior of Automobiles, in short IDBA, by using a language that specializes in the definition of the highest level of abstraction. The resulting model will clearly define, for each situation, the desirable behavior. Thus, the specification will determine for each scenario the optimum (possible) behavior of the automobile in terms of speed, trajectory, and angular moment. However, this high-level specification language is not suitable to represent situations such as how should be corrected the torque transmitted to each wheel or how should the brakes act on each wheel. In such a context, one may wonder how a test can indicate to the IUT that a breaking action on the rear wheels has to be performed under a overturn. If the specification language implementation by following a fixed procedure protocol. This is so because the specification language does not allow to express these details. For example, if we fix the procedure protocol when an overturn appears then we are forcing the IUT to follow that procedure, even though this information is not reflected in the specification. However, it is obvious that the test will be using a specific protocol of desirable behavior. Otherwise, it would not be able to propose different actions to the IUT, being these the basic operations to stimulate the IUT. In order to solve the previously stated problem we will impose two conditions.

First, we need a more complete definition of the specification where lower abstraction levels are somehow included. Let us remark that even though a high level language can be used to provide key information about the desired behavior of the system, the system itself must indicate some lower level operations allowing to perform the desired functionalities. Thus, the specification of the whole system must be done in several steps and by (potentially) using different specification languages for each level of abstraction.

Second, the definition of tests will be also given by levels/units. The tester has to use the same levels of abstraction as the ones in the specification. In order to test a certain level of abstraction of the IUT the tests will represent activity plans for that level. Nevertheless, each of the interactions between the test and the IUT will be carried out by using auxiliary (possibly lower level) operations. These operations have to be tested beforehand with respect to the lower levels of abstraction where they are defined. Besides, lower levels of abstraction are tested by using operations of lower levels of abstraction, and so on. In general, the definition of a test to check the behavior of the IUT at a level of abstraction needs the definition of all the levels of the test from that level down to the lowest level. Thus, in order to define tests we will use a bootstrapping approach. The behavior of the units belonging to the lowest level will be tested as usual. The difference comes when testing the behavior of a higher unit and, more precisely, when defining tests for these units. If a test is devoted to check a unit belonging to a certain level of the IUT then it will *use* and *invoke* IUT operations belonging to lower levels as part of its own definition. Before we use these IUT operations, we need to be confident that they are correctly implemented. Thus, we require that these IUT operations have already been tested by other (lower level) tests. This procedure yields a recursive testing methodology where units belonging to lower levels must be tested before the ones corresponding to higher levels.

2.2 Basic definitions

Next we introduce some notation to formally define *multi-level* specifications and tests. Intuitively, a *specification* can be seen as a set of services, that is, functionalities that the system is supposed to provide. Each service can be either an *input* or an *output*, being the main difference who is responsible of its initialization: The *outside world* or the *own system*, respectively. Each service is defined by means of an expression in a certain specification language. This expression indicates the operations that take place to perform that service. A given service can depend on other services provided by the specification and/or by other lower level sub-specifications. In particular, an input service can be defined by using an output one, that is in turn defined in terms of an input service, and so on. The organization of services in units allows to precisely define how a unit depends on other units.

DEFINITION 1 Let us suppose that the system contains n different units. For all $1 \leq i \leq n$, a *specification* S_i is a tuple $(L_i, I_i, O_i, \alpha_i)$, where L_i is the *language* to define S_i, $I_i = \{s_1, \ldots, s_n\}$ denotes the set of *input services* of S_i, $O_i = \{s_{n+1}, \ldots, s_m\}$ denotes the set of *output services* of S_i, and $\alpha_i \subseteq \{1, \ldots, n\} - \{i\}$ denotes the set of *specifications below* S_i. For all $j \in \alpha_i$, let $S_j = (L_j, \{s_1^j, \ldots, s_{a_j}^j\}, \{s_{a_j+1}^j, \ldots, s_{b_j}^j\}, \alpha_j)$. Each service s_r is defined by an *expression* in the language L_i that may depend on any other service of either S_i or on services defined in S_k, for some $k \in \alpha_i$. That is, for any service $s_r \in I_i \cup O_i$ we have

$$s_r = f_r(s_1, \ldots, s_m, s_1^1, \ldots, s_{b_1}^1, \ldots, s_1^k, \ldots, s_{b_k}^k)$$

If $\alpha_i = \emptyset$ then we say that the specification S_i is *simple*. We assume that S_1 represents the *highest level* specification, that is, for all $1 \leq j \leq n$ we have $1 \notin \alpha_j$ and for any $j \neq 1$ we have that there exists $1 \leq k \leq n$ such that $j \in \alpha_k$.

Let us consider the sub-specifications $S_1, S_2, \ldots, S_n$. The levels of the specification are recursively defined as:

- The first level contains those specifications S_j such that $\alpha_j = \emptyset$.

- For all $i > 1$, the i-th level contains those specifications S_j such that for all $k \in \alpha_j$ we have that S_k belongs to an already defined level (that is, a level lower than i).

- We finish the process when we find i such that S_1 belongs to level i.

For a given specification language L, we denote by Specs_L the set of all specifications in language L. We denote the set of specifications in language L that do *not depend* on any other specification, that is, $\alpha = \emptyset$, by $\text{Specs}_L^\emptyset$. $\quad\Box$

Let us consider the *tree* of sub-specifications included in a specification. Each of these sub-specifications defines a different *unit*. There is a distinguished sub-specification, S_1, denoting the *root* of the tree. Specifications at the same level of the tree denote a *level*. Let us remark that neither individual

A sub-specification denotes some functionalities of *interaction* of the system with the environment, where each of them may be defined in terms of operations belonging to lower levels. These functionalities are called *services*. On the contrary, functionalities provided by a component do no need to interact with the environment. This difference will be relevant for testing purposes.

Let us take up again the running example of interactive driving system agents. The highest level of abstraction is given by the behaviors considered acceptable, at each time, by the driver. Essentially, the specification will provide a unique output service *"adequate speed, trajectory within the road, and angular position on the trajectory."* This service will be defined in terms of more basic operations such as *"modify the speed"*, normally a reduction, performed by the BAS and ABS agents, *"change the trajectory,"* performed by EHPS and ESP agents, and *"angular position tangent to the trajectory,"* in charge of CBC and EBD agents. These operations are atomic for the intermediate level of abstraction but they have to be defined in a greater detail for lower levels.

EXAMPLE 2 Let us consider the specification of the output operation *"taking a bend"* at the highest level of abstraction. In order to specify this service in terms of operations of the *interactive driving system* unit, we could consider the following sequence:

- (Output) Turn the steering wheel.

- (Input) Put the foot on the brake pedal.

- (Output) The front wheels turn following the steering wheel and the vehicle decelerates.

- (Input) The driver panics because the new trajectory is not correct. He quickly overturns the steering wheel. In addition, he might step down the brake.

- (Output) As a consequence, the vehicle underturns and follows a right trajectory.

- (Input) Different sensors detect, on the one hand, a violent movement on the steering wheel and, on the other hand, a lost of trajectory since the rotation speed of the front wheels is slower than the one of the rear wheels.

- (Output) An *underturn scenario* from the vehicle is identified.

- (Input) IDS follows the protocol to correct an underturn. This is done by reading the sensors of the agents which is formed of. Once the right trace to the braking systems (mainly, braking the wheels of the inside side of the bend, or even also braking both rear wheels via CBC and EBD).

- (Output) The vehicle comes back into the road trajectory (if it is possible from the physics' point of view).

- (Input) IDS returns the control of the brakes to the driver. The vehicle corners in the right way.

The previous dialogue can take different bifurcations depending on the actions on the controls, the speed, the angle of the bend, how slippery the road is, etcetera.   □

Next we introduce a general notion of *test suite*. This concept will allow us to abstract the underlying test derivation methodology. We only assume that there exists a fix criteria to construct test suites (see [Zhu et al., 1997] for a good survey on coverage criteria). Since the purpose of the following definition is to generalize current test derivation algorithms, where specifications do not have multiple *levels*, we consider that the given specification is simple. We will extend this notion to multi-level specifications in the forthcoming Definition 5.

DEFINITION 3 Let L be a specification language and $S = (L, I, O, \emptyset) \in$ Specs_L be a specification. We denote the set of tests for the language L by Tests_L. We say that a test $T \in \text{Tests}_L$ is *simple* if it stimulates only services belonging to $I \cup O$. We denote the set of simple tests for the language L by $\text{Tests}_L^{\emptyset}$.

A *simple test suite* for the language L and the specification S is any element belonging to $\mathcal{P}(\text{Tests}_L^{\emptyset})$.   □

As an additional condition on tests we assume that they provide the output service $fail$ to denote that a failure has been found. In the following definition we introduce a general testing framework. As usual in formal testing, we consider that there exists a formal language to construct a precise model to describe the behavior of the IUT. In our setting we suppose, again as usually, that specifications and implementations are described in the same formal language.

DEFINITION 4 Let L be a specification language, $S \in \text{Specs}_L$ be a specification, and $T \in \text{Tests}_L$ be a test. If the interaction of S and T may trigger the execution of a service a then we denote this event by $\text{Produce}(L, S, T, a)$.

Let $S \in \text{Specs}_L^{\emptyset}$ be a simple specification and $I \in \text{Specs}_L^{\emptyset}$ be an IUT. Let F be a simple test suite for L and S. We say that I *passes* F if for all $T \in F$ we have that $\text{Produce}(L, I, T, fail)$ does not hold.   □

2.3   Formal definition of the testing process

As we pointed out before, the proposed methodology considers that the IUT is a *black box*. So, we cannot assume any internal structure. In particular, when we speak about a given *unit of the IUT*, we mean the implementation in the IUT of some services that are *logically* grouped in the specification as a unit. Similarly, when we speak about *level of the IUT* we mean the *implementation* of the corresponding units in the IUT, that is, a set of sets of services. If the IUT is correct then these services must be correctly implemented, but their physical structure in the IUT is indeed not considered. In order to test the conformance of a given unit with respect to a specification, we will create tests to stimulate the IUT according to some operations used in that unit. However, each of these operations has to be performed according to its specification. Since the IUT is supposed to correctly implement all of the units, the test should be allowed to take and use operations provided in lower levels.

However, the implementation of the corresponding units conforming these levels could be *faulty*. Therefore, before we use the operations given in units belonging to a lower level, we will have to *check* their correctness. More precisely, the correctness of the capabilities provided by those units has to be assessed. In order to do that, we will *test* them. Following the same idea, testing the units belonging to a lower level may require to consider the functionalities condensed in an even lower level of the IUT. So, first of all we will have to check the correctness of those units. The same reasoning is repeated until we infer that we need to check the units corresponding to the lowest level. The tests needed to check the correctness of level 1 do not use any lower unit/level. Thus, they can be used exactly as they are generated by the corresponding test derivation algorithm for level 1. Once we have tested this level of the IUT, we will use the contained capabilities as part of the implementation of the tests that check the units belonging to the immediately higher level, and so on.

Let us remark that using the services provided by a unit of the IUT as part of a test implementation does not consist in *breaking* this part and connecting it to the test. Since IUTs are black boxes, this cannot be done. Instead, using an IUT unit consists in taking the *whole* IUT and invoking and using *only* some of its services: The services that are logically grouped as the considered unit in the specification.

The next definition formalizes this process. We derive a set of *multi-level* tests from a set of *simple* tests. In tests belonging to the latter set, all services are *atomic*. Thus, they do not need any further definition. In order to obtain the set of multi-level tests, we modify the aforementioned simple tests so that all the tests contain the definition of all lower levels. The operations from these units are taken directly from the IUT.

To pass a test suite created for checking the i-th level of the IUT (for some $i > 1$) requires that lower units are correct with respect to the corresponding units of the specification. In order to be confident in this correctness (although it will not be a *proof* of it), we will recursively apply a suitable test suite to the immediately lower units/level of the IUT. If this test suite is passed then we will use the services appearing in these units to construct services of the tests that check the capabilities corresponding to units appearing at level i.

DEFINITION 5 Let us consider a specification $S = (L_S, I_S, O_S, \alpha_S)$, an implementation under test $IUT = (L_I, I_I, O_I, \alpha_I)$, and a simple test suite for L_S and S, $F = \{(L_S, I_1, O_1, \emptyset), \ldots, (L_S, I_n, O_n, \emptyset)\}$. We say that the set $\{(L_S, I_1, O_1, \alpha_I), \ldots, (L_S, I_n, O_n, \alpha_I)\}$ is a *multi-level test suite* for L_S, S, and IUT.

Let G be a multi-level test derivation suite for L_S, S, and IUT. We say that *IUT passes G* for S if the following two conditions hold:

(1) For all $S' = (L', I', O', \alpha') \in \alpha_S$ there exists $i \in \alpha_I$ such that IUT_i passes G' for S', where G' is a test derivation set for L', S', and IUT_i.

(2) For all $T \in G$ we have that $\texttt{Produce}(L_S, IUT, T, fail)$ does not hold.
$\qquad\qquad\qquad\qquad\qquad\qquad\qquad\qquad\qquad\qquad\qquad\qquad\qquad\qquad\square$

Let us note that the anchor case of the previous recursive definition is applied only when we test a simple system. In this situation, there is no element to consider in clause (1), so that this case trivially holds.

3.   CASE STUDY: INTERACTIVE DRIVING SYSTEM

In this section we present the application of our methodology to our running example: Interactive Driving System Plus by Opel. IDS Plus enables the suspension, brake and steering systems to *talk* to each other. It senses the driving condition and synchronizes the performance of every component of the chassis to adapt and respond. IDS Plus consists mainly of the following three agents:

- *Electro-Hydraulic Power Steering*, in short EHPS, is a remarkable innovation, intelligent enough to sense the *adequate* driving speed. It requires little effort at low speeds (e.g. for parking) and increased effort at high speeds. This ensures safety and complete control.

- *Electronic Stability Program*, in short ESP, basically generates an opposite force to the one which tries to take the vehicle out of the good trajectory. It is composed of the following units:

    - *Anti-Lock Braking System*, in short ABS, guarantees that at any moment the rotation speed of all the wheels are the same and corresponds with the speed of the vehicle during a braking action. It has five sensors to determine those speeds and two electric valves per wheel in order to be able to modify the braking force on any wheel. Its functioning depends on the CBC.

    - *Cornering Brake Control function*, in short CBC, allows to apply braking force individually to each wheel. This helps the car main-

- *Brake Assist System*, in short BAS, recognizes a panic braking situation. In such an emergency, this system releases brake power with a faster built up, considerably reducing braking distance. It acts on the electro valves of the wheels and takes the necessary pressure from an electronic pump which can provide around 150 bar inside the brake circuit.

- *Electronic Brake-force Distribution*, in short EBD, senses the brake force the driver applies and distributes it proportionally to the mass shift of the car. This helps to improve braking performance even when the car is loaded.

- *Traction Control*, in short TC, ensures that the vehicle never loses grip of the road, even at high speeds on slippery and wet surfaces.

- *Shock Absorbers Control*, in short CDC, modifies the consistency of the shock absorbers as a function of the angle of the steering wheel and the speed and rock of the vehicle.

These entities can be seen as agents whose behavior consist in performing their work on their particular domains fulfilling the requirements described above. They have to put all their input/output information via a *Controlled Area Network Bus* to the IDS controller. Moreover, the IDS controller, attending more general intentions, will give some new operation instructions to each unit. In order to specify these agents we may consider three different levels of abstraction. At the lower level, every agent among ABS, BAS, CBC, EBD, and TC needs to verify that its input sensors and its hardware mechanisms work properly. At the intermediate level, the agents corresponding to EHPS, ESP, and CDC have to satisfy their own goal, that is, they have to calculate the necessary response in view of the data collected by the sensors. At the highest level, IDS, it has to be ensured that the system follows the intentions of the driver.

Next we briefly describe how our testing approach is applied to this system. Since the IDS controller is the highest level unit, testing this unit implies creating some tests that will stimulate the IUT by proposing some *extreme* situations. In order to allow the resulting tests to communicate with the IUT, we need to endow them with a procedure to allow them to transmit the signals according to the protocol committed by all the agents. Actually, the IUT contains an implementation of the lower-level units that allows it to perform these operations. We will take these units as part of the implementation of each test.

However, the implementation of the lower level units could be faulty. For example, the implementation of the functionalities grouped in the ESP could present mistakes. Hence, before we use it to define our tests we need to check its correctness. In order to do that, we generate a new test suite to check the correctness of the sequences of operations executed as part of a *trajectory correction* in the ESP unit. Tests will be able to perform its operations by interacting through operations belonging to the lowest units of the IUT. These units define how these operations are performed in terms of basic communication operations.

Once we have tested the ABS, CBC, BAS, EBD, and TC units of the IUT we can use its operations as part of the tests that will check the correctness of the ESP unit. If the testing of functionalities belonging to the EHPS, ESP, and CDC units does not find an error then we can use the operations belonging to these units to define tests that will be used to test the highest level unit. Let us remind that by applying these tests to the IUT we will obtain a diagnosis about the correctness of the highest level unit of the IUT and, by extension, about the correctness of the lower units and of the whole system.

4. CONCLUSIONS

We have presented a testing methodology for testing complex embedded systems. In general, each component is specified by using a different language. These languages can be, in general, very different. The proposed methodology is defined in a recursive way and is based on the idea of testing at first lower levels and by continuing with higher levels, up to the highest one. Testing the correctness of the functionalities of each unit of the IUT allows us to *use* these operations as part of the tests that will check the behavior of units located in higher levels of the IUT. In order to illustrate our approach we have applied it to the interactive driving system developed by Opel.

REFERENCES

Bird, R. and Wadler, P. (1988). *Introduction to Functional Programming*. Prentice Hall.

Booch, G., Rumbaugh, J., and Jacobson, I., editors (1998). *The Unified Modeling Language User Guide*. Addison-Wesley.

Hindriks, K., de Boer, F., van der Hoek, W., and Meyer, J.-J. (1998). Formal semantics for an abstract agent programming language. In *Intelligent Agents IV, LNAI 1365*, pages 215–229. Springer.

ITU92 (1992). ITU. Recommendation Z.100: CCITT Specification and Description Language (SDL).

Kiczales, G., Lamping, J., Menhdhekar, A., Maeda, C., Lopes, C., Loingtier, J.-M., and Irwin, J. (1997). Aspect-oriented programming. In *11th European Conference on Object-Oriented Programming, LNCS 1241*, pages 220–242. Springer.

LOTOS (1988). A formal description technique based on the temporal ordering of observational behaviour. IS 8807, TC97/SC21.

Opel (2005). Description of the IDS. http://www.opel.com.

Rao, A. (1996). AgentSpeak(L): BDI agents speak out in a logical computable language. In *Agents Breaking Away, LNAI 1038*, pages 42–55. Springer.

Szyperski, C. (1998). *Component Software: Beyond Object-Oriented Programming*. Addison-Wesley.

Zhu, H., Hall, P., and May, J. (1997). Software unit test coverage and adequacy. *ACM Computing Surveys*, 29(4):366–427.

ENHANCING INTERACTION SUPPORT IN THE CORBA COMPONENT MODEL

Sylvain Robert[1], Ansgar Radermacher[1], Vincent Seignole[2], Sébastien Gérard[1], Virginie Watine[2] and François Terrier[1]

[1]*CEA-LIST, DRT/LIST/DTSI/SOL, CEA Saclay, 91191 Gif sur Yvette Cedex, France;* [2]*Thales Alice pilot program, Thales Communications, 91300 Massy, France*

Abstract: Even if promising with respect to software complexity management, component-based approaches, like CCM and EJB, have until now fall short in achieving their breakthrough in the real-time and embedded community. Our aim is to adapt one of these approaches - namely the CCM - to the specific needs of this area. In such a process, we have identified several crucial points, among which is interaction management. The current CCM runtime interaction support is actually poor and lacks flexibility. That is the reason why, drawing our inspiration from similar works of the ADLs field, we propose to gather all interaction-related processing in connectors. This paper details the rationale underlying our choice, and outlines all modifications needed to introduce the connector meta-element in the CCM. It also illustrates the relevance of CCM connectors in the scope of a telecommunication use case.

Keywords: CCM, ADL, Components, Connectors, Real Time, Embedded, Interaction

1.   INTRODUCTION

The current trend of real time embedded software is towards complexity. Complexity of the developed software, of course, but also complexity of the development processes. Component-based approaches, like CCM[2] or EJB[11], are likely to help developers coping with this issue. However, they have until now been considered to be poorly adapted to embedded software design, notably because of their associated runtime infrastructures which consume too much resources (e.g. memory footprint). For instance, using the CCM implies using a CORBA-compliant middleware layer, which is generally not affordable in the embedded domain. Hence, a gap has to be bridged, before these approaches can spread in embedded software development practices.

We aim to bridge this gap in the scope of the CCM approach, within ongoing collaborative research projects[*]. In such a process, we have identified three main steps. First, CCM containers shall be extended with real-time specific support (e.g. scheduling). Then, deployment guidance (i.e. the way the application is installed and launched on the target) has to be adapted. At last, our execution framework should also be usable on systems with limited memory resources. This latter goal is achieved by two measures: (i) choosing a lightweight version of the CCM[1], (ii) making it possible to use light (which means lighter than CORBA) execution infrastructures, like real time operating systems.

The paper focuses on the second aspect, i.e. the integration of new interaction mechanisms that reduce the dependencies to CORBA. As a side effect, these interactions offer more design flexibility. The approach we propose adds a brand new entity in the CCM: the *connector*. While components are loci for business logic, connectors are loci for interaction management logic[8]. They encapsulate all interaction-related processing, thus providing a better separation of concerns. Integrating connectors with CCM is not straightforward, since it imposes a modification of all CCM facilities (e.g. extending the IDL language to be able to define connectors, or adapting deployment and configuration). In the following, we describe our approach to this technical issue and illustrate its relevance an example. The structure of this paper is as follows: Section 2 is an introductive overview of CCM. In Section 3, we describe our view of the CCM connector concept, and show how connectors integrate with the original CCM development process. We also give a short illustration of the introduced concepts. Eventually, section 4 gives a short overview of related work, before concluding.

2.   AN OVERVIEW OF THE CCM

The CCM specification[2] covers the whole software development process, from specification to components packaging. It is completed by the OMG[†] Deployment & Configuration specification[5], which provides guidelines for applications configuration and deployment. Describing all CCM facilities

---

[*] The IST COMPARE project (http://www.ist-compare.org) and the ITEA MERCED project (http://www.itea-merced.org)
[†] Object Management Group, http://www.omg.org

would be tedious and not relevant in the context of this paper. Thus, in the following, we sketch only CCM main features: the component model, the execution architecture, and the development process.

In the CCM, components are basically software entities providing services to any of their counterparts. Conversely, they specify the services they need to execute properly. In CCM terminology, a component owns facets (i.e. provided interfaces) and receptacles (required interfaces). On top of that, components may own event sources and sinks, which are the event based equivalents of receptacles and facets. Attributes may also be defined for each component, mostly to enable components configuration at instantiation. Components are defined and declared thanks to a specific language, the Interface Definition Language (IDL). Writing components specifications in IDL is the first step in a CCM application development process. As an example, we provide the declaration of a component "C", providing a port "a_intf" of "IMyIntf" type.

```
component C {
        provides IMyIntf a_intf; // A facet
        consumes E a_E; // An event sink
};
```

The CCM proposes an execution model based on the *component-container* pattern, with the objective to separate business (components) and non-functional (containers) concerns. Containers are the glue between components and the underlying execution / communication platform. They mediate all interactions between components, be they remote or co-located. The container is in particular responsible for providing to the component a *context object*, which can then be used by the component to perform various actions: for instance retrieving a reference to a facet of another component, or publishing an event.

Two main development processes may be differentiated: developing a (single) CCM component and building an application using existing CCM components. The first consists in developing a component corresponding to an interface specification. Fig. 1 shows the successive phases of such a process. Once the interface of the component is written using the IDL, a component skeleton (written in the targeted implementation language) may be obtained using an IDL compiler. This skeleton has then to be completed by the functional (or business) code, and the whole is compiled, in order to obtain a component implementation. This latter step is repeated as many times as necessary: for instance, in order to obtain one Linux, and one Windows implementation. At last, the implementations of the component are packaged together with the component descriptors (XML files describing the contents of the packages) and IDL files.

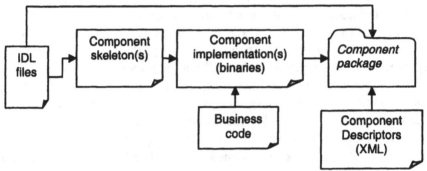

Figure 1. Developing a CCM component

Supposing that all components needed for a given application are identified and the corresponding packages are available, the CCM provides further guidance[5] to properly build, configure, and run the application. First, the application architecture (components instances, connections) have to be defined in dedicated (XML) assembly files. These files are used as an input to a deployment tool, which is then in charge of components instantiation and configuration, also performs the specified connections, and eventually launches the application.

3.   CCM CONNECTORS OVERVIEW

In this section, we highlight the interest we have found in defining connectors for CCM and outline the modifications made to CCM in order to integrate this new artifact. The impact of connectors on the CCM development process is also evaluated. In the end, we provide a short illustration of connectors usage.

3.1   Why a CCM connector?

In its native field (Architecture Description Languages[9]), the *connector*[7] is a clearly distinguished entity (from components), dedicated to interaction management. Depending on the work considered, the capabilities of "connectors" may vary a lot. For instance in Unicon[8], the connector is given numerous functional features: a type, an interaction protocol, and other functional features like real-time ones. The elements that may be considered as connectors are also very different from one work to another: sometimes, all kinds of interaction supports are considered (from pipes to scheduler) and even HW artefacts may be parts of the application architecture design[6].

In the scope of the CORBA component model, introducing connectors would have two major impacts: enriching CCM interactions models (CCM originally supports only synchronous method invocation and a specific form of event delivery), and making CCM components interactions *independent from CORBA*. This latter issue is particularly important for embedded systems, since the HW platforms can scarcely afford embedding a CORBA implementation. An additional motivation is that the way interactions are dealt with is part of the application domain's expertise. Thus, building reusable interaction media enables to gather and reuse (i.e. capitalize) software practitioners' knowledge on interaction management. At last, it is obvious that connectors could facilitate component assembly (for instance, two components having provided/required interfaces of different types, but potentially compatible could be linked by means of an "adaptation" connector).

3.2 CCM connectors main features

A CCM connector is an artifact that mediates some interactions between two or more components, while performing intermediary processing. Since components are potentially distributed, it is obvious that connectors are not monolithic, but fragmented. A connector is actually an aggregation of what we call *connector fragments*, each of these fragments being linked to and co-localized with a participant in the interaction. For instance, Fig. 2 shows the deployment view of a connector split into two fragments that are co-located with the components using them. Each fragment has to be bound to the component that will use it. Please note that the connection between a component and a connector fragment is always a *local method invocation*. The remote connection, if necessary, occurs only between the two connector fragments. A major point is that the way the communication between the connector fragments is performed does not forcedly rely on CORBA, i.e. *the communication layer used is specific to the connector under consideration.*

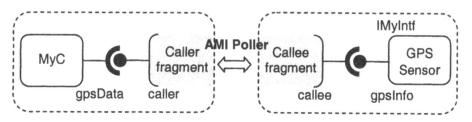

Figure 2. Distributed connector fragments

Connector fragments are connected to the components participating to the interaction. This means that these fragments have to *exhibit CCM ports* that match those of the components. Hence, the abstract model of connector fragments has to be the same as the one of components, basically a combination of (provided and required) ports. However, due to the introduction of connectors, ports will only define the interface in terms of operations and are not responsible for the interaction mechanism that is chosen. Therefore, event-based ports are no longer desirable, for they require using a CORBA middleware event service. Thus, in a CCM design using connectors, components and connector fragments *will only exhibit receptacles and facets*. At last, it is quite obvious that connector fragments will - like components - require configuration means. Hence, we have decided that connector fragments will own attributes as well.

While working on connectors definition, it has rapidly occurred to us that from a methodological point of view, two classes of connectors had to be distinguished. We call those two categories *adaptive* and *fixed* connectors. Adaptive connectors have the particularity that their definition is not fixed, but templated. They ensure a well-defined interaction mechanism (e.g. asynchronous method call), but the interfaces they exhibit are strictly dependent on those of the components they are connected to. Adaptive connectors are interesting in situations where a given interaction mechanism is likely to be used for a variety of interface definitions. For instance, a connector for asynchronous invocations would not be useful, if its port would provide always the same interface: it has to be possible to instantiate the connector and its ports with a certain interface. The advantage of adaptive connectors is that they impose no constraints on components. Fixed connectors have, on the contrary, a fixed set of provided and required interfaces. Therefore, they constrain the definition of the components. Actually, these connectors are very similar to CCM components, excepting their fragmented (and distributed) structures. From a methodological point of view, these two types of connectors are fundamentally different. Adaptive connectors will be preferably used to connect already existing components. On the contrary, using fixed connectors requires an early awareness from the component designer, who will have to define the components in accordance with the connectors he plans to use. Moreover, depending on the class of connectors used, the development processes (and the corresponding support tools) will be different, as shown in the next section.

3.3   A CCM design with connectors

For fixed connectors, the process is the same as for components. Connectors are first described in IDL. For this purpose, we have extended the IDL with the *connector* keyword, and customized accordingly our IDL compiler. Then, based on this specification, several implementations are produced. For instance, one implementation running on top of CORBA, and another that uses Java RMI. These implementations and the IDL are eventually packaged together with descriptor files (an extension has been made on the OMG D&C specification[5] that enables connectors-related features descriptions).

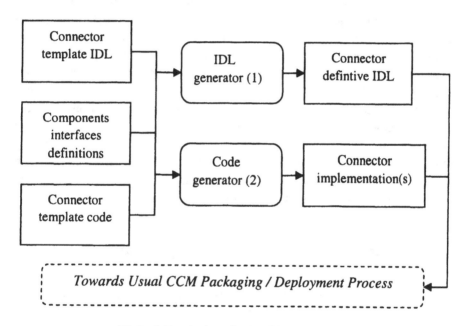

Figure 3. Developing adaptive CCM connectors

The development of adaptive connectors involves more steps. Since these connectors must have the capability to adapt themselves to components interfaces, what shall be provided initially are connector's "raw material", and the associated generation tool. Raw materials are a (template) connector IDL description and one or more (template) connector implementation(s). The generators enable definitive IDL and connector code generation. The corresponding generation process is schematized in Fig. 3. The template declarations are performed by means of IDL extensions we propose. For instance, here follows the template declaration of a connector RemoteMethodCall, with an ISyncInterface template parameter.

```
connector RemoteMethodCall<ISyncInterface> {
        provides ISyncInterface to_caller;
        uses ISyncInterface to_callee;
};
```

In the section dealing with CCM introduction, we indicated that the CCM specification also describes the application building and deployment process. Connectors can be integrated well in this process, since they have basically the same shape as components. It was only necessary to define an extension of the OMG D&C specification[5] to add a connector meta-element in the deployment artifacts. Connectors are packaged strictly the same way as components: an archive (e.g. .zip) is built, which contains connector IDL description, connector implementation(s), and the corresponding descriptor files. However, in the case of adaptive connectors, all connector items have to be obtained *prior to packaging*. With connectors, the deployment process is as follows: (1) Instantiate components and connector fragments on their respective nodes; (2) perform connections between (co-localized) components and connectors fragments; (3) perform connections between remote connector fragments (note that this step depends on the communication mechanisms used by the considered connector implementation); and (4) launch the application. Note that from components point of view, nothing has changed: they obtain a reference for each of their facets without "being aware" that this reference points to a connector fragment.

3.4   Using connectors with CCM: an illustration

In order to test and assess our approach, we are currently carrying out an experimental design. Our application will simulate voice transmission through a simplified UMTS[10] protocol stack. In this scope, we have defined a set of connectors that have significantly eased our design. For instance, we have designed a connector which ensures a "slotted aloha" access protocol. This protocol, which is frequently used in the telecommunication domain, is the following:

- The client initiate the slotted aloha protocol
- A randomly temporized call is performed on the server until the client receives a positive or negative acknowledgement, or the maximum number of calls is reached

Using a "slotted aloha" connector, the process is as follows: (1) the connector is properly configured (e.g. maximum number of calls); (2) the client component initiates the protocol by calling a method of the connector – the call is asynchronous, so the client may then keep on its own processing; (3) the connector performs the slotted aloha protocol by randomly calling server component, and waits for an acknowledgement. The process is stopped when an acknowledgement is received, or the maximum number of calls is reached; (4) The connector continuously exhibits the acknowledgement status, which can be polled any time by the client component. Using a connector in this case offers several advantages. First, a better separation of concerns, since all the protocol is managed by the connector instead of being ensured by the client component. Then, the connector can be easily reused. For instance, in the UMTS protocol stack, we will use it at two different places, only by modifying connector configuration.

4. RELATED WORK

Besides the foundations in the ADL domain[7], the Qedo (QoS Enabled Distributed Objects) project[12] develops a CCM implementation that adds interaction via streaming, but it does not provide a general framework to add new interaction mechanism. The QuO (Quality Objects) project at BBN[13] adds Quality of service and connectors (as well a connector setup language, CSL) to CORBA. The integration of QuO into the CCM implementation CIAO has been investigated[14] and has led to some aspects also considered by us. However, their intent was more on the resource management and allocation aspects than on fine-grain interaction support. Eventually, we shall precise that even if we closely follow ongoing works on CORBA at the OMG (e.g. minimum CORBA[3] or real-time CORBA[4]), we have no direct relation with these latter, for our focus is strictly on the CCM.

5. CONCLUSIONS AND PERSPECTIVES

We have described in this paper our strategy to improve interaction support in the CORBA Component Model. By analogy with Architecture Description Languages, we have defined a new entity, called "connector", which is dedicated to interaction management. Using CCM connectors enables a better separation between business logic and non-functional logic. Connectors also capitalize interaction management expertise, while reducing design efforts. And, most important in the scope of embedded systems, connectors make CCM-based applications independent from CORBA. We have performed all necessary modifications to the CCM, and are currently assessing our approach on a use-case. The first feedbacks from the design are positive, and we plan to have further usage of connectors. But CCM enhancement with regards to real-time and embedded systems design (which is the global target of the projects we are involved in) remains an ongoing work. In particular, further real-time support has to be provided by the execution framework (container) to the applicative components. In the next parts of the projects, we plan for instance to evaluate the inclusion of scheduling facilities at framework level.

REFERENCES

1. Lightweight CORBA Component Model – OMG draft adopted specification, Object Management Group, 2003.

2. CORBA Components, version 3.0, Object Management Group, 2002.

3. Minimum CORBA specification, version 1.0, formal/02-08-01, Object Management Group, 2002.

4. Real-time CORBA specification, version 1.2, formal/05-01-04, Object Management Group, 2005.

5. Specification for deployment and configuration of component based applications - draft adopted specification, OMG, 2003.

6. Towards a Taxonomy of Software Connectors, N. R. Mehta, N. Medvidovic and S. Phadke, ICSE 2000.

7. Software Connectors and their role in component development, D. Bálek & F. Plášil, DAIS'01.

8. Abstractions for Software Architecture and Tools to support them, M. Shaw, Robert Deline et al., Software Engineering, vol. 21, number 4, 1995.

9. A Classification and Comparison Framework for Software Architecture Description Languages, N. Medvidovic, R. N. Taylor, IEEE transactions on software engineering, vol. 26, n. 1, 2000.

10. General UMTS Architecture v5.0.1, 3rd Generation Partnership Project, Technical Specification Group Services and System Aspects, 2004.

11. Enterprise JavaBeans Specification version 2.1, Sun Microsystems, 2003.

12. Qedo, QoS Enabled Distributed Objects. http://www.qedo.org

13. Using QDL to Specify QoS Aware Distributed (QuO) Application Configuration, P. Pal et al., Proceedings of ISORC 2000, The 3rd IEEE International Symposium on Object-Oriented Real-time distributed Computing, March 15 - 17, 2000, Newport Beach, CA, http://quo.bbn.com/

14. A Qos-aware CORBA component model for distributed real-time and embedded system development. Nanbor Wang and Chris Gill. OMG Real-time and embedded workshop 2003, Arlington VA. see http://www.omg.org/ workshops/proceedings/

OBJECT ORIENTATION PROBLEMS WHEN APPLIED TO THE EMBEDDED SYSTEMS DOMAIN

Júlio C. B. Mattos[1], Emilena Specht[1], Bruno Neves[1], Luigi Carro[1,2]

[1] *Federal University of Rio Grande do Sul, Informatics Institute, Av. Bento Gonçalves, 9500 - Campus do Vale - Porto Alegre, Brasil*
[2] *Federal University of Rio Grande do Sul, Electrical Engineering Dept.*
Av. Oswaldo Aranha 103 - Porto Alegre, Brasil

Abstract: Software is more and more becoming the major cost factor for embedded devices. Nowadays, with the growing complexity of embedded systems, it is necessary to use techniques and methodologies that in the same time increase the software productivity and can manipulate the embedded systems constraints like memory footprint, real-time behavior, power dissipation and so on. Object-oriented modeling and design is a widely-know methodology in software engineering. This paradigm may satisfy the software portability and maintainability requirements, but it presents an overhead in terms of memory, performance and code size. This paper presents some experimental results that shown that, for some OO applications, more than 50% of the execution time is taken just for the memory management. This is a huge overhead that cannot be paid by many embedded systems. This way, this paper shows experimental results and indicates a solution of this problem in order to reduce execution time, while maintaining memory costs as low as possible.

Keywords: Embedded Systems, Embedded Software, Object Oriented

1. INTRODUCTION

The fast technological development in the last decades exposed a new reality: the widespread use of embedded systems. Nowadays, one can find these systems everywhere, in consumer electronics, entertainment, communication systems and so on. In embedded applications, requirements like performance, reduced power consumption and program size, among others, must be considered. Many of these products today contain software and probably in the future even more products will contain software. In many cases software is preferred to a hardware solution because it is more flexible, easier to update and can be reused. Software is more and more becoming the major cost factor for embedded devices [1,2].

Over the years, embedded software coding is traditionally developed in assembly language, since there are stringent memory and performance limitations. [3]. The best software technologies use large amounts of memory, layers of abstraction, elaborate algorithms, and other approaches that are not directly applicable. However, the hardware capabilities have improved, and the market demands more elaborate products, increasing software complexity. But, the existing software methodologies are not adequate for embedded software development. This development is very different from the one used in the desktop environment. Embedded software development should address constraints like memory footprint, real-time behavior, power dissipation and so on. Thus, it is necessary to adapt the available techniques and methodologies, or to create novel approaches that can manipulate the embedded systems constraints.

Object-oriented modeling and design is a widely-know methodology in software engineering. Object oriented analysis and design models include various modeling abstractions and concepts such as objects, polymorphism, and inheritance to model system structure and behavior. Using higher modeling abstractions that are closer to the problem space make the design process and implementation easier, and besides, these abstractions provide a very short development time and a lot of code reuse. Nevertheless, the object-oriented design paradigm presents an overhead in terms of memory, performance and code size [4].

Using object-oriented design the developers need an object-oriented language to do the implementation. Over the past few years the developers have embraced Java, because this technology can provide high portability and code reuse for their applications [5,6]. In addition, Java has features such as efficient code size and small memory footprint, that stand out against other programming languages, which makes Java an attractive choice as the specification and implementation language of embedded systems. However, developers should be free to use any object oriented coding style and the whole package of advantages that this language usually provide. In any case, one must also deal with the limited resources of an embedded.

The Java language deallocates objects by using garbage collection [7]. Garbage collectors have advantages freeing programmers from the need to deallocate the objects when these objects lost their reference, and helping to avoid memory leaks. However, garbage collectors produce an overhead in program execution and a non-deterministic execution.

It is widely known that design decisions taken at higher abstraction levels can lead to substantially superior improvements. Software engineers involved with software configuration of embedded platforms, however, do not have enough experience to measure the impact of their algorithmic decisions on issues such as performance and power.

In this way, this work proposes a pragmatic approach, transforming, as many dynamic objects to static ones, in the goal to reduce execution time, while maintaining memory costs as low as possible. This change should deal with the objects after the programmer has coded the application, and before the execution – when the memory management and garbage collector act. This approach is also compliant with classical OO techniques and embedded systems requirements.

This paper is organized as follows. Section 2 discusses related work in the field of OO and procedural programming comparison and techniques to improve the memory management system. Section 3 describes some Java Object-Oriented applications analysis to make the problem characterization. Section 4 presents our proposed approach based on a case study. Finally, section 6 draws conclusions and introduces future work.

2. RELATED WORK

There are several works that present some optimizations and techniques to produce better results in memory management. These works present optimizations to reduce the memory and performance overhead, to be able real-time applications and so on. In [8] a hardware mechanism (co-processor) to support the runtime memory management providing real-time capability for embedded Java devices is presented. This approach guarantee predictable memory allocation time. Chen [9] presents management strategies to reduce heap footprint of embedded Java applications that execute under severe memory constraints and a new garbage collector. Another work [10] of the same author focuses on tuning the GC to reduce energy consumption in multibanked memory architecture.

In [4], the object oriented programming style is evaluated in terms of both performance and power for embedded applications. A set of benchmark kernels, written in C and C++, is compiled and executed on an embedded processor simulator. The paper has been shown that oriented objected programming can significantly increase both execution time and power consumption.

Shaham [11] presents a heap-profiling tool for exploring the potential for space savings in Java programs. The output of the tool is used to direct rewriting of application source code in a way that allows more timely garbage collection of objects, thus saving space. The rewriting can also avoid allocating some objects that are never used making space savings and in some cases also to improvements in program runtime. This approach is based on three code rewriting techniques: assigning the null value to a reference that is no longer in use, remove code that has no effect on the result of the program and delay the allocation of an object until its first use.

Our proposed approach starts from a more radical point of view. Instead of trying just to improve the code written by the programmer, we tries to transform, as many dynamic objects to static ones, in the goal to reduce execution time, while maintaining memory costs as low as possible. Thus, it provides a large design space exploration for a given application.

3.   PROBLEM CHARACTERIZATION

In this work, we have analyzed some Java Object-Oriented applications that may run on embedded systems. It is well known that the object-oriented programming paradigm significantly increases the dynamic memory used, producing considerably overhead in terms of performance, memory and power. The goal of this section is to characterize the exact amount of overhead one has to pay to effectively use the OO paradigm.

In this work we analyzed some Java applications that can be found in embedded systems. The applications we used as benchmarks are:

- MP3Player - is an MP3 decoder implementation. This algorithm reads an MP3 file and translates it in an audio signal. This code is a version based on a description available on [12].
- SymbolTest – is a simple application that displays Unicode char ranges and different fonts types [13].
- Notepad - is a text editor with simple resources [14].
- Address Book - is an application used as electronic address book that stores some data (like name, address, telephone number, etc.) [15].
- Pacman – is the well-known game with a labyrinth and rewards [16].

It is important to mention that except for the MP3 application, none of the above applications has been coded by the authors. A completely blind analysis has been performed, in order to avoid influence of a particular code style.

To generate the application results representing the dynamic behavior of the application, an instrumentation tool was developed. It is based on BIT

(Bytecodes Instrumentation Tool) [17], which is a collection of Java classes that allow the construction of customized tools to instrument Java byte-codes. This instrumentation tool allows the dynamic analysis of Java Class files, generating a list of objects information (objects allocated, object time life, etc.), memory use and performance results.

Table 1 shows some object information like the total allocated objects for some instance execution, and the number of allocation instructions. This number of allocation instructions shows the instructions that perform the memory allocation task. Each one of these instructions can create several objects (objects with the same type) because it can be located in a method that is called several times, or can be located in a loop, for example. The table 1 shows that during MP3 execution 46,068 objects were created by only 101 allocation instructions, and hence some allocation instructions create more than one object. During the execution the Garbage Collector collects from the memory the objects that have lost their reference. The table also presents the results from the other applications.

Table 1. Object Results

Application	Total allocated objects	Number of allocation instructions
MP3	46,068	101
SymbolTest	27	16
Notepad	184	66
AddressBook	28	14
Pacman	2,547	30

Table 2 shows some memory results. Two results are shown: total memory allocated during the application execution and the maximum memory used during the application. Using object-oriented programming the total memory allocated should be larger, because there is an intensive memory use. However, the memory necessary to run the application should be enough to store just the objects used in the moment (it depends on GC implementation, considering a GC implementation that all objects that lose their reference are colleted immediately). It is clear from table 2 that there is a huge waste on memory resources, since only a fraction of the allocated memory is effectively used in a certain point of the algorithm.

The table 3 presents the results in terms of performance and the overhead caused by garbage collector making the allocation and deallocation of the objects. The performance results are shown as the number of executed instruction. The overhead caused by GC was calculated based on a GC implementation in software targeting the FemtoJava processor and Sashimi Tool [18]. This implementation is based on the Reference Counting algorithm that has a low memory overhead. At each object manipulation the garbage collector needs to make some changes in the respective object counter, and as soon as a counter reaches zero, the corresponding memory block becomes available to a new object. The cost of allocation and deallocates is about 696 instructions on average.

Table 2. Memory results

Application	Total memory allocated (bytes)	Maximum Memory utilization (bytes)
MP3	10,080,512	23,192
SymbolTest	1,509	625
Notepad	9,199	4,580
AddressBook	867	185
Pacman	216,080	456

The plot in figure 1 shows some statistics about the overhead that might be expected by dynamic allocation and deallocation. The figure shows the overhead caused in different applications considering a cost of 1 to 1000 instructions per allocation/deallocation.

As it can be seen from figure 1, for some applications the memory allocation needed to support the OO paradigm can represent more than 50% of the execution time is taken just for the memory management, thus the CPU spends more time and energy just managing memory, instead of actually executing the target application. This is a huge overhead that cannot be paid by many embedded systems.

It is interesting to notice what happens when the cost of allocation/deallocation is increased. In some application more than 80 % of the execution time is used by memory management system. In the case of the FemtoJava processor, its Garbage collector takes 696 instructions, and the cost of each application can be easily seen to surpass 35% for most applications.

Table 3. Performance results

Application	Performance (instructions)	GC Overhead (%)
MP3	85,767,756	37.40
SymbolTest	67,342	27.91
Notepad	136,621	93.86
AddressBook	24,435	79.84
Pacman	2,091,684	84.85

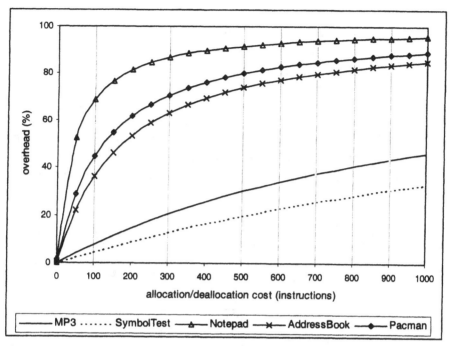

Figure 1. Object-Oriented Overhead

4. THE PROPOSED APPROACH

When a programmer uses an object-oriented design paradigm, the application objects can be statically or dynamically allocated. When the programmer uses static allocation the memory footprint is known in compilation time. Hence, in this approach, normally, the memory size is big, but there is a lower execution overhead while dealing with the dynamic allocation (produced by the memory manager). On the other hand, when the programmer uses a dynamic allocation, there is an overhead in terms of performance, but the memory size decreases because the garbage collector removes the unreachable objects.

The experimental results in section 3 have shown that, for some OO applications the largest part of the execution time is taken just for the memory management. However, if the designer allocates memory in a static fashion, the price to be paid is a memory much larger than actually needed, with obvious problems in cost, area and power dissipation.

In section 3, table 1 shows that during MP3 execution 46,068 objects were created by only 101 allocation instructions, and hence some allocation instructions create more than one object. The main idea of the proposed approach is transforming, as many dynamic objects to static ones.

According the table 3, there are 101 possible objects transformation in MP3 application. Table 4 presents 7 different allocation instructions in terms of the number of objects that each instruction allocates and the size of the object. The comparison between the number of total allocated objects by the application with the number of allocated objects by the first instruction allocation (first row) shows that just one allocation instruction is responsible by 62.51 % of allocations. Transforming this allocation instruction in a static way, the results in terms of GC overhead can be extremely improved. The table 4 also presents that other allocation instructions can improve the results too. But when a static transformation occurs, this transformation implies in a memory increase.

Table 4. MP3 Allocation instruction

Allocation instruction	Number of allocated objects	Object Size (bytes)
#1	28,800	64
#2	1,728	144
#3	1,728	36
#6	1,600	72
#8	1,536	144
#11	900	2,048
#36	25	4,608

Table 5 shows the results after the static transformations with the same allocation instructions of the table 4. These results show the performance in terms of instruction, the percentage reduction in relationship on original code (total OO code) and the memory increase necessary to make the static transformation. It is interesting to notice that the static transformation in only one allocation instruction can improve the performance results in 23.47 % paying only 0.28 % of memory increase.

Table 5. MP3 results after static transformation

Allocation instruction	Performance (instructions)	Reduction (%)	Memory Increase (%)
#1	65,636,556	23.47	0.28
#2	84,559,884	1.41	0.62
#3	84,559,890	1.41	0.16
#6	84,649,356	1.30	0.31
#8	84,694,092	1.25	0.62
#11	53,700,828	0,73	8,83
#36	85,750,231	0.02	19.87
#1+#2	53,612,844	24.88	0.90
#1+#2+#11	53,609,244	25.61	9.73

The other allocation instructions present different results in terms of performance gain and memory increase. These values can seem insignificantly, but these transformations can be grouped taking more advantages. The two last rows show the results of the combination of the allocation instruction 1 and 2, and the combination of the 1, 2 and 11. These combinations show, as example, that grouping different static transformations can be obtained a great number of possibilities with different characterization in terms of performance and memory overhead. Thus, the process of search the best combination according the systems requirements is a hard task.

The table 6 also presents that the total memory allocated can be reduced taking more advantages in terms power saving. Table 2 shows that the MP3 application uses 10,080,512 bytes and when the proposed approach is applied the reduction can be excellent.

Table 6. MP3 total memory allocated results

Allocation instruction	Total memory allocated (bytes)	Reduction (%)
#1	8,237,320	18.28
#2	9,831,880	2.47
#3	10,018,504	0.62
#6	9,965,512	1.14
#8	9,859,524	2.19
#11	8,237,320	18.28
#36	9,965,316	1.14
#1+#2	7,988,688	20.75
#1+#2+#11	6,145,496	39.04

5.   CONCLUSIONS AND FUTURE WORK

This paper shows that in the same time oriented-object programming increases the software productivity satisfying the software reusability and maintainability requirements, it presents a critical overhead in terms of performance and memory.

The paper proposes a technique to management this problem, transforming as many as possible dynamic objects to static ones, as reducing execution time, while maintaining memory costs as low as possible. Thus, it provides a large design space exploration for a given application.

As a future work, we plan to implement a tool making possible the transformation of dynamic objects to static ones in automatic way. Furthermore, this tool can be able to allow an automatic selection of the best object organization (combinations of static and dynamically objects) for given application based on systems requirements. We also plan to evaluate the amount of power savings obtained.

REFERENCES

1. Graaf, B., Lormans, M., Toetenel, H. Embedded Software Engineering: The State of the Practice. IEEE Software, (Nov./Dec. 2003), 61-69.
2. Embedded Systems Roadmap 2002. http://www.stw.nl/progress/Esroadmap/ /ESRversion1.pdf.
3. Lee, E. What's Ahead for Embedded Software ?. IEEE Computer, New York, Sept. 2000, 18-26.
4. Chatzigeorgiou, A.; Stephanides, G. Evaluating Performance and Power of Object-Oriented Vs. Procedural Programming in Embedded Processors. In Proceedings of 7th Ada-Europe International Conference on Reliable Sofware Technologies. LNCS 2361. Springer-Verlag Berling Heidelberg, 2002.65-75.
5. Mulchandani, D. Java for Embedded Systems. Internet Computing, 31(10), May 1998, 30–39.
6. Lawton, G. Moving Java into Mobile Phones, IEEE Computer, vol. 35, n. 6, 2002, 17-20.
7. Richard. Jones; Rafael D. Lins. Garbage Collection: algorithms for automatic dynamic memory management. Chichester: John Wiley, 1996.
8. Lin, C.; Chen, T. Dynamic memory management for real-time embedded Java chips. In Proceedings of Seventh International Conference on Real-Time Computing Systems and Applications, 2000.
9. Chen, G. et al. Heap compression for memory-constrained Java environments. In Proceedings of the 18th annual ACM SIGPLAN conference on Object-oriented programming, systems, languages, and applications, Anaheim, California (2003), 282-301.
10. Chen, G. et al.Tuning Garbage Collection for Reducing Memory System Energy in an Embedded Java Environment. ACM Transactions on Embedded Computing Systems, vol. 1, n. 1, November 2002, 27–55.
11. Shaham, R.; Kolodner, E.; Sagiv, M. Heap profiling for space-efficient Java. In Proceedings SIGPLAN Conf. on Prog. Lang. Design and Impl., ACM Press, 2001. 104-113.
12. Javalayer. Java MP3 Player. Available at http://www.javazoom.net/javalayer/ /sources.html(2004).
13. Sun Microsystems. SymbolTest. Available at http://java.sun.com/j2se/1.3/docs/ /guide/awt/demos/ symboltest/actual/index.html
14. Sun Microsystems. Notepad. Available at http://java.sun.com/j2se/1.3/docs/ /relnotes/demos.html
15. Brenneman, Todd R. Java Address Book (ver. 1.1.1). Available at www.geocities.com/SiliconValley/2272.
16. Pacman Silver Edition. Available at http://www.netconplus.com/antstuff/pacman.php
17. Lee, H.B.; Zorn, B.G. BIT: A Tool for Instrumenting Java Bytecodes, USITS'97 - USENIX Symposium on Internet Technologies and Systems, Dec. 1997.
18. Ito, S. A.; Carro, L.; Jacobi, R. Making Java Work for Microcontroller Applications, IEEE Design & Test, vol. 18, no. 5, Sep-Oct, pp. 100-110.

TOC-BISR: A SELF-REPAIR SCHEME FOR MEMORIES IN EMBEDDED SYSTEMS

Gustavo Neuberger, Fernanda Lima Kastensmidt, and Ricardo Reis
Universidade Federal do Rio Grande do Sul (UFRGS) - Instituto de Informática
CP15064, CEP91501-970, Porto Alegre, Brazil email: {neuberger,fglima,reis}@inf.ufrgs.br

Abstract: Memories are important components in embedded systems, since complex systems require more and more amount of data storage. Upcoming memories are more and more required to guarantee reliability for secure applications in the presence of massive soft and hard errors. This work proposes a fault tolerant customizable technique that combines EDAC, which can correct soft errors, and a built-in self-repair approach based on online testing and a Content Addressable Memory (CAM), which can tolerate hard errors. The goals of this approach are ensuring the correct operation of the system, extending the lifetime of the component, and improving the yield. This digital system was described in VHDL and synthesized in FPGA. The approach is customizable in terms of EDAC code, test algorithm and CAM size. The main advantage of the customization is to choose the best tradeoff between the number and type of tolerated and corrected errors compared to the area overhead and performance penalties for a target application.

Keywords: Self-Repair, Embedded Memories, Fault-Tolerance, EDAC Code

1. INTRODUCTION

The technological evolution to very deep submicron processes with drastic device shrinking, power supply reduction, and increasing operating speeds has significantly increased the sensitivity of integrated circuits to multiple faults[1]. Faults can be classified by their effects: transient or permanent. In this paper, transient faults will be identified as soft errors and permanent faults as hard errors. Soft errors occur due to radiation effects and noise. Technological scaling increases device vulnerability to radiation, as charged particles that were once negligible are now much more likely to produce upsets at ground level[2]. Hard errors occur due to manufacturing defects and, more recently, radiation effects, such as total ionization dose or heavy ion strike, which can provoke faults with permanent effects[3, 4, 5].

One of the main advantages of developing fault tolerant techniques for soft and hard errors is to keep the memories operating in hostile environments without being replaced, even in the presence of multiple faults. Techniques usually are able to cope with one or other type of error and in many cases they are only able to detect them. The challenge is to develop a methodology that can be easily applied to commercial memories to detect and correct soft and hard errors, or at least cope with them.

Many fault tolerance techniques have been proposed to detect and correct soft errors, such as, error detection and correction codes (EDAC). Hamming code[6] and Reed-Solomon code[7] are good examples of high-level design techniques able to correct single and multiple soft errors. However they have some limitations. The first drawback of EDAC codes is their inefficiency in protecting rarely executed code addresses or data, for instance, error handling routines. In this case, latent errors remain undetected during a long period of time and consequently upsets can accumulate. This can overcome the protection of many fault-tolerant techniques that are based on single error detection and correction. An upset in this case must be detected and corrected before a second one occurs. Even the fault-tolerant architectures based on multiple upset corrections must periodically remove the latent errors. It must avoid a state where there are so many upsets that can no longer be corrected. The second deficiency of EDAC codes is that, although they are used to detect and tolerate hard errors in commercial memories, they can not eliminate the cause of the hard error, and in presence of both types of errors, EDAC codes will fail in the case of a soft error in the same address as a hard error.

Hard errors can be detected by a test that alters the memory contents continually. For detecting defects during the memory lifetime, transparent online testing techniques[8, 9] have been used. However, these techniques are not able to tolerate the detected defects. This drawback is usually ignored because once the memory is tested, all defects due to fabrication process are detected, and only soft errors will affect the memory. However, in very deep submicron technologies, hard errors can often appear during the lifetime due to radiation, which makes it necessary to develop a fault-tolerant technique able to tolerate hard errors. In addition, memories able to tolerate a set of defects can help to reduce yield losses, in such way that memories with pre-mapped defects can be sold in the market, as the use of fault tolerance techniques will be able to cope with these hard errors. This can reduce the cost of manufacturability.

Current methods found in literature are not able to cope with soft and hard errors at the same time during the normal memory operation, which is crucial today for high-reliability memories. This work proposes a fault-tolerant customizable technique that combines EDAC, which can correct soft errors, and a built-in self-repair approach based on online testing and a Content Addressable Memory (CAM), which can tolerate hard errors. The objectives of this methodology are to guarantee the correct operation of the device in the presence of soft and hard errors, extending the lifetime of the component by tolerating hard errors due to radiation, as well as improving the yield, by tolerating manufacturing defects.

This digital system was described in VHDL and prototyped in a Xilinx FPGA. The approach is customizable in terms of EDAC code, test algorithm and CAM size. The main advantage of having a customizable fault-tolerant methodology is to choose the best tradeoff between the number and type of tolerated and corrected errors compared to the area overhead and performance penalties for a target application.

This paper is organized as follows: section 2 shows the related work on tolerant techniques against soft and hard errors. Section 3 describes the developed built-in self-repair system, the detailed implementation of the method in an embedded system programmable platform and the advantages of the customization of this platform in terms of flexibility. The area and performance results are evaluated in section 4. Conclusions and future work are discussed in section 5.

2. MOTIVATION

With the development of the IC technology, complex systems can be built in a single chip (System-on Chip, SoC). Modern FPGAs include microprocessors, memories and several other specialized components, and a full system can be designed in a single FPGA. Even a very large system that uses external microprocessors and memories can use an FPGA to implement a set of more complex specialized functions. The main benefit of an FPGA is the re-programmability, useful in several applications. For example, in space applications, reprogramming the FPGA after the launch, to correct errors, improve performance or increase features, can reduce the mission cost. However, in general, the systems need big amounts of memory. In space applications, and also at ground level, the memories are the component most susceptible to faults.

Considering the case of a system composed by a microprocessor, a memory and several hardware cores running in parallel in an FPGA, the memory can have its reliability increased with only the inclusion of one more core in the FPGA, responsible to test and repair the memory. This solution can be very attractive, since it does not increase the cost, if the FPGA still has available enough logic blocks to implement the test and repair system, impacting only the performance and power. Figure 1 shows the scheme of this possible system.

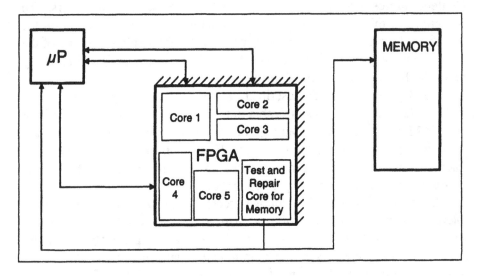

Figure 1. Scheme of a System Composed of Microprocessor, Memory and FPGA

3.   RELATED WORK

Recent works have been concerned about the effects of multiple faults in memories[10]. Multiple soft errors can occur in VDSM memories due to the incident angle of the charged particle, to the logic cell density or to the time between faults. If the time between faults is too short, faults can accumulate in the memory. Consequently, standard error correction codes such as Hamming code may not be enough in many applications.

Thaller[11] has proposed the Transparent Online Memory Test (TOMT) for soft and hard errors detection. It combines parity or Hamming code with March tests to perform active fault detection over the whole memory, warning the system. A March test consists of a sequence of March elements. A March element consists of a sequence of operations applied to every cell, in either one of two address orders: increasing ($\Uparrow$) or decreasing ($\Downarrow$).

The TOMT is completely transparent for the user. It does not affect the memory usage by the processor. The drawback of this scheme is that it only detects the faults, sending an error message to the processor when a problem occurs. The scheme is not able to correct on-the-fly the hard error and to continue the user's application. Figure 2 shows the schematic of the TOMT unit used to perform the active test in the memory. The system is placed between the processor and the memory and it is transparent to both.

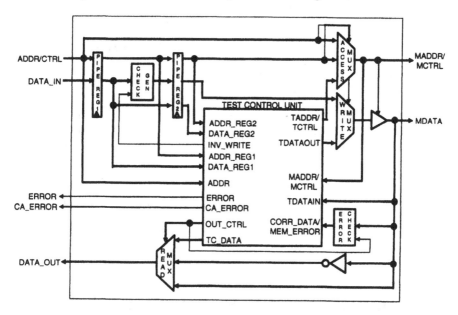

Figure 2. TOMT Unit Schematic[11]

A BISR system is proposed by Zappa[12], using a programmable BIST together with a Flash memory to store the defective words. The BIST can be programmed with different March tests, to detect different types of hard faults. However, as this system does not perform online BISR, it must stop the operation of the SRAM to make the test. Another deficiency is its incapacity to handle soft errors. Figure 3 shows the architecture of this system.

As seen previously, recent published related works are not able to detect and correct soft errors at the same time they are able to cope with hard errors. Next section presents an online built-in self-repair (BISR) customizable for memories able to detect and correct soft errors and to tolerate hard errors in VDSM memories, ensuring the correct operation of the application without interruption.

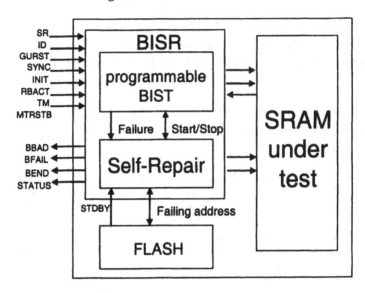

Figure 3. BISR Scheme using a Flash Memory

4.   DEVELOPING A CUSTOMIZABLE ONLINE BUILT-IN SELF-REPAIR SYSTEM

The proposed Transparent Online Customizable Built-in Self-Repair system, named TOC-BISR, is based on the TOMT unit[11], with a set of modifications in order to tolerate the soft and hard errors instead of only warning the processor in the case of occurrence of them. The new BISR method is composed of:

- Test control unit presented by Thaller[11], that controls the March test and the generation of addresses to send to the memory; which was re-implemented in a programmable platform for further customization,

- EDAC encoder and decoder blocks, to correct soft errors in the read data;

- Content-Addressable Memory (CAM), to store redundant addresses to tolerate hard errors;

- Extra logic (inverters and multiplexers) to route the data from/to the processor and the memory.

The test control unit uses the same algorithm as TOMT[11], being composed of a word-level algorithm and a bit-level algorithm, performing a March test in the whole memory. It is important to emphasize that the processor always has the priority to access the memory over the test algorithm. However, if the processor wants to read the same address that is currently under testing, it must read from the backup register instead of the memory. At this moment, the data stored in the memory can be wrong, because it can be in the middle of the March algorithm.

In order to cope with soft errors, an EDAC encoder and decoder must be placed in series with the data path, differently than in TOMT[11], where parity or Hamming is used in parallel only to detect the error. Any EDAC code can be used, but in the first implementation Hamming code was used to simplify the encoding and decoding circuits. In the future, it is planned to use other codes to increase the fault tolerance to multiple errors, like Reed-Solomon codes.

Concerning tolerance to hard errors, a possibility is to remap the faulty address into another address, or extra memory area. In this work, a CAM is used to store the data together with the faulty addresses. When the processor requires a certain address, both the main memory and the CAM are read in parallel. If the address is found in the CAM, the data stored in the CAM is sent to the processor; otherwise, the data stored in the memory is used. The figure 4 shows what is stored in the CAM, and CAM inputs and outputs.

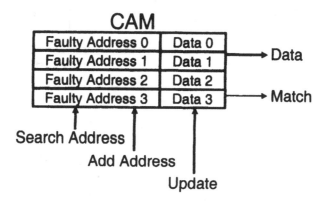

Figure 4. Content-Addressable Memory Scheme

The search address signal, figure 4, is used to check if an address is present in the CAM. If yes, then the match signal goes high, and the data signal contains the data associated to that address. This means that the current address requested by the processor correspond to a location with a hard error in the main memory, which has been previously detected by the test algorithm (in this case, March). The data stored in the memory is ignored, and the data stored in the CAM is used instead. The *add* address signal inserts a new faulty address in the CAM. The insertion occurs when the March test finds a hard error in the main memory. Finally, the update signal is used to write a new data in an address that is faulty. In this case, the data is updated in the current address stored in the CAM.

Figure 5 shows the final schematic of the TOC-BISR system. In addition to all blocks that were inserted in the original method presented in TOMT[11]: the CAM, Hamming encoder and decoder, and CAM mux; the error signal of the test control unit now must be sent to the CAM instead of being an error signal to the processor, as well as the faulty address. The final proposed method is capable of tolerating soft and hard upsets.

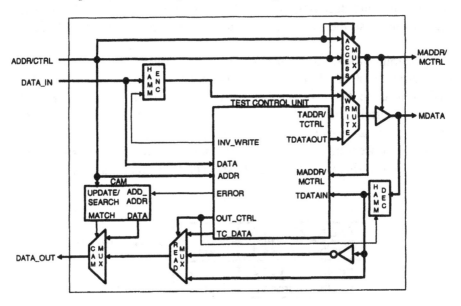

Figure 5. TOC-BISR System

The use of a configurable platform offers additional advantages for the customization of the TOC-BISR. The reconfigurability of FPGAs can be used to increase the features of the TOC-BISR unit, such as: changing the EDAC code to increase the tolerance to multiple soft errors, the March algorithm to increase the fault coverage of hard errors, and the size of the CAM to increase the tolerance to a maximum number of addresses containing hard errors. It would be possible to use the whole available set of logic of the FPGA to implement the TOC-BISR unit, with the largest possible CAM, a complex EDAC code and the most efficient March test. However, it is much more attractive to have a programmable platform to attend the needs of each case, or extra power could be dissipated and performance lost without reason. For example, the system could be initialized with a very small CAM, and only if the CAM becomes full, it is reprogrammed to have a larger size.

The TOC-BISR unit implemented in an FPGA can be integrated transparently in a system, being placed between the processor and the main memory. The figure 6 shows the TOC-BISR unit integrated in a system.

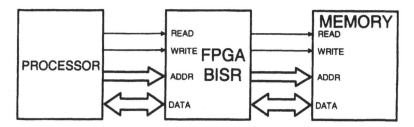

Figure 6. System Integration of the TOC-BISR

For evaluation purposes, the TOC-BISR customizable method was described in VHDL and implemented in a Xilinx FPGA (VirtexE family). An 8-bit address was used, with 16-bit data, and 16 available positions in the CAM. There is no pre-defined CAM component in the Virtex FPGA. There are solutions to implement a CAM using embedded RAM memories (BlockRAMs) available in most FPGA families from Xilinx[13].

All the TOC-BISR circuit must also be protected against soft and hard errors by definition as well. Normally in an ASIC, the sensitive parts to soft errors are mainly the memory elements: the registers inside the test control unit and the CAM. But all the logic can be sensitive to hard errors. Consequently, the most appropriate solution for protection is the Triple Modular Redundancy (TMR). In the case of the FPGA, TMR is also the most suitable method to protect against soft and hard errors. According to the circuit, there are also other methods that can be used for fault tolerance in the FPGA and they can be applied in the TOC-BISR[14].

5. EXPERIMENTAL RESULTS

Some comparisons were made with different implementations using the FPGA platform, after the design of the TOC-BISR unit and its description in VHDL. The comparisons are in terms of online testing and soft error tolerance approaches, aiming at evaluating the drawback of fault tolerance efficiency compared to area and performance overhead. The results shown in this section are based in the synthesis of the TOC-BISR VHDL code in the Xilinx FPGA VirtexE-XCV300EPQ240[15]. Although the TOC-BISR core was developed to protect any commercial memory, in the experimental result, the protected memory is embedded in the same FPGA that contains the TOC-BISR approach.

Table 1 shows the results of the clock period obtained in the usage of the memory by itself and with Hamming code. It also shows the area to implement the Hamming code. The area is given by number of Lookup Tables (LUTs). The results are for a memory with 8-bit address and 16-bit data. In addition to the area for the encoder and decoder, the error correction code uses some extra RAM area for the parity bits. A 5-bit parity for a 16-bit word data is used in the Hamming code version.

Table 1. Results for standard and error correction code memories

	No Protection	Hamming EDAC
Clock Period	7.5 ns	13.2 ns
#LUT4	N/A	51

Table 2 presents the results of the TOMT unit[11] with Hamming code implemented in parallel for error detection only; a modified TOMT unit with Hamming code implemented in series, for autonomous soft error correction, and the proposed TOC-BISR unit. The table 2 shows the results obtained for these units.

Table 2. Results for TOMT and BISR Units

	TOMT[11]	TOMT[11] + Hamming	TOC-BISR
Clock Period	13.3 ns	17.63 ns	17.73 ns
#LUT4	463	443	680

The TOC-BISR unit does not change drastically the clock period compared with the previous unit, because the CAM and the main memory with Hamming protection are read in parallel, and the CAM access time is smaller than the Hamming decoding, not altering the total clock period. However, there is an increase in area of about 50% to implement the extra logic in the CAM, together with one BlockRAM, as already explained in previous section. In an ASIC implementation, the CAM can be more efficiently implemented in terms of area, with few SRAM cells and no extra surround logic, but it does not give the flexibility of size customization as the one proposed here.

The performance penalties seen are more than twice the period of the no-protected memory. This can be explained by the EDAC code insertion in the critical path, which happens with all memories protected by this technique. For large memories, the delay for the EDAC code can represent a small increase of the memory time access time in percentage. However, an increase of at least 50% in delay was already expected, and it can be a reasonable price to pay to ensure fault tolerance for soft and hard errors. In terms of area, the results are quite good, since it uses about only 10% of the available logic in the FPGA in the case of VirtexE-XCV300.

The customization of the TOC-BISR can be done with little extra cost. For example, changing the EDAC to Reed-Solomon code, it would be expected to increase the delay and the area due to the code about 50% compared to the memory protected with Hamming code[11]. The March algorithm could be changed with no cost for the application. The algorithm only changes the total time expended performing the test in the whole memory. Finally, the CAM can have its size increased with almost no cost in performance, and a linear increase in area cost.

6. CONCLUSIONS

This paper has presented a transparent online customizable built-in self-repair (TOC-BISR) system to protect commercial memories against soft and hard errors. The first implemented version uses Hamming code combined with a March test algorithm together with a CAM, which is used to remap addresses with permanent faults.

Results show that the presence of the CAM did not significantly increase the clock period compared to a similar approach that performs only soft error correction and online testing. The main advantage of the proposed approach is the flexible customization after the design. New EDAC codes and testing algorithms can be used to update and improve the fault tolerance of the system, as well as, the CAM size can be updated to tolerate a large number of hard errors in the memory. Future works include the study of some parallelism techniques in order to reduce the performance overhead, and the investigation of other options to store the defective addresses, such as using a Flash memory.

REFERENCES

1. K. Johansson, B. Dyreklev, B. Granbom, M. C. Calvet, S. Fourtine, O. Feuillatre, "In-Flight and Ground Testing of Single Event Upset Sensitivity in Static RAMs", IEEE Transactions on Nuclear Science, Vol. 45, pp. 1628-1632, 1998.
2. A. Johnston, "Scaling and Technology Issues for Soft Error Rates", 4th Annual Research Conference on Reliability, October, 2000.
3. T. R. Oldham, K. W. Bennett, J. Beaucour, T. Carriere, C. Polvey, P. Garnier, "Total Dose Failures in Advanced Electronics from Single Ions", IEEE Transactions on Nuclear Science, Vol. 40, pp. 1820-1830, 1993.
4. P. Cheynet, R. Velazco, R. Ecoffet, S. Duzellier, J. P. David, J. Loquet, "Comparison Between Ground Tests and Flight Data for Two Static 32KB Memories", Proceedings of European Conf. Radiation and Its Effects on Components and Systems, pp. 554-557, 1999.
5. J. P. David, J. Loquet, S. Duzellier, "Heavy Ions Induced Latent Stuck Bits Revealed by Total Dose Irradiation in 4T Cells SRAMs", Proceedings of European Conf. Radiation and Its Effects on Components and Systems, pp. 80-86, 1999.
6. R. W. Hamming, "Error Detecting Codes", Bell System Technical Journal, Vol.26, no. 2, April 1950.
7. A. D. Houghton, "The Engineer's Error Coding Handbook", London: Chapman & Hall, 1997.

8. D. C. Huang, W. B. Jone, S. R. Das, "An efficient parallel transparent BIST method for multiple embedded memory buffers", Proceedings of International Conf. VLSI Design, pp. 379-384, 2001.
9. M. G. Karpovsky, V. N. Yarmolik, "Transparent memory BIST", Proceedings of International Workshop on Memory Technology, Design and Testing, pp. 106-111, 1994.
10. R. A. Reed, M. A. Carts, P. W. Marshall, O. Musseau, P. J. McNulty, D. R. Roth, S. Buchner, J. Melinger, T. Corbiere, "Heavy Ion and Proton Induced Single Event Multiple Upsets", IEEE Transactions on Nuclear Science, Vol. 44, Issue 6, pp. 2224-2229, December 1997.
11. K. Thaller, A. Steininger, "A Transparent Online Memory Test for Simultaneous Detection of Functional Faults and Soft Errors in Memories", IEEE Transactions on Reliability, Vol. 52, Issue 4, pp. 413-422, December 2003.
12. R. Zappa, C. Selva, D. Rimondi, C. Torelli, M. Crestan, G. Mastrodomenico, L. Albani, "Micro Programmable Built-In Self Repair for SRAMs", Proceedings of International Workshop on Memory Technology, Design and Testing (MTDT), pp. 72-77, 2004.
13. H. T. Vergos, D. Nikolos, "Performance Recovery in Direct-Mapped Faulty Caches via the Use of a Very Small Fully Associative Spare Cache", Proceedings of International Computer Performance and Dependability Symposium, pp. 326-332, 1995.
14. F. L. Kastensmidt, G. Neuberger, L. Carro, R. Reis, "Designing and Testing Fault-Tolerant Techniques for SRAM-based FPGAs", ACM Computer Frontiers Conference, 2004.
15. Xilinx Inc., "Virtex™ 2.5 V Field Programmable Gate Arrays", Xilinx Datasheet DS008, v2.4, October, 2000.

INTEGRATION OF EMBEDDED SOFTWARE WITH CORPORATE INFORMATION SYSTEMS*

Ricardo J. Machado, João M. Fernandes
Dept. Sistemas de Informação & Dept. Informática
Universidade do Minho, PORTUGAL

Abstract: This paper describes a methodology and corresponding tools to support the development of information systems, by integrating and interconnecting a network of embedded devices, that supervise processes in industrial environments, with the corporate information system of an organization. We discuss in detail how the LabVIEW environment was customized, so that it effectively supports a component-based and data-flow approach in the development of the gateway responsible for the integration.

Keywords: Integration of Embedded Software, Design Methodology, Network and Communication Systems, System Architectures

1.   INTRODUCTION

Nowadays, internet makes electronic commerce and electronic business a reality. Therefore, organizations are starting to base their logistic processes in the internet, in an attempt to guarantee a continuous satisfaction to their clients. However, the industrial organizations still feel that the organizational supporting processes do not include their true business, which are the production of goods and services [1].

This new reality forces an important re-structuring on the organizations and gives rise to the need of supporting and controlling the information of their production processes, especially in real-time, anywhere, and at any level of management [2].

* This work has been supported by projects STACOS (POSI/CHS/48875/2002) and METHODES (POSI/CHS/37334/2001)

The integration of real-time shop-floor applications, which we designate industrial control-based information systems (ICIS), with the corporate, or management, information system (MIS) is currently a question of survival for any industrial organization that is dependent on the information and communicant technologies. The typical network topology of the final MIS+ICIS solution is presented in fig. 1, where two distinct "zones" can be identified: (1) the first one corresponds to the shop-floor network supporting the ICIS implementation (in our approach, a CAN network of several embedded devices and one gateway executing LabVIEW software); (2) the second one corresponds to the Ethernet network supporting the MIS implementation by using typical ERP (enterprise resource planning) and POS (plant operations system) software.

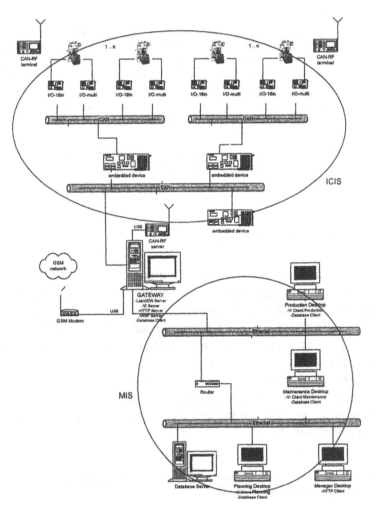

Figure 1 - Network topology for typical MIS+ICIS solutions.

Monitoring and supervision of industrial processes require huge investments in technical solutions based on real-time embedded technologies, especially developed to interconnect the production equipments with the MIS applications. To make CIM (computer integrated manufacturing) [3] an effective reality for an organization, without dependencies from proprietary solutions, we need to fill the gap that exists between the MIS and the ICIS technologies [4].

CIM levels integration have already been handled by the definition of specific industrial communications protocols, namely MAP (manufacturing automation protocol), TOP (technical and office protocol) and MMS (manufacturing message specification). However, the same degree of sophistication was not yet achieved for the applications, which are crucial to feed MIS with truly relevant information flows.

In this context, we have witnessed the relatively low success of the SCADA (supervision, control, automation and data acquisition) applications, due mainly to their low degree of flexibility, whose main examples are WINCC, INTOUCH, and BridgeVIEW. It is important to notice that the CIM levels 0 and 1 are well supported in what concerns the physical control of industrial processes, since industrial equipments usually embed a control system to make their operation more automatic. Thus, the "big" problems are on the systems that monitor and supervise processes and equipments.

Even recent efforts on the definition of standards [5], technologies [6] and methodological frameworks [7] to support the enterprise application integration [8] have failed to support the specific characteristics of industrial information systems. These approaches have not been able to support the design of middleware capable of filling the semantic gap amongst MIS and ICIS.

Under these circumstances, it seems clear that we need technical solutions to easily interconnect the lower CIM levels (0 to 2) with the higher ones (3 and 4). These solutions must necessarily use real-time embedded (and eventually distributed) systems to manage the information flow among the lower CIM levels, and also between these ones and the higher levels [9].

The strategies for the technological integration of MIS and ICIS must also take into consideration that the differences between those two types of information systems can be classified in four groups [10]:

(1) temporal, since a MIS handles time scales that typically are within the days or weeks (in some cases, months or even years are also common), while a ICIS must work with time frames that are measured in seconds or even in milliseconds;

(2) informational, since for a MIS the information is handled under the transactional semantics, while a ICIS is typically described under a event-driven model of computation;

(3) operational, because a MIS directly supports operations of planning and scheduling of the production process and a ICIS supports the control and the supervision of the industrial equipments;

(4) cultural, since a MIS is oriented towards the organizational business, whilst a ICIS focuses on the industrial processes.

2.   SOFTWARE ENGINEERING WITH LABVIEW

Allowing non-technical persons to be able to program is becoming not only advantageous but also needed, taking into account the constant changes in requirements and the scarceness of programmers to handle all applications [11]. Therefore, anyone could program a small application according to his own needs and requirements, without the need to follow a software engineering process. This is already a reality for spreadsheets, for example, since anyone (namely those without a computer engineering background) can create his tables and introduce his formulas without knowing the details of the computational engine that is hidden by the graphical interface. This does not happen, in any sense, in the case of embedded systems, with respect to the development activities. However, the use of the LabVIEW tool allows the integrations of physical modules (hardware) and algorithmic modules (VIs - LabVIEW virtual instruments) and increases the abstraction level [12]. This permit the development of components (VIs and virtual models of hardware) with a clear separation between their interface and implementation [13], to directly support the construction of solutions at the system-level and following a component-based design approach.

An important aspect that must be taken into account is to study how adequate is the LabVIEW specification language to the specific working area where the environment is being used. Thus, we need to reinterpret the way applications are to be developed through the definition of the language subset to be used and to produce of a set of guidelines that constitute an architectural reference for developing applications.

One of the main differences that LabVIEW presents with respect to the conventional textual languages is that it follows a data-oriented paradigm (data-flow and data-driven), in the sense that the execution of the programs is controlled by the availability of data and their flow. Thus, the results of the computations (data tokens) are directly transported between instructions, and the data items produced by an instruction are replicated to feed all the instructions that further need them to continue the computational flow. This approach is completely the opposite of the traditional model of computation, known as von Neumann, where the execution of a program is controlled by the sequence of instructions written by the programmer (control-driven).

In LabVIEW, the data-flow approach is mainly reflected on the specification of:

(1) parallelism (concurrency), since it is inherent to the data-flow and is frequently independent of the structural replication of the control units;

(2) reactions of the asynchronous events, since it is often needed to take into consideration the computational context where the event occurs;

(3) hierarchy, since the violation of the hierarchical levels and the termination of activities on computational sub-levels put some difficulties in the gateway design.

We must reinforce the idea that in data-driven programming the data semantics is stronger than in control-driven programming, since there is a direct relation between its availability and an implicit control over the flow of computational execution. In data-driven approach, this execution is typically concurrent and asynchronous in contrast with sequential and synchronous execution of the traditional control-driven programming.

3. GATEWAY DESIGN

To adapt the LabVIEW platform as the development environment for the gateway, responsible for the integration of the MIS and the embedded devices, the tasks next described have been undertaken by the authors.

3.1 Virtual Modeling

The virtual models of the embedded devices must be created in LabVIEW through the implementation of VIs that possess: (1) an interface that contains all the attributes previously formalized through an interface schematics; (2) an implementation that ensures the electronic and run-time access to the corresponding device.

Fig. 2 illustrates an example of the LabVIEW virtual model of an embedded device, as well as the internal attributes that belong to the device access interface. The access to the attributes of an embedded device is accomplished through *unbundle* constructors.

3.2 Access to the Embedded Devices

To assure the electronic and run-time access to the embedded devices in LabVIEW, it is necessary to build a thread in Windows OS, independent of the thread executing the algorithms of the final solution. This new thread aims to multiplex the single physical access to the industrial network (CAN server). The implementation of this CAN server is based on the construction of a bi-directional queuing system that guarantees the storage and forwarding of the data packets sent from a virtual model to its corresponding embedded device and vice-versa.

This thread is needed, since several embedded devices may be connected to the network, and consequently the corresponding virtual models will be used, potentially in parallel, by the application in LabVIEW.

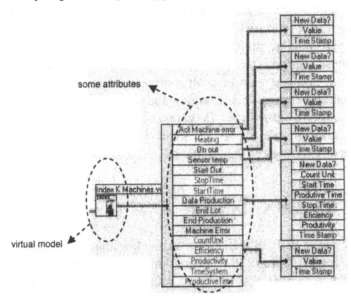

Figure 2 - Virtual model of an embedded device and the "unbundle" of some attributes.

The communication between the LabVIEW application and the embedded devices requires the definition of a communication protocol that implements a layer of services on top of the CAN protocol (VAP) to ease the end-to-end transport of information. This protocol also provides a set of communication services, such as send attributes (*putData( )*), send immediately attributes (*putDataNow( )*), ask attributtes (*getData( )*), ask recent attributes (*getFreshData( )*), parameterize embedded devices, and announce the arrival of new embedded devices (see [14] for more details).

The definition of the VAP protocol followed some of the techniques typically adopted in group communications [15], by using a network of embedded devices that support:

(1) redundancy of embedded devices to permit fault-tolerance;

(2) usage of time stamps in all attributes of the embedded devices;

(3) uniform treatment of a set of embedded devices that handle similar messages (broadcast and multicast communication), both as consumers and producers;

(4) dynamic management of computational resources connected at any time to the network.

In this last topic, it is important to highlight the fact that the connection (or disconnection) of a "new" embedded device is automatically detected by the gateway, behaving as the group server. This implements a truly *plug & play* technology for embedded devices, seen as dynamic components of the distributed system.

3.3   Library of components

To ease on the development of the gateway, a library of components (VIs) was implemented. This library includes several VIs, which are grouped in the following categories:
(1) communication with the CAN network to send and receive data packets;
(2) interaction with structured documents, typically stored in databases, using SQL (structured query language) commands;
(3) sending and reception of SMTP mail messages;
(4) sending and reception of SMS messages to and from entities connected to GSM (global system for mobile communications) networks;
(5) virtual modeling of embedded devices to use in the construction of the gateway software.

3.4   Architecture of the gateway software

The software of the gateway must be developed according to well-defined architectural patterns; such as the *multi-level ICIS* pattern [14]. Apart from that, the gateway software must be structured into the following units:
(1) declaration, where all the embedded and I/O devices that integrate the final solution must be declared (fig. 3);
(2) initialization, where some communication services to be used in the final solution are initialized (fig. 4);
(3) parameterization, where the VIs corresponding to the embedded devices of the final solution are parameterized (fig. 5);
(4) interconnection, where the final solution is developed at the algorithmic point of view (fig. 6).

Some of the interconnection mechanisms between the four aforementioned structural units of the gateway software may be automatically inserted at the very beginning of the development, if the designers use explicitly a LabVIEW wizard developed by the authors to supports this task.

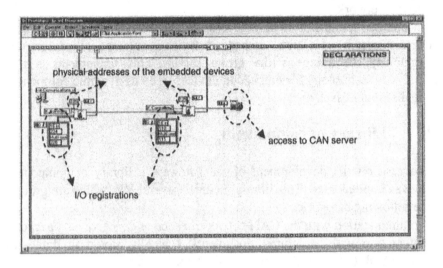

Figure 3 - Declaration of the embedded and I/O devices.

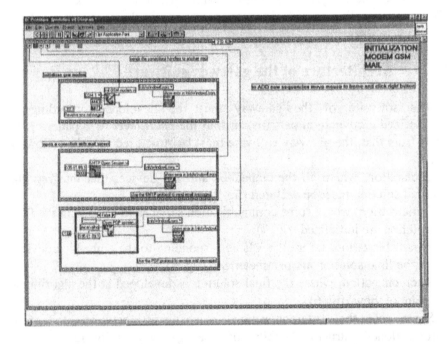

Figure 4 - Initialization of the communication services.

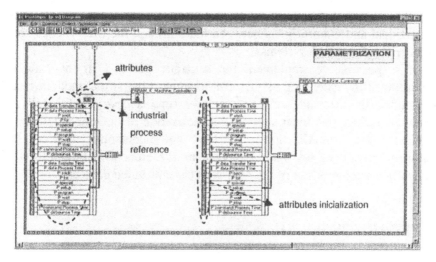

Figure 5 - Parameterization of the virtual models of the embedded devices.

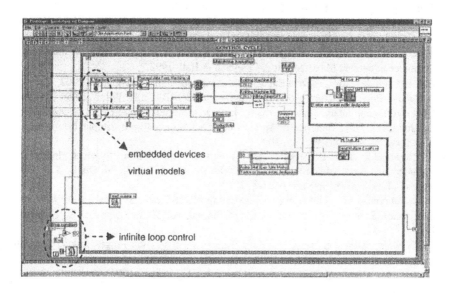

Figure 6 - Interconnection of the MIS with the embedded devices.

4. CONCLUSIONS

The implementation of industrial information systems demands the integration of the industrial networks of embedded devices that supervise the industrial equipments and processes, with the corporate information systems. This integration can be executed at the application level, by developing a semantic gateway capable of dealing with the temporal, informational, operational and cultural gaps between the ICIS and the MIS "zones" of the industrial information systems.

It is possible to implement the semantic gateway in the LabVIEW environment by extending its platform to support the virtual modeling of the embedded devices, as well as their run-time access. Additionally, the gateway design flow must support the declaration of the embedded and I/O devices, the initialization of the communication services, the parameterization of the virtual models of the embedded devices and the logically interconnection of the MIS with the embedded devices.

REFERENCES

[1] A. W. Sheer, Business Process Engineering: Reference Models for Industrial Enterprises, Springer-Verlag, 2nd edition, 1994.
[2] The New Productivity Factor, LIPRO Holding AG, 1999.
[3] J. B. Waldner, CIM: Principles of Computer-Integrated Manufacturing, John Wiley & Sons, 1992.
[4] B. Scholz-Reiter, CIM Interfaces: Concepts, Standards and Problems of Interfaces in Computer Integrated Manufacturing, Chapman & Hall, 1992.
[5] EIA-836 standard for CM Data Exchange and Interoperability, EIA, June, 2002.
[6] R. Zahavi, Enterprise Application Integration with CORBA, John Wiley & Sons, 1999.
[7] UML Profile and Interchange Models for Enterprise Application Integration, OMG, 2001.
[8] D. Linthicum, Next Generation Application Integration – From Simple Information to Web Services, Addison-Wesley, 2002.
[9] R. J. Machado, J. M. Fernandes, Heterogeneous Information Systems Integration: Organizations and Methodologies, PROFES'02, pp. 629-643, M. Oivo, S. K. Sirviö (editors), LNCS 2559, Springer-Verlag, 2002.
[10] R. R. Derynck, T. Hutchinson, Integrating Real-Time Systems with Corporate Information Systems, The Hewlett Packard Journal, vol. 50, no. 1, pp. 26-28, November, 1998.
[11] T. Williams, Object-Oriented Methods Transform Real-Time Programming, Computer Design, pp. 101-118, September, 1992.
[12] J. Jehander, Graphical Object-Oriented Programming in LabVIEW, Application Number no. 143, National Instruments, October, 1999.
[13] R. J. Machado, J. M. Fernandes, A Petri Net Meta-Model to Develop Software Components for Embedded Systems, ACSD'01, pp. 113-122, IEEE CS Press, 2001.
[14] R. J. Machado, J. M. Fernandes, A Multi-level Design Pattern for Embedded Software, DIPES 2004, pp. 247-256, B. Kleinjohann, G. R. Gao, H. Kopetz, L. Kleinjohann, A. Rettberg (editors), Kluwer AP, 2004.
[15] K. P. Birman, The Process Group Approach to Reliable Distributed Computing, Communications of the ACM, vol. 36, pp. 36-53, December, 1993.

AUTOMATIC GENERATION OF COMMUNICATION ARCHITECTURES

Dongwan Shin
Andreas Gerstlauer
Rainer Dömer
Daniel D. Gajski
Center for Embedded Computer Systems
Information and Computer Science
University of California, Irvine
{dongwans,gerstl, deomer, gajski}@ics.uci.edu

Abstract: In this paper, we propose automatic generation of bus-based communication architectures from an abstract model reflecting only the communication topology. Tasks include protocol selection for each bus, master/slave assignment for each component, interrupt handling and addressing for synchronization between components, and arbitration to resolve multiple accesses on a bus. We present a set of experimental results demonstrating how the proposed approach works on typical system designs. Experimental results show the benefits of our methodology and demonstrate the effectiveness of automatic model generation for communication design.

1.   INTRODUCTION

With ever increasing SoC complexities, design of system communication structures is becoming an in increasingly important factor and bottleneck. Together with time-to-market pressures, communication design requires extensive design space exploration in a short amount of time. Typically, designers use models of a system to validate and evaluate different designs. Traditionally, these models are manually written, which is a tedious, error-prone task, and time-consuming task, severely limiting exploration opportunities.

In order to tackle these problems, we propose a communication design flow with automatic generation of communication models from a virtual architecture model. Figure 1 shows the communication design flow [5]. Design starts with the architecture model which reflects the structure

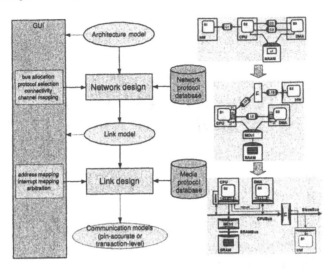

Figure 1.   Communication design flow.

of processing components/elements (PEs), but where communication is done abstractly on a message-passing level. Communication design is then divided into two tasks: *network design* and *link design.*

During network design, the topology of the communication architecture is defined and abstract message passing channels between processors are mapped into communication between adjacent stations of the communication architecture. The network topology of communication stations connected by logical link channels is defined, bridges and other communication elements are allocated as necessary, and abstract message passing channels are routed over sets of logical link channels. The result of the network design step is a link model of the system which represents the topology of the communication architecture and in which stations communicate via untyped, logical links.

During link design, logical links between adjacent stations are then grouped and implemented over an actual communication medium (e.g. system busses). For each group of links to be implemented over a single, shared medium, a communication protocol is selected and parameters such as addresses and interrupts for synchronization are assigned to each logical link.

As a result of the communication design process, a pin-accurate or transaction-level communication model of the system is generated. Communication models are fully structural where components are connected via busses and communicate in a timing-accurate manner based on media protocol timing specifications.

In this paper, we concentrate on the link design task and we will present our approach to speeding up the link design process by enabling automatic model refinement. The rest of the paper is organized as follows. Section 2 gives an overview of related work. Section 3 shows our refinement-based link design flow and Section 4 looks at the individual tasks of link refinement. Finally, we present experimental results in Section 5 and wind up with a summary and conclusion.

2. RELATED WORK

Recently, system-level design languages have been proposed as vehicles for so-called transaction-level modeling (TLM) for communication abstraction [4] [7]. However, TLM proposals so far focus on simulation only and they lack the path to vertical integration of models for implementation and synthesis.

There are several approaches dealing with automatic generation of communication architectures [2] [3]. These approaches, however, are usually based on target architecture templates and limited in their support for general architectures and applications. Furthermore, most of the work has been done in optimizing communication architectures for specific designs [6] [8]. Finally, approaches that deal with optimization and automatic decision making for communication synthesis [11] [9] are usually lacking support for generating implementations for those decisions.

In previous work [1], we proposed an automatic communication refinement flow. In this paper we extend this work to support more general architectures with networks of interconnected busses, realistic communication mechanisms and advanced synchronization primitives.

3. LINK DESIGN

Link design implements the functionality of link layer, media access layer and protocol layer and inlines them into corresponding components. The link layer defines the type of a communication station (e.g. master/slave on a bus) for each of its incoming or outgoing links. It is also responsible for implementing synchronization between communication stations, e.g. via interrupts or by polling in case of interrupt sharing.

The media access layer is responsible for slicing blocks of bytes into bus words. Furthermore, it resolves simultaneous bus accesses of components through arbitration. Depending on the arbitration scheme chosen, additional arbitration components are introduced into the system as part of the media access layer.

Finally, the protocol layer is responsible for driving and sampling the external pins according to the protocol timing diagrams and thereby matching the transmission timing on the sender and receiver sides.

3.1   Inputs and Outputs

Link design starts from a link model, which represents the topology of the communication architecture. Components on the top level of the design communicate with each other via logical link channels. Each channel provides *send/receive* methods for enable data transactions with message passing semantics.

During the design process, the user provides a set of design decisions such as protocol selection for each bus, master/slave assignment for components, address and interrupt assignment for logical links, and arbitration scheme and bus access priorities.

With these inputs, the link refinement tool produces an output communication model that reflects the bus architecture of the system. In the output model, the top level of the design consists of system components connected by wires of the system busses. The components themselves are refined down to bus-functional models that communicate via ports.

3.2   Databases

Link design is supported by a media database that consists of a database of bus protocols and a database of associated bus-functional component models.

3.2.1   Bus database.

The bus database contains models of busses including associated protocols. Bus models in the bus database consist of a stack of two layers: protocol layer and media access layer. At the bottom of the stack, the protocol layer is connected to the actual bus wires and it implements the primitives defined by the bus protocol for data transfers, synchronization and arbitration. On top of the protocol layer, the media access layer provides an abstraction of external communication into data links and memory accesses by using and combining bus primitives to regulate media accesses and slice abstract data into bus words.

Each protocol layer can have two separate sides with different implementations for bus masters and bus slaves. Each layer provides a protocol implementation for one single component connected to the bus. Protocol layer models connect to the bus wires through ports of the model and pins of the component. Layers are stacked on top of each other and connect via interfaces where the media access layer calls the methods of the protocol layer beneath it.

3.2.2   Bus-functional component database.   For components with fixed, pre-defined interfaces and communication functionality, the component database has to contain a bus functional model of the component. A bus functional component model accurately describes the component interface at the pin level and it provides a simulation model of communication aspects of the component.

For programmable components with flexible computation behavior but fixed, pre-defined interfaces and communication functionality, a bus functional model with at least two layers has to be provided in the database: a top level bus functional layer describing the component pin interface on the outside and an internal, empty hardware abstraction layer (HAL) describing the interface for accessing the bus medium from the software on the inside. In addition, the HAL has to provide templates of interrupt handlers for each external interrupt line of the processor.

4.   LINK REFINEMENT

Link refinement is the process of transforming the input link model into a communication model based on the user-supplied decisions. The refinement process can be divided into five major steps, namely, channel grouping, bus functional model instantiation, synchronization synthesis, arbiter/interrupt controller insertion, and bus wiring. be further divided into sub-steps.

In the following, we will outline transformations for link refinement. More details about this process can be found in [10]. We will use a simple example (Figure 2(a)) where 2 PEs (*PE1* and *PE2_OS*), 1 IP (*IP1*), a shared memory (*M1_LK*) and a bridge (*Bridge*) are allocated. They are communicating using message passing channels *L1* and *L2*. The design decision for link design are made as shown in Figure 2(b). For example, the channel *L1* is assigned to interrupt *intA* and address *0x00020000*.

4.1   Channel grouping

The first task of link refinement is channel grouping which combines different links mapped onto a bus. Message passing channels between components will be grouped into transactions over a single, shared bus and unique bus addresses will be assigned to each link and each memory interface or slave register mapped onto the bus.

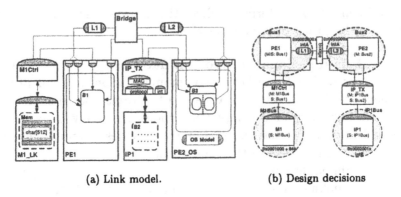

(a) Link model.   (b) Design decisions

Figure 2.   An example of link model and design decision.

4.2   Bus-functional component instantiation

As a next step, bus functional models for components with fixed, predefined bus interfaces (e.g. programmable processors, IPs, bridges and system memories) are taken out of the bus-functional component database and instantiated in the design.

Bus functional models for programmable components have to include a definition of the interrupt capabilities of the component. The top level bus functional shell defines the interrupt pins available at the physical component interface and the hardware abstraction layer (HAL) model provides corresponding empty interrupt handler templates. During link refinement, interrupt lines from slaves are connected to the interrupt pins of programmable components and interrupt handlers in the HAL are generated by filling the templates. Finally, interrupt tasks triggered by the HAL interrupt handlers are generated in the operating system of the processors.

4.3   Synchronization synthesis

In order to preserve the semantics of the original input model, synchronization between components has to be introduced whenever necessary. The link layer is responsible for implementing synchronization through interrupts and/or polling. Link layers have different implementations depending on the type of station (master/slave). Methods on the master side wait for interrupt from slaves before invoking media access layer methods to perform the actual data transfer. On the slave side, a slave will send an interrupt to notify the master about any data transfer request. In case of memory or register (memory-mapped I/O) accesses, slave components are assumed to be always ready and no extra synchronization is necessary.

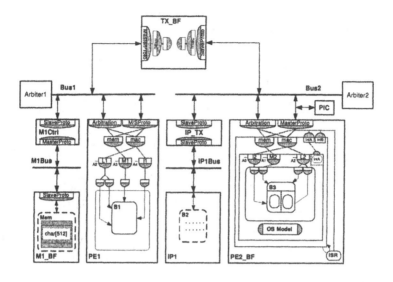

Figure 3. Communication model example.

4.4 Arbiter/Interrupt controller insertion

If multiple master components are connected to a bus, arbitration becomes necessary to resolve conflicting accesses of bus masters. The arbitration mechanism will be instantiated from the bus database as part of the bus protocol master implementation. All masters are assigned additional arbitration ports connected to the arbiter on the bus. The arbiter will be instantiated at the top level of a design together with the arbitration wires. Based on design decisions, we generate a priority-based or round-robin arbitration component.

If a master communicates with more than one slave, it will require an interrupt controller to handle synchronization requests from multiple slaves. For each slave on a bus, an interrupt port is created and connected to the corresponding interrupt wire on the bus. Finally, an interrupt controller is generated and inserted into the bus master component.

4.5 Bus wiring

After all bus-functional models of processing and communication elements are generated and/or inserted from the database, components at the top of the design need to be connected to each other through bus wires. Bus-functional component models define the bus ports of each station. Connections between port and busses are defined through the

Table 1.   Design decisions for link design.

Examples		Traffic (bytes)	Channel (num.)	Medium (master/slave)
JPEG	A1	2244	6	DSP Bus (DSP/IP)
	A2	3420	13	DSP Bus (DSP/(IP,HW))
Vocoder	A1	46944	12	DSP Bus (DSP/HW)
	A2	140832	36	DSP Bus (DSP/2 HWs)
	A3	154524	42	DSP Bus (DSP/3 HWs)
	A4	57160	29	2 DSP Bus (2 DSPs/2 HWs)
MP3	A1	0	0	CF Bus (CF)
	A2	169747	66	CF Bus (CF/4 HWs) 4 Handshake Bus (4 HWs)
Baseband	A1	178500	19	CF Bus ((CF,DMA)/(IP,DMA,MEM) DSP Bus (DSP/(5 HWs)

port mapping. Finally, interrupt and arbitration lines are connected based on the priorities selected by the user.

As a result, the final communication model of the design is generated. Figure 3 shows the communication model for the example from Figure 2. Logical link channels from the link model have been inlined into the connected components. Media access and protocol layer channel adapters are taken out of the bus database, inserted into the bus functional model of the corresponding components and connected to the logical link adapters. Additional communication elements such as interrupt controllers (*PIC*) and arbiters (*Arbiter1* and *Arbiter2*) are inserted into the design. Inside programmable components (*PE2*), interrupt service routines (*ISR*) and interrupt handling methods (*intA* and *intB*) are generated and inserted for synchronization with other system components (*PE1* and *IP1*).

5.   EXPERIMENTAL RESULTS

Based on the described methodology and algorithms, we developed a link refinement tool for automatic generation of communication models. We performed experiments using four industrial strength examples: a JPEG encoder (*JPEG*), a voice codec (*vocoder*), an MP3 decoder (*MP3*) and a baseband platform (*Baseband*) which combines a JPEG encoder with a voice codec. For each example, we implemented several different architectures. Table 1 shows the total traffic, the number of logical link channels and the allocated architecture each.

Table 2. Experiment results of link refinement.

Examples		Lines of Code			Tool	Man.	Gain
		Link	BF	Mod. (*ins.* + *del.* − *DB*)	(sec)	(hr)	
JPEG	A1	3464	5250	351 (1867 − 1618 + 102)	0.10	35.1	421
	A2	3755	5655	303 (1975 − 1768 + 96)	0.10	30.3	364
Vocoder	A1	10980	11740	341 (794 − 487 + 34)	0.31	34.1	409
	A2	11415	12205	405 (841 − 487 + 51)	0.33	40.5	486
	A3	12276	13096	489 (897 − 487 + 77)	0.39	48.9	587
	A4	14033	15220	757 (1309 − 674 + 122)	0.84	75.7	908
MP3	A1	29959	31666	375 (1822 − 1584 + 137)	0.44	37.5	450
	A2	33905	36361	1198 (2724 − 1818 + 292)	1.06	119.8	1437
Baseband	A1	20227	23027	1288 (3150 − 2212 + 350)	1.02	128.8	1545

Table 2 shows the results of link refinement. Overall model complexities are given in terms of code size using lines of code (LOC) as a metric. Results show significant differences in complexity between input and generated output models due to extra implementation detail added between abstraction levels. To quantify the actual refinement effort, the number of modified lines is calculated as the sum of lines inserted and lines deleted whereas code coming from database models is excluded. We assume that a person can modify 10 LOC/hour. Thus, manual refinement would require several hundred man-hours for reasonably complex designs. Automatic refinement, on the other hand, completes in the order of seconds. In order to compute the productivity gain, we assume that design decisions (address/interrupt assignment, arbitration) for link refinement can be done in 5 minutes. Results show that a productivity gain of around 1000 times can be expected using the presented approach and automatic model refinement.

6. CONCLUSIONS

In this paper, we presented a methodology to automatically generate communication models from a representation of the communication topology and abstract communication channels going across. During this link design process, logical links between adjacent components are grouped and implemented over a system bus and link, MAC and protocol layers are implemented at the interfaces of components.

Using several industrial-strength examples, the feasibility and benefits of the approach have been demonstrated. Huge productivity gains can be obtained using automatic link refinement. Our main contribution in the paper is the automation of a time consuming and error prone process to achieve better designer productivity, thus enabling designers to explore a large part of the design space in a shorter amount of time.

REFERENCES

[1] S. Abdi, D. Shin, and D. D. Gajski. Automatic communication refinement in system-level design. In *Proceedings of the Design Automation Conference*, pages 300–305, June 2003.

[2] I. Bolsens, H. D. Man, B. Lin, K. V. Rompay, S. Vercauteren, and D. Verkest. Hardware/Software co-design of the digital telecommunication systems. *Proceedings of the IEEE*, March 1997.

[3] W. O. Cesario, A. Baghdadi, L. Gauthier, D. Lyonnard, G. Nicolescu, Y. Paviot, S. Yoo, A. A. Jerraya, and M. Diaz-Nava. Component-baed design approach for multicore SoCs. In *Proceedings of the Design Automation Conference*, pages 789–794, June 2002.

[4] M. Coppola, S. Curaba, M. Grammatikakis, and G. Maruccia. IPSIM: SystemC 3.0 enhancements for communication refinement. In *Proceedings of the Design Automation and Test Conference in Europe*, pages 106–111, March 2003.

[5] A. Gerstlauer, D. Shin, R. Dömer, and D. D. Gajski. System-level communication modeling for Network-on-Chip synthesis. In *Proceedings of Asian South Pacific Design Automation Conference*, pages 45–48, January 2005.

[6] G. Gogniat, M. Auguin, L. Bianco, and A. Pegatoquet. Communication synthesis and HW/SW integration for embedded system design. In *Proceedings of the International Workshop on Hardware-Software Codesign*, pages 49–53, March 1998.

[7] T. Grötker, S. Liao, G. Martin, and S. Swan. *System Design with SystemC.* Kluwer Academic Publishers, March 2002.

[8] P. Knudsen and J. Madsen. Integrating communication protocol selection with partitioning Hardware/Software codesign. In *Proceedings of the International Symposium on System Synthesis*, pages 111–116, December 1998.

[9] R. B. Ortega and G. Borriello. Communication synthesis for distributed embedded systems. In *Proceedings of the International Conference on Computer-Aided Design*, pages 437–444, November 1998.

[10] D. Shin, A. Gerstlauer, and D. D. Gajski. Communication link synthesis for SoC. Technical Report CECS-TR-04-16, Center for Embedded Computer Systems, University of California, Irvine, June 2004.

[11] T.-Y. Yen and W. Wolf. Communication synthesis for distributed embedded systems. In *Proceedings of the International Conference on Computer-Aided Design*, pages 288–294, November 1995.

ABSTRACT COMMUNICATION MODELING

A Case Study Using the CAN Automotive Bus

Gunar Schirner and Rainer Dömer
Center for Embedded Computer Systems
University of California Irvine
hschirne@uci.edu, doemer@uci.edu

Abstract: Communication modeling is a critical issue in specifying SoCs. It is needed for accurately predicting the timing behavior of the system. Fast simulation capabilities are a key in this environment, for coping with the complex design choices during the specification process. Recently, Transaction Level Models (TLM) have been proposed to speedup communication simulation at the cost of accuracy.

This paper reports on a case study, where an automotive communications protocol, the Controller Area Network (CAN), has been captured at different levels of abstraction, where specific features of the protocol, such as bit stuffing, are reflected in the model, or abstracted away. The resulting models have been measured in an experimental setup in terms of performance and accuracy. The paper will analyze the results and evaluate the benefits and drawbacks of these TLM and pin-accurate models. In conclusion it will be shown for which applications the models are suitable, with respect to their speed/accuracy trade off.

Keywords: Transaction Level Modeling, Communication Modeling

1. INTRODUCTION

The System-On-Chip (SoC) design faces a gap between the production capabilities and time to market pressures. The design space, to be explored during the SoC design, grows with the improvements in the production capabilities, while at the same time shorter product life cycles force an aggressive reduction of the time-to-market. Addressing this gap has been the aim of recent research work. As one approach, abstract models have been introduced to tackle the design complexity.

Fast simulation capabilities are required for coping with the immense design space that is to be explored; these are especially needed during early stages of the design. This need has pushed the development of Transaction Level Models (TLM) [6], which are abstract models that execute dramatically faster than synthesizable, bit-accurate models.

Transaction level modeling, however will come with the drawback of a decreased accuracy. This paper will analyze the performance gains of transaction level modeling and show the drawbacks in accuracy. The analysis is based on a case study of the Controller Area Network (CAN) bus, which is a standard bus protocol used in the automotive industry.

This paper will first introduce the main features of the CAN bus. Based on a feature selection a set of models with different levels of abstraction will be proposed and their design will be described. Following that the implemented models will be measured in an experimental setup and their results will be analyzed, to conclude with a set of models suitable for the desired application.

1.1   Related Work

System level modeling has become a more important issue over the recent years, as a means to improve the SoC design process. Languages for capturing these models have been developed, such as SpecC [3] or SystemC [6]. Furthermore capturing and designing communication systems using transaction level models has received research attention.

Sgroi et al. [11] address the SoC communication with an Network-on-Chip (NoC) approach. They propose partitioning of the communication into separate layers that follow the OSI structure. Software reuse is promoted with an increase of abstraction from the underlying communication framework.

Siegmund and Müller [12] describe with SystemC^{SV} an extension to SystemC, and propose modeling of an SoC at different levels of abstraction. They describe three different levels: the physical description at RTL level, a more abstract model that covers individual messages, and a most abstract level that deals with transactions.

[1] describes how the CAN bus is modeled using the above mentioned extension SystemC^{SV}. The work also shows the three abstraction levels, but does not give any experimental results on performance or accuracy.

In [2] Caldari et al. describe the results of capturing the AMBA rev. 2.0 bus standard in SystemC. The bus system has been modeled at two levels of abstraction, fist a bus functional model on RTL level and second a model on TLM level. Their TLM model reached a speedup of 100 over the RTL level model.

2.   INTRODUCTION CAN BUS

The Controller Area Network (CAN) is a serial communications protocol, introduced by the Robert Bosch GmbH [10], that was designed with a focus on automotive applications.

CAN is a serial multi master broadcast bus. Messages, with up to 8 bytes user data, are received by all bus nodes and distinguished by the message identifier. Each bus node decides using local rules whether to process the message. The message identifier also serves as a message priority. If multiple senders attempt a transmission, the collision free CSMA/CA arbitration will guarantee that the highest priority message will succeed undisturbed.

The CAN bus defines two bus states: recessive (1) and dominant (0). A CAN data frame has the basic format shown in Figure 1. After transmitting the start of frame bit, the message identifier is transmitted with the most significant bit first. During transmission, each sender compares the send and receive signal. A sender that has send recessive bit but a detects a dominant bit will back off from transmission. Another sender must have started a higher priority message.

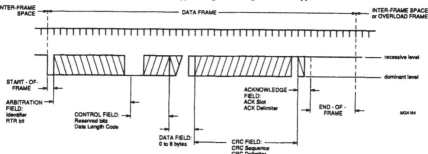

Figure 1.   CAN Data Frame (Source [9]) .

In order to ensure correctness of the received data, each CAN message includes a 15-bit CRC. In case of a CRC mismatch, a retransmission of the frame is triggered. The protocol also defines elaborate error detection and error confinement rules for protection against faulty bus nodes.

The CAN serial protocol operates without a centralized clock. Each bus node synchronizes on the bit stream of the sender. A bit stuffing rule guarantees sufficient edges for this synchronization. After transmitting 5 bits of equal polarity, a bit of opposite polarity is introduced.

In summary, the following properties are candidates for abstraction:
- Serial protocol
- Bit synchronization
- Error detection and confinement
- Bit error detection using a 15 Bit CRC
- Bit stuffing
- Arbitration, bus access controlled by CSMA/CA

The following section describes our modeling of the CAN bus. For each model a subset of the above listed features is selected.

3.   MODELING

A layered architecture was chosen for the communication system modeling in order to cope with the complexity of communication. Following the ISO OSI reference model [8], the CAN specification falls within the second layer, the data link layer. For modeling of the CAN bus the media access control (MAC) and the protocol sublayer, both sublayers of the data link layer, are considered as well as the physical layer.

The OSI layer definition is based on functional concerns. An alternative view, suitable for describing the models, focuses on the granularity in which user data is handled. The **media access layer** provides services for the transmission of a contiguous block of bytes, called a **user transaction**. This layer divides the arbitrary sized user transaction into smaller bus transactions and transfers them using the protocol layer. The **protocol layer** transfers data as **bus transactions**, which are bus primitives (e.g. a CAN data frame with up to 8 bytes data), and uses the physical layer services. The **physical layer** implements a **bus cycle** access to sample and drive individual bus wires.

Figure 2 shows how the above defined data granularity levels can be analyzed with respect to time. A user transaction is successively split into the smaller elements: bus transaction and finally bus cycles.

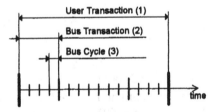

Figure 2.   Time decomposition of a user transaction.

Using a system level modeling approach, each layer was implemented as a separate channel using a system description language (SDL)[1].

3.1   Transaction Level Model

The Transaction Level Model TLM is the most abstract model - it only implements the media access layer. The user data, handled at the user transaction granularity, is transferred in one chunk, regardless of the size. The bus access is checked only once per user transaction.

---

[1]SpecC [3] was used as the SDL of choice, SystemC could be used just as well.

In the implementation, the user data is transferred using a single *memcpy*. The timing is simulated by a single *waitfor* statement, covering the whole user transaction. Neither the CRC nor bit stuffing are observed, since both would require a bit inspection of each message. For an increased performance concurrent bus access is avoided using a semaphore, hence the concurrency resolution relies on the simulation environment and does not observe the message identifier.

3.2 Arbitrated Transaction Level Model

The Arbitrated Transaction Level Model (ATLM) simulates the bus access with a bus transaction granularity (CAN frames), at the protocol layer level. It uses the MAC layer implementation of the later described bus functional model to split user transactions into bus transactions.

The ATLM accurately models the arbitration for each bus transaction (CAN frame) based on the message identifier. It collects all requests during start of frame, and proceeds with the highest priority message. The bus simulation has been implemented without an own flow of execution, in order to maximize execution performance.

Two variants of the ATLM model have been defined. The first, the ATLM (a), performs a bitwise inspection of the frame in order to calculate the CRC and perform stuff bit handling: a stuff bit is inserted/removed each time 5 bits of equal polarity are found. With the bit stuffing, the physical frame length depends on the frame content. The second model, the ATLM (b), does neither calculate the message CRC and nor does it handle stuffing bits. It avoids the costly bit inspection and is expected to execute faster than the ATLM (a), however at the cost of accuracy.

3.3 Bus Functional Model

The bus functional model is a synthesizable model bus model that covers all timing and functional properties of the bus definition. It is a pin accurate and cycle accurate model of the bus.

The bus functional model implements all features of the specification. It protects the data by the CRC, handles stuff bits and performs arbitration. The frame data is send and received serially and the nodes clock is synchronized to the bit stream according to [10] and [7].

Table 1 summarizes the features implemented by a model and shows at which granularity user data is handled. Each model has been implemented in the SDL with the following amount of code lines (excluding testbench): TLM: 250, ATLM (b): 475, ATLM (a): 550, BF: 1400. The model performance and accuracy is analyzed in the following section.

Feature	Bus Functional Model	ATLM (a)	ATLM (b)	TLM
serial transmission	yes	no	no	no
bit synchronization	yes	no	no	no
error detection, confinement	yes	no	no	no
CRC calculation	yes	yes	no	no
bit stuffing	yes	yes	no	no
arbitration	yes	yes	yes	no
data granularity	bus cycle	bus transaction	bus transaction	user transaction

Table 1.   Summary of features supported or abstracted away in the models.

4.   ANALYSIS

This chapter will explore how the implemented models can be used for system modeling. Two main aspects will be examined. First, simulation performance will be evaluated, since a performance gain is the main premise of abstract modeling. Second, the accuracy of the more abstract models will be examined. Weighting the speed benefits against the accuracy drawbacks allows the designer to decide on speed/accuracy trade-off applicable for a particular design stage.

4.1   Performance

The performance of each model has been measured in a scenario with two bus nodes: one acting as a master, one as a slave. A user transaction is transferred a constant number of times, without any delay in between. The simulation time (also referred as real time or wall clock time) for executing all repetitions of the user transaction was measured and the average execution time for a single user transaction was calculated. All tests have been performed on a Pentium 4, 2.8 GHz.

The results of performance measurements in terms of simulation time are shown in Figure 3. The x-axis denotes the size of a user transaction in

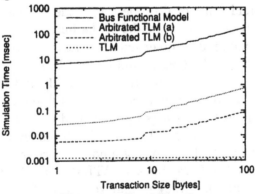

Figure 3.   Simulation time

Feature	Bus Functional Model	ATLM (a)	ATLM (b)	TLM
simulation time [ms]	27.4	0.12	0.015	0.0012
simulation bandwidth [MByte/sec]	0.0006	0.127	1.05	12.3
speedup over bus functional model	1	228	1879	22124
speedup over next more accurate model	1	228	8	12

Table 2. Model performance comparison for sending 16 bytes.

bytes. The y-axis denotes the time the simulation spends for transferring of one user transaction. Table 2 compares the performance of the models for a 16 bytes user transaction.

The performance measurements confirm the expectations: the simulation speed increases with an increase of abstraction. The TLM model executes the fastest. Its execution time is independent of the transaction size, since a constant number of operations is executed for each transfer (one *memcpy* and one *waitfor*). Transferring 16 bytes (via multiple CAN messages) takes 0.0012 ms.

The next slower model is the ATLM (b), which does not model bit stuffing and CRC. Since the ATLM models the data transfer at the level of bus transactions (CAN messages), a step is noticeable in the graph for each 8 bytes - an additional CAN message is needed for transferring the user data. The execution time increases linearly with the amount of bus transactions. A 16 byte transaction is transfered in 0.015 ms.

The ATLM (a) performs 8 times slower than the ATLM (b), since it inspects every bit of the message for the bit stuffing and the CRC calculation. The effect of the additional effort can be seen by the increase of simulation time within one frame. Transferring a 16 bytes user transaction takes 0.12 ms.

The bus functional model is two orders of magnitude slower than the ATLM (a). The additional effort of serially transmitting the data and performing the bit synchronization requires more computing power. Additionally to the increased functionality, the structure of the implementation reduces the performance. For each bus node two additional threads of execution are required, one for the bit stream processor and one for the bit timing logic. It takes 27.4 ms for transferring 16 bytes.

4.2 Accuracy

In the previous section, the gain of speedup by using models at higher level of abstraction was quantified. Now we will evaluate, which accuracy limitations the designer has to accept for achieving the higher simulation speeds. However, unlike the performance measurements before, it is hard to define a single expressive number that allows comparing the accuracy of the different models. The actual accuracy depends heavily on the environment and the actual application at hand.

4.2.1   Test Setup.

A generic test setup with 4 bus nodes was used. Two nodes act as masters and two nodes act as slaves. During the test, each master transfers a predefined set of 5000 user transactions. The user transactions vary in message id, in length and content of the transaction (1 - 16 bytes) and in the delay between two transactions (simulating local computation). All varying parameters are linear random distributed. Each master sends from an exclusive range of message ids. One master will send messages with high priority ids (0-511), the other emits messages with low priority (ids 512-1023).

During the test execution, the start time and duration (each in simulated time) of each individual user transaction is recorded, separately for each master. The test is repeated once for each implemented bus model. Since the same set of user transactions is transferred by each model, their results are comparable and can be analyzed.

Bus contention is a major concern for bus usage in general. It is expected, that model accuracy varies significantly with bus contention. Therefore the described test was repeated for different bus contentions.

The bus contention can not be controlled directly in this test. Instead, the maximum delay between two user transactions of a master has been varied between test runs. Varying the maximum delay influences the bus utilization and, since two masters access the bus during the test, it correlates to the amount of bus contention. The actual amount of contention during was measured during test execution of the bus functional model.

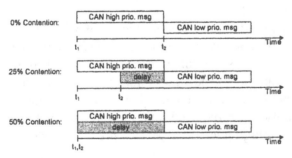

Figure 4.   Example of bus contention.

For this paper, the contention is defined as the overlap between user transactions as shown in Figure 4. The actual amount of contention, as a result of a particular maximum transaction delay, has been measured with the bus functional model. For each CAN bit time, it was measured whether one or two user transactions where active. A user transaction is active if the application is blocked for completion of the transaction. This definition of an active transaction is independent from the actual state of the bus node (e.g. pending, arbitration, active transmission). Given this basic definition, the contention is defined for this paper as:

$$contention = 100 * \frac{bus\ cycles\ with\ two\ active\ user\ transactions}{bus\ cycles\ with\ at\ least\ one\ active\ user\ transaction} \tag{1}$$

4.2.2   Analysis Based on Transfer Duration.   As described above, a test run yields a execution record of each individual user transaction. The following paragraphs will describe the analysis of the measured data.

The transfer duration of an individual user transaction is an important measure for predicting the application latency due to bus access. Therefore, in a first step, the accuracy of the models has been evaluated with respect to the transfer duration. For this purpose, the error of an individual user transaction is defined as:

$$duration_{std} : \quad transfer\ duration\ as\ per\ CAN\ standard$$
$$duration_{test} : \quad transfer\ duration\ in\ model\ under\ test$$
$$error_i \quad = \quad 100 * \frac{|duration_{test} - duration_{std}|}{duration_{std}} \tag{2}$$

Given this error definition, a timing accurate model exhibits 0% error. It was avoided to directly express the accuracy in percent, since a particular model may have an error of more than 100% (i.e. the model under test predicts more than twice the simulated time).

The first set of graphs, Figure 5a for the high priority master and Figure 5b for the low priority master, show the average timing error for a user transaction for different amounts of bus contention.

Figure 5a shows that the ATLM (a), which includes bit stuffing and CRC calculation, performs as accurate as the bus functional model (both graphs lie on top of the x-axis). This result has to be seen in perspective to the restrictions of the test, which are: no propagation delay between sending and receiving on the CAN bus, all delays between user transactions are multiple of the CAN bit time and the test starts aligned to the bit clock of the first sender. With this restrictions, reasonable for a simulation environment only, all bus accesses are performed aligned to the CAN bit clock, and no sub cycle information is needed. In this situation the additional capabilities of the bus functional model, i.e. bit synchronization, are not exercised and both the bus functional model and the ATLM (a) perform with 100% accuracy.

The ATLM (b), due to the lack of modeling the bit stuffing and CRC, performs inaccurately. For messages in the high priority range, the in-

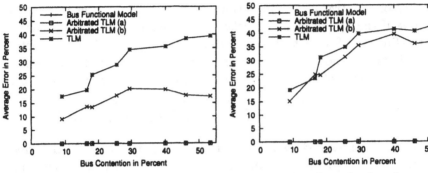

Figure 5a.   Duration based error for   *Figure 5b.*   Duration based error for
high priority messages.   low priority messages.

accuracy starts with 10% for low contention situations and platoes after linearly rising to 20% inaccuracy at 30% contention. With the lack of the bit stuff modeling, an individual message transfer is - depending on its content - shorter than in the bus functional model. Therefore, the arbitration interaction between the two senders differs. With an increasing contention the user transactions of the low priority band increasingly influence the high priority transactions. However an earlier started low priority transaction, which may consist of multiple CAN frames, can delay a later started high priority user transaction only for up to one frame. A second started CAN frame of the low priority transaction will lose arbitration, which leads to the plateau in inaccuracy at 30%.

Looking at the same scenario with reversed priorities, this limitation does not apply. A low priority user transaction may be delayed for a full high priority user transaction consisting of many CAN frames. Hence, the timing error of the ATLM (b) increases without a plateau for the low priority user transactions (Figure 5b) with increasing contention.

The TLM model, which simulates bus access on the level of user transactions only, both high and low priority give a uniform result. For both cases the inaccuracy increases with the bus contention. As to be expected, the TLM achieves the most inaccurate results (40% inaccuracy at 45% contention).

4.2.3   Analysis Based on Cumulative Transfer Duration.

The accuracy analysis based on the transfer duration is a measure to predict the application latency due to bus traffic. Additionally, the overall timing (e.g. when does the application finish?) is of interest for design decisions. For this, the same experimental results have been evaluated in terms of the cumulative transfer time, which is the sum of the user transaction durations. Figure 6a and Figure 6b show the results of the accuracy based on the cumulative transfer time.

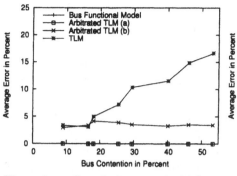

Figure 6a. Cumulative error for high priority messages.

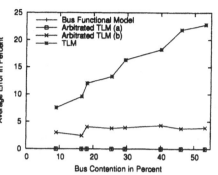

Figure 6b. Cumulative error for low priority messages.

The cumulative transfer time analysis reveals: mispredictions of the ATLM (b) for individual CAN frames average out during the test, since the model correctly captures arbitration. Regardless of priority a constant error of about 4% is measured. This can be attributed to not modeling the bit stuffing (which in average adds 4% bits). The TLM, with its coarse grain contention resolution independent of priority, shows for both priority ranges a linear increasing inaccuracy.

5. CONCLUSION

This paper has reported on a case study, based on the CAN bus, for abstract communication modeling. Three major models have been implemented: the bus functional model, the arbitrated transaction level model (ATLM) and the transaction level model (TLM). Additionally, two variances have been created for the ATLM.

The usability of the models has been evaluated. With respect to the simulation performance, a speedup of two magnitudes was measured from the bus functional model to the ATLM (a). With each further increase of abstraction (to the ATLM (b), and TLM) an additional speedup of one order of magnitude was measured.

A detailed analysis of the simulation accuracy of each model has been done. Based on the analysis results, Table 3 lists the fastest model, that yields acceptable results for a given environment and simulation focus.

Environment Condition	Applicable Model
• no overlap between masters bus access • early stage in design	TLM
• main focus on application finish time	ATLM (b)
• main focus on individual transfer delay	ATLM (a)
• synthesizable • using propagation delay	bus functional

Table 3. Model selection

The TLM can only be used in very early stages of the design. Its accuracy, for individual and cumulative transfer time, degrades heavily with increasing bus contention. The still fast ATLM (b) is applicable in scenarios, where the main focus is on the application finish time. This model is not suitable for predicting an individual transfer delay, since the duration based analysis has not shown acceptable results.

The ATLM (a), which includes bit stuffing and CRC calculation, has shown 100% accuracy given the test restrictions (e.g. no propagation delay). It is the fastest model that accurately predicts the delay of an individual transfer in all contention situations. The bus functional model is necessary as a synthesizable model, or in case the simulation includes propagation delay on the simulated CAN bus.

REFERENCES

[1] Denny Brem and Dietmar Müller. Interface based system modeling of a CAN using SVE. In *EkompaSS Workshop*, Hanover, Germany, April 2003.

[2] M. Caldari et al. Transaction-level models for AMBA bus architecture using SystemC 2.0. In *DATE*, Munich, Germany, March 2003.

[3] Daniel D. Gajski et al. *SpecC: Specification Language and Design Methodology*. Kluwer Academic Publishers, 2000.

[4] A. Gerstlauer et al. System-Level Communication Modeling for Network-on-Chip Synthesis. In *ASP-DAC*, Shanghai, China, January 2005.

[5] A. Gerstlauer and D. Gajski. System-level abstraction semantics. In *ISSS*, Kyoto, Japan, October 2002.

[6] Thorsten Grötker, Stan Liao, Grant Martin, and Stuart Swan. *System Design with SystemC*. Kluwer Academic Publishers, 2002.

[7] Florian Hartwich and Armin Bassemir. The Configuration of the CAN Bit Timing. http://www.can.bosch.com/, 1999.

[8] Internation Organization for Standardization (ISO). *Reference Model of Open System Interconnection (OSI)*, second edition, 1994. ISO/IEC 7498 Standard.

[9] Philips. P8xC592: 8-bit microcontroller with on-chip CAN. http://www.semiconductors.philips.com, 1996.

[10] Robert Bosch GmbH. *CAN Specification*, 2.0 edition, 1991. http://www.can.bosch.com/.

[11] M. Sgroi et al. Addressing the system-on-a-chip interconnect woes through communication based design. In *DAC*, June 2001.

[12] R. Siegmund and D. Müller. SystemC^{SV}: An Extension of SystemC for Mixed Multi-Level Communication Modeling and Interface-Based System Design. In *DATE*, Munich, Germany, March 2001.

ADAPTABLE SWITCH BOXES AS ON-CHIP ROUTING NODES FOR NETWORKS-ON-CHIP

Ralf Eickhoff, Jörg-Christian Niemann, Mario Porrmann, Ulrich Rückert
Heinz Nixdorf Institute, System and Circuit Technology, University of Paderborn
Fürstenallee 11, 33102 Paderborn, Germany
{eickhoff,niemann,porrmann,rueckert}@hni.upb.de

Abstract: Due to continuous advancements in modern technology processes which have resulted in integrated circuits with smaller feature sizes and higher complexity, current system-on-chip designs consist of many different components such as memories, interfaces and microprocessors. To handle this growing number of components, an efficient communication structure must be provided and incorporated during system design. This work deals with the implementation of an efficient communication structure for an on-chip multiprocessor design. The internal structure of one node is proposed and specified by its requirements. Furthermore, different routing strategies are implemented. Moreover, the communication structure is mapped on a standard cell process to examine the achieved processing speed and to determine the area requirements.

Keywords: Switch Box, Networks-on-Chip, System-on-Chip, Multiprocessor Architectures

1.   INTRODUCTION

Due to upcoming improvements in semiconductor processes it is possible to integrate a huge amount of components on a single chip. Consequently, different Intellectual Property (IP) cores have to cooperate and to communicate with each other. Thus, when designing the system, an efficient communication structure must be provided, which is able to manage the traffic between all components. On the one hand, many existing approaches known from computer networks can be adapted to networks-on-chip (NoCs). For example, a circuit-switching network or a packet-switching network can be established and the performance and flexibility trade-off has to be solved. On the other hand, these networks-on-chip differ from traditional computer networks. In a packet-switched network-on-chip, for example, the packet size will mostly be much smaller than in a computer network. Furthermore, the geometrical dimensions of such a network are much smaller compared to computer networks. Consequently, lower latency and higher throughput can be achieved. In this paper, we present a network-on-chip, which is based on the packet switching approach. It is able to handle the traffic between an unlimited but known number of modules.

After a short account on how the design of the network-on-chip was motivated, the implementation is presented in section 2 where the topology of the network and the topology of each node are shown. In section 3 two different routing strategies are analyzed. In section 4 we present first results of a synthesis of this network structure.

1.1   Motivation

Due to increasing traffic in computer networks and due to the growth of the whole network there is an increasing demand to manage the traffic [2]. For this task, a general purpose processor is not efficient for the required performance whereas an application-specific instruction processor (ASIP) such as a network processor (NPU) is more suitable. Today, these complex architectures can be integrated into one single chip due to modern design techniques, as mentioned in the introduction.

In the GigaNetIC project [9] we aim at developing high-speed components for networking applications based on massively parallel architectures. A central part of this project is the design, evaluation, and realization of a parameterizable network processing unit. The proposed architecture is based on massively parallel processing, enabled by a multitude of processors, which form a homogeneous array of processing elements arranged in a hierarchical system topology with a powerful communication infrastructure. Four processing elements are connected via an on-chip bus to a so-called switch box [10], cf. figure 1, which allows a forming of arbitrary on-chip topologies. Hardware accelerators support the processing elements to achieve a higher throughput and help to reduce energy consumption. Following a top-down approach, network applications are analyzed and partitioned into smaller tasks. The tasks are mapped to dedicated parts of the system, where a parallelizing compiler exploits inherent instruction level parallelism. The hardware has to be optimized for these programming models in several ways. Synchronization primitives for both programming hierarchies have to be provided and memory resources have to be managed carefully. Furthermore, the shown dimension of the system is only one example of our multiprocessor system. The number of parallel operating processors can be further increased. As a core component of our architecture, we use a 32 bit RISC CPU, the S-Core, which has been designed in our research group [6]. By changing the number of ports of the switch boxes the topology of the on-chip network can be arbitrarily formed including meshes, butterfly networks or tori [1]. For our first implementation we have chosen a mesh topology due to efficient hardware integration (cf. section 4).

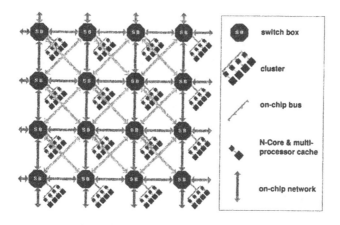

Figure 1.   Architecture of the network processor proposed in the GigaNetIC project

2.   IMPLEMENTATION OF THE NETWORK-ON-CHIP

As in computer networks, different requirements have to be considered in order to find an efficient implementation for a special application. An important issue of a common network is the underlying graph. This has a strong impact on several parameters of the network affecting latency, throughput etc. When the topology of the network is fixed each switch box can be designed due to its requirements. The inputs for example, have to face tasks like storing and delivering packets. In the following these packets will be referred to as flits, which represent the atomic transportation units in our approach [7].

2.1   Topology of the network

The network-on-chip can be evaluated with the methods known in computer networks. Consequently, the existing models can be adapted to characterize the network and the topology can be described by a graph. Besides common similarities in respect to the modeling of a network, some differences are still present. Compared to a computer network, a network-on-chip is marked by several differences [5]:

- different geometrical dimension; a system-on-chip obtains short distances to other nodes

- parallel communication structures are easier to establish on a chip without high costs

- higher bandwidth due to parallel communication structures

- deterministic and periodic traffic

- smaller packet size

Consequently, these characteristics have to be considered in the network topology. For the application as a network processor the on-chip network has to meet the following requirements:

- regular communication structure

- high scalability during design time

- good re-use

- high performance

Moreover, as the production process maps the communication structure on a two-dimensional surface a regular communication structure is provided by a two-dimensional graph. Thus, the 2-d grid, the 2-d torus and the binary tree are well suited to achieve a regular communication structure. The binary tree provides a small bisection bandwidth which results in high throughput requirements next to the root of the tree. Thus, a communication link that allows higher throughput in comparison to the other links of the net has to be established. This also leads to an irregular structure.

The grid and the torus provide a regular communication structure and have no technical limits in respect to a growing number of nodes. Consequently, these structures can be used when a new design of the network processor contains more computing arrays and thus more nodes. The main disadvantage of a torus is the circular connection. This causes longer interconnection delays at the boundaries, and leads to lower operating speed in a globally synchronous design [8].

We have chosen the grid as the topology for the network-on-chip. In order to provide a high scalability during design time slight modifications have been implemented. The nodes are not only connected to their direct neighbors but also to their neighbors lying on the diagonal, causing a shorter diameter of the whole network, as can be seen in figure 1. Compared to a conventional grid, this introduces a higher connectivity and a shorter diameter.

2.2   Structure of each switch box

When the topology of the network-on-chip is determined, each switch box of the net has to handle the information streams, which are split into several flits by the processor array. Thus, the switch box has to handle each flit independently and autonomously. One task provided by this node is to store the flits. Moreover, in order to relieve the connected processor array the switch box has to route the flit through the net autonomously. This requires a routing decision inside each box and a communication structure between the input and

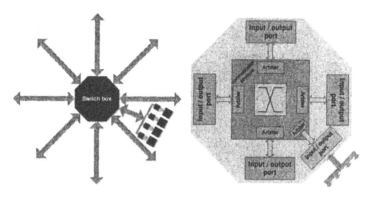

(a) switch box with an inter switch box connectivity of nine

(b) internal structure of each switch box with a connectivity of five, one port for the connected processor array

Figure 2.   Structure and connectivity of each switch box in the middle of the grid

output ports of every node. Figure 2(b) shows the structure of our approach. Here, due to a generic description the whole number of input and output ports can be changed during design time easily and all components are adapted to the number of ports.

One requirement of each box is to store the flits. Due to independent information streams, a distributed memory approach is used in contrast to shared memory by implementing FIFOs in each port. FIFO structures are able to achieve a higher performance and, compared to shared memory, do not need a complex control structure. In contrast, the FIFOs in each port establish a queuing line and the head-of-line-blocking problem has to be faced if only one queue is provided [4]. Thus, in every input port one queue of FIFOs is used for each output, known in literature as *virtual-output-queuing* (VOQ) [11]. Inside the output ports no parallel queue has to be established since this function can be transferred to the input port of the adjacent switch box.

For the communication structure inside each switch box, a crossbar is established in order meet the high performance requirements inside each box. A bus structure is not able to guarantee high throughput because one participant blocks all the other accesses even though these might be disjunctive. Anyway, at each output port an arbiter must be provided because two or more inputs could deliver their flits to the same output. A suitable solution to arbitrate these accesses is to provide a round-robin arbiter for each output. Our approach uses a modification of [3] to improve the operating speed. Thus, only two of the proposed arbitrary stages are established with the result of a non-bijective mapping. This leads to a pipeline length of two stages and, consequently, a shorter latency.

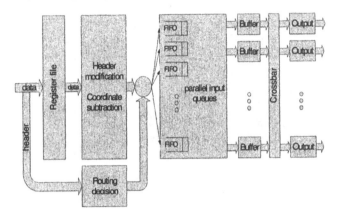

Figure 3.   Structure of an input port

2.3   Structure of one port

As mentioned earlier, each switch box has to store each flit at the input or output in a virtual output queue. This task can be managed by an input or an output or by both. Consequently, the function of an output of one node can be transferred to the input of the next neighbor so that complexity is reduced. It suffices to use the storage function in the output port if the interconnection delay between two switch boxes becomes too long. In contrast, if only one storage queue is provided at the output port, head-of-line-blocking will occur also. Thus, nearly the same input structure must be used at the output. So long as the critical path is not determined by the interconnection delay, the output of the crossbar can be directly connected to the input of the neighboring node.

Besides storing the flits and separating them into parallel input queues every input has to change the header of a flit that contains information about its destination. Thus, the structure shown in figure 3 is developed. Here, the flits are stored in a register file because of the routing decision, which takes computation time. In parallel to this decision the header modification is applied and each flit is stored in a FIFO. Multicast and broadcast functions can also be implemented.

3.   ROUTING STRATEGY

In our approach the information is split into several flits that are routed through the net to the target node. In contrast to a circuit-switched network the path through the net is not reserved and each node handles the flits autonomously. Two different strategies can be used to determine the path through the network. Due to the underlying grid topology, Cartesian coordinates can be used to determine the destination node. Each flit consists of a header that includes a two-dimensional destination vector. This vector relatively points to the target node from the current position in the network. Thus, the vector has to be modified if one flit is sent to a neighbor node.

3.1 Dynamic routing

The flits have to be delivered from the source node to its destination. Instead of establishing a central routing decision at the initial node, the dynamic routing is used inside each switch box, especially inside each input port (cf. figure 3). Central routing algorithms such as Dijkstra or Bellman-Ford algorithms require a global knowledge of the network. This would result in extensive hardware if this task is transferred into the switch box relaxing the processor array. Moreover, these algorithms need information about the communication costs, which are mainly based on the actual traffic in a system-on-chip design since the network and the communication structure between two nodes are regular. Thus, due to high throughput these costs change immediately. This results in another optimal path through the network.

The connectivity of each switch box can be increased (see section 2) resulting in additional output ports. Here, each output port is identified by its coordinates and is allocated by costs stored in registers. Each flit is temporarily stored at the input and the information about the header is extracted. With this information, the corresponding quadrant is chosen so that we have a subset of all outputs. The output port with the minimum cost is selected. Then, the flit is stored in the according FIFO queue, the header modification is performed and, with this, the relative position of the flit changes.

3.2 Static routing

By using this strategy the way of each flit through the network is predetermined. When arriving at an input port, the header information is extracted and the flit is switched to the output port depending on the quadrant (x-y routing). For a switch box with a connectivity of four, this results in a transmission to positive or negative x/y direction. First, the corresponding column is chosen by switching the flit to the node at which the x coordinate of the vector equals zero. As long as the y coordinate is unequal to zero the flit is switched in y direction. After storing the flit the header modification is the same for both routing strategies.

This technique chooses the shortest way through the net if a grid with a connectivity of four is used as topology. If the connectivity increases this technique is inefficient and must be adapted. If the x coordinate or y coordinate has already been reached the flit is sent into the remaining y direction or x direction. If no corresponding row or column is reached the next node is chosen depending on the ratio of both coordinates. Thus, the flit covers the largest distance toward its destination so that the shortest way through the net will

Table 1. Results of synthesis on UMC 130 nm @1.2 V (one switch box)

number of flits[1]	ports per switch box	delay bc/wc[2] [ns]	frequency [GHz]	area [mm^2]	power bc/wc [W]	throughput bc/wc [Gbit/s]
dynamic and static routing						
5	5	0.80/1.78	1.25/0.56	0.5621	2,966/0.855	200/90
10	5	0.86/1.85	1.16/0.54	0.9019	2.954/0.834	186/86
20	5	0.90/1.80	1.11/0.55	1.8059	2.886/0.930	177/89
5	9	1.00/2.25	1.00/0.44	1.8488	2.799/0.745	288/128
10	9	1.09/2.30	0.92/0.43	2.9209	3.101/0.803	264/125
20	9	1.13/2.46	0.88/0.41	5.5675	3.579/0.859	255/117
5	17	1.50/3.10	0.66/0.33	6.6744	2.805/0.756	363/175
static routing only						
5	5	0.72/1.63	1.39/0.61	0.5542	3.368/0.932	222/98
10	5	0.77/1.57	1.30/0.64	0.8803	3.185/0.990	208/102
20	5	0.75/1.56	1.33/0.64	1.7329	3.469/1.045	213/102
5	9	0.95/2.00	1.05/0.50	1.7827	2.901/0.857	303/144
10	9	0.92/2.00	1.08/0.50	2.8223	3.411/0.931	313/144
20	9	0.99/2.10	1.01/0.47	5.5881	3.886/1.024	291/137
5	17	1.10/2.50	0.91/0.40	6.5350	2.804/0.942	494/218

also be found with these modifications when the connectivity is bigger than the standard connectivity of a grid.

Both possibilities (dynamic and static routing) are implemented in our system. After a flit has been received, it is stored in one of the parallel queues based on the static or dynamic routing. Depending on application demands the routing strategy can be changed immediately by special control flits. Before storing the flit, the header has to be modified due to a change in the position because no storage elements are being provided at the outputs. Thus, the destination vector has to be modified before leaving the queue. Additionally, a header modification behind the queues would have increased the critical path substantially.

4.   SYNTHESIS OF ONE NODE

In this section, we analyze the on-chip network related to latency, throughput, area, and power consumption, in dependence on storage capacity and connectivity of the switch box. A first prototype has been implemented on

---

[1] stored in each FIFO
[2] best case and worst case conditions

a modern standard cell technology provided by UMC (0.13 μm@1.2 V). Our approach for the communication structure is designed in such a way that several parameters such as flit width, storage capacity of the FIFO structures and the header size and, with this, the whole dimension of the mesh can be easily changed before synthesis.

Table 1 gives an overview of the synthesis results for various storage capacities and various connectivities of each switch box while the width of one flit is set to 32 bit including an eight bit destination vector (although these parameters can be changed later). The connectivity is changed by increasing the number of ports. The table shows the critical path delay, the area of one node, and the power consumption at a certain connectivity. The power is computed with Synopsys Design Power for the maximum speed of each switch box version. The width of the destination vector is fixed because the expected size of the system will be in this dimension. Due to the sign-magnitude representation of the vector a $2^3 \times 2^3$ grid^3 can be addressed, which is suitable for the proposed multiprocessor.

It can be concluded from table 1 that the dynamic routing has a negative impact on the network due to a longer critical path and higher area consumption. Thus, the implementation of both routing strategies has to be considered in dependence on the application. If only static routing is provided a compact design with less area consumption and higher throughput, based on a higher system clock, is achieved, whereas dynamic routing can relieve edges of traffic with the help of cost tables (e.g., in an universal coprocessor design). Furthermore, the proposed network can handle a throughput of 20 Gbit/s per port in each direction if a flit size of 32 bit is assumed. Throughput can be enhanced if the number of parallel interconnections is further increased by using a larger flit size.

5.   CONCLUSION

In this work, a network-on-chip for an on-chip multiprocessor design has been proposed. The topology was chosen as a grid to provide a regular communication structure and a good re-use possibility for further implementations. Moreover, each node has been designed to handle the traffic autonomously and provides a good scalability with growing networks. Two routing strategies have been implemented in the switch box design and are analyzed in respect to their performance and resource requirements. Providing a maximum throughput of about 500 Gbit/s, a prototypical implementation has been designed by using a 130nm CMOS technology.

---

^{3}Thus a $64 \cdot 4 = 256$ processor array can be implemented.

Acknowledgement

The project outlined in this work was funded by the Federal Ministry of Education and Research (Bundesministerium für Bildung und Forschung), registered there under 01M3062A. Theauthors of this publication are fully responsible for its contents. This work was supported in part by Infineon Technologies AG, especially the department CPR ST, Prof. Ramacher and by the German Research Council DFG, SFB 376.

REFERENCES

[1] A. Brinkmann, J.-C. Niemann, I. Hehemann, D. Langen, M. Porrmann, and U. Rückert. On-Chip Interconnects for Next Generation System-on-Chips. In *Proc. of the 15th Annual IEEE International ASIC/SOC Conference*, pages 211 – 215, September 2002.

[2] U. Brinkschulte, J. Becker, and T. Ungerer. CARUSO - an approach towards a network of low power autonomic systems on chips for embedded real-time applications. In *18th International Parallel and Distributed Processing Symposium (IPDPS'04) - Workshop 2*, Apr. 2004.

[3] A. Gupta, F. G. Gustavson, M. Joshi, and S. Toledo. Design and implementation of a fast crossbar scheduler. *ACM Transactions on Mathematical Software*, 24(1):74–101, 1998.

[4] M. J. Karol, M. G. Hluchyj, and S. P. Morgan. Input versus output queueing on a space-division packet switch. *IEEE trans. on commun.*, COM-35:1347–1356, 1987.

[5] S. Kumar. On packet switching networks for on-chip communication. In A. Jantsch and H. Tenhunen, editors, *Networks on Chip*, chapter 5. Kluwer Academic Publishers, 2003.

[6] D. Langen, J.-C. Niemann, M. Porrmann, H. Kalte, and U. Rückert. Implementation of a risc processor core for soc designs fpga prototype vs. asic implementation. In *Proc. of the IEEE-Workshop: Heterogeneous reconfigurable Systems on Chip (SoC)*, Hamburg, Germany, 2002.

[7] Z. Lu and A. Jantsch. Flit admission in on-chip wormhole-switched networks with virtual channels. In *Proceedings of the International Symposium on System-on-Chip 2003*, Nov. 2004.

[8] J. Muttersbach, T. Villiger, H. Kaeslin, N. Felber, and W. Fichtner. Globally-asynchronous locally-synchronous architectures to simplify the design of on-chip systems. In *Proc. 12th International ASIC/SOC Conference*, pages 317–321, Sept. 1999.

[9] J.-C. Niemann and et al. A holistic methodology for network processor design. In *Proc. of the Workshop on High-Speed Local Networks held in conjunction with the 28th Annual IEEE Conference on Local Computer Networks*, pages 583 – 592, Oct. 2003.

[10] J.-C. Niemann, M. Porrmann, and U. Rückert. A scalable parallel soc architecture for network processors. In *IEEE Computer Society Annual Symposium on VLSI (ISVLSI)*, Tampa, FL., USA, 2005.

[11] Y. Tamir and G. Frazier. High-performance multiqueue buffers for VLSI communication switches. *15th Annual International Symposium on Computer Architecture*, pages 343–354, 1988.

INTEGRATION OF TWO COMPLEMENTARY TIME-TRIGGERED TECHNOLOGIES: TMO AND TTP

R. Obermaisser[1], E. Henrich[2], K.H. Kim[2], H. Kopetz[1], M.H. Kim[3]
[1]*Vienna University of Technology, Vienna, Austria*
[2]*University of California, Irvine, CA, 92697 U.S.A*
[3]*KonKuk University, Seoul, Korea*

Abstract: The TMO model for real-time distributed object-computing supports the specification of temporal constraints with respect to a global time base and provides execution engines for ensuring that these constraints are met at runtime. This paper describes a solution for supporting TMO applications on top of the Time-Triggered Architecture, a system architecture that meets the dependability requirements of safety-critical applications. Thereby, the TMO model advances to the domain of safety-related and safety-critical systems. Due to an ongoing trend in transportation systems (e.g., automotive industry) of increasing functionality and complexity, this domain can benefit from the intuitive and programmer-friendly TMO scheme. We realize TMO on top of the TTA by establishing a Kernel Abstraction Layer (KAL) for the TTP/RTAI-Linux platform. This KAL maps the platform services used by the TMO support middleware to the service of the TTP protocol and the operations of RTAI-Linux. KAL also layers event-triggered communication for remote method invocations and multicast channels on top of the purely time-triggered TTP protocol.

Keywords: Real-time Systems, Distributed Object-Computing, Time-triggered Control

1.   INTRODUCTION

Distributed object computing is a widely accepted model for conquering the complexity of large distributed systems. Each object represents a nearly-independent subsystem (Simon, 1996, chap. 8) that is designed without being influenced by the internal details of other objects.

The Time-triggered Message-triggered Object (TMO) model (Kim et al., 1994) has extended distributed object computing to the area of distributed real-time computing in an intuitively appealing form. TMO combines the complexity management benefits of the object-oriented paradigm with the ability to explicitly specify temporal constraints in terms of global time in natural forms. In addition, TMO execution engines based on several major platforms (e.g., Windows NT (Kim and Ishida, 1999), Windows CE (Gimenez and Kim, 2001), and Linux (Kim et al., 2002)) have been developed. An execution engine consists of a commercial operating system (OS) kernel, middleware devised to support TMOs, and libraries of object classes for a particular programming language which wraps the services of the middleware and collectively serve as an approximation of an ideal TMO programming language. An execution engine honors the temporal constraints specifications by managing execution resources judiciously.

With the increasing functionality of electronics in safety-related and safety-critical real-time applications, the need for programming models that facilitate the effective management of growing complexity in this domain has become acute. Currently, in embedded system design such as the design activities in the automotive domain, assembly and C language are still prevalent (VDC, 2003). The distributed object computing paradigm can be exploited to reduce design costs, time-to-market, and the number of software-related recalls. A prerequisite for applying this technology to safety-related and safety-critical applications is the ability to certify the resulting systems. In this regard, the underlying distributed computing platform must be based on an architecture that supports safety-critical fault-tolerant computing.

This paper describes an approach for distributed real-time object computing on a platform architecture that is appropriate for safety-critical applications. We realize TMO on top of the Time-Triggered Architecture (TTA) (Kopetz and Bauer, 2003). Formal analysis (Rushby, 2002) and experiments (Ademaj et al., 2003) have demonstrated that the TTA with its communication protocol TTP is appropriate for the implementation of applications in the highest criticality class (e.g., class A according to RTCA DO-178B (RTCA, 1992)).

The realization of TMO on TTP platforms is an integration of two complementary time-triggered technologies that work at different levels. The TTP technology offers formally verified architectural services, such as a clock synchronization service with high precision, a communication service with low latency and low jitter, and error containment between components. The TMO technology builds higher-level services by making use of the services of TTP platforms and wrap them onto a uniform Application Programming Interface (API) for real-time distributed computing object programming. It exploits the services of TTP in exchanging messages for remote method invocations and in realizing logical multicast communication channels, as well as in global synchronization of the executions of application and middleware threads.

Furthermore, the integration of TMO and TTP enables distributed real-time object computing for applications with sub-millisecond-level temporal precision requirements. Low transmission latencies and low jitter are important factors for realizing a high degree of quality-of-service in control loops. In addition, a global time base with a precision in the range of a few microseconds enables design of a certain class of real-time applications in the form of distributed object computing, which was not possible before (Kim et al., 2005).

This paper is structured as follows. Section 2 gives an overview of the TMO model and describes the requirements for an underlying platform. The TTA, which is employed as the platform for TMO in this paper, is the focus of Section 3. In Section 4, we discuss the Kernel Abstraction Layer (KAL) for the TTP/RTAI-Linux platform. Section 5 provides results on the temporal performance of the implementation and discusses the merits of integrating TMO and TTP.

2.   TIME-TRIGGERED MESSAGE-TRIGGERED OBJECTS

TMO is a natural and syntactically minor but semantically powerful extension of conventional objects (Kim, 2000). Significant extensions realized by the TMO scheme are summarized below.

(1) *Globally referenced time base*: All time references in a TMO are references to global time in that their meaning and correctness are unaffected by the location of the TMO.

(2) *Distributed computing component*: TMOs distributed over multiple nodes may interact via remote method calls. TMOs can also interact via logical multicast channels called Real-time Multicast and Memory-replication channels (RMMC).

(3) *Spontaneous method (SpM)*: TMO introduces a new type of methods, spontaneous methods (SpMs) (also called time-triggered methods), which are clearly separated from the conventional service methods (SvMs). The SpM executions are triggered by the real-time clock at points in time specified as constants during design time, whereas the SvM executions are triggered by service request messages from clients.

(4) *Basic concurrency constraint (BCC)*: This rule prevents potential conflicts between SpMs and SvMs and reduces the designer's efforts in guaranteeing timely service capabilities of TMOs. Under BCC, the activation of

an SvM triggered by a message from an external client is allowed only to the extent of not disturbing any SpM execution.

(5) *Guaranteed completion time (GCT) and deadline for result arrival:* The TMO incorporates deadlines in the most general form. Basically, for output actions and method completions of a TMO, the designer guarantees and advertises execution time-windows bounded by start times and completion times. In addition, deadlines can be specified in the client's calls for SvMs for the return of the service results.

2.1   Basic Structure of TMOSM

TMO Support Middleware (TMOSM) is a TMO execution support middleware model which can be easily adapted to most COTS platforms. Prototype versions of TMOSM currently exist for Windows XP, Windows CE and Linux. Within TMOSM, the innermost core is a super-micro thread called the WTST (Watchdog Timer & Scheduler Thread). It is a "super-thread" in that it runs at the highest possible priority level. It is also a "micro-thread" in that it manages the scheduling / activation of all other threads in TMOSM.

2.2   Requirements for an Underlying Platform

TMOSM relies on many system services provided by the underlying OS kernel in order to complete its tasks. The OS-dependent functionality has been grouped into a separate module called Kernel Adaptation Layer (KAL) so that the porting work can be easily achieved by plugging in a new native implementation of KAL built on the host OS.

The KAL specification precisely defines the functionality and timeliness requirements imposed on the underlying platform (i.e., hardware, OS kernel and C++ compiler) by TMOSM. The major components of KAL are described below:

(1) Time services: The scheduler in TMOSM, WTST, relies on a timer to trigger its execution. Since all threading activities in TMOSM are scheduled by WTST, the resolution and the precision of the timer are crucial to the performance of TMOSM. To achieve reasonable performance, TMOSM demands a timer with at least 100 microsecond-level precision. In addition, KAL should support the creation and setting of a timer object representing the current system time. This timer must have a 64-bit horizon and a resolution of one microsecond.

(2) Thread services: TMOSM has two major requirements regarding the threading support by KAL. First, KAL must be able to create a thread with the highest priority in the system. WTST needs to be given this priority so that it can run immediately each time it becomes ready and it may not be preempted by other threads. This is essential to guarantee the timely and predictable schedule of all activities in the TMOSM. Secondly, the thread

should be light-weighted, namely, threads should share the same process address space. This is necessary in order to limit the overhead incurred in the context switches that occur with high frequency in TMOSM.

(3) Synchronization services: Events are primarily used to synchronize the activities of different threads in TMOSM. There are two major requirements regarding the event support by KAL. First, the delivery of an event must be reliable. Events cannot be lost even when multiple events are signaled simultaneously. The other requirement is that a thread can wait for multiple events, and the arrival of any of those events should resume the execution of the waiting thread.

(4) Communication services: KAL supports the standard socket operations, in particular, sending and receiving UDP packets through a socket.

3. TIME-TRIGGERED ARCHITECTURE

The Time-Triggered Architecture (TTA) provides a computing infrastructure for the design and implementation of dependable distributed real-time systems (Kopetz and Bauer, 2003). Structuring rules guide the designer in the decomposition of the overall system into components that can fail independently. In addition, the TTA offers to system designers a validated stable baseline of generic architectural services for the development of applications.

3.1 System Structure

The basic building block of the TTA is a node computer, which is a self-contained composite hardware/software subsystem (system component). A cluster is a set of nodes that are interconnected by two redundant communication channels. For the interconnection of nodes, the TTA distinguishes between two physical interconnection topologies, namely a TTA-bus and a TTA-star. A TTA-bus consists of replicated passive buses. Every node is connected to two independent guardians, which use the a priori knowledge about the points in time of communication activities to prevent communication outside a node's time-slot. In the TTA-star topology, the interconnection of nodes occurs via two replicated central guardians. The star topology has the advantage of a higher level of independence, since guardians are located at a physical distance from nodes (Ademaj et al., 2003).

3.2 Architectural Services

The TTA provides four services essential for cost-effective construction of real-time fault-tolerant systems, which are implemented by the Time-Triggered Protocol (TTP):

- **Deterministic and Timely Transport of Messages.** The TTP protocol uses *Time Division Multiple Access* (TDMA) to control the media access to the two independent communication channels. The periodicity of the message transmissions is defined within a *cluster cycle*. Information about the points in time of all message transmissions during a cluster cycle is contained in a static message schedule. The cluster cycle is divided into a sequence of *TDMA rounds* and each TDMA round is partitioned into time slots. Slots are statically assigned to nodes in a way that allows each of them to send a message during the TDMA round.
- **Fault-Tolerant Clock Synchronization.** TTP provides fault-tolerant clock synchronization via the Fault-Tolerant Average (FTA) clock synchronization algorithm (Lundelius and Lynch, 1984) in order to establish a global time base without relying on a central time server.
- **Strong Fault Isolation.** Although a *Fault Containment Region* (FCR) can demarcate the immediate impact of a fault, fault effects manifested as erroneous data must be prevented from propagating across FCR boundaries (Lala and Harper, 1994). For this reason, the TTA provides *error containment* within an FCR for message timing failures recognized within the fault hypothesis of the TTA (Kopetz, 2004). In addition, the TTA offers a reliable distributed computing platform by ensuring that a message is either consistently received by all correct nodes or detected as being faulty at all correct nodes.
- **Membership service.** The membership service provides nodes with consistent information about the operational state of every node in the cluster.

4.   IMPLEMENTATION OF TMO ON THE TTA

This section describes the RTAI-Linux / TTP platform employed for the integration of TMO and TTP. In addition, we describe the adaptations of KAL in order to realize the platform services required by TMO. We have mapped the communication and time services of KAL to TTP, while realizing thread and synchronization services with RTAI-Linux operations.

4.1   Platform

The basic platform comprises a cluster of TTP monitoring nodes (TTTech, 2002) interconnected by a redundant 25 Mbps TTP network. Each node is equipped with a TTP C2 communication controller and a Motorola embedded PowerPC processor MPC855T. The TTP monitoring node uses the embedded real-time Linux variant, Real-Time Application Interface (RTAI) (Beal et al., 2000), as its OS kernel. RTAI combines a real-time hardware abstraction layer (RTHAL) with a real-time application interface for making Linux suitable for hard real-time applications.

4.2   Kernel Abstraction Layer

The Kernel Abstraction Layer (KAL) provides classes for accessing the OS kernel services from the TMO support middleware. The purpose of KAL is to simplify the porting of the TMO execution engine to different kernel platforms.

4.2.1   Time Services

The time services of KAL support the creation and destruction of time objects, the setting of time handlers, and the determination of the current time. KAL timers support a "horizon" of 64 bits and a granularity that depends on the quality of the employed clock synchronization algorithm. For adapting TMO to TTP, we have extended the horizon of the TTP global time (see Section 3.2) from 16 bit to 64 bit at a granularity of $5\mu s$. This horizon corresponds to $2.9 \cdot 10^6$ years, thus preventing a timer overflow within the lifetime of the system.

Another purpose of the time services is the periodic activation of WTST which is in turn responsible for causing the scheduling of the other middleware and application threads. WTST uses the synchronization services of KAL in order to wait for multiple events, including an event triggered by the signaled timer. The TTP handler does the signaling of this event at the beginning of each TDMA round, which has a duration of 3 ms in the TTP communication schedule. This way, the scheduling of WTST is synchronized with the underlying time-triggered TTP communication.

4.2.2   Thread Services

The realization of KAL's thread services involves RTAI operations for the creation of fixed-priority, light-weighted processes designated as *real-time tasks*. RTAI priorities for real-time tasks range from 0 (highest), which is assigned to WTST, to 0x3fffFfff (lowest). Linux is assigned priority 0x7fffFfff, which is considered a non-real-time task.

4.2.3   Synchronization Services

RTAI does not provide events that can directly meet KAL's requirements regarding synchronization services. Instead, semaphores are used, as illustrated in Figure 1. Setting an event and waiting for an event are easily achieved by signaling and waiting for an associated semaphore. When a thread waits for multiple events, it actually waits for one semaphore shared by multiple events, e.g. multiple events are represented by the same semaphore. Also, to ensure that no event gets lost when several of them occur at the same time, events are recorded into a circular buffer inside KAL when they are set. Operations on the event buffer are protected by disabling all hardware interrupts.

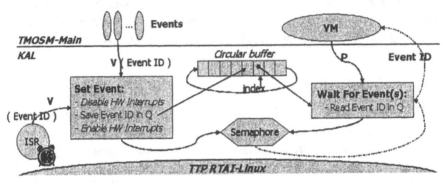

Figure 1. Threads Synchronization Using Semaphores

4.2.4   Communication Services

KAL provides to TMOSM-Main a socket interface, which is the de facto standard API for TCP/IP. Sockets can be dynamically created and destroyed and each socket is assigned a local name via a port number. The socket is assumed to queue messages in order to process messages exactly once.

TTP, on the other hand, provides a temporal firewall interface (Kopetz, 1997) for the periodic exchange of state variables. The sender deposits information into the Communication Network Interface (CNI) according to the information push paradigm, while the receiver must pull information out of the CNI. The TTP protocol autonomously carries the state information from the CNI of the sender to the CNI of the receivers at a priori specified global points in time. Since applications are often interested in the most recent value of a real-time entity, old state values are overwritten by newer state values.

For each TDMA round and each node in the cluster, the CNI contains a dedicated state variable. At a particular node n the state variable associated with n at this node's CNI is written by the application, while all other state variables are read by the application. The communication system behaves inversely, reading the state variable associated with n before broadcasting its contents via the network. All other state variables are updated with the contents of messages received from other nodes. The global point in time of a message reception not only denotes the identity of the sending node, but also determines the state variable in the CNI that is to be overwritten.

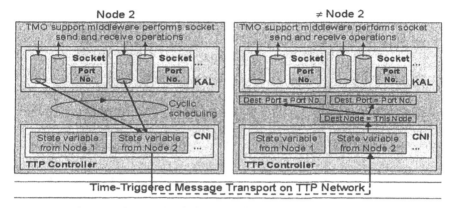

Figure 2. Transmission at Node 2 (left) and Reception by Another Node (right)

Since the temporal firewall interface of TTP is purely time-triggered, we have implemented event-triggered sockets on top of TTP in KAL. Each socket contains an incoming and an outgoing message queue. TMOSM-Main inserts messages that need to be broadcast into the outgoing queue, while KAL removes the messages and puts them into the CNI. The incoming message queue contains messages that have been received from other nodes.

As depicted in Figure 2, a node's slot in the TDMA scheme is shared among the sockets in that node. For sending messages to other nodes, KAL goes through all sockets in the node in a circular fashion. If the currently checked socket contains a message that needs to be broadcast, then KAL copies the message into the CNI of the TTP controller. Consequently, the message will be autonomously transferred to the CNIs of all other nodes by the underlying TTP protocol.

TTP Header 2 Bytes	Length 1 Byte	Dest. Node 1 Byte	Source Port 2 Bytes	Dest. Port 2 Bytes	Horizon Extension 3 Bytes	Data 183 Bytes

Figure 3. Message Format

Figure 3 depicts the syntactic structure of a message stored in the CNI. In addition to the 16 bit TTP header, each message contains information about its length, a source address, a destination address, and up to 183 data bytes. The destination address comprises the 8 bit identifier of the receiver TTP node in combination with a 16 bit port number. The source address is specified as a 16 bit port number. Since TTP sends all messages of a node exclusively within the slots reserved for the respective node, the identity of the sender is implicitly known.

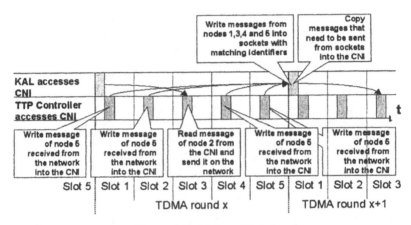

Figure 4. Activities at Node 2

In order to copy messages between the event message queues of the sockets and the TTP CNI as described above, KAL is activated at the beginning of each TDMA round. In any particular node n, KAL reads the CNI areas belonging to the nodes other than node n (local node). In addition, KAL writes the CNI area belonging to node n, if node n needs to send during the starting TDMA round. KAL accesses the CNI in time-triggered manners and is thereby implicitly synchronized with the TTP communication controller. Figure 4 illustrates this scheme for node 2 in an ensemble of five nodes. This design prevents the transmission and reception of partially updated messages.

5.   DISCUSSION

This section discusses the temporal performance of TMOs on top of the TTA and the benefits with respect to dependability that are gained through the reliable underlying time-triggered architecture.

5.1   Temporal Performance

While control algorithms can be designed to compensate a known delay, delay jitter brings an additional uncertainty into a control loop that has an adverse effect on the quality of control (Kopetz, 1997). In case of low jitter or a global time-base with a good precision, state estimation techniques allow to compensate a known delay range between the time of observation and the time of use of the observed image of the real-time entity. State estimation uses a model of a real-time entity to compute the probable state of the real-time entity at a future point in time. In systems of TMOs layered on top of TTA, clock synchronization is performed at the hardware level resulting in a global time base with a precision of 5 μs. Furthermore, communication jitter can be minimized by devising conflict-free time-triggered schedules at design time for both processing activities (e.g., SpM methods) and communication activities (e.g., messages for remote method invocations and those exchanged via multicast channels).

5.2   Improved Dependability

The integration of TMO and TTP improves the reliability of application TMOs through the fault-tolerance mechanisms of the underlying TTA services (i.e., fault-tolerant communication service, fault-tolerant clock synchronization, fault isolation between components). The fault isolation capability of the TTA ensures that a fault within the fault hypothesis of the TTA (Kopetz, 2004) does not impact the temporal behavior and the consistency of message exchanges between correct components.

Based on these properties of the architecture, it is possible to realize fault-tolerant TMO applications with active redundancy with relative ease. An example for such a configuration is Triple Modular Redundancy (TMR), which comprises three replica deterministic TMOs that compute the same outputs on different components that fail independently. Due to the consistency guarantees and the determinism of the TTA, such a configuration can mask an arbitrary failure of a single component, when performing an exact voting on the outputs of the three replicas.

6.   CONCLUSION AND FUTURE WORK

The TMO model is a powerful extension of distributed object-computing for the domain of real-time systems. TMO supports the specification of temporal constraints in a natural form and provides a model for execution engines for ensuring that these constraints are met at runtime.

The establishment of a TMO execution engine on top of a base architecture suited for ultra-dependable applications is an important step towards enabling economical construction of safety-related and safety-critical applications and effective management of growing complexity in such constructions. The TTA, which has been employed for the realization of TMO in this paper, is such an architecture. Its constituent communication protocol TTP has been validated through formal analysis and fault injection experiments.

A considerable side effect of the TMO / TTP integration is the availability of a global time base with microsecond granularity to TMO applications, as well as multicast communication channels and remote method invocations with small jitter. Jitter-sensitive applications (e.g., control loops) and applications with the requirement for high-precision timestamping can benefit from this improvement.

ACKNOWLEDGEMENTS

This work has been supported in part by the European IST project DECOS under project No. IST-511764, by the NSF under Grant Number 03-26606 (ITR), and by the Software Research Center, KonKuk Univ.

REFERENCES

Ademaj, A., Sivencrona, H., Bauer, G., and Torin, J., Evaluation of fault handling of the Time-Triggered Architecture with bus and star topology. In *Proc. of the International Conference on Dependable Systems and Networks*, 2003.

Beal, D., et al., RTAI: Real-time application interface. *Linux Journal*, April 2000.

Gimenez, G., and Kim, K.H., A Windows CE implementation of a middleware architecture supporting time-triggered message-triggered objects. In *Proc. of 25th Annual International Computer Software and Applications Conference*. 2001.

Kim, H.-J., Park, S.-H., Kim, J.-G., Kim, M.-H., and Rim, K.W., TMO-Linux: a Linux-based real-time operating system supporting execution of TMOs. In *Proc. of 5th IEEE International Symposium on Object-Oriented Real-Time Distributed Computing*. April 2002.

Kim, K.H., "APIs for Real-Time Distributed Object Programming", *IEEE Computer*, 2000.

Kim, K.H., and Ishida, M., An Efficient Middleware Architecture Supporting Time- Triggered Message-Triggered Objects and an NT-based Implementation. In *Proc. of 2nd IEEE CS International Symposium on Object-Oriented Real-time Distributed Computing*, 1999.

Kim, K.H. et al., Distributed Computing Based Streaming and Play of Ensemble Music Realized Through TMO Programming. In *Proc. of 10th IEEE International Workshop on Object-oriented Real-time Dependable Systems*. 2005.

Kim, K.H. et al., Distinguishing Features and Potential Roles of the RTO.k Object Model. In *Proc. of IEEE Computer Society Workshop on Object-oriented Real-Time Dependable Systems*. Dana Point, October 1994.

Kopetz, H., and Bauer, G., The time-triggered architecture. *IEEE Special Issue on Modeling and Design of Embedded Software*. 2003.

Kopetz, H., *Real-Time Systems*, Design Principles for Distributed Embedded Applications. Kluwer Academic Publishers. 1997.

Kopetz, H., The Fault Hypothesis for the Time-Triggered Architecture. In *Proc. of the IFIP World Computer Congress*. 2004.

Lala, J.H., and Harper, R.E., Architectural principles for safety-critical real-time applications. *Proc. of the IEEE*, 82:25–40. 1994.

Lundelius, J., and Lynch, N., A new fault-tolerant algorithm for clock synchronization. In *Proc. of the 3d Annual ACM Symposium on Principles of Distributed Computing*. 1984.

RTCA. DO-178B: *Software Considerations in Airborne Systems and Equipment Certification*. Radio Technical Commission for Aeronautics, Inc. 1992.

Rushby, J., An overview of formal verification for the time-triggered architecture. *Formal Techniques in Real-Time and Fault-Tolerant Systems*, Lecture Notes in Computer Science, pages 83–105, Springer-Verlag, 2002.

Simon, H., *The Sciences of the Artificial*. MIT Press, 1996.

TTTech Computertechnik AG. TTP Monitoring Node – A TTP Development Board for the Time-Triggered Architecture, March 2002.

Venture Development Corporation (VDC). Current Practices and Emerging Requirements in the Automotive Vertical Market. *Embedded Developers' Demand and Requirements for Commercial OSs and Software Development Tools, Volume I*. Natick, 2003.

ASSESSING THE USE OF RT-JAVA IN AUTOMOTIVE TIME-TRIGGERED APPLICATIONS

Marco A. Wehrmeister[1], Fernando H. Athaide[2], Fabiano C. Carvalho[1], Carlos E. Pereira[2]

[1]*Computer Science Institute, Federal University of Rio Grande do Sul, Brazil*
  {mawehrmeister, fhataide, fccarvalho}@inf.ufrgs.br
[2]*Electrical Engineering Department, Federal University of Rio Grande do Sul, Brazil*
  {cpereira}@eletro.ufrgs.br

Abstract: Distributed embedded real-time systems are becoming widely used in several areas of application, including automotive systems. Most of these applications have severe timing constraints and are safety critical. A key component in distributed embedded real-time systems is to ensure a deterministic and reliable communication among distributed embedded systems. Especially in the automotive area, which is considering the possibility of replacing the major part of mechanical and/or hydraulic systems for electronic systems, the importance of a correct behavior in the electronic communication system plays a key role. This paper presents an platform-based embedded real-time system design methodology which can be used in automotive embedded real-time system design. The use of the proposed method is demonstrated through a steer-by-wire case study implemented using a Java platform.

Keywords: Embedded Real-Time Systems, RT-UML, RT-Java, Time-Triggered Architecture, Steer-By-Wire

1. INTRODUCTION

Recent advances in the areas of electronics and informatics have enabled the use of embedded computational systems in different application areas. In the automotive sector, the so called "x-by-wire" systems have been investigated as a cost-effective alternative to replace mechanical and hydraulic systems. The "x" in "x-by-wire" represents the basis of any safety related application, such as steering, braking, suspension control or multi-airbag systems. These applications should greatly increase overall vehicle safety by assisting the driver to find solutions in critical situations. X-by-wire systems have hard timing constraints and must present a deterministic predictable behavior[1]. Most of x-by-wire systems are implemented as distributed embedded real-time systems. The design of this kind of system is recognized as a very complex activities. It has to deal with the (co-)design of hardware and software components – including a communication infrastructure – as well as due to the safety and reliability constraints from the application domain. Thus the entire distributed embedded real-time systems must be deterministic and reliable. The time-triggered architecture - TTA (see for instance Kopetz and Bauer[5]) has been successfully applied to some automotive applications and can be considered a interesting deployment architecture.

From a high-level perspective, the object-oriented paradigm appears as an interesting alternative to tackle the complexity in the design of distributed real-time embedded systems. Object oriented methodologies using the Unified Modeling Language (UML)[12] are widely accepted, specially in the development of software-intensive systems [7,8,9,10]. However, the application of object-oriented concepts in the area of distributed embedded real-time systems is still a research area.

This paper presents the Platform-Based Embedded Electronic Systems design methodology, or simply SEEP (project acronym in Portuguese), applied to a time-triggered distributed embedded system design. The SEEP methodology encompasses all development phases, including modeling, analysis, validation, and synthesis tools to support the development of optimized real-time embedded systems. The approach is based on the reuse of hardware and software components and on the configuration of predefined FPGA-based architectural platforms.

The remaining of this paper is organized as follows. Section 2 compares event-triggered and time-triggered systems. Section 3 gives a brief overview on the design methodology proposed in the SEEP project. Section 4 shows the application of the SEEP's design methodology to the development of a steer-by-wire system. Finally, Section 5 draws conclusions and signals future work directions.

2. EVENT-TRIGGERED VS. TIME-TRIGGERED SYSTEMS

There has been an intense debate in the real-time community on which of the two approaches, event-triggered or time-triggered, has more advantages in the design of distributed embedded real-time systems (see for instance, Kopetz and Bauer[5]). In the event-triggered model, all communications and processing activities initiates when a significant event occurs (for instance, the system enters into a new state). In the time-triggered approach, all activities are started periodically at predetermined instants.

Event-triggered systems usually require lower network bandwidth since a new message transmission is only needed if the value to be transmitted is distinct from the previous one. A drawback of this approach is that missing messages may cause synchronization problems, which can be detected only at the sender. In time-triggered systems, messages are transmitted periodically so, both sender and receiver can detect a communication fault. In this case, although missing messages may temporarily lead to synchronization loss, they can be detected at the receiver because all message transmission instants are known *a priori*. Time-triggered systems are considered to be predictable and more composable than event-triggered due to the temporal regularity of its communication pattern. However event-triggered systems are recognized as more flexible than time-triggered systems.

The Time Triggered Architecture (TTA) (Kopetz and Bauer[5]) proposes a communication system that is executed autonomously, controlled by a time-triggered schedule (Time Division Multiple Access - TDMA). In TTA, the tasks read/write state messages from/to Communication Network Interface (CNI), at predefined instants known *a priori*. Therefore, the communication controller reads the messages from CNI and transmit them, also at instants known a priori, for all other nodes in the network. This transmission overwrites the previous received messages on all other CNIs in the cluster. Execution times of the periodic fetch and delivery actions are stored into the message scheduling table (Message Descriptor List – MEDL) on each communication controller.

An important feature of the CNI, is that it separates the local processing within a node from the global interactions among the nodes. It consists of two unidirectional data-flow interfaces, one from the host computer to the communication system and the other one in the opposite direction.

2.1   Time-Triggered Scheduling

In a time-triggered scheduling strategy, the static scheduler activates tasks in a strictly sequential order, which is stored in a dispatcher table. The dispatcher table is executed cyclically, providing a periodic task execution scheme. A time-triggered task does not have a static priority, its activation time is configured in the dispatcher data structure. If a task is running and another task becomes active (its activation instant arrives), the current task will be preempted and the other task will run. After termination, the preempted task will continue its execution. All time instants related the activation of tasks are stored into a dispatch table that follows the temporal characteristics of the application domain and the precedence relations among tasks. The dispatch table is defined during system configuration phase and takes into account the specified timing requirements. That means that task scheduling is done offline and therefore all time instants related to task activations are know *a priori*.

An example of a scheduler that follows these characteristics is the OSEKtime[3]. According to the OSEKTime specification, there is no task synchronization via blocking mechanisms. An RTOS that implements this offline schedule approach is the TTP-OS[6], which is a time-triggered operating system with TTP communication system support. An example of time-triggered tasks activations, showed in figure 5, illustrates six time-triggered tasks (TTTask) distributed on different nodes, which are activated at different times.

3.   SEEP PROJECT

The SEEP project proposes a complete and integrated methodology for the analysis, design, implementation, and test of real-time embedded systems. An overview of the proposed design methodology, which extensively supports design space exploration activities, is depicted in figure 1 (interested readers on a detailed description of the SEEP project are referred to Wehrmeister *et al.*[13]).

The SEEP approach aims to ensure a smooth transition between development phases, from RT-UML[2] specification to implementation. The transition from higher to lower abstraction levels is facilitated by the use of a real-time Java API[14], whose underlying facilities are customizable and optimized according to the application requirements and available platforms. This API includes high-level real-time constructs and therefore avoids the use of low-level system calls to implement the specified temporal behavior. Furthermore, using the provided API it is possible to design concurrent real-time Java applications and synthesize them into a dedicated Java processor[15].

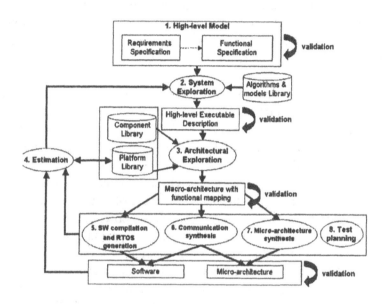

Figure 1. The SEEP design methodology

The mapping from RT-UML specification diagrams to the RTSJ-based API is discussed in Becker *et al*,[11] on which a clear link between real-time requirements and the programming entities that provide their implementation is established. The main idea of this approach is to enhance the traceability as well as the readability of timing constraints from a model-based requirement model to implementation.

3.1   Target Hardware Platforms

Currently, two platforms are being considered within the SEEP project. The first one is based on a family of customizable Java processors, implemented on commercial FPGAs, while the second one is a commercial platform, containing a large FPGA with two PowerPC processors cores. In this paper we will focus on the customizable Java platform.

In SEEP methodology, one of the possibilities is to use Java source code to represent the high-level executable description. Using the SASHIMI environment[15], both a VHDL description for a dedicated Java processor and the respective program memory code (application code) are generated. This CAD environment automatically synthesizes an Application Specific

Instruction Set Processor (ASIP) microprocessor (named FemtoJava) for a target application, using only the subset of instructions used by the designed application. This Java processor implements a Java execution engine in hardware through a stack machine compatible, but restricted, Java Virtual Machine (JVM) specification. A customized control unit for the FemtoJava processor is generated, supporting only the opcodes used by that application. The control unit of the synthesized processor is thus directly proportional to the number of different opcodes needed by the application software, therefore optimizing the final footprint based on application requirements.

In order to express more clearly timing constraints in the source code of real-time embedded application, an API based on the Real-Time Specification for Java (RTSJ) was developed[14]. This specification introduces the concept of schedulable objects, which are instances of classes that implement the Schedulable interface, such as the RealtimeThread. It also specifies a set of classes to store parameters that represent a particular resource demand from one or more schedulable objects. For example, the ReleaseParameters class (superclass from AperiodicParameters and PeriodicParameters) includes several useful parameters for the specification of real-time requirements. Additionally, RTSJ supports the expression of other useful concepts for real-time systems development, such as time values (absolute and relative time), timers, periodic and aperiodic tasks, and scheduling policies. The term 'task' derives from the scheduling literature, representing a schedulable element within the system context. It is also a synonym for schedulable object. For a detailed description of the RTSJ-base API see Wehrmeister *et al.*[14].

4.   CASE STUDY

This paper presents a case study, on which the SEEP methodology is applied to the development of a steer-by-wire system that follows the time-triggered model of computation. This application presents hard real-time requirements that must be accomplished for safety reasons. Johannessen[4] presents a steer-by-wire system that has six nodes interconnected through a TTP/C network (see Figure 2). This steer-by-wire system has three steering modes: two-wheel steering (normal), four-wheel steering and parallel steering.

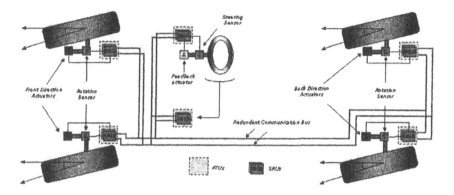

Figure 2. Steer-By-Wire Systems Architecture [Johannessen[4]]

The steer-by-wire system proposed in this case study includes two subsystems: the steering wheel subsystem that runs on the computational node located in the steering wheel; and 4 wheel subsystems that run on each wheel. The first subsystem is responsible for sampling the steering wheel rotation angle and disseminating this information to the wheel nodes through the communication network. This subsystem also has to provide feedback force to the steering wheel, based on the angle and the velocity of the wheels. The wheel subsystems must sample the angle and speed, and then send these two values to the steering wheel node. Also, the wheel computational nodes have a controller task that controls the rotation angle according to the steering wheel position and selected steering mode. The wheel angle depends directly on the steering wheel angle applied (by the driver) and the selected steering mode. It is important to highlight that due to limitations in papers' length, the discussion on this paper will focus in the timing aspects only, despite the fact that authors are aware that fault-tolerant aspects represent a fundamental issue in safety-critical applications.

The design process started with the construction of a high-level object model using RT-UML. Diagrams used in the model are: Use Cases, Collaboration, and Class Diagrams. Particularly the last two diagrams are decorated with the stereotypes and tag-values define by the RT-UML profile[2].Figure 3 and 4 depicts two collaboration diagrams for the steer-by-wire system: one for the steering wheel node (figure 3) and other for the wheel node (figure 4).

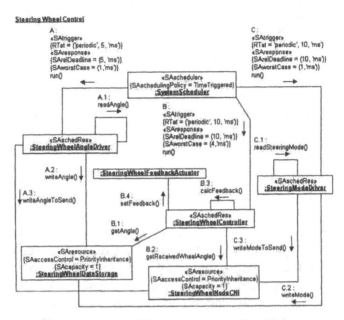

Figure 3. Collaboration Diagram for Steering Wheel Subsystem

In figure 3, the stereotype «SAtrigger» represents a periodic activation for active objects. Three active objects have been identified: the SteeringWheelAngleDriver that samples the steering wheel angle and stores this value in the shared memory (SteeringWheelDataStorage object); the second active object is the SteeringModeDriver which provides the steering mode selected by driver to the steering wheel subsystem, this value is stored in the shared memory and in the CNI; finally, the third active object is the SteeringWheelControler that is responsible to perform the control of this subsystem. It includes the control algorithm responsible for feedback force, the calculation of the steering wheel's rotation angle and the storage of the computed values in CNI for transmission to the other nodes. Additionally, a stereotype «SAresponse» specifies task's deadline and worst-case execution time (WCET). Similarly, in figure 4 the «SAtrigger» and «SAresponse» stereotypes identify the real-time constraints of active objects in the wheel node system, an information included in the time-triggered dispatch table.

In the "system design exploration" phase, algorithms and components libraries are selected to optimize the steer-by-wire system for a given platform (see for instance Mattos *et al.*[16] for further details). For the present case study, it is assumed that the Java programming language is chosen for coding the selected algorithm, so that programs that make use of the RTSJ-based API (see Wehrmeister *et al.*[14]) are generated.

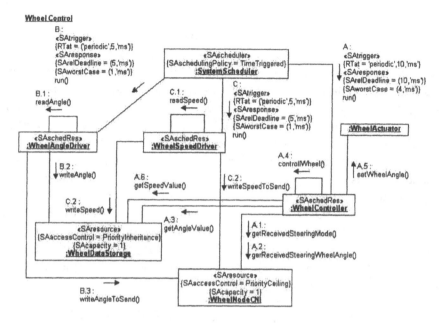

Figure 4. Collaboration Digrams for Wheel Subsystem

When applied to classes, the RT-UML stereotypes correspond to Java classes that may extend classes from a RTSJ-based API, e.g. «SAschedRes. Stereotype tags that are relevant in the context of the runtime application are mapped to RTSJ-based API class attributes. Class constructors should accept initialization values for such attributes. When applied to methods, stereotypes correspond to methods implemented in the generated class or in one of its attributes. The tasks characteristics, modeled in the collaboration diagrams presented in figures 3 and 4, are used as basis to build the dispatch table (as mentioned previously this is done offline and based on application time requirements). Figure 5 depicts the generated dispatch table where the predefined task activation instants can be observed.

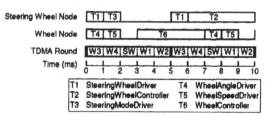

Figure 5. Task and comunication schedules

Figure 5 also shows the TDMA round that drives the communication among steer-by-wire nodes where SW stands for the steering wheel node and Wn for the other four wheel node. Figure 6 depicts the performed mapping, showing the generated source code for the real-time class SteeringWheelControl, which includes objects responsible for the periodic force feedback control applied to the steering wheel. The period and deadline information derive from tags specified in the collaboration diagram in figure 4. They are represented, respectively, by the «SATriggers» and «SAResponse» stereotypes of the RT-UML. As it can be seen in the code, two distinctic method: *mainTask()* and *exceptionTask()* are generated. The former represents the task body, i.e., the code executed when the task is activated. This is a periodic task, on which periodic activation is implemented as a loop with execution frequency being controlled by calling the *waitForNextPeriod()* method. This method controls the task execution based on the dispatch table generated by the offline scheduler. The *exceptionTask()* method represents an exception handling code that is triggered in case of deadline misses, i.e., if the mainTask() method does not finish within the established deadline.

```
01   public class SteeringWheelController extends RealtimeThread {
02       private static PeriodicParameters
03                              releaseParams = new
04   PeriodicParameters(
05                              null, // start time
06                              null, // end tTime
07                              TimeObjects._10_ms, // period
08                              TimeObjects._4_ms, // cost
09                              TimeObjects._10_ms);
10   //deadline
11       // Other class attributes...
12       public void mainTask() {
13           while (true) {
14             // control actions
15             // ...
16               waitForNextPeriod();
17           }
18       }
19       public void exceptionTask() {
20           // exception handling code is inserted here
         }}
```

Figure 6. SteeringWheelControl class source code

After having generated the source code using the RTSJ-based API, this code is then compiled using a standard Java compiler and the synthesis of the embedded real-time system is performed. The resulting class files are used as input to the SASHIMI tool[15] and analyzed in order to generate VHDL files that will customize the FemtoJava processor. It is important to highlight that the size of the generated FemtoJava control unit is proportional to the number of distinct Java opcodes used by the application software. In the final step, the resulting binary is loaded into the FPGA. In the synthesis process of the steer-by-wire application, the generated software occupies 410 bytes of RAM to store all objects in steering wheel node and 426 bytes on each wheel node. The code size needed by application objects for each node type is, respectively, 3259 and 3374 bytes. This case study was simulated using the Cycle Accurate COnfigurable Power Simulator (CACO-PS)[17] considering a FemtoJava processor running at 10 Mhz. The simulation results are showed in table 1 (timing information in milliseconds).

Table 1. Steer-By-Wire simulation data

Task	Predefined Activation Instant	Real Activation Instant	Delay	Task WCET
Steering Wheel Node				
SteeringWheelAngleDriver	0	0,2316	0,2316	0,4830
	5	5,2316	0,2316	0,4830
SteeringModeDrive	1	1,2316	0,2326	0,4805
SteeringWheelController	6	6,2338	0,2338	2,3789
Wheel Nodes				
WheelAngleDriver	0	0,2316	0,2316	0,4830
	7	7,2316	0,2316	0,4830
WheelSpeedDriver	1	1,2316	0,2316	0,4830
	8	8,2338	0,2338	0,4830
WheelController	3	3,2316	0,2316	2,9017

The simulation results present a satisfactory behavior of the steer-by-wire system over the FemtoJava processor without deadline misses that can be seen on real activations instants and WCET of all tasks. The response times are consistent in relation to temporal specification contained in the dispatcher data structure of the communication nodes.

5.   CONCLUSIONS

In this paper a case study showing how the object-oriented methodology proposed within the SEEP project can be mapped to a time triggered architecture is presented. The paper shows the integration of the design phases, from a requirements specification using the RT-UML profile to an implementation that makes use of a RTSJ-based API and a customizable real-time Java processor. The obtained results indicate that the use of object orientated paradigm and the RT-UML to design time-triggered systems can be an interesting alternative to conventional project methods. Timing requirements can be extracted from RT-UML model, through the stereotypes and tagged values that decorate diagram elements and provide the required information to build the time-triggered application dispatch table as well as to generate the application code. The results also indicate that a RTSJ-based programming language can be used in time-triggered systems.

REFERENCES

1. X-By-Wire Team, "X-By-Wire Safety Related Fault Tolerant Systems in Vehicles," Project No. BE 95/1329, Tech. Report, 1998.
2. OBJECT MANAGEMENT GROUP, "UML Profile for Schedulability, Performance, and Time Specification," http://www.omg.org/cgibin/doc?ptc/02-03-02, March 2002.
3. OSEK Group, "Time-Triggered Operating System Specification 1.0. OSEKtimeOS 1.0," OSEK/VDX group, July 2001.
4. Johannessen, P, "Project SIRIUS 2001: A University Drive-by- Wire Project ," Dept. of Computer Eng., Chalmers University of Technology, Goteborg, Sweden, , Tech. Report 01-14, 2001.
5. Kopetz H., Bauer Gunther, "The Time-Triggered Architecture," Proceedings of the IEEE Special Issue on Modeling and Design of Embedded Software, October 2002.
6. TTTech GROUP, "TTPOS Time-Triggered Operating System with TTP Support," White Paper http://www.tttech.com/technology/docs/general/TTTech-TTPOS.pdf, 2004.
7. Jong, G., "A UML-Based Design Methodology for Real-Time and Embedded Systems," Proc. of Design, Automation and Test in Europe Conference and Exhibition, France, March 2002.
8. Axelsson, Jakob, "Real-World Modeling in UML," Proceedings of International Conference on Software and Systems Engineering and their Applications, France, December 2000.
9. Chen, Rong; Sgroi, Marco; Lavango, Luciano; Martin, Grant; Sangiovanni-Vincentelli, Alberto; Rabaey, Jan, "UML and Platformbased Design. Norwell," Kluwer 2003. p. 107-126.
10. Nebel, Wolfgang; Oppenheimer, Frank; Schumacher, Guido, "Object-Oriented Specification and Design of Embedded Hard Real-Time Systems," Proceedings of Internation Conference on Chip Design, Laxenburg: IFIP, 2000. p. 285-296.
11. Becker, Leandro B.; Holtz, Rudy; Pereira, Carlos E, "On Mapping RT-UML Specifications to RT-Java API: Bridging the Gap," Proceedings of the IEEE International Symposium on Object-Oriented Real-Time Distributed Computing, 2002.
12. Booch, Grandy; Rumbaugh, James; JacobsonN, Ivar. The Unified Modeling Language User Guide. Reading, Massachusetts: Addison-Wesley, 1999.
13. Wehrmeister, Marco A.; Becker, Leandro B.; Wagner, Flavio R.; Pereira, Carlos E. "On Object-Oriented Platform-based Design Process for Embedded Real-Time Systems". Proceedings of the IEEE International Symposium on Object-Oriented Real-Time Distributed Computing, 2005.
14. Wehrmeister, Marco A.; Becker, Leandro B.; Pereira, Carlos E. "Optimizing Real-Time Embedded Systems Development Using a RTSJ-based API". Proceedings of Workshop On Java Technologies For Real-Time And Embedded Systems, 2004.
15. Ito, S.; Carro, L; Jacobi, R.P. "Making Java Work for Microcontroller Applications". IEEE Design & Test of Computers, vol. 18, n. 5, 2001, p. 100-110
16. Mattos, J. C. B.; Brisolara, L.; Hentschke, R.; Carro, L.; Wagner, F. "Design Space Exploration with Automatic Generation of IP-based Embedded Software". Proceedings of the IFIP Working Conference on Distributed and Parallel Embedded Systems, 2004.
17. Beck Filho, A.C.; Mattos, J.; Wagner, F.R.; Carro, L. "CACO-PS: A General-Purpose Cycle-Accurate Configurable Power Simulator". Proceedings of Symposium on Integrated Circuits and Systems Design, 2003.

DISTRIBUTED CONTROL STRUCTURE OF THE NBP TEST TRACK WITH LINEAR MOTOR DRIVEN VEHICLES

Andreas Pottharst, Horst Grotstollen
University of Paderborn, Institute for Power Electronics and Electrical Drives,
D-33095 Paderborn, Germany,
Phone: ++49-5251-602206, fax: ++49-5251-605483,
Email: pottharst@lea.upb.de, grotstollen@lea.upb.de

Abstract: This paper describes the drive control structure of the Railcab system realized at a test track at the University of Paderborn based on a distributed data processing system. The drive of this railway system, a doubly-fed linear motor, consists of two active parts distributed on the vehicles and along the track, which both have to be powered. Safe operation of the Railcabs is guaranteed by a mechanism synchronizing the current controllers via different communication channels (CANopen and radio). This measure makes possible to control the phase shift between the magnetic fields of primary and secondary which is a must for drive control. Finally measurement results are presented to prove the functionality of the described synchronization mechanism.

Keywords: Railway system, Railcab, Doubly-fed Linear Motor, Drive Control, Distributed Signal Processing

1.   INTRODUCTION

At University of Paderborn a new railway system called Railcab is under investigation. This system is characterized by the following features [1]:
- Instead of trains travelling in accordance with a fixed schedule autonomous shuttles travelling on request are used for transportation of passengers and cargo. By this change short time for transportation can be achieved without high-speed operation because passengers can travel any

time and do not loose time by changing trains. On the other hand cargo does not spend most of transportation time on switch yards where trains are formed and split.

- On main routes all shuttles travel with approximately the same speed of about 160 km/h; neither passenger traffic and cargo traffic nor short distance traffic and long distance traffic are separated.
- Railcabs traveling on the same section of track can form convoys and save energy by reducing the wind resistance.
- When arriving at its destination a vehicle has to leave the main track for disembarking people or unloading cargo. With regard to long reaction time of conventional switches this causes a problem when a vehicle has to leave a convoy. Therefore the system makes use of passive switches in combination with active steering of the shuttle's axes.
- For driving the vehicles linear motor technology is used which allows to generate great force and to climb steep slopes. With linear motor generation of thrust force is performed without moving and wearing parts which results in high reliability of the drive system. Furthermore realization of active steering is simplified because wheels are not used for driving.
- With regard to size of Railcabs and great number of vehicles there is a great interest in transferring energy to the vehicles without using pantographs or contact rails.

The basic principles of Railcab system are under investigation at the test track of NBP project which was installed in scale 1:2.5 at University of Paderborn in 2003 (see figure 1). The track has a total length of 530 m and consists of a circle and a straight section which are connected by a switch.

a) Track with plant control and one power supply station

b) NBP railway vehicle: *railcab*

Figure 1: Test track and vehicle of Railcab system

The doubly-fed linear motor used for driving a Railcab consists of two parts. The primary is installed between the rails and two pairs of secondaries are fitted below the undercarriages. The primary generates a traveling magnetic field by means of a three-phase winding. The secondaries also have three-phase windings. By this means the magnetic field of the secondaries can be shifted with regard to the Railcab. Operating Railcabs in the asynchronous mode has two important advantages: First, vehicles travelling on the same primary segment are able to drive with different speeds, so relative motion between different Railcabs becomes possible which is required for forming convoys. Second, by asynchronous operation of the motor energy transmission from the primary to the secondary and to the on-board power supply system of a Railcab becomes possible [2] and neither overhead wires nor contact rails are required.

To realize this asynchronous operating mode of the motor with the advantages given above, a vehicle control structure based on along the track distributed systems becomes necessary, because the linear motor's thrust force depends on the current vectors in secondary and primary [3]. These currents (frequency and amplitude) are controlled by sterically separated systems.

2.   SIGNAL PROCESSING AND COMMUNICATION SYSTEM OF THE TESTING PLANT

Signal processing and communication system of test track used for control of a single vehicle is shown at figure 2.

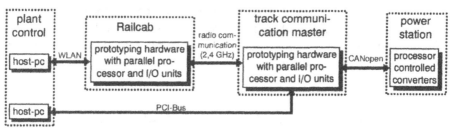

Figure 2: The Railcab system test track

In accordance with the procedures required for a fully automated operation of the testing plant the data and signal processing system is divided into three parts which are distributed to a central control room (plant control), the Railcab and the power stations distributed along the track which receive information from the vehicle via a track communication master.

Each motion of the shuttle is commanded and controlled at a central control room. By means of two host PCs the reference for the vehicle's position or destination, respectively, is set here as well as the maximum speed permitted during motion. This information is sent to the vehicle by WLAN radio transmission. In return data are received from the vehicle which are used for monitoring the experiment, measuring significant parameters and performing fault diagnostics.

On board the vehicles dSPACE prototyping hardware with parallel processors (power PCs) and several I/Os are used for controlling speed and position of the vehicle. In particular references for the frequencies, phase angles and amplitudes of the linear motor's currents are generated here with a sampling rate of 4 kHz. References of secondary currents are delivered directly to the signal processing units of the on-board power converters where closed loop control of currents is performed with a sampling rate of also 4 kHz. In addition to drive control, which is described in more detail afterwards, the prototyping hardware has also to control the charge of an on-board battery and operation of all hydraulic units used for steering of the undercarriages and for suspension and tilting of the carriage.

Closed loop control of primary currents is performed by the track-side power converters feeding the 84 primary sections. Therefore the references of primary currents are sent from the vehicle to a track communication master which is placed at one of four stationary power plants at which the power converters are installed. For this data transmission radio communication at 2.4 GHz is used. By the communication master references for amplitude, frequency and phase angle of primary current are transmitted to the power converters via CANopen and only those power converters are activated which are responsible for feeding the stator sections on which the vehicle is present. Primary current references are updated with a repetition rate of 50 Hz.

For operation of more than one vehicle radio communication between vehicles is also required when forming convoys and while driving in a convoy. Up to now this communication is not implemented at the track and not shown at figure 2, but tests have already been made at HIL test rigs.

3.   SYNCHRONIZATION MECHANISM FOR VEHICLE-TO-TRACK COMMUNICATION

Magnitude and sign of the torque or force generated by an electric motor depend on the phase shift between magnetic fields of primary and secondary. Therefore synchronization of primary and secondary currents - which generate the traveling fields of both windings - is the most important control task at any drive. With doubly-fed linear motor this task is extremely difficult because primary and secondary and their power supplies are distributed to stationary track and moving vehicle. To perform force control reliably and as exactly as required a special synchronization mechanism has been implemented [4]. At figure 3 a communication diagram of this synchronization mechanism, which is based on radio links of the distributed control systems, is given.

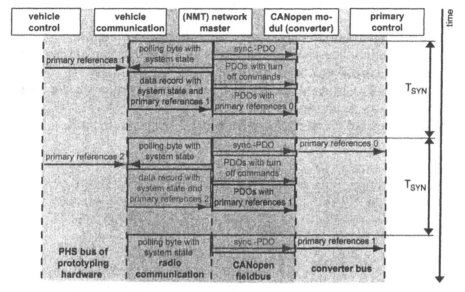

Figure 3: Diagram of communication sequences

Data transmission from vehicle-side motion control to track-side current controllers is performed within two sampling periods of the track-side network master (NMT). At the beginning of the first period data transmission of references ('references 1' in figure 3) is initiated by the NMT by sending a polling byte to the vehicle via radio communication. After receiving this polling byte, which is used to indicate error states of the communication channel or of primary sections, the primary references are sent from the vehicle's control to the NMT.

During the second period the references are transmitted from the NMT to all power converters placed along the track. At the beginning of the third period - exactly when sending the polling byte to the vehicle - the NMT sends a synchronization process data object (PDO) to the respective power converters via CANopen causing the power converters to replace the previous references (references 0) by the new values. By demanding for new reference values from the motion control and activating already transmitted values at the power converters at exactly the same time a well-defined transmission time and a deterministic behavior of the control system is achieved as necessary for adjusting the magnetic fields of primary and secondary with sufficient accuracy.

4.   STRUCTURE OF DRIVE CONTROL

Basic task of the drive control is to control the linear motor's primary and secondary current in such a way that
1. the magnitudes of currents do not exceed the permitted limits,
2. speed and position are in accordance with the references delivered from the plant control and
3. the energy transferred to the on-board power system via the motor matches the requirement.

The structure of the control solving these tasks is shown at figure 4.

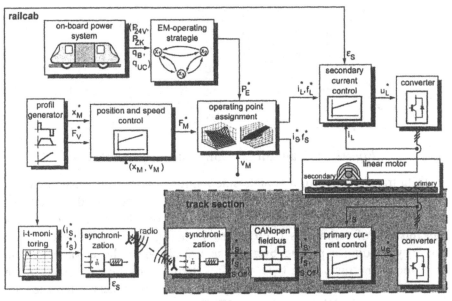

Figure 4: Linear drive control structure

The first requirement, limitation of currents, is fulfilled as usual by closed loop control which is performed by microprocessors on the power converters with a sampling rate of 4 kHz.

For motion control profiles for position, speed and force are determined onboard the shuttle from the information delivered from the central control room. Under consideration of actual conditions the force reference is calculated. Thrust force depends on primary current I_1 and secondary current I_2 and on the special phase shift α between the magnetic traveling fields produced by these currents.

$$F_M = -\frac{3\pi}{\tau_P} L_{12} \cdot I_1 I_2 \sin \alpha$$

where τ_P and L_{12} are the pole pitch and the coupling inductance of linear motor, respectively.

Obviously torque is generated with minimum current and minimum losses when the secondary magnetizes perpendicularly to the magnetic field of the primary winding or when angle $\alpha = \pm\pi/2$, respectively. Furthermore it is important to notice that the angle must not leave the range $0 < |\alpha| < \pi/2$ because otherwise thrust force will change its direction and motion control will become unstable. Phase shift α between traveling waves depends not only on the phases of primary and secondary but also on the vehicle's position where an angle of $\alpha = \pi/2$ refers to a length of a half pole pitch ore $\tau_P/2 = 60$ mm, respectively. Consequently the position of the vehicle must measured with a relatively high accuracy.

As can be seen from the above equation the product of primary and secondary current is determined by the demand on thrust force. The final setting of the current references is performed at the module Operating Point Assignment where the current ratio is established under consideration of different aspects: On the one hand, limitations of voltages and currents as well as the influence of the current ratio on efficiency have to be considered. On the other hand frequency of primary current is calculated from the actual speed and the frequency required in the secondary winding for energy transfer [2].

Closed loop control of stator current is performed at the track-side in accordance with magnitude and frequency reference delivered by the on-board drive control which are updated every 20 ms. With regard to delay time caused by radio communication, it is impossible to perform the most important task - synchronization of primary and secondary field of linear motor - by control of the primary current. With regard to operation of several vehicles on the same stator section it is also suitable to adjust each vehicle's magnetic field to the traveling wave of the primary.

As can be seen from the figure the actual position of the primary field is calculated from the frequency reference being sent to the track. At this calculation it is essential to consider the delay time caused by data transmission (44 ms) and the motion of the traveling field during the sampling period. If error of position angle is not considered safe operation of the Railcab is not possible and control can become instable.

5. MEASUREMENT RESULTS

At figure 5 measured response of speed control to a step of speed reference from 0 to 5 m/s are presented. During all the process shown reference of power to be transferred from the primary into the on-board supply system of the Railcab is 4 kW (1 kW for each secondary winding).

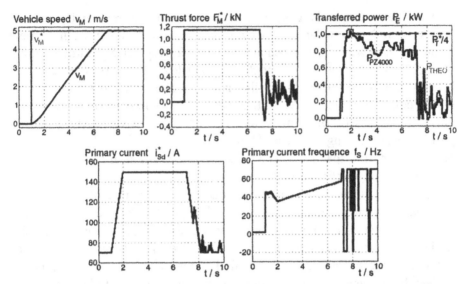

Figure 5: Step response of speed control with control of energy transfer

As can be seen from the plots measured thrust force and speed match the references determined by the profile generator very well. In contrast the transferred power which was measured with a power analyzer (PZ4000) shows an aberration from its reference. The error becomes extremely high after acceleration is terminated which confirms that noteworthy energy transfer is only possible while a relevant amount of thrust force is generated by the linear motor.

While high thrust force is present during acceleration error of transferred power rises up to 20 %. This has different reasons: First, when speed and frequencies increase voltages of power converters reach their limits. Second, in contrast with position and speed the transferred power is not subject of a closed loop control which compensates parameter variations and edge effects of the linear motor [5].Third, errors of measured vehicle position and remaining dead time effects of data transfer from Railcab to track (dead time is not an integer literal multiple of the Railcabs controller sampling time) cause an error of phase shift between magnetic fields of primary and secondary which cannot be compensated.

Strong disturbances of thrust force can be observed after acceleration. They are caused by the rims of wheels touching the rails which happens because at time of measuring steering mechanism was not in operation.

Finally the measurements in figure 5 document the functionality of the synchronization mechanism of the drive control based on a distributed hardware structure works. In spite of continuous changes of primary current and frequency a safe operation of the linear motor driven Railcab with energy transfer in the required dimension becomes possible.

6.   CONCLUSION

After one year of commissioning the drive of test track with its distributed control, signal processing and communication system was fully in operation. Due to energy transfer via the linear motor the vehicles can be driving for unlimited time without any stop for charging the onboard battery.

Present and future work is devoted to improve the onboard power management and implement a set of capacitors (power caps) [6] which are capable of higher currents than the NiCd battery used onboard the vehicle for energy storing and make possible to store all energy delivered by the drive at braking.

Last not least, another system for communication is under development [7]. The system is based on a distributed active network with a dynamic changing number of communication units which will increase the data rate and so fasten up the control dynamic of this railway system.

REFERENCES

[1]   Grotstollen, H.; Henke, M.; Richard, H.-A.; Sander, M.: *Erprobung des Verkehrssystems der Neuen Bahntechnik Paderborn*, 4. int. Heinz Nixdorf Symposium, HNI Verlagsschriftenreihe Band 82, Paderborn, 2000, S. 247-264.

[2]   Pottharst, A; Baptist, K; Schütze, O.; Böcker, J.; Fröhleke, N.; Dellnitz, M.: *Operating Point Assignment of a Linear Motor Driven Vehicle Using Multiobjective Optimization Methods*, 11th International Power Electronics and Motion Control Conference, EPE-PEMC 2004, Riga, Lettland.

[3]   Henke, M.; Grotstollen, H.: *Control of a Linear Drive Test Stand for the NBP Railway Carriage*, Symposium on Linear Drives for Industrial Applications, LDIA 2001, Nagano, Japan, S. 332 - 336.

[4]   Pottharst, A.; Schulz, B.; Böcker, J.: *Kommunikationssysteme einer Anlage mit doppelt gespeistem Linearmotor*, Fachmesse und Kongress SPS/IPC/DRIVES, Nürnberg, November 2004, S. 635 – 643.

[5]   Gieras, J.F.: *Linear Induction Drives*. Clarence Press, Oxford, 1994

[6]   Li, R.; Pottharst, A.; Fröhleke, N.; Böcker, J.:*Energy Storage Scheme for Rail-guided Shuttle using Ultracapacitor and Battery*. 11th International Power Electronics and Motion Control Conferences, EPE-PEMC 2004, September 2004, Riga, Latvia.

[7]   Zanella, M.; Lehmann, T.; Hestermeyer, T.; Pottharst, A.: *Deterministic and High-Performance Communication System for the Distributed Control of Mechatronic Systems Using the IEEE1394a*, IFIP Working Conference on Distributed and Parallel Embedded Systems, DIPES 2002, Montreal, Canada.

TOWARDS A REAL-TIME COMMUNICATION NETWORK FOR AUTONOMOUS RAIL VEHICLES

André Luiz de Freitas Francisco, Bernd Schulz, Christian Henke

University of Paderborn – RtM
Pohlweg 98, D-33098 Paderborn, Germany
Tel:. +49 5251 605576, Fax: + 49 5251 605579,
Email: Andre.Francisco@RtM.upb.de

University of Paderborn – LEA
Warburger Str. 100, D-33098 Paderborn, Germany
Tel:. +49 5251 605486, Fax: + 49 5251 605483,
Email: schulz@lea.upb.de, henke@lea.upb.de

Abstract: This paper presents a communication network architecture aimed at supporting the operation of autonomous rail vehicles. The implicit dynamism of this application imposes the design of special mechanisms to guarantee real-time and fault-tolerant data communication, even when logical networks are dynamically created, destroyed or reconfigured. To cope with this requirement, a new protocol is used to build up dynamic communication channels, which are mapped in a hierarchical physical network. The propulsion of the vehicles is based on linear motors placed along the rail track and, for this reason, the cars must not only communicate with each other, but also with the linear motors they are passing by.

Keywords: Real-time Communication, Mechatronic Systems, Hardware Design

1.   INTRODUCTION

Mechatronic systems are gradually becoming larger and more complex. Moreover, especially for applications in the automotive, transportation or aerospace domains, there is increasingly the necessity to interconnect a large amount of components in order to realize the required functions in a distributed manner. For this reason, data communication systems play an important role in the design of new mechatronic systems and must be carefully designed to guarantee real-time and possibly fault-tolerant behavior.

In this paper we deal with the data communication requirements for the RailCab project [7], which is a train system that consists of autonomous vehicles, also called shuttles. Linear motors placed along the rail track and installed on the vehicles are used for propulsion and braking. This technology also allows shuttles to build up or leave vehicle-convoys while moving. To implement such features, a real-time and fault-tolerant communication system to support the management of dynamic logical networks is required. However, the requirements of data communication systems for conventional trains are different [4], because they are mainly meant for traffic control and not necessarily for establishing links between several trains. In addition, the need for the vehicles to control linear motors sections on the track, to decide with other shuttles which convoy strategies to take and to control velocity and distance with respect to other vehicles are all factors that lead to a higher bandwidth utilization.

This paper is organized as follows. In section 2 we briefly introduce a communication protocol to support the functions previously described. Section 3 presents the data network infrastructure concept for the RailCab track and in section 4 we show how dynamic networks can be implemented using the new protocol. Finally we present the hardware used to test the new components and some concluding remarks.

2.   THE TRAILCABLE PROTOCOL

The communication system described in this paper can be implemented using the TrailCable communication protocol, which is described in more details in [3]. A network based on this protocol is built up with point-to-point, full-duplex communication links made up of electrical cables or fiber optics. Every node can have one or more ports, and for each port a unique link to a neighbor can be established. Once such a physical infrastructure is available, it is possible to create logical channels as indicated by the example in figure 1.

Each node dynamically assigns the available data links to currently active real-time communication tasks by means of a scheduling algorithm such as the Earliest Deadline First (EDF) [1]. To guarantee real-time behavior, before a new communication task can be admitted into the network an acceptance test must be executed based on the characteristics of the real-time channels, such as arrival rate, length and deadline of the data packets. Thus, the logical communication channels are limited by factors such as link bandwidth, maximum transmission latency or the number of available message identifiers. The scheduling operation and the routing of frames are controlled by data structures stored locally in each node, the so called *scheduling tables*.

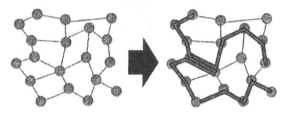

Fig. 1 – A set of communication channels

The TrailCable protocol also implements special mechanisms to cope with fault-tolerance of the real-time data channels, including redundancy of the data links and bandwidth guardians to prevent that traffic overload (that can only be caused by faults) interfere with the correct scheduling of the remaining tasks.

The choice to use the TrailCable is justified by the fact that managing dynamic networks under real-time conditions can be supported by this new protocol, as will be shown in the following sections.

3.   NETWORK INFRASTRUCTURE

Before looking in details how dynamic networks are built up, it is necessary to present the communication infrastructure to be used. To construct the physical network for the RailCab track we initially assume that three main components must be interconnected: The servos that control the linear motors, the Shuttle/Track Communication Points (STCP) and the section manager. Their functions are the following:

- *Servo* – equipment that controls the linear motors based on the following reference values: frequency f and current I of the desired stator wave, position x and length l of the convoys or a single vehicle.
- *STCP* – because different technologies can be used for transmitting data between the rail track and the moving shuttles, we use the so called STCPs to abstract the components that are responsible for establishing this wireless communication.
- *Section managers* – are computers that collect the information of all shuttles in a certain track section, such as position and velocity. The data

are then used for different functions, ranging from distributing the reference values to the linear motor servos to supporting the convoy formation phase.

A test-track (fig. 2) of about 530m (scale 1:2,5) for the RailCab project was built at the University of Paderborn and is used to evaluate different subsystems. We start by showing how the current network infrastructure looks like and suggest afterwards a new concept that can be scaled up to larger systems.

Fig. 2 – The RailCab test-track

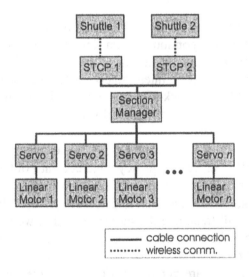

Fig. 3 – Current test-track infrastructure

The current infrastructure of the test-track [6] consists of 83 linear motor sections that are installed along the rail and the respective servos. One section manager controls all servos via a CAN bus interface and is also connected to two STCPs (radio modems), one for each of the two vehicles that can travel simultaneously on the test-track. An architecture representation of this system is depicted in figure 3.

Although the presented architecture meets the current test-track communication requirements, it is clear that such a centralized structure can not be scaled up for larger systems as a lot of problems would arise. In the typical application scenarios, the nodes (servos, STCPs and servo managers) are linearly distributed over great distances on the track and therefore factors like communication latency, cabling effort, required bandwidth, electrical interferences, fault-tolerance, among others, prohibit a centralized approach.

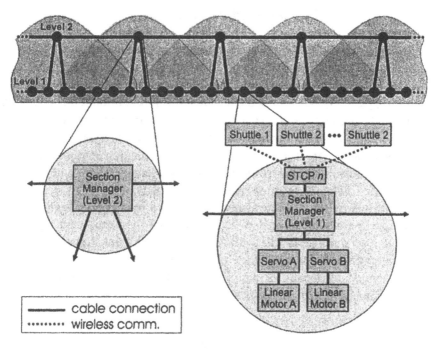

Fig. 4 – The new network concept

To build up a scalable network, the topology shown in figure 4 can be employed. Each node at the lowest level consists of a section manager, a STCP and two linear motors with their respective servos. Via the STCP, the shuttles currently traveling over the correspondent track section can communicate with the fixed network infrastructure. The real-time data communication channels passing through different section managers can be mapped in the hierarchical network using the same procedure that is used in figure 1.

For the sake of clarity, the connections in the figure 4 are represented as simple point-to-point links, but the communication topology can be constructed to tolerate link errors, as shown if figure 5. In this scenario, even if a single link fails, the system is able to continue working properly as the data interfaces are replicated. The topology in figure 5 is therefore robust enough to support a limited number of not consecutive node failures, because at least one alternative route would still be available.

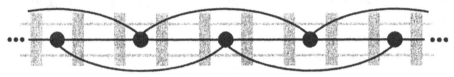

Fig. 5 – A redundant topology

It can also be seen in figure 4 that a higher communication level made up of interconnected section managers (level 2) exists. The objective of this second level is not to overload the primary communication path by transmitting packets node by node over great distances. Should this necessity exist, the data packets are transmitted from a section manager of level 1 to the correspondent section managers of level 2, which then forward the message via the upper "shortcut" links to the destination region. Once the message is received by the respective section managers of level 2, it is directed to the final node (section manager of level 1).

The reason why the section managers build up overlapping regions (fig. 4) is to cope with fault-tolerance. Should one of the section managers of level 2 fail, a second one is still available to assume the functionalities of the faulty neighbor. Another advantage of the presented architecture is that it can be extended by means of additional hierarchy levels if bandwidth or other communication requirements should increase.

4.   DYNAMIC NETWORKS

Now that the basic network topology was presented, it is possible to show how the communication channels between different shuttles are maintained when the vehicles are moving. During normal operation, communication channels can be reconfigured, added, and removed dynamically. A possible scenario, which consists of three shuttles, is depicted in figure 6a. The nodes A to F build up the "level 1" segment identified in the figure 4. For the sake of simplicity in fig. 6a, we will consider only the data flow from left to the right, but the concept also applies for the inverted direction. It can be seen in figure 6a that every participating node has the same *scheduling table,* where the *ID* 1 indicates that the information received by a node was generated at its direct neighbor, the *ID* 2 at a neighbor one hop away and so on. This is possible due to the fact that when a data packet is forwarded by a node, the *ID* of the message is replaced by a new one.

a)

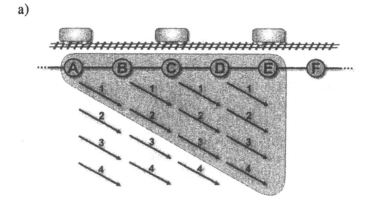

b)

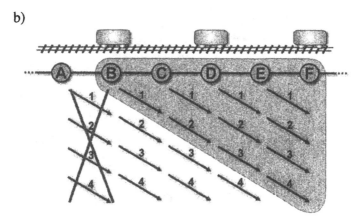

Fig. 6 - Maintenance of dynamic channels

When shuttles keep moving along the track and change their position (figure 6b), it is not necessary to alter all *scheduling tables* at all nodes. Instead, the reconfiguration process takes place only at the channel ends. The link from node A to node B is not needed anymore as soon as the left-most shuttle has reached the position B. Therefore, node A becomes idle and its scheduling and routing operations can be partially disabled. From this moment, node B turns into the new origin. At the channel end, the communication channel must be expanded by activating node F with the same *scheduling table* used by the other participants.

The employment of reusable IDs instead of exclusive addresses represents an elegant manner to cope with the described "moving" logical networks, because the management of the communication links can be done by means of similar data structures in the different nodes.

In the given example, a logical network consists of 5 nodes, but the concept can be also extended for larger clusters, by including additional entries in the *scheduling tables*.

5.   INITIAL IMPLEMENTATION

To test the concepts described throughout this paper on the test track, three electronic boards have been developed. The first one is adapted from [8] and consists of a PowerPC MPC555 microcontroller, an FPGA, an Ethernet interface, and four LVDS ports. The second one is a bridge from the TrailCable protocol to the interface used by the motor servos [2]. The third board couples the electrical LVDS interface to fiber optics (fig. 7).

Fig. 7 – Evaluation Hardware

The TrailCable protocol is being entirely implemented in FPGAs, using the VHDL programming language and the Xilinx ISE 7.1 development suite. Data rates up to 32Mbps for links of about 100 meters (using the fiber optics adapter) can be reached using the current hardware. The size of the data packets is initially restricted to 128 bytes and the packet forwarding operation in a node takes less than 1μs. In order to construct the communication protocol in a resource efficient manner, special components of the FPGA architectures, such as distributed and block memories are used to reduce the area needed by the protocol functions in the programmable logic devices. This is done because resource efficiency is also a factor that should be taken into account when building embedded systems.

6. CONCLUSION

A concept to build up the data communication network of a new train system was presented in this paper. It is based on the TrailCable protocol, which allows real-time data channels to be dynamically reconfigured, besides providing fault-tolerance capabilities.

Using the approach presented, it is possible to create overlapping logical networks that are used for two purposes: to create a hierarchical topology for organizing the data flow and to establish "moving" logical subnets. In the latter case, the shuttles within a certain area are able to communicate with each other, abstracting the fact that they are moving.

Due to the physical behavior of the system, shuttles do not need to communicate with all others over a long track, but mainly with their neighbors. For this reason, the proposed architecture still allows the scalability of the system, what can be done, for example, by adding extra hierarchy levels in the network physical structure.

Finally, to implement and validate the concepts described in this paper, a new hardware platform was specially constructed and an optimized architecture for the TrailCable protocol is being developed to allow a resource efficient implementation for the network to be tested at the RailCab test-track.

REFERENCES

[1] Buttazzo, G. *"Hard Real-Time Computing Systems – Predictable Scheduling Algorithms and Applications"* Kluwer Academic Publishers, Boston/Dordrecht/ London, 1997.

[2] de Freitas Francisco, A. L.; Rettberg, A.; Hennig, A.: *Hardware Design and Protocol Specification for the Control and Communication within a Mechatronic System.* In: Proceedings of IFIP Working Conference on Distributed and Parallel Embedded Systems (DIPES'04). Toulouse, France. Kluwer Academic Publishers, 23-26 August 2004

[3] de Freitas Francisco, A. L.; Rammig, F. J.: *Fault-Tolerant Hard-Real-Time Communication of Dynamically Reconfigurable, Distributed Embedded Systems.* In: 8th IEEE International Symposium on Object-oriented Real-time distributed Computing. Seattle, Washington, USA. May 18-20, 2005.

[4] European Train Control System (ETCS) Project. Available online at: http://etcs.uic.asso.fr/.

[5] Kandlur, D., Shin, K. G. & Ferrari, D. *"Real-Time communication in point-to-point networks"*. IEEE Trans. on Parallel and Distributed Systems, Oct. 1994, pp. 1044-1056.

[6] Pottharst, A.; Schulz, B.; Böcker, J.: *"Kommunikationssysteme einer Anlage mit doppelt gespeistem Linearmotor"*. In: Fachmesse und Kongress (SPS/IPC/DRIVES). Nürnberg, Germany, 2004

[7] University of Paderborn. *The RailCab Project*. Available online at: http://www.railcab.de. 2004.

[8] Zanella, M.; Robrecht M.; Lehmann, T.; Gielow, R.; de Freitas Francisco, A. L.; Horst, A.: *"RABBIT: A Modular Rapid-Prototyping Platform for Distributed Mechatronic Systems"*. In: Proc. of the 14th Symposium on Integrated Circuits and Systems Design; Brasília, Brazil, 2001.

TOWARDS RUN-TIME PARTITIONING OF A REAL TIME OPERATING SYSTEM FOR RECONFIGURABLE SYSTEMS ON CHIP *

Marcelo Götz, [1] Achim Rettberg [2] and Carlos Eduardo Pereira [3]

[1] *Heinz Nixdorf Institute*
University of Paderborn, Germany
mgoetz@uni-paderborn.de

[2] *C-LAB*
University of Paderborn, Germany
achim@c-lab.de

[3] *Departamento de Engenharia Eletrica*
UFRGS - Universidade Federal do Rio Grande do Sul - Brazil
cpereira@eletro.ufrgs.br

Abstract: Reconfigurable computing have successfully been designed taking into advantage the supporting of architectures based on the FPGAs and CPU. Moreover, the new hybrid FPGAs (e.g. Virtex-II Pro™), provides a hardcore general-purpose processor (GPP) embedded into a field of programmable gate arrays. Together with the ability to be partially reconfigured, those chips are very attractive for implementation of run-time reconfigurable embedded systems. However, most of the efforts in this field were made in order to apply these capabilities at application level, leaving to the Operating System (OS) the provision of the necessary mechanisms to support these applications. This paper present an approach for run-time reconfigurable Operating System, which take advantage of the new hybrid FPGA chips to reconfigure itself based on online estimation of application demands. The paper focus on run-time assignment and reconfiguration of OS services over a hybrid architecture. The proposed model uses a 0-1 Integer programming strategy for assigning OS components over a hybrid architecture, as well as an alternative heuristic algorithm for it. In addition, the evaluation of the reconfiguration costs are presented and discussed.

Keywords: Reconfigurable Computing, System-on-Chip, Real Time Operating System

*This work was developed in the course of the Special Research Initiative 614 - Self-optimizing Concepts and Structures in Mechanical Engineering - University of Paderborn, and was published on its behalf and funded by the Deutsche Forschungsgemeinschaft.

1.   INTRODUCTION

Nowadays, the usage of Field Programmable Gate Array (FPGA) in the field of Reconfigurable Computing (RC) has become widely used. In particular the capability of a FPGA to be run-time reprogrammed makes its use for reconfigurable systems very attractive Even more attractive is the emerging hybrid FPGAs, which has a hardcore or softcore general purpose processor (GPP) surrounded by a large field of reprogrammable logic. These new components open several interesting possibilities to design reconfigurable architectures for Systems on Chip (SoC). [2].

One of the challenges of our research is to provide support for run-time reconfigurable architectures, which may be used for self-optimizing systems. Such systems are used to realize and implement the control of transportation system like that one described in [1]. In dynamic environments, where application requirements may dynamically change, the concept of reconfigurable operating systems appears, which is emerging as new research field.

Differently from the normal approach where the design of such operating system (OS) is done offline, the proposed approach suggests the use of new partial reconfigurable architectures in order to support the development of a hardware/software reconfigurable operating system [6]. In this proposed architecture, the RTOS is capable to adapt itself to current application requirements, tailoring the RTOS components for this purpose. Therefore, the system continuously analysis the requirements and reconfigure the RTOS components at the hybrid architecture optimizing the use of system resources. Hence, the system is capable to decide on-the-fly which RTOS components are needed and also to which execution environment (CPU or FPGA) they will be assigned.

The paper focuses on an online partitioning algorithm for a real-time operating system services, which tries to minimize the whole resource utilization and the reconfiguration costs of the components.

The remaining of the paper is organized as follows: Section 2 presents a brief state-of-the-art analysis regarding hardware implementation of OS services their flexibilities. Then, section 3 shortly presents the architecture used. Section 4 presents the system formulation using 0-1 Integer Programming (BIP) and the reconfiguration costs evaluation. An analysis of the run-time execution of this evaluations, with an heuristic algorithm for the components assignment problem are presented in section 5. Section 6 presents some evaluation results using MATLAB to compare the proposed heuristic algorithm with the optimal solution provided by BIP. Finally, some conclusions and future work are shown in section 7.

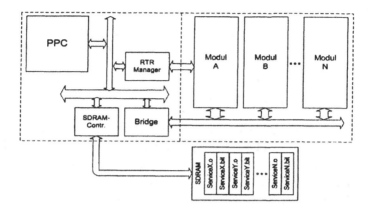

Figure 1. Proposed architecture based on a Virtex-II Pro™FPGA.

2. RELATED WORK

The idea of implementing OS services in hardware is not new. Several works in the literature, [12],[11],[10],[13],[15] and [14] show that hardware implementation may significantly improve performance and determinism of RTOS functionalities. The overhead imposed by the operating system, which is carefully considered in embedded systems design due to usual lack of resources, is considerably decreased by having RTOS services implemented in hardware. However, up to now all approaches have been based on implementations that are static in nature, that means, they do not change during run-time even when application requirements may significantly change.

In the field of reconfigurable computing, reconfiguration aspects have been concentrated at application level (see [7], [18] and [16]). At the OS level the research are limited to provide run-time support for those applications (see [10], [3], [20] and [19]).

In the approach presented in this paper we expand the usage of those concepts and the hardware support to the OS level. Additionally, based on the state-of-the-art analysis, for a self-optimized reconfigurable RTOS none such similar approach has been proposed yet.

3. ARCHITECTUIRE

Our target architecture is composed of one CPU, configurable logic elements (FPGA), memory and a bus connecting the components. Most of these elements are provided in a single CHIP, such as the Virtex II Pro™, from Xilinx company. The RTOS services that are able to be reconfigured are stored on an external SDRAM chip in two different implementations: as software object and as FPGA configuration bitstream (see Figure 1).

The Run-Time Reconfiguration (RTR) block (see [5]) provides the necessary services to the RTOS to manage the FPGA resources: module placement, loading and allocation. More detailed information about this architecture can be seen in [9] and [8].

4. PROBLEM DEFINITION

The problem of assigning RTOS components over the two execution environments can be seen as a typical assignment problem. Therefore, we decided to model the problem using Binary Integer Programming (BIP) [17] and [21]. A set of available services is represented as $S = \{s_{i,j}\}$, where every service i has its implementation for CPU ($j = 1$) or FPGA ($j = 2$). Every component has an estimated cost $c_{i,j}$, which represents the percentage of resource from the execution environment used by this component. On the FPGA it represents the circuit area needed by the component and at CPU it represents the processor used by it. Note that these costs are not static, since the application demands are considered to be dynamic. This topic will be addressed later on in subsection 4.2.

4.1 OS Service Assignment

The assignment of a component to either CPU or FPGA is represented by the variable $x_{i,j}$. We say that $x_{i,j} = 1$ if the component i is assigned to the execution environment j, and $x_{i,j} = 0$ otherwise. As some of the components may not necessary be needed by the current application, they should neither be assigned to the CPU ($j = 1$) nor to the FPGA ($j = 2$). Therefore, to proper represent this situation we consider that this component should stay at memory pool ($j = 3$). As we are focusing on the resource utilization optimization between CPU and FPGA we define that a component i placed on the memory pool ($j = 3$) does not consume any resource ($c_{i,3} = 0$). The definition of a third assignment place for an OS component is more useful for reconfiguration costs estimation, that will be seen in section 4.2.

The resources are limited, which derive two constraints for our BIP formulation: the maximum FPGA area available (A_{max}) and the maximum CPU workload (U_{max}) reserved for the operating system. Thus, the total FPGA area (A) and total CPU workload (U) used by the hardware components and the software components, respectively can not exceed their maximums. These constraints are represented by

$$U = \sum_{i=1}^{n} x_{i,1} c_{i,1} \leq U_{max}, \qquad A = \sum_{i=1}^{n} x_{i,2} c_{i,2} \leq A_{max}$$

We also consider that a component i can be assigned just to one of the execution environment: $\sum_{j=1}^{3} x_{i,j} = 1$ for every $i = 1, ..., n$.

To avoid that one of the execution environment would have its usage near to the maximum, we specify a constraint to keep a balanced resource utilization (B) between the two execution environments: $B = |w_1 U - w_2 A| \leq \delta$. Where δ is the maximum allowed unbalanced resource utilization between CPU and FPGA. The weights w_1 and w_2 are used to proper compare the resource utilization between two different execution environments. If the resource used from an execution environment are not near to its maximum, it will have the capability to absorb some variation of the application demands. This characteristic are useful for real-time system in order to avoid the application to miss its deadlines due to workload transients. Note that this approach cannot guarantee hard real time constraints. However, for soft real-time systems it is useful.

The objective function used to minimize the whole resource utilization is defined as

$$min\{\sum_{j=1}^{3}\sum_{i=1}^{n} c_{i,j} x_{i,j}\}$$

The solution of this BIP are the assignment variables $x_{i,j}$, which we define as being a specific system configuration: $\Gamma = \{x_{i,j}\}$.

4.2   Reconfiguration Costs

As is has been said in the section 4, the application requirements are considered to change over system life time. These modifications are represented by changes of the component costs $c_{i,j}$. This leads to the fact that a certain system configuration Γ may no longer be valid after application changes. Therefore, a continuously evaluation of the components partitioning is necessary. Whenever the systems reaches a unbalanced situation ($|w_1 U - w_2 A| > \delta$), the RTOS components should be reallocated in order to bring the system again in the desired configuration. In this situation, not just the new assignment problem need to be solved (Γ') again, but also the costs (time) necessary to reconfigure the system from Γ to Γ' need to be evaluated. This evaluation is necessary since we are dealing with real-time system. Thus, we have a limited time available for reconfiguration activities.

The reconfiguration cost of every component represents the time necessary to migrate a component from one execution environment to the other one. Therefore, we need to specify for every possible migration of a component its correspondent cost. As it was shown in section 4.1, our model assumes three different environments ($j = \{1, 2, 3\}$). The definition of the environment $j = 3$ (memory pool) is necessary to proper represent the case where a new OS service arrives in the system. This happens when the application requires a service that is neither at CPU nor at FPGA available, but it is stored at the memory pool. The same is valid for a service that leaves the system (it is not more needed by the application). So, we define for a component i a 3×3 size migration costs matrix R_i. Let $R_i = \{r^i_{j,j'}\}$, where j and j' are the current and new execution environment of component i.

If $x_i = \{x_{i,1}, x_{i,2}, x_{i,3}\}$ and $x'_i = \{x'_{i,1}, x'_{i,2}, x'_{i,3}\}$ are the current and new assignment of the component i, then the complete reconfiguration cost K (total reconfiguration time) of the system is defined as:

$$K = \sum_{i=1}^{n} x_i^T R_i x'_i$$

In our current approach the migration costs associated which a component includes all necessary steps to remove a component from one execution environment to the other one. These steps represents the time to program the FPGA with a component or link the software component with in the CPU programm, translate the context between different execution environments (when necessary), and also read the component instance from memory pool.

5.   RUN-TIME ANALYSIS

As our operating system is being designed to support real-time applications, a deterministic behavior for service assignment and system reconfiguration need to be used in order to handle application time constraints.

5.1   Heuristic Algorithm for Assignment Problem

The solution of an BIP finds an optimal solution for the assignment problem. For a small set of components this approach is very suitable. However, it is too computationally complex to solve all problem sizes. Therefore, we are currently using an heuristic greedy based algorithm for this problem.

The algorithm starts selecting the component that has the smallest cost among them needed by the current application and it assigns this component to the correspondent execution environment. It then selects the component that has the smallest cost among the remaining unassigned ones so that it tries to keep the usage of CPU resource U equal to the FPGA resource A. This process is repeated until all components have been assigned. The algorithm terminates by checking if the CPU and FPGA resources usage constraint are fulfilled: $U \leq U_{max}; A \leq A_{max}$. If so, the algorithm returns a valid assignment solution, or an error otherwise. It can be seen that this algorithm has a polynomial complexity of $O(n^2)$, since we have just one *for* loop which produce n searches in a list of (maximum) n elements. This algorithm is also shown in Algorithm 1.

Note that this algorithm do not take into consideration the balancing constraint δ. So, there is no guarantee that it will provide a solution which fulfills this constraint. Therefore, a second algorithm is proposed that improves the balancing B in order to meet the δ constraint. It is based on Kernighan-Lin

---

Algorithm 1 Heuristic for service assignment

$C_1 = \{c_{i,1}\}$ Set of components available for CPU ($j = 1$)
$C_2 = \{c_{i,2}\}$ Set of components available for FPGA ($j = 2$)
$X_1 = \{x_{i,1}\}$ Assignment of CPU components
$X_2 = \{x_{i,2}\}$ Assignment of FPGA components
$C = C_1 \cup C_2; \quad X = X_1 \cup X_2; \quad U = A = 0$
n = number of components
for $k = 1$ to n **do**
  if $U \leq A$ **then**
    Find an unassigned component i among $\{c_{i,1}\}$ so that it has the smallest cost.
    Assign this component to CPU: $x_{i,1} = 1; x_{i,2} = 0$
  else
    Find an unassigned component i among $\{c_{i,2}\}$ so that it has the smallest cost.
    Assign this component to FPGA: $x_{i,2} = 1; x_{i,1} = 0$
  end if
  $U = C_1 X_1^T$
  $A = C_2 X_2^T$
  if $U > U_{max}$ or $A > A_{max}$ **then**
    Exit with error: "Not feasible"
  end if
end for
return X

---

algorithms [4] and it aims to obtain a better balancing B than the first one by swapping pairs of components between CPU and FPGA. The algorithm receives as input the assignment solution X provided by the first algorithm which has $nc_1 = \sum_{i=1}^{n} x_{i,1}$ components assigned to CPU and $nc_2 = \sum_{i=1}^{n} x_{i,2}$ components assigned to FPGA. The maximum number of pairs that are possible to be swapped is defined as: $max\_pairs = min(nc_1, nc_2)$.

By moving a component i, previously assigned to the CPU, to the FPGA ($\{x_{i,1} = 1; x_{i,2} = 0\} \Rightarrow \{x_{i,1} = 0; x_{i,2} = 1\}$), we have a new balancing B: $B_{new} = |B_{current} - s_i|$, where $s_i = \{c_{i,1} + c_{i,2}\}$. Similarly, by moving a component i from FPGA to CPU, the new balancing B will be: $B_{new} = |B_{current} + s_i|$. Thus, swapping a pair of components o, p ($\{x_{o,1} = 1; x_{o,2} = 0\}; \{x_{p,1} = 0; x_{p,2} = 1\}$), the new balancing B is defined as: $B_{new} = |B_{current} - s_o + s_p|$. Similarly, $B_{new} = |B_{current} + s_o - s_p|$ if $\{x_{o,1} = 0; x_{o,2} = 1\}; \{x_{p,1} = 1; x_{p,2} = 0\}$. Additionally, we define G_{op} as the gain obtained in the balancing B by swapping a pair o and p of components:

$G_{op} = B_{new} - B_{current}$. A gain below 0 means an improvement obtained in the balancing B.

Algorithm 2 Heuristic for balancing B improvement

$X_1^{init} = \{x_{i,1}\}$ Initial assignment of CPU components
$X_2^{init} = \{x_{i,2}\}$ Initial assignment of FPGA components
$X^{init} = X_1^{init} \cup X_2^{init}$
$X^{new} = X^{init}$
$B^{init} = |U^{init} - A^{init}|$
$B^{new} = B^{init}$
$m = max\_pairs$ maximum number of pairs
repeat
    for $k = 1$ to m **do**
        Find the pair o, p ($\{x_{o,1} = 1; x_{o,2} = 0\}; \{x_{p,1} = 0; x_{p,2} = 1\}$ or $\{x_{o,0} = 0; x_{o,2} = 1\}; \{x_{p,1} = 1; x_{p,2} = 0\}$) so that o and p are unlocked and G_{op} is minimal
        if $G_{op} < 0$ **then**
            Swap o and p changing the current assignment $\Rightarrow X^{new} = (X^{new}$ with o and p swapped)
            $B^{new} = B^{new} + G_{op}$
            Lock o and p.
        end if
    end for
until $G_{op} \geq 0$ OR $B^{new} < \delta$ OR all pairs are locked
return X^{new}

The algorithm stars trying to swap all possible pairs and storing the gain obtained by every try. It than chooses the one which provides the smallest gain. If this gain is bigger than or equal to zero, none swap is able to provide an improvement in the balancing B and the algorithm stops. Otherwise, the pair that provides the smallest gain are swapped and locked (no longer a candidate to be swaped). This process is repeated until all pairs have been locked or no improvement can be obtained by any interchange or if the δ constraint has been fulfilled. The algorithm terminates by returning the new assignment solution X that provides a better (or at least an equal) balancing B than the solution provided by the first one. The algorithm for balancing B improvement is shown in Algorithm 2.

5.2   System Reconfiguration

For real-time applications, the reconfiguration time must also be taken under consideration. Depending on the decision of the assignment algorithm (which generates a new system configuration Γ') the total system reconfiguration time

K required may be bigger than the current time allowed by the application. Therefore, the reconfiguration of the OS components need to be done separately in time in order to still able the application to meet its time constraints. It means that a schedule for components reconfiguration needs to be found. Some technics for component reconfiguration scheduling are currently being investigated. However, this topic will not be treated in the scope of this paper.

6.   EXPERIMENTAL RESULTS

For system evaluation of the run-time assignment problem, we made some simulations using MATLAB tool. We generated a number of 100 different systems having randomly costs: $1\% \leq c_{i,1} \leq 15\%$ and $5\% \leq c_{i,2} \leq 25\%$; and fixed size: $n = 20$ components. The maximum FPGA resource was defined to be 100% ($A_{max} = 100$), as well as for the CPU ($U_{max} = 100$). The components assignment were calculated for every system using the 0-1 Integer Programming (optimal solution) and the heuristic algorithm (first and second one). The average value of total cost ($U + A$) and the absolute difference cost ($|w_1 U - w_2 A|$) were compared for different values of δ (the resource usage balancing restriction): $(0.5, 1, 2, 3, 4, 5, 10, 20, 30, 40, 50 \ and \ 60)$.

The solutions provided by the first heuristic algorithm were very similar to the optimal one, if the δ constraint has values around ($\delta \approx 10\%$), concerning the fulfil of this constraint (see Figure 2, Heuristic-1). The smaller the δ the poor the results given by the first heuristic algorithm. This was expected to be so, since the first algorithm do not consider the balancing restriction.

The appliance of the second algorithm over the solution provided by the first one deliver a better balancing B. However, an increase in the total cost

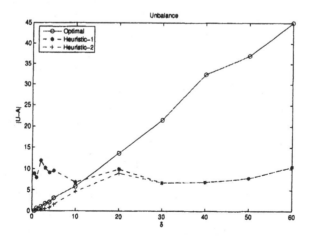

Figure 2.   Unbalance average for different δ constraints.

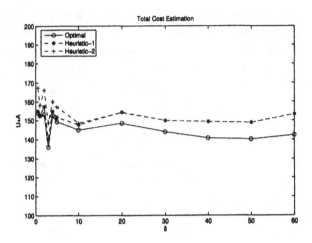

Figure 3.   Total cost assignment average for different δ constraints.

assignment was verified for the cases where the second algorithm achieved an improvement in the balancing B ($\delta <\approx 10\%$). Nevertheless, the total cost assignment achieved by this heuristic algorithm were quite satisfactory: maximum of 15% bigger if compared with the optimal case (see Figure 3, Heuristic-2).

7.   CONCLUSIONS AND FUTURE WORK

In this paper we have presented our investigation towards a run-time reconfigurable RTOS running over a hybrid platform, focusing in the OS service assignment and system reconfiguration. Looking at the related work, we are quite convinced that this is a novel approach for a self-optimized RTOS.

A shortly presentation of the hardware architecture based on a Virtex-II Pro™FPGA was also presented. The 0-1 Integer Programming model of the system and the reconfiguration cost evaluation have been presented. Additionally, considerations of a run-time execution of this technics, in order to support real-time applications have been discussed.

As a future work, the investigation of a proper OS components assignment algorithm which takes into consideration the application time constraints and the integration of the communication costs among the components are going to be made. Technics to able the run-time reallocation of the components over an hybrid architecture will be investigated. Moreover, a reconfiguration scheduling of the components, necessary to bring the system to a new configuration ($\Gamma \Rightarrow \Gamma'$) are going to be made.

REFERENCES

[1] http://nbp-www.upb.de/.

[2] David Andrews, Douglas Niehaus, and Peter Ashenden. Programming models for hybrid cpu/fpga chips. *Computer - Inovative Thecnology for Computer Professionals*, 37:118–120, January 2004. IEEE Computer Society.

[3] Krishnamoorthy Baskaran, Wu Jigang, and Thamipillai Srikanthan. Hardware partitioning algorithm for reconfigurable operating system in embedded systems. In *Sixth Real-Time Linux Workshop*, pages 117–123, November 2004. Singapore.

[4] Petru Eles, Krzysztof Kuchcinski, and Zebo Peng. *System Synthesis with VHDL: A Transformational Approach*, chapter 4, pages 114–119. Kluwer Academic Publishers, 1998.

[5] Björn Griese. Eingebettete prozessoren in rekonfigurierbaren strukturen. Studienarbeit, Schaltungstechnik, Heinz Nixdorf Institut, Universitat Paderborn, feb 2003.

[6] Marcelo Götz. Dynamic hardware-software codesign of a reconfigurable real-time operating system. In *International Conference on Reconfigurable Computing and FPGAs 2004 (ReConFig04)*, pages 330–339. Mexican Society of Computer Science, SMCC, 20-21, September 2004.

[7] J. Harkin, T. M. McGinnity, and L. P. Maguire. Modeling and optimizing run-time reconfiguration using evolutionary computation. *Trans. on Embedded Computing Sys.*, 3(4):661–685, 2004.

[8] Heiko Kalte, Mario Porrmann, and Ulrich Rückert. A prototyping platform for dynamically reconfigurable system on chip designs. In *Proceedings of the IEEE Workshop Heterogeneous reconfigurable Systems on Chip (SoC)*, Hamburg, Germany, 2002.

[9] Boris Kettelhoit, Alexander Klassen, Carlos Paiz, Mario Porrmann, and Ulrich Rückert. Rekonfigurierbare hardware zur regelung mechatronischer systeme. In *3. Paderborner Workshop: Intelligente mechatronische Systeme*, HNI-Verlagsschriftenreihe, 2005.

[10] Paul Kohout, Brinda Ganesh, and Bruce Jacob. Hardware support for real-time operating systems. In *International Symposium on Systems Synthesis*, pages 45–51. Proceedings of the 1st IEEE/ACM/IFIP International conference on HW/SW codesign and system synthesis, 2003.

[11] P. Kuacharoen, M. Shalan, and V. Mooney. A configurable hardware scheduler for real-time systems. In *International Conference on Engineering of Reconfigurable Systems and Algorithms (ERSA)*, pages 96–101, June 2003.

[12] Jaehwan Lee, Vicent John Mooney III, K. Ingström, Anders Daleby, T. Klevin, and Lennart Lindh. A comparison of the rtu hardware rtos with a hardware/software rtos. In *ASP-DAC2003, (Asia and South Pacific Design Automation Conference)*, page 6, 2003. Japan.

[13] Jaehwan Lee, Kyeong Ryu, and Vincent John Mooney III. A framework for automatic generation of configuration files for a custom hardware/software rtos. In *International Conference on Engineering of Reconfigurable Systems and Algorithms (ERSA*, June 2002.

[14] Lennart Lindh. Fasthard - a fast time deterministic hardware based real-time kernel. In *IV Euromicro Workshop on Real-Time Systems*, pages 21–25, June 1992.

[15] Lennart Lindh and Frank Stanischewski. Fastchart - a fast time deterministic cpu and hardware based real-time-kernel. In *EUROMICRO'91*, pages 12–19, 1991. Paris, France.

[16] Jean-Yves Mignolet, Vincent Nollet, Paul Coene, Diederik Verkest, Serge Vernalde, and Rudy Lauwereins. Infrastructure for design and management of relocatable tasks in a heterogeneous reconfigurable system-on-chip. In *DATE*, pages 10986–10993, 2003.

[17] George L. Nemhauser and Laurence A. Wolsey. *Integer and combinatorial optimization.* Wiley-Interscience, 1988.

[18] Heather Quinn, Laurie A. Smith King, Miriam Leeser, and Waleed Meleis. Runtime assignment of reconfigurable hardware components for image processing pipelines. In *FCCM*, pages 173–, 2003.

[19] Herbert Walder and Marco Platzner. A runtime environment for reconfigurable hardware operating systems. In *FPL*, pages 831–835, 2004.

[20] Grant Wigley and David Kearney. The development of an operating system for reconfigurable computing. In *FCCM*, April 2001.

[21] Laurence A. Wolsey. *Integer Programming*. Wiley-Interscience, 1998.

COMPONENT CASE STUDY OF A SELF-OPTIMIZING RCOS/RTOS SYSTEM

A reconfigurable network service[*]

Björn Griese, Simon Oberthür, Mario Porrmann
Heinz Nixdorf Institute, University Paderborn
Fürstenallee 11, 33102 Paderborn, Germany
bgriese@hni.upb.de, simon@oberthuer.net, mario@hni.upb.de

Abstract: In highly dynamic scenarios a real-time communication/real-time operating system (RCOS/RTOS), which can fulfill all upcoming demands of the application, is normally very extensive. These RCOS/RTOS systems are heavy-weighted and produce much overhead. System resources for an application or a system service are often reserved for worst-case scenarios and are not usable for other applications. We present a self-optimizing RCOS/RTOS with an integrated flexible resource management. Our RCOS/RTOS adapts its services to the application demands and redistributes temporarily unused resources to other applications under hard real-time conditions. The benefit of our system is shown by means of a self-optimizing communication service. The main building block of this communication service is a reconfigurable dual-port Ethernet switch. Using dynamically reconfigurable hardware to implement the switch enables an adaption of the switch to changing requirements during run-time.

Keywords: RCOS, RTOS, Self-Optimization, Resource Management, Ethernet Switch, Dynamic Reconfiguration

1.   INTRODUCTION

Increasing complexity is one of the major problems in today's automotive industry. To deal with this complexity an approach is to build mechatronic systems in a self-reflecting, self-adaptive and self-optimizing way. Such self-optimizing applications have highly dynamic resource requirements and versatile demands to system services. To fulfill every upcoming demand a standard operating and communication system would have to be very extensive

[*]This work was developed in the course of the Collaborative Research Center 614 - Self-Optimizing Concepts and Structures in Mechanical Engineering - Paderborn University, and was published on its behalf and funded by the Deutsche Forschungsgemeinschaft.

and would have a high overhead. We have developed a dynamic real-time communication/real-time operating system (RCOS/RTOS) for such systems to fulfill the upcoming demands efficiently. The RCOS/RTOS optimizes the infrastructure of the services and redistributes the released resources to the applications. Even resources of an application, which are temporarily unused but guaranteed (e.g. for error recovery), can be temporarily provided to other application under hard real-time conditions.

In this paper we give an overview of the self-optimizing concept in our RCOS/RTOS in section 2. This includes the mechanism of getting necessary information from the applications about their upcoming resource requirements, the modelling of the reconfigurable system services and the optimization of these services and of the system resources. Subsequently, the concepts are illustrated considering as an example a concrete reconfigurable system service: A reconfigurable RCOS service.

The basis of our reconfigurable RCOS are dual-port network nodes. Each node consists of two external network interfaces that connect the node to its neighbors and an internal interface to an embedded processor. In order be able to adapt the network nodes to changes in protocols and interface requirements, which can not be foreseen, we use reconfigurable hardware for the implementation of the network interfaces.

The nodes handle two different types of data streams: data originated from or terminated at the processor and streams that are simply passed through. If network traffic is rather small or if real-time requirements are low or even nonexistent, comparatively simple network interfaces are sufficient, which occupy only a few resources. In this case, data packets are forwarded from one port to another by a software implementation on the embedded processor. This causes a high load for the processor, the internal bus and the memory while the FPGA resources can be utilized by other applications. If the software implementation is not able to deliver the required performance, e.g., due to increasing bandwidth or real-time requirements, the two separate interfaces are substituted by a single integrated hardware switch during run-time. This switch is able to forward data packets autonomously and, as a consequence, manages a much higher amount of traffic. However, the structure of this switch is more complex and requires additional FPGA resources, which are no longer available for other applications.

A prototypical implementation of the dynamic RCOS/RTOS has been realized on the RAPTOR2000 System, a Rapid Prototyping System developed at the System and Circuit Technology research group at the University of Paderborn [5]. Xilinx Virtex-II Pro FPGAs are used, which comprise two embedded PowerPC processors. The Ethernet switch is implemented either in software or in hardware, as detailed in section 3.

Then we show an example scenario (section 4) in which the benefit of a self-optimizing RCOS/RTOS system with this RCOS component is shown.

2. SELF-OPTIMIZING RCOS/RTOS SYSTEM

For building an RCOS/RTOS system, which optimizes itself and provides the released resources optimally to the applications, we had to answer the three following questions:

1. How can we get information about the dynamic resource requirements during run-time of an application? A suitable interface between the application and the operating system is required.
2. How can we describe the design space for reconfiguration of the RCOS/RTOS system? A model is required that describes the dependencies between the system services.
3. Based on this information: Which is an adequate system configuration? A resource management system is required to activate/deactivate the system services and to release resources for the applications.

Our self-optimizing RCOS/RTOS system consists of three components (illustrated in figure 1), which deal with the questions mentioned above: Profile Framework, Online TEReCS and Flexible Resource Management (FRM).

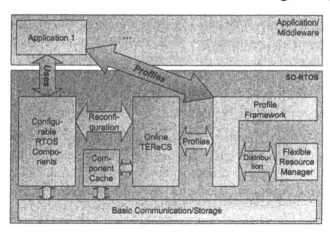

Figure 1.   Overview of the self-optimizing RCOS/RTOS system

2.1   Profile Framework

The Profile Framework, described in detail in [9], has two main purposes: The first purpose is to get information about the dynamic resource requirements of the application and of the system services. The knowledge about the resource requirements of the applications is necessary to optimize the system by deactivating services that are currently not required. The resource requirements of the system services are necessary to determine the amount of resources, which can be released and to guarantee that applications and system services get their required resources under hard real-time conditions. The second purpose is to provide released resources from deactivated system services to the applications.

By means of this framework the developer can define a set of profiles per application. Profiles describe different *service levels* of the application, including different quality and different resource requirements. Furthermore, the states of deactivated/activated system services are mapped to profiles by Online TEReCS.

A single profile contains the following information:

Resource requirements: The *maximum* and *minimum resource usage* per resource of the application if the profile is active.

Maximal assignment delay: All resource allocations of an application require an announcement to the FRM. The maximal delay is the worst case time the assignment of the resource can be delayed by the FRM from the announcement until its allocation.

Switching conditions: The information, between which profiles a switching is possible, and the worst-case execution times (WCET) for activating and deactivating the profiles.

Profile quality: By means of this value the profiles of an application can be ordered according to their quality. Thus, the FRM knows, which profile to prefer when trying to increase the system quality by selecting a profile for activation.

2.2   Online TEReCS

On the basis of the offline configurator TEReCS (Tools for Embedded Real-Time Communication Systems) [1] an online configurator Online TEReCS has been developed for our customizable component based RCOS/RTOS library DREAMS (Distributed Real-time Extensible Application Management System) [3].

The Online-TEReCS component has knowledge of the design space of the customizable components, maps system services into profiles, and is responsible for the low-level reconfiguration of the system services. The knowledge about the design space of the RCOS/RTOS components is stored by the RCOS/RTOS system developer in an AND/OR service dependency graph [2]. For the online case of the configuration a coarse grained hierarchy of this graph is used on the system service level – one service can be composed of many components. Thus, the overall decision space is more restricted and the number of generated profiles is easy to manage.

Each service that is provided in the system is treated as a resource of the system and is managed by the FRM. For a system service, which can be in a deactivated or in an activated state, two profiles are created. One profile for the activated and one profile for the deactivated state. In the profile for the activated state the service specifies the required resources to fulfill its task. In the profile for the deactivated state the service occupies the resources it provides in the activated state. Hereby, it is guaranteed that the services can only be deactivated if the provided services are not required.

2.3 Flexible Resource Manager

The major goal of the FRM [9] is to optimize the resource utilization and the over-all system quality by selecting profiles for activation under the actual conditions. To maximize the utilization the FRM puts the resources, which are held back for worst case resource requirements of an application, at other application's disposal. Normally, an application acquires as much resources as it requires for worst-case scenarios. Thus, the application has always enough resources for its tasks and can fulfill its service at any time. These resources are only required when the worst-case scenario occurs. In our approach the FRM tries to minimize this internal waste of resources, by making these resources temporarily available to other applications under hard real-time conditions.

The FRM is responsible for switching between the profiles of the applications and system services under the defined switching conditions. The decision is made based on a quality function, which considers the actual resource requirements, the importance of an application, and the quality of the profiles. To guarantee hard real-time conditions, an acceptance test for profile activation is integrated in the optimization process.

3. RECONFIGURABLE COMMUNICATION SERVICE

The dynamically reconfigurable Ethernet switch consists of a software and a hardware switch. The software switch comprises two Ethernet Media Access Controllers (MACs), which are connected to the system bus of the network node. For each port of the switch, one Ethernet MAC is required. The switching decision is made by the processor. The whole Ethernet traffic is transferred over the system bus, which results in a high processor and system bus load.

In contrast to the software switch, the switching decision of the hardware switch is carried out in the internal logic of the switch. Every packet that is not destined for the processor is processed and forwarded to the calculated output port by the hardware switch. Therefore, the processor and the system bus are released from performing network infrastructure tasks.

The hardware switch consists of two independent cross-connected sub switches, which are connected to the system bus. The sub switch component is an extension of the Ethernet MAC mentioned above. It integrates an additional buffer for receiving and forwarding the packets that are not destined for the processor. One sub switch component is able to forward packets in one direction. Because of this hierarchical structure of our switch, the Ethernet software driver for both the Ethernet MAC and the hardware switch are the same.

To comply with the real-time requirements of the network service it is important to maintain the connection to the neighboring nodes without loosing packets, while the network interface is reconfigured. Hence, we have introduced a method to reconfigure network interfaces without loosing packets [12]. The reconfiguration strategies are based on a parallel instantiation of both switch implementations, which allows a fast transition from the software switch to the hardware switch and vice versa. To hand over interface control from the current configuration to the new configuration we use the Inter Frame Gaps (IFG) of the applied Ethernet protocol. Because the IFG does not appear simultaneously on both directions the transmit process and the receive process can be switched separately by the hardware multiplexer, which controls the access to the Media Independent Interface (MII).

The reconfiguration from a software switch to a hardware switch is shown in figure 2. The dashed arrows represent copy operations of the processor, and transmitted packets respectively. The solid arrows represent new arriving Ethernet packets. The figure illustrates the state after the hardware switch is loaded. At the first IFG the multiplexer can handover the receive signals from the software implementation to the hardware implementation. Moreover, the processor has to copy the packets that still reside in the receive buffer of the software switch to the transmit buffer of the hardware switch. If the transmit buffer of the software switch is empty, the multiplexer can handover the transmit signals to the new configuration.

3.1   Profiles of the Ethernet switch

The two implementations of the Ethernet switch are mapped into one profile each by Online-TEReCS. Additionally, a third profile is created, in which the reconfiguration between both switch variants is done. We assume that the node will be in a network in which transit traffic goes through the Ethernet switch component. This means it can not be disabled completely. In table 1 we show the defined settings of the three profiles.

The first profile includes the software switch, while the second profile includes the hardware switch. The quality of both profiles is zero, because in the quality function of the FRM only applications should be considered. The goal of the FRM is to maximize the quality of applications, not of the system

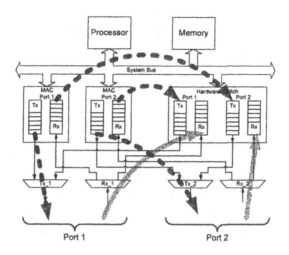

Figure 2. Packet flow during reconfiguration

System service or application	Impor-tance	Profile							
				Resource requirements				WCET	
		Profile name	Profile quality	FPGA		Bandwidth			
				in Slices	Delay	MBit/s	Delay	Enter	Leave
Ethernet switch	0.0	SW	0	1981	0 ms	86	0 ms	1 ms	1 ms
		HW	0	4573	0 ms	0	0 ms	1 ms	1 ms
		reconf.	0	6554	0 ms	0	0 ms	10 ms	1 ms
BW manager	1.0	standard	0	0	0 ms	1-100	15 ms	10 ms	1 ms
Self-opt. application	1.0	normal	0	0	0 ms	0	0 ms	1 ms	1 ms
		accel.	0	3000	0 ms	0	0 ms	10 ms	1 ms

Table 1. The profiles of the example scenario

services. System services are indirectly optimized by deactivating them and releasing their acquired resources, thus allowing the FRM to activate a profile of an application with higher quality.

To simplify the example only the requirements for FPGA resource and for bandwidth are shown in the table, additional resource requirements like memory or CPU are hidden. The minimum and maximum required space on the FPGA is constant in each profile. Once activated the profiles do not allocate additional space on the FPGA. Both profiles allocate the required space on the FPGA in their initialization phase. This is the reason why the maximal assignment delay is zero.

The resource 'bandwidth' has a special significance for this communication system service: It is the resource the service provides to the system. The maximum bandwidth provided is 100 MBit/s, which can only be provided by the hardware profile of the Ethernet switch. The hardware/software variant can only provide 14 MBit/s. Therefore, the Ethernet switch blocks the unavailable bandwidth by allocating 86 MBit/s in the software profile. This guarantees that the FRM does not activate this variant if a bandwidth larger than 14 Mbit/s is required. This kind of modeling is necessary because the FRM operates on a fixed quantity of resources.

As mentioned above, handing over the communication service without packet loss from the software switch to the hardware switch requires a coexistence of both switch implementations. In the short period of reconfiguration the third profile provides the FPGA resources that are necessary for both switch implementations. Only if packet loss and an interruption of the connection is tolerable it is possible to just deactivate the current configuration and replace it with the new one. In this case the third profile is dispensable.

4.   CASE STUDY: OPTIMIZATION EXAMPLE

To show the benefit of our self-optimizing RCOS/RTOS we present an example scenario. The scenario consists of three components, which define profiles. The presented Ethernet switch component, a bandwidth manager, and a self-optimizing application. In table 1 we show the defined settings of the profiles the components define.

Bandwidth manager.   The Ethernet switch is responsible for delivering packets to components on the node and for transit traffic through the node. To guarantee communication under hard real-time conditions bandwidth reservation is applied. By means of the bandwidth manager applications from other nodes can reserve bandwidth in the Ethernet component of this node. The manager allocates the amount of bandwidth at the local FRM for the remote application.

The Bandwidth manager defines only one profile because it cannot be deactivated nor has any implementation alternatives. It is implemented in software, thus no FPGA resources are required. The minimum and maximum bandwidth requirements range from 1 MBit/s to 100 Mbit/s with an assignment delay of 15 ms. This delay allows the activation of the Ethernet switch's software implementation in order to release FPGA resources. If more bandwidth is required enough time is available to load the hardware implementation. 1 MBit/s is reserved for the communication between the bandwidth managers of the whole communication system (e.g. for the reservation protocol). The remaining bandwidth is allocated if reservations are made by the bandwidth manager.

Self-optimizing application.   The self-optimizing application is a component that tries to optimize another application component (e.g., a mechatronic feedback controller). The optimization process can be accelerated, e.g., by a floating point unit (FPU) implemented in the FPGA. The PowerPC processor of our system does not provide an integrated FPU, so if no FPU is loaded into the FPGA floating point calculations are performed in software with a large overhead. The FPU requires 3000 slices of the FPGA resource and accelerates a 32-bit floating point multiplication by the factor of 44. For system services and application 7.000 slices of the FPGA are available in the system. This means, only the hardware Ethernet switch or the FPU can be executed on the FPGA, not both at the same time. Our self-optimizing resource management system deactivates the hardware Ethernet switch by activating the software profile of the switch if a bandwidth less than 14 MBit/s is required in the system. If a higher bandwidth is required, the floating point acceleration of the application is deactivated and the hardware switch is activated.

5. RELATED WORK

The idea to use reconfigurable logic for the integration of network applications into the network interface has been realized, e.g., by Underwood et al. [11]. Comparable network interfaces have been used for server and network applications, e.g., webservers, firewalls [4], and virus protection [6]. Furthermore, it has been shown that Switched Ethernet is appropriate for low-latency hard real-time communication [7].

Customization and configuration is not a new approach for adapting a system to the requirements of an application. In the field of (real-time) operating systems various approaches for customization have been proposed.

SYNTHESIS [8] adapts its code by partially evaluating and recompiling condition statements depending on available input data at run time. This can result in changing compare instructions and conditional jumps by unconditional jumps and vice versa. This eventually leads to the elimination or integration of complete code fragments. Likewise, the operating system K42 [10] includes system support for online reconfiguration by a hot-swap mechanism using C++ virtual function tables.

6. CONCLUSION

In this paper, we have presented the concept and design of a self-optimizing RCOS/RTOS systems for dynamic, self-optimzing applications. Our RCOS/ RTOS system deactivates system services or activates slim version of the service, which are restricted in functionality, if the service or the full version is not required. In addition to an efficient use of resources our system includes support for upcoming application demands. This concept of redistributing temporally unused resources is not only applicable for system services but also for the applications itself. Thus, the resources of the system can be utilized much better, even under hard real-time conditions. Furthermore, the internal waste of resources for worst-case resource consumptions are minimized. To facilitate this, possible system services and applications have to provide additional information about their resource requirements and about corresponding conditions by means of the Profile Framework. The benefit of our system is shown by an example of a communication service, which we have implemented on our platform for self-optimizing systems.

REFERENCES

[1] C. Böke. *Automatic Configuration of Real-Time Operating Systems and Real Time Communication Systems for Distributed Embedded Applications*. Dissertation, Universität Paderborn, Heinz Nixdorf Institut, Entwurf Paralleler Systeme, 2004.

[2] R. P. Chivukula, C. Böke, and F. J. Rammig. Customizing the Configuration Process of an Operating System Using Hierarchy and Clustering. In *Proc. of the 5th IEEE International Symposium on Object-oriented Real-time distributed Computing (ISORC)*, pages 280–287, Crystal City, VA, USA, 29 April – 1 May 2002. IFIP WG 10.5. ISBN 0-7695-1558-4.

[3] C. Ditze. *Towards Operating System Synthesis*. Phd thesis, Department of Computer Science, Paderborn University, Paderborn, Germany, 1999.

[4] D. Friedman and D. Nagle. Building firewalls with intelligent network interface cards. Technical report, 2001.

[5] H. Kalte, M. Porrman, and U. Rückert. A prototyping platform for dynamically reconfigurable system on chip designs. In *Proceedings of the IEEE Workshop Heterogeneous reconfigurable Systems on Chip (SoC)*, 2002.

[6] J. W. Lockwood, J. Moscola, M. Kulig, D. Reddick, and T. Brooks. Application of hardware accelerated extensible network nodes for internet worm and virus protection. In *Proceedings of the International Working Conference on Active Networks (IWAN)*, 2003.

[7] J. Löser and H. Härtig. Low-latency hard real-time communication over switched ethernet. In *Proceedings of the 16th Euromicro Conference on Real-Time Systems (ECRTS 04)*, 2004.

[8] H. Massalin. *Synthesis: An Efficient Implementation of Fundamental Operating System Services*. Phd thesis, Columbia University, 1992.

[9] S. Oberthür and C. Böke. Flexible resource management - a framework for self-optimizing real-time systems. In B. Kleinjohann, G. R. Gao, H. Kopetz, L. Kleinjohann, and A. Rettberg, editors, *Proceedings of IFIP Working Conference on Distributed and Parallel Embedded Systems (DIPES'04)*. Kluwer Academic Publishers, 23 - 26 Aug. 2004.

[10] C. Soules, J. Appavoo, K. Hui, D. Silva, G. Ganger, O. Krieger, M. Stumm, R. Wisniewski, M. Auslander, M. Ostrowski, B. Rosenburg, and J. Xenidis. System support for online reconfiguration, 2003.

[11] K. D. Underwood, R. R. Sass, and W. B. Ligeon. A reconfigurable extension to the network interface of beowulf clusters. In *Proceedings of the IEEE Conference on Cluster Computing (Cluster 2001)*, 2001.

[12] E. Vonnahme, B. Griese, M. Porrmann, and U. Rückert. Dynamic reconfiguration of real-time network interfaces. In *Proceedings of the 4th International Conference on Parallel Computing in Electrical Engineering (PARELEC 2004)*, pages 376–379, Dresden, Germany, 7 - 10 Sept. 2004.

A JITTER-FREE OPERATIONAL ENVIRONMENT FOR DEPENDABLE EMBEDDED SYSTEMS

Christo Angelov[1], Jesper Berthing[2] and Krzysztof Sierszecki[1]
[1]*Mads Clausen Institute for Product Innovation, University of Southern Denmark, Grundtvigs Alle 150, 6400 Soenderborg, Denmark;* [2]*Center for Software Innovation, Stenager 2, 6400 Soenderborg, Denmark*

Abstract: The paper presents a new real-time kernel architecture featuring component-based design, as well as advanced algorithms based on Boolean vectors and bitwise vector processing of kernel data structures. These have been consistently applied to all aspects of task management, as well as task synchronization and communication. Hence, the execution time of system functions no longer depends on the number of tasks involved, resulting in predictable, jitter-free operation of kernel subsystems. This approach has been further extended to time management resulting in a new type of kernel component, which can be used to implement Distributed Timed Multitasking - a novel computational model providing for predictable jitter-free execution of hard real-time tasks as well as distributed transactions in a dynamic scheduling environment.

Keywords: Hard Real-Time Systems; Boolean Vector Processing; Distributed Timed Multitasking

1.   INTRODUCTION

Modern embedded systems have to comply with stringent requirements with respect to system safety and dependability. There are essentially two approaches to task scheduling for dependable embedded systems: static scheduling vs. predictable dynamic scheduling using algorithms developed in modern Real-Time Scheduling Theory[1]. The former approach is widely used with safety-critical systems in application areas such as aerospace and military systems, automotive applications, etc.[1,2]. However, static scheduling has a major disadvantage: its application results in closed systems that are generally difficult to re-configure and maintain. This is in contradiction to the requirement for an open and flexible system architecture that must support software reuse and reconfiguration.

The second approach is more promising but it requires the development of a new generation of so-called *safe* real-time kernels, which provide a secure and predictable environment for application tasks. That is accomplished through a number of specific features, such as predictable task scheduling, safe task interaction, extensive timing and monitoring facilities, and predictable kernel behaviour[3]. Unfortunately, available real-time kernels, with the exception of some experimental designs, do not meet the above requirements. In particular, most of them are implemented using linked-list queues resulting in substantial and largely varying overhead (kernel jitter), which complicates considerably task schedulability analysis[4,5]. Therefore, it can be argued that the elimination of kernel jitter will make it possible to precisely estimate task and transaction response times early in the design process, taking into account kernel execution effects.

The above problem has been addressed in the MicroC/OS kernel where the ready task queue and event queues have been implemented as two-dimensional bit patterns[6]. This solution makes it possible to execute task insertion/deletion operations in constant time, irrespective of task priority, but that is not possible with multiple tasks (e.g. multiple tasks released simultaneously by one and the same event).

On the other hand, dynamic scheduling inherently introduces the problem of task execution jitter, which is detrimental to control system behaviour. One way of eliminating this effect is to enforce constant execution time on kernel execution paths via dummy code, and likewise - enforce task execution times within worst-case execution time bounds, as suggested for the *Asterix* real-time kernel[7]. That solution is expected to result in highly predictable and reproducible system behaviour but it could have a negative side effect, i.e. substantially increased kernel overhead and reduced system utilization. Another option is to combine static and dynamic scheduling within a hybrid real-time kernel[8].

However, an even better approach has recently emerged, i.e. *Timed Multitasking* - a powerful yet elegant and conceptually simple computational model, which effectively eliminates task execution jitter[9]. Under that model task I/O drivers are executed atomically at precisely specified time instants (i.e. task release and deadline instants), whereas application tasks are executed in a dynamic scheduling environment. Hence, task jitter is of no consequence, as long as the tasks finish execution before their deadlines. Ultimately, timed multitasking makes it possible to engineer real-time systems combining high flexibility inherent to dynamic scheduling and predictable operation, which is typical for statically scheduled systems.

It must be noted that this is an event-driven model, as against purely time-triggered models featuring atomic execution of task I/O drivers and split-phase execution of periodic tasks, e.g. *Giotto*[10]. In principle, that model accommodates all kinds of events, such as periodic timing events, aperiodic external and internal events, message arrival events, etc., and its implementation is not strictly related to a specific compiler or operating system. However, the existing implementation supports only local communication via interconnected ports implemented as shared data structures[9]. Another limitation comes from the fact that each task has to use its own set of timers (e.g. period, offset and deadline timers), which could result in considerable kernel overhead. That overhead might be substantially reduced by developing an integrated time manager capable of servicing multiple tasks simultaneously, e.g. tasks whose periods or deadlines expire at one and the same time instant.

The above problems have been addressed while developing the *HARTEX* kernel architecture, which is presented in the paper. Our approach is to eliminate linked lists and instead, use Boolean vectors (bit-strings) in order to emulate system queues[3]. Queues can thus be processed through <u>bitwise</u> Boolean operations resulting in jitter-free execution of kernel functions, independent of the number of tasks involved. This technique has been recently extended to time management resulting in a new type of kernel component, which can be used to efficiently implement Distributed Timed Multitasking - a novel computational model providing for predictable jitter-free execution of hard real-time tasks as well as distributed transactions in a dynamic scheduling environment.

The paper is structured as follows: Section 2 gives an overview of the main features of the *HARTEX* architecture. Section 3 presents jitter-free task management using Boolean vectors and bitwise vector operations on kernel data structures. Section 4 extends this approach to static time management - a newly developed technique that has been used in the latest timed-multitasking version of the kernel. Section 5 presents transparent task communication using content-oriented message addressing, in the context of both time-triggered and event-triggered distributed transactions.

2.   HARTEX ARCHITECTURE

HARTEX (HArd Real-Time Executive for Control Systems) is a safe real-time kernel, which has been conceived as an operational environment for component-based embedded applications conforming to the *COMDES* (formerly *ASPS*) model of distributed computation[3,11,12].

The *HARTEX* architecture exhibits a number of novel features, which are briefly summarized below:

- Component-based architecture supporting kernel reconfiguration and scalability
- Integrated task and resource scheduling via the System Ceiling Priority Protocol – a non-blocking synchronization protocol providing for predictable and efficient management of shared resources
- Boolean vector processing of kernel data structures, resulting in very low overhead and constant execution time of system functions, hence jitter-free operation of kernel subsystems
- Predictable jitter-free execution of real-time tasks in a distributed timed multitasking environment, using an advanced clock synchronization mechanism and a new type of time manager - the Static Time Manager
- Event notification via Boolean vector semaphores, providing for the instantaneous broadcast/multicast of events to multiple receiver tasks
- Integrated communication protocol supporting transparent content-oriented message addressing within local and/or remote interactions, including both state message and event message communication

Component-based design is an important feature of the *HARTEX* architecture. A number of reconfigurable kernel components have been specified and implemented: task managers supporting basic and/or extended tasks; dynamic and static time managers; external event manager; integrated time/event manager; task I/O manager, resource manager; software bus, etc. These can be used to configure various types of operating systems – from small kernels for stand-alone microcontrollers to distributed real time operating systems.

However, the main innovation of the architecture is the use of Boolean vector processing, which is presented in subsequent sections.

3.   JITTER-FREE TASK MANAGEMENT

The *HARTEX* Task Manager provides support for both basic (non-blocking) and extended (blocking) tasks, in accordance with the state transition diagram shown in Fig. 1-a. Its ready task queue is emulated by a Boolean vector - the *Active Tasks Vector (ATV)* having as many bits as there are tasks in the system, whereby $ATV[i] = 1$ denotes an active task of priority i and task number i. Another vector is used to specify task operational status, i.e. the *Enabled Tasks Vector (ETV)*: task i is enabled (disabled) if $ETV[i] = 1(0)$.

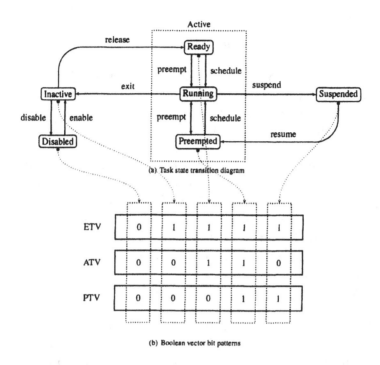

(a) Task state transition diagram

(b) Boolean vector bit patterns

Figure 1. HARTEX state transition diagram and Boolean vector bit patterns

An active task can be in one of three substates: *ready*, *running* and *preempted*. Ready and preempted tasks are differentiated by means of the *Preempted Tasks Vector (PTV)* where $PTV[i] = 1(0)$ denotes a preempted (ready) task of the same ATV bit position. The running task is specified by an auxiliary variable – the *Running Task* as well as its corresponding ATV bit which is reset only after the task has been finished. Extended real-time tasks may have their ATV bit temporarily reset while being suspended. Basic tasks can never be suspended but they might be eventually preempted by higher-priority tasks.

The state encoding for various task states is shown in Fig. 1-b. It has been specifically designed to reduce the execution time of task state transition operations and corresponding task management primitives, which are effectively reduced to bit manipulation. Moreover, the use of the above encoding technique makes it possible to simultaneously execute multiple identical operations involving different tasks through bitwise operations on Boolean vectors. This is done in *constant* time, no matter how many tasks are involved in the operation, as illustrated by the primitive *release(tasks)*. Its argument is a Boolean vector specifying the tasks to be released (e.g.

vector 10101010b specifying tasks 1, 3, 5 and 7). That operation is executed as follows:

```
release(tasks)
{
    ATV = ATV OR (tasks AND ETV);
}
```

The execution time of the above primitive is in the (sub)microsecond range depending on the platform used, e.g. 4 μs in an 8-bit *ATmega103* microcontroller running at 4 Mhz and operating on 16-bit vectors. With linked-list queues, the same operation might take from tens to hundreds of microseconds depending on the number of tasks involved even in relatively high-end processors. For instance, it has been shown experimentally that 20 periodic tasks are released in 570 μs in an *M68020*-based computer running under the *Olympus* kernel, as against 76 μs for a single task[4].

Most other primitives are executed in the same manner, resulting in substantially reduced overhead and jitter-free execution, e.g. operations on Boolean vector semaphores[3] and communication primitives that use such semaphores (see section 5)

Likewise, task scheduling is facilitated by the Boolean vector data structure. The task manager determines the highest priority active task to be executed by finding the highest priority non-zero bit in the *ATV*. This is done via a bit search procedure, which takes constant time to execute, and in some processors this can be accomplished with a single instruction (e.g. the BSF instruction in the Intel family of microprocessors). In fact, the scheduling algorithm is somewhat more involved because it implements integrated task and resource scheduling using the so-called System Ceiling Priority Protocol (known also as the Stack-Sharing Priority Ceiling Protocol[1]).

Timed multitasking introduces an important extension to the conventional multitasking model, i.e. *split-phase* execution of real-time tasks, whereby task I/O drivers may be executed separately from the main task body. Specifically, task input drivers are executed when the task is released and output drivers – when the task deadline arrives, or when the task comes to an end (if no deadline has been specified). This requires the introduction of a separate kernel component – the *Task I/O Manager*, which is actually implemented as the highest priority system task.

When activated, the Task I/O Manager invokes all output drivers, and subsequently – all input drivers that have been registered for execution. I/O drivers are registered using two additional Boolean vectors – the *Output Drivers Vector (ODV)* and the *Input Drivers Vector (IDV)*. Specifically, input drivers are registered for execution by the corresponding task release events, e.g. periodic timing events, sporadic external and internal events, or message arrival events. Output drivers are registered for execution by deadline timing events and in some cases by the task itself when it comes to an end (if no deadline has been specified).

Task I/O drivers are atomic pieces of code, whose execution time is negligible compared to that of the task body. These may be physical I/O drivers or communication drivers that are used to transparently exchange labeled messages (signals) between interacting local and/or remote subsystems[11,12]. This has resulted into an extended variant of the basic timed multitasking model called *Distributed Timed Multitasking*, which is now supported by the latest version of *HARTEX* (see subsequent sections).

4.   TIME MANAGEMENT FOR JITTER-FREE EXECUTION OF REAL-TIME TASKS

This section presents a kernel component - the *Static Time Manager (STM)*, which can be used to implement time-triggered transactions in the context of Timed Multitasking and its extended variant.

The Static Time Manager uses a table specifying the behaviour of a set of periodic hard real-time tasks. The latter consists of k records corresponding to superperiod time instants $0, 1, 2, ..., k-1$. Each instant is defined with an offset from the beginning of the superperiod. Accordingly, each table entry has the following format:

{*offset, tasks_with_deadline, tasks_to_release*},

where *tasks_with_deadline* is a Boolean vector specifying the tasks whose deadline expires at the time instant given by *offset*, and *tasks_to_release* is another Boolean vector specifying tasks that have to be released at that same instant.

The Static Time Manager processes the scheduling table in the following manner:

```
with every clock tick do {
  update current time;
  if ( current_time < schedule[I].offset) return;
  else {
    generate   a   deadline   violation   vector   if   some
    tasks_with_deadline have not finished execution and
    disable those tasks;
    register   the   output_drivers   of   tasks   that   have
    finished   execution   in   the   Output   Drivers   Vector
    (ODV);
```

```
    release  tasks  specified  by  the  tasks_to_release
    vector if not disabled (i.e. register those tasks in
    the Active Tasks Vector (ATV);
    register the input_drivers of released tasks in the
    Input Drivers Vector (IDV);
    I = I + 1 (mod (schedule length));
    release the Task I/O Manager;
    invoke the Task Manager;
  }
}
```

The above algorithm is executed using Boolean vector processing techniques, as follows:

- A deadline violation vector (DVV) is generated, and the corresponding tasks - disabled:

```
DVV = ATV & tasks_with_deadline;
ETV = ETV & ~DVV;
```

- Output drivers are registered for execution with the task I/O Manager:

```
tasks_finished = tasks_with_deadline & ~ATV;
for all tasks in tasks_finished {
    ODV = ODV | task.output_drivers;
}
```

- Tasks are released for execution:

```
ATV = ATV | (tasks_to_release & ETV);
```

- Input drivers are registered for execution with the task I/O Manager:

```
tasks_released = (tasks_to_release & ETV);
for all tasks in tasks_released {
    IDV = IDV | task.input_drivers;
}
```

- The Task I/O Manager is released and the Task Manger – invoked:

```
release(taskIOManager);
preempt();
```

The Task I/O Manager is treated as a high(est) priority system task. It executes the registered output drivers, then – input drivers and exits, whereupon the Task Manager invokes the next highest-priority application task registered in the *ATV*.

The superperiod table is processed in this manner upon successive tick interrupts, which amounts to the operation of multiple free-running timers measuring intervals such as period, offset and deadline for all tasks involved. It is obvious that the presented timing mechanism implements a static schedule with respect to <u>timed input/output and task release actions</u>, whose operation is largely similar to that of a rotating drum sequencer used in some mechanical devices. Therefore, it has been denoted as the *Static Time Manager*, and alternatively – the *Drum Sequencer*.

Timed multitasking can be extended to distributed systems via signal drivers used to transparently exchange messages between local and/or remote tasks (see next section). However, a distributed application would require synchronized operation of multiple drum sequencers running concurrently in various network nodes.

5. TASK COMMUNICATION FOR DISTRIBUTED TIMED MULTITASKING

Application tasks interact by exchanging *signals*, i.e. messages having unique communication variable identifiers. That follows from the *COMDES* component model, which presumes that subsystems interact by exchanging signals via communication objects called *signal drivers*[11,12]. The latter may be viewed as a special class of task I/O drivers within the timed multitasking model of computation. Accordingly, these can be invoked at precisely specified time instants resulting in time-triggered communication between subsystems and encapsulated tasks[11]. Alternatively, it is possible to invoke signal drivers when a task is released by a sporadic event (input drivers) and at the end of task execution (output drivers), which is typical for event-triggered communication within phase-aligned transactions.

Signal driver operation is supported by the *HARTEX* message exchange layer[3]. Messages are actually exchanged by means of communication primitives, which are invoked by signal drivers in order to transparently transfer data from the source to the destination message buffers of interacting local and/or remote subsystems. Each message has a unique source buffer associated with an output signal driver (or the underlying network layer), and one or more destination buffers that are associated with the corresponding input signal drivers and receiver tasks (see Fig. 2).

HARTEX communication primitives are invoked with communication variable identifiers (names) within an implicit message addressing scheme, which is known as content-oriented message addressing, e.g. *broadcast_state_variable(TEMPERATURE)*. The variable name is subsequently used to transparently route a message to local and/or remote receivers. To that end, each message is uniquely specified by a kernel data structure - a Message Control Block (MCB) containing relevant information such as source buffer address, message length, receiver tasks, local and/or remote type of communication, blocking or non-blocking interaction, etc. In local communication the message identifier is used as an index for the corresponding MCB, whereas in remote communication it is mapped onto a network message identifier (e.g. a CAN identifier).

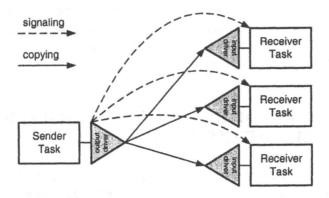

Figure 2. Transparent communication via content-oriented message addressing

The message exchange layer may use the services of the underlying event notification layer in order to signal message arrival to one or more receiver tasks. However, receiver notification is needed only in event-driven communication, i.e. in sequential (phase-aligned) transactions where the receivers are released by message arrival events. In that mode of operation the input signal drivers are invoked by the Task I/O Manager, immediately after the task has been released by the message arrival event and its input drivers - registered in the *Input Drivers Vector.* Accordingly, the output drivers are invoked after the task has exited and its output drivers - registered in the *Output Drivers Vector.* This is explained below in the context of non-blocking state message communication.

The output signal driver composes the message into the corresponding source buffer and sends it off via the primitive *broadcast_state_variable(var_name).* In case of local communication, the broadcast primitive invokes a vector semaphore operation, i.e. *signal_and_release(semaphore, receivers).* This is used to notify receiver tasks about message arrival and release some or all of them, whereby the corresponding input drivers are registered for execution. In case of remote communication the message is queued for transmission and subsequently copied into a receiver-node source buffer. The underlying network layer is then responsible for signalling message arrival to the remote receivers, as explained above.

After message arrival notification, the message is copied from the source buffer to the corresponding destination buffer for each receiver task. That is done by the corresponding input signal driver, which is invoked by the Task I/O Manager immediately after the receiver task has been released. It is actually accomplished with a kernel primitive invoked by the driver, i.e. *receive_state_variable(var_name, destination_buffer)*. Message copying has to be atomic, and in local communication this is guaranteed by the non-preemptive execution of signal drivers. In remote communication it might be necessary to use a protocol providing for mutual exclusion between an interrupt-driven network-layer driver and the input signal driver executing a *receive_state_variable* operation, e.g. the *NBW* protocol[13].

Vector-semaphore signalling primitives are executed in constant time[3], and on the other hand, each input driver is responsible for copying the message into its destination buffer, on per driver/task basis. That is why the broadcast primitives execute in constant time no matter how many receivers are involved.

Time-triggered communication is conceptually simpler, since receiver tasks need not be signalled. Obviously, that is not necessary because receiver tasks are released, and signal drivers - invoked by the Static Time Manager at precisely specified time instants, whereby message copying is executed within input drivers as explained above. Consequently, the Task Manager activates released tasks only after their input drivers have been executed and the corresponding messages - received (see section 4).

6.   CONCLUSION

This paper has presented advanced task management and interaction techniques featuring Boolean vectors and parallel (bitwise) vector operations on kernel data structures, which have been developed for the *HARTEX* family of real-time kernels. That approach has been consistently applied to all aspects of task management and interaction: task scheduling, task execution request generation, task synchronization and communication. This has resulted in considerably reduced kernel overhead and jitter-free execution of kernel subsystems, whereby the execution time of system operations depends no longer on the number of tasks involved.

That is an outstanding feature with important implications. On the one hand, low kernel overhead results in faster task response and increased processor schedulability. On the other hand, constant duration of kernel operations makes it possible to precisely estimate task response times taking into account kernel execution effects, which will contribute to higher systems safety and predictability.

Ultimately, this technique has made it possible to efficiently implement a timed multitasking version of the *HARTEX* kernel providing for predictable jitter-free execution of hard real-time tasks in single-computer and distributed environments. Under that kernel task I/O drivers are executed atomically at precisely specified time instants, whereas tasks are executed in a preemptive priority-driven environment and may have termination jitter. However, jitter is effectively eliminated, as long as tasks finish execution before their deadlines.

The presented techniques have been validated in a series of distributed motion control experiments, and jitter-free behaviour has been demonstrated during the execution of transactions with one-period delay from sampling to actuation, transactions with offsets as well as transactions with decoupled (pipelined) execution of transaction tasks.

REFERENCES

1. Liu, J.W.S.: Real-Time Systems. Prentice Hall (2000)
2. Kopetz, H.: Real-Time Systems. Design Principles for Distributed Embedded Applications. Kluwer Academic Publishers (1997)
3. Angelov, C., Ivanov, I., and Burns, A.: HARTEX - a Safe Real-Time Kernel for Distributed Computer Control Systems. Software: Practice and Experience, vol. 32, N3, (2002) 209-232
4. Burns, A., Tindell, K., and Wellings, A.: Effective Analysis for Engineering Real-Time Fixed-Priority Schedulers. IEEE Trans. on Soft. Eng., 21, (1995) 475-480
5. Katcher, D., Arakawa, H., and Strosnider, J.: Engineering and Analysis of Fixed-Priority Schedulers. IEEE Trans. on Soft. Eng., 19, (1993) 920-934
6. Labrosse, J.: MicroC/OS-II. The Real-Time Kernel. CMP Books (2002)
7. Thane, H., Pettersson, A., Sundmark, D.: The Asterix Real-Time Kernel. Proc. of the 13th Euromicro International Conference on Real-Time Systems, Delft, Netherlands (2001)
8. Isovic, D.; Norström, C.: Components in Real-Time Systems. Proc. of the 8th International Conference on Real-Time Computing Systems and Applications, Tokyo, Japan (2002)
9. Liu, J., Lee, E.A.: Timed Multitasking for Real-Time Embedded Software. IEEE Control Systems Magazine: Advances in Software Enabled Control, February (2003) 65-75
10. Henzinger, T.A., Horowitz, B., and Kirsch, C.M.: Embedded Control Systems Development with Giotto. Proc. of the Conference on Languages, Compilers and Tools for Embedded Systems LCTES'01, Salt Lake City, USA (2001)
11. Angelov, C., and Sierszecki, K.: Component-based Design of Software for Distributed Embedded Systems. Proc. of the 10th IEEE International Conference on Methods and Models in Automation and Robotics, Miedzyzdroje, Poland (2004)
12. Angelov, C., and Sierszecki, K.: A Software Framework for Component-Based Embedded Applications. Proc. of the Asia-Pacific Software Engineering Conference APSEC'2004, Busan, Korea, Dec. 2004
13. Kopetz, H., Reisinger, J.: The Non-Blocking Write Protocol NBW - a Solution to a Real-Time Synchronisation Problem. Proc. of the IEEE Real-Time Systems Symposium (1993) 131-137

PARTITIONING METRICS FOR IMPROVED PERFORMANCE AND ECONOMY OF DISTRIBUTED EMBEDDED SYSTEMS

Augustin Kebemou
Fraunhofer-Institut für Software- und Systemtechnik (ISST)
Mollstrasse 1, 10178 Berlin, Germany
augustin.kebemou@isst.fraunhofer.de

Abstract: *This paper describes some metrics which can be applied to optimize the constrained partitioning of very large distributed software/hardware systems. These metrics are tailored for software component models for UML specifications. The use of clear defined metrics allows us to capture more aspects of the design (abstraction level, aggregation and causality relations between the components). Besides, the appropriate formalization of these metrics has a great impact on the results that can be obtained from the partitioning regarding both the performance and the economy of the system under design.*

Keywords: Software Component, Metrics, Codesign, Partitioning, Automotive

1. INTRODUCTION

Embedded systems are used in live facilities where the principal requirements include safety, performance and security. A very large embedded system may consist of several parts which are geographically separated, like those in a car. Automotive systems are complex systems with software and hardware that are constantly in execution. The functionalities of such systems are located on different physical components (subsystems) which do not only cooperate with each other, but also depend on each other. Anyhow, it will be necessary to design all the parts of the system simultaneously to ensure that they will conjointly meet the given performance and economy goals. This is otherwise called codesign. Thus, effective design methods are required.

Each of the functionalities expected from a system can be specified by a function which implements it. Hardware/software codesign proposes a concurrent design of the hardware and the software parts of the system in order to meet the best trade-off between performance and costs. Some really large embedded systems offer a very big set of functionalities which can only be modeled by thousands of high level functions. For these systems, the modeling languages commonly used in the current codesign methodology for the partitioning offer a poor structuring, since the abstraction level is comparable with the one of programming languages like C or Ada [9]. We overcome this scarceness by using a modeling language which can handle the specification of the artifacts of very large systems at every abstraction level. We use the unified modeling language UML, which in the new version 2.0 extended with the component-based design paradigm simplifies the modeling of software/hardware systems [4] through a port concept. The port concept provides abstraction by means of aggregation mechanisms and information hiding principles [2, 8] for the design complexity management. Furthermore, the UML provides a graphical visualization of the logical system architecture independently of the granularity of the specification.

The partitioning of the specification of a large technical system is a challenging task since it is not enough to partition the functionalities of a system among the various subsystems; more important is to achieve a partition which satisfies the system constraints. Thus the challenge of the partitioning task is to find the best system architecture including the right distribution of the functions among the subsystems and the right hardware components and communication facilities.

We propose a partitioning heuristic the input of which is a functional logical specification. We use a set of metrics to guide the partitioning of the specification before we conjointly design the subsystems which we have methodically determined. This paper will particularly present the partitioning metrics we use at the early steps of the partitioning task.

The paper is organized as follows: The next section presents the motivations of the metric guided partitioning in the automotive engineering and a summary of some works considering the necessity of measurements in the system development. The section 3 introduces briefly a component-based system specification metamodel defined for mixed software/hardware Systems. The following section presents the partitioning metrics and section 5 presents some concrete advantages derived from a metric guided partitioning application in the automotive engineering.

2. RELATED WORK AND MOTIVATION

A typical example of the complexity of embedded systems is the amount of Electric/Electronic (E/E) systems providing the comfort, the performance and the security in the automobile. It is quite difficult to imagine what the car of the future will look like. Even if ESP (Electronic Stability Program), ACC (Active Cruise Control), ABS (Anti Blocking System for the brakes) and airbags are nowadays mainstream, it is clear that on the way to build the cars which will drive autonomously, more and more functionalities will be added to the system automobile. The mastering of the design of such systems is a great challenge because the system consists of subsystems which are distributed on different physical locations, needing to cooperate with each other in order to fulfill the required functionalities. Some important design constraints can be formulated as follows: the monetary cost of the product with regard to the time to market and the material usage have to be hold minimal by providing concurrently high functionality and performance. The volume, the weight and the energy consumption of automotive systems must not grow proportionally to the number of the embedded functionalities.

In the current practice, the OEM (Original Equipment Manufacturer) partitions the functionalities according to vague estimations or to experience, without any helpful documentation. Then he orders some electronic control units (ECU), each implementing a part of the functionalities and plug them together. Consequently, the real time constraints are not easy to achieve, due to the communication difficulties between sensors, ECUs and actuators. There are more material resources installed into the system as obligatory necessary making the cost/performance ratio poor. To solve the communication problems, they design better and better communication protocols (e.g. CAN and family, MOST, Flex Ray, LIN) or they add the communication bandwidth by adding new buses. This alone will not definitely solve this problem actually challenging the industrial research. Suitably localized functions communicate cheaper. A goal-oriented approach of the partitioning, which can be automated is the key to master the costs and the performance requirements of automotive systems.

Since system level models are abstractions of implementation, metrics of interest are required to evaluate system models and the partitioning state space of such mix software/hardware systems. Metrics are commonly used to estimate/predict the costs and schedules of the product and the process by which it is developed. Product metrics measure the product quality at any stage of the development. In the software engineering, product metrics may measure the size and the complexity of either the model or the final code [3, 7, 18]. Process metrics may estimate the overall development time, the average experience of the staff or the type of the methodology used. Software process metrics are summarized in [5, 10]. Particularly, some general metrics have been proposed [6, 10, 11, 15] to evaluate the quality of object oriented system design. But the known software and OO design metrics concentrate on the characterization of software programs or OO Models. They can not consider the constraints of heterogeneous software/hardware systems.

Two key metrics are used in the software/hardware codesign partitioning to define the quality of a partition: performance and hardware size. Since the partitioning in the software/hardware codesign is basically the process of deciding, for each subsystem, whether the required functionality is more advantageously implemented in hardware or in software, these metrics mostly address especially the 2-way clustering issues. Closeness metrics are used in [12, 14] to predict the benefit of grouping any two specification objects. Closeness metrics have been defined on fine-granularity : logical, arithmetical operations or assignments [16] and on coarse-grainularity obejcts [13]. In a great work, Vahid and Gajski [17] presented some "closeness metrics for the system-level functional partitioning", with VHDL-level specifications input. We redefined these metrics to close the area of distributed systems with geographical separation constraints. Our metrics are tailored for the particular concept of software components in order to enable the investigation (structural analysis) of UML-level models for constrained distributed embedded systems.

3.   INPUT PRESENTATION

We specify large systems using a ULM-like modeling language. At the logical level, a set of system functionalities are represented by logical functions. We encapsulate the logical functions in software components. A software component has an internal behavior, an input and an output interface. The component interfaces are the communication facilities of the components. They are represented by two sorts of ports: the input ports at the input interfaces and the output ports at the output interfaces. The inter-component communication is modeled by means of signal transfer over logical connectors, which we simply name connectors. Each connector represents the fact that in a logical channel the connected components share a set of signals called connector interface. With this architecture, the communication can be modeled independently from the internal behavior of the components. This components concept can be used at every granularity level of the specification. So we can build a logical model of the system under construction as a network of communicating components. Figure1 shows the metamodel of the logical component network and Figure2 shows a part of a functional specification.

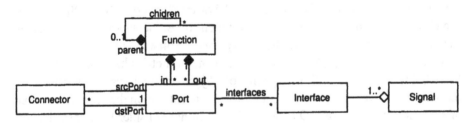

Figure 1.   The metamodel of the logical specification

We add descriptive attributes to our model elements. The attributes describe the implementation requirements and the external behavior of the components, especially their communication requirements. The required memory, the maximum execution time, the average execution period of the function illustrate the kind of information which describe a function. Ports are attributed by the maximal cycle time of signal calls, the security level, etc. Each signal has a resolution, a priority, a transmission/access frequency (accfreq) and so on. The logical model gives sufficient information at least to measure the closeness between the functions. That is to predict the benefits of grouping any two logical components. The partitioning can now be driven.

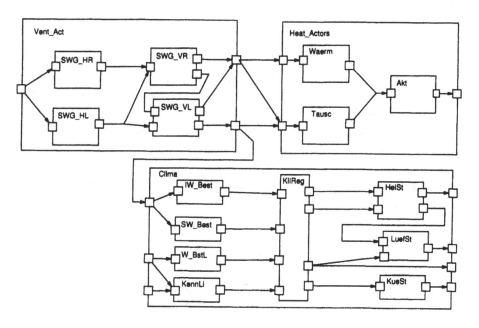

Figure 2.   Example of a functional specification

We can formally define the functional model as a tuple as follows:

$$
\begin{aligned}
G &= \langle F, P, S, C \rangle \\
F &= \{components\} \\
P &= I \oplus O;\, I = \{input\ ports\}\ \text{and}\ O = \{output\ ports\} \\
S &= \{signals\}\ ;\ signal = \langle src, dst \rangle\ \text{where}\ src, dst \in F \\
C &= \{connectors\};\ connector = \langle src, dst, Int \rangle \\
&\quad \text{where}\ src \in O,\ dst \in I\ \text{and}\ Int \subseteq S.
\end{aligned}
$$

This is a graph which nodes represent the functions/components of the specification and the edges are the connectors. The ports are inherent parts of the nodes. Each connector is labeled with the signals it transports.

4.   PARTITIONING METRICS

Since the specification language provides a component de-/composition mechanism (hierarchical aggregation), we define the partitioning metrics between two sets of components. A set of components can be seen as a bundle of components of the same abstraction level or a package. For illustration, figure 2 shows 3 sets of components. We use appropriate normalization factors in order to combine and to fairly compare the values resulting from the measurements.

4.1   The connection metric

The connection measures the number of interfaces shared between two sets of logical components. It is advantageous to implement two functions which have a common great number of communicating interfaces together on the same component. Doing so, we intent to reduce the inter-components communication. The connection of two sets of components is the number of connectors connecting a function of the first set with a function of the second set.

Assume that the operator $AccessedConnectors(f)$ returns the set of connectors transporting at least one signal s for which $s.src \in f$ or $s.dst \in f$; $AccessedConnectors(f) = \{c \in C | \exists s \in c.Int; s.src \in f \vee s.dst \in f\}$
The connection metric is formalised as follows:

$$
\begin{aligned}
Connection(F_i, F_j) &= |commonConnectors_{i,j}|/Norm \\
commonConnectors_{i,j} &= C_i \cap C_j \\
C_i &= \bigcup_{f \in F_i} AccessedConnectors(f) \\
C_j &= \bigcup_{f \in F_j} AccessedConnectors(f) \\
Norm &= |C_i \cup C_j|(local) \\
&= |C|(global)
\end{aligned}
$$

C_i respectively C_j represent the sets of the logical connectors which are associated with the ports of the functions F_i respectively F_j.
$commonConnectors_{i,j}$ is the set of connectors commonly accessed by F_i and F_j. The local normalization factor is the set of the connectors accessed by F_i or F_j. $Connection(F_i, F_j)$ is the normalized number of connectors accessed by both F_i and F_j.

4.2   The communication metric

The communication measures the estimated amount of data transferred between two sets of components. The communication provides a different information as the connection. For example, if two components communicate 8 bytes of user data over a connector and 2 bytes over another one, the connection will consider two connectors, whereas the communication will consider the total number of bits shared between the two components (10 bytes). It is important to keep this metric different from the connection because the connectors are often differently constrained. We compute the communication by the means of the operator $AccessedConnectors$.

$$Communication(F_i, F_j) = com_{i,j}/Norm$$
$$com_{i,j} = \sum_{c \in commonConnectors_{i,j}} comWeight(c)$$
$$comWeight(c) = \sum_{s \in c.Int} s.accfreq \times s.resolution$$
$$Norm = \sum_{c \in C_i \cup C_j} comWeight(c)(local)$$
$$= \sum_{c \in C} comWeight(c)(global)$$

$comWeight(c)$ represents the amount of data (in bits) transfered through the connector c during an average activation time of the component $c.src$. $com_{i,j}$ is the total amount of data shared between the function sets F_i and F_j during an average activation time of the functions F_i and F_j. The local normalization factor is the total amount of data transferred between F_i, F_j and any other function of the specification whereas the global normalization factor is the total amount of data transferred around all the specification during an average activation time of the functions F_i and F_j.

4.3 The common accessors metric

Grouping two sets of components which have a great common set of accessors (e. g. a sensor) can improve the quality of the communication and therefore the performance of the system.

Let's assume that the operator $Accessors(f)$ returns the set of logical components $(f_i) = \{f_1, f_2, \ldots f_n\}$ for which exists at least one signal s so that $(s.src = f$ and $s.dst \in (f_i))$ or $(s.src \in (f_i)$ and $s.dst = f)$. We observe that each function is its own accessor (i. e. $\forall f; f \in Accessors(f)$).

$$CommonAccessors(F_i, F_j) = |commonAccessorSet_{i,j}|/Norm$$
$$commonAccessorSet_{i,j} = allAccessor_i \cap allAccessor_j$$
$$allAccessor_i = \bigcup_{f \in F_i} Accessors(f)$$
$$allAccessor_j = \bigcup_{f \in F_j} Accessors(f)$$
$$Norm = |allAccessor_i \cup allAccessor_j| \ (local)$$
$$= |F| \ (global)$$

$allAccessor_i$ represents the set of logical components that share at least one signal with a function contained in F_i. $commonAccessorSet_{i,j}$ is the set of all components communicating with both a function contained in the component F_i and a function contained in F_j. $CommonAccessors(F_i, F_j)$ returns the normalized number of the components accessing F_i and F_j, where the local normalization factor is the number of the logical functions communicating with a function contained in F_i or in F_j and the global normalization factor is the number of all components of the specification.

4.4   The communication constraint metric

Embedded systems typically are subject to real time, hard security and performance constraints which are considerably influenced by the inter-components communication. The precedent metrics have not taken these important constraints into consideration. When partitioning the logical specification of highly constrained heterogeneous systems, the number of channels and the amount of data shared between two components shall not always be sufficient as closeness indicators. For example, although the brake control unit communicates more often with other functions than with the crash-avoidance sensor, the designer would decide to favorite this relatively rarely activated connector on the basis of the interpretation of the values of the communication constraint metric.

We define *cons* as the set $\{e_1, e_2, \ldots, e_n\}$ of the given communication constraints. Since we globally map the connectors rather than the signals on buses, we assume that all signals transferred over a connector are equally constrained. That's what we mean bellow by constrained connectors (*consConnectors*). We assume that the operator $consConnectors_{e,i,j}$ returns the set of the connectors common to the component sets F_i and F_j that are subject to a given constraint e.

$$
\begin{aligned}
ComCons(F_i, F_j) &= \sum_{e \in cons} \alpha_e Cons_e(F_i, F_j) / \sum_{e \in cons} \alpha_e \\
Cons_e(F_i, F_j) &= consCom_{e,i,j} / Norm \\
consCom_{e,i,j} &= \sum_{s \in commonConsSig_{e,i,j}} s.accfreq \times s.resolution \\
commonConsSig_{e,i,j} &= \bigcup_{c \in consConnectors_{e,i,j}} c.Int \\
Norm &= \sum_{e \in cons} consCom_{e,i,j} \text{ (local)} \\
&= \sum_{e \in cons; F_i, F_j \in F} consCom_{e,i,j} \text{ (global)}
\end{aligned}
$$

$commonConsSig_{e,i,j}$ (common constrained signals) is the set of signals exchanged between the component sets F_i and F_j which are involved in the achievement of the constraint e. $consCom_{e,i,j}$ (constrained communication) is the volume of data (in bits) exchanged between the component sets F_i and F_j over the connectors which are subject to the constraint e. $Cons_e(F_i, F_j)$ is the normalized heaviness of the communication between F_i and F_j which is constrained by e. The local normalization factor is the volume of data shared between the component sets F_i and F_j over all common connectors, each being subject to at least one of the given communication constraints. The global normalization factor is the volume of the constrained data transported around the whole specification. $ComCons(F_i, F_j)$ considers all chosen constraints on the communication between the component sets F_i and F_j and returns the normalized communication constraint.

The designer is free to choose the values parameter α_e that reflect the weight and the importance of each constraint e for a given communication.

4.5   The sequenceness metric

Implementing two components which are defined to run sequentially on the same processor is obviously advantageous. Thus, grouping sequentially executing components of the logical functional specification will take benefits from these advantages.

Let's assume that the operator $Sequent(f_1, f_2)$ returns 0 if f_1 and f_2 could be executed concurrently and 1 if not.

$$
\begin{aligned}
Sequenceness(F_i, F_j) &= sequentPairs_{i,j}/Norm \\
sequentPairs_{i,j} &= \textstyle\sum_{f_1 \in F_i, f_2 \in F_j} Sequent(f_1, f_2) \\
Norm &= |F_i| \times |F_j| \text{ (local)} \\
&= \frac{|F| \times (|F|-1)}{2} \text{ (global)}
\end{aligned}
$$

$sequentPairs_{i,j}$ is the number of pairs of functions contained in $F_i \times F_j$ which could execute sequentially. The local normalization factor is the number of all possible pairs of functions of the set $F_i \times F_j$. The global normalization factor represents the number of all pairs of functions around the whole specification.

4.6   The resource sharing metric

The resource sharing metric measures the likelihood that two logical components should share the same resource. A resource can be a physical hardware or any hardware-closed logical object like message frames (shared between signals) in the case of serial bus transmission. If the resource sharing constraint is not dictated from the system requirements, i. e. some functions are designed a priori to run on the same physical component while other pairs of functions must exclude each other (for example because of electromagnetic incompatibilities), we can hardly measure the resource sharing with the available information. An example of resource sharing criteria could be the fact that different functions which never run at exactly the same time could use the same hardware resource (e. g. a reconfigurable processor, FPGA). Just as well, if some components are supposed to implement each a particularly constrained algorithm for which they need an adequate optimized processing element to run, it will be likely to group them together. This is the case of using an ASIP for the optimized computation paths or ASSPs, ASICs. Therefore, although the partitioning is done on the logical structural specification, the resource sharing metric can not only be evaluated from the structure of the system. It also depends on the components behavior. Details will be presented in a coming work.

5.   RESULTS

We applied the metrics on a functional specification containing 4 functions representing the features of a part of the chassis of a car. The specification was originally partitioned and mapped on four different ECUs communicating through a CAN Bus. CAN [1] is an event triggered bus concept used in the automotive industry, by which the messages are identified rather than the sender. After we decomposed the aggregations contained in the model, we clustered the resulting refined specification of 18 low level atomic functions in a bottom-up manner using a simple closeness function adding different metrics unweighted together. The partitioning function only considered the connection, the communication and the communication constraint metric.

To investigate the effects of the partitioning on the communication, we had to consider both the performance of the system and the order of the messages necessary for the inter-components communication that results from the dependencies between the tasks loaded on different ECUs. The performance has been measured by the ability of the bus to react to asynchronous (i. e. which are not predictable) external events at the working time. That is the possibility for the controller to access the bus within a predefined period of time after buffering the signal corresponding to an asynchronous event requiring emergency handling, in order to write a "CAN-message" containing this signal. Short latencies are easy to achieve in such a low bus load constellation, when the message priorities are consequently distributed. Since we were interested in the dependability of the system upon the economy of data transfer more than on other performance attributes, the most significant result was the number of messages transmitted over the bus.

For the measurements, we fixed the data rate on the bus to 250 kbits/s and the message length in the range from 0 to 4 bytes user data. Each of the different system architectures have been proved to realize the principal functionalities of the system. These include the mean computation time for the constrained functions, the maximum response time of the components (i.e latency due to the time to wait for the permission to access the bus), the transmission delay, which depends on the data rate, the length of the message and the topology of the system. All of them important as automotive systems underly real-time requirements [19]. We exited the functions in a way that we could simulate the maximum bus work case corresponding to each partition, by stimulating the functions in a way that every component would transmit the maximum number of messages on the bus as it was possible, in order to simulate the worst case of the bus regular operation regarding its load. The external/environmental events have been created by artificial functions representing some virtual sensors. Under these conditions all asynchronous events could be handled. This was not surprising as we mentioned above, simply because of the reduced size of the specification under experimentation, but could not hide the significance of the results of our interest, namely the number of messages exchanged through the bus. For the partitions of 1,..,6 parts, table 1 shows the approximated augmentation(+)/ diminution(-) in percent of the number of messages exchanged through the bus in comparison to the original 4-parts partition.

Number of parts	1	2	3	4	5	6
Variation of the inter-components communication	-100	-12	-5	0	+21	+45

Table 1. Effects of the partitioning on the serial bus communication

The partition with 2 parts appeared to be the best one when combining the inter-components communication and the geometrical advantages (i. e. peer-to-peer communication with sensors, gateways and actuators which are not in the bus network).

6. CONCLUSION AND COMING WORK

We have defined some powerful metrics which we use to distribute a software component-based specification on different physical components. These metrics are particularly useful when the different components must be geographically separated since they optimize the inter-components communication constraints. The metrics aim at helping the experienced designer to verify and document his assumptions, while the novice will get guidance in the partitioning task. Since the resource sharing requirements depend at least partially on the functional behavior of the components and on the mapping and scheduling strategies, a next paper will introduce further useful metrics additionally to the behavioral specification of such very large, highly constrained distributed systems and thereupon will complete the opened metrics definitions.

REFERENCES

[1] *CAN Specification Version 2.0, Part A, Part B; Robert Bosch GmbH.*

[2] *Systems Modelling Language (SysML) Specification, OMG UML for SE RFP, 2004.*

[3] A. J. Albrecht and Jr. J. E. Gaffney. Software Function, Source Line of Code, and Development Effort Prediction: A Software Science Validation. *IEEE Trans. Software Eng., Vol 9 Number 6, pp. 639-648*, 1983.

[4] M. Bjoerkander and C. Kobryn. UML 2.0 - Der nächste Schritt. *Elektronik Automotiv, Germany; pp. 30-33*, April 2002.

[5] B. W. Boehm. Software Engeeniering Economics. *IEEE Trans. Soft. Eng. Vol 10, Number 1*, 1984.

[6] S. R. Chidamber, D. P. Darcy, and K. F. Kemerer. Managerial Use of Metrics for Object-Oriented Software: An Exploratory Analysis. *IEEE Transactions on Soft. Eng. Vol 24, Number 8, pp 629-639*, 1998.

[7] M. H. Halstead. *Elements of Software Science*. New York: Elsevier North-Holland, 1977.

[8] M. Jeckle, C. Rupp, J. Hahn, B. Zenger, and S. Queins. *UML 2 Glasklar*. Hanser Verlag ISBN 3-446-22575-7, 2004.

[9] R. Kamdem. *Contribution au Partitionement Materiel/Logiciel des Systemes Temps Reel pour les Applications de Controle d'Experiences*. PhD thesis, Univ de provence; France, 1999.

[10] Chris. F. Kemerer. An Empirical Validation of Software Cost Estmation Models. *ACM, Vol 30, Number 5 , pp. 416-429*, 1987.

[11] M. Marchesi. OOA Metrics for the UML. *Proc. of the 2nd Euromikro Conference on Software Maintenance and Reengineering*, 1998.

[12] M. C. McFarland. Using bottom-up design techniques in the synthesis of digital hardware from abstract behavioral descriptions, pp 474 - 480. *Annual ACM IEEE Design Automation Conference archive Proceedings of the 23rd ACM/IEEE conference on Design automation*, 1986.

[13] R. Niemann and P. Marwedel. Hardware/Software Partitioning Using Integer Programming. *IEEE/ACM Proc. of EDAC 96, pp 473-479*, 1996.

[14] C. A. Papachristou and W. Zhao. Architechtural Partitioning of Control Memory for Application Specific Programmable Processors. *Proceedings of the 1995 IEEE/ACM international conference on Computer-aided design, December 1995*, December 1995.

[15] R. Reissing. *Bewertung der Qualität objectorientierter Entwürfe*. PhD thesis, Uni Stuttgart; Germany, 2002.

[16] W. Rosenstiel, E. Barros, and X. Xion. A Method for Partitioning UNITY Language in Hardware and Software. *Proc. of The European Conf. on Design Automation*, 1994.

[17] F. Vahid and D.D. Gajski. Closeness metrics for system-level functional partitioning. *IEEE Proceding 1995, 328-333*, 1995.

[18] Tong Yi, Fangjun Wu, and Chengzhi Gan. A Comparison of Metrics for UML Class Diagrams. *ACM SIGSOFT, SE Notes, Vol 29, Number 5*, Sep 2004.

[19] K. M. Zuberi and K. G. Shin. Scheduling Messages on Controller Area Network for Real-Time CIM Applications. *IEEE Trans. Robotics and Automation, pp 310-314,*, April 1997.

TEMPORAL GRAPH PLACEMENT ON MESH-BASED COARSE GRAIN RECONFIGURABLE SYSTEMS USING THE SPECTRAL METHOD

Florian Dittmann
Heinz Nixdorf Institute, University Paderborn
Fuerstenallee 11, 33102 Paderborn, Germany
roichen@upb.de

Christophe Bobda
University of Erlangen-Nuremberg
Am Weichselgarten 3, 91058 Erlangen, Germany
christophe.bobda@informatik.uni-erlangen.de

Abstract: Coarse grain architectures need domain specific place and route methods. The existence of such methods provided, algorithms can be executed in time and space on the processing elements of coarse grain reconfigurable systems. Additionally, the short reconfiguration time and reduced power requirements comparing to FPGA makes coarse grain systems worth to be scrutinized as alternative execution platforms. By help of spectral methods, which target quadratic distance optimization of graphs, we can achieve short communication distances. This paper shows how to use the spectral method for efficiently scheduling processing elements of coarse grain reconfigurable devices by combining the spectral method and ASAP scheduling.

Keywords: Coarse Grain Reconfigurable Computing, Temporal Placement

1.   INTRODUCTION

The advent of multimedia into our life seems just to have started. We are surrounded by multiple electronic devices in every situation and independent of our location (sometimes referred to as nomadic computing). Presumably, the amount of services will even increase further. Yet, more services also means an increase in the amount of requirements, i. e., different/new protocols, decoding and encoding methods, compression techniques, etc. Due to often used advanced concepts, these requirements demand for special purpose hardware (e.g. ASICs), as general purpose processors often cannot meet the speed requirements. Reconfigurable systems, which facilitate the combination of the performance of ASICs and the flexibility of general purpose processors, seem to be worth to be scrutinized as an alternative.

Thereby, the realm of mobile devices often comprises power constraints. Power-intensive FPGAs as reconfigurable devices are only of limited value as processing units for mobile devices. Coarse grain reconfigurable architectures seem to be an alternative. They comprise path-widths greater than 1 bit, which enables more area-efficient operation. Additionally, they do not have such a huge routing area overhead and poor routability compared to FPGAs (Hartenstein, 1997). Further, coarse grained architectures provide operator level configurable function blocks, word level datapaths, and powerful and very area-efficient datapath routing switches. They are often used to speed up computational intensive loops (Hartenstein, 2001).

The limited routing capabilities of coarse grained devices demands for advanced compilation and mapping methods. Connections between random processing elements often is impossible. However, local connection facilities are often numerously available. In order to avoid additional computation delays due to poor routing, mapping algorithms should particularly target at short wire lengths. In this paper, we introduce an approach how to find a placement for mesh-like coarse grain reconfigurable architectures, which explicitly aims at nearby placement when the communication is intensive. Therefore, we use the spectral method as introduced by Hall, 1970. The quadratic objection of the spectral method is capable to reduces long wires.

The rest of this paper is organized as follows. We review related work, before we introduce our topology abstraction, including the modeling of the problem. In Section 4, we introduce the spectral method for data flow graphs. Section 5 shows how we combine the spectral method and ASAP scheduling to temporally place data flow graphs on the processing elements of coarse grain reconfigurable devices. Finally, we conclude.

2.   RELATED WORK

Coarse grain reconfigurable devices are not widespread. Consequently, their compilation, mapping and placement concepts are sparsely present in the literature.

Recent work in the area was done by Bansal et al., 2004, performing network topology exploration. The authors propose a consecutive place-

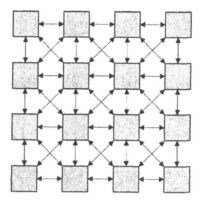

Figure 1. Topology abstraction of mesh-based coarse grain reconfigurable devices.

ment (topology traversal). The concept abstracts from heterogenous architectures and produces reasonable results. They do not focus on the possibility to reuse processing elements in directly succeeding cycles.

Lee et al., 2003 present a generic reconfigurable architecture targeting coarse grain architectures. They describe a compilation approach to manage the memory bottleneck that typically limits the performance of many applications. Their mapping flow comprises three steps, the first targets the processing elements mapping, the second operation grouping on processing element lines, and the third the arrangement of lines including stacking and time multiplexing.

Nageldinger, 2001 differentiates the necessary design steps for coarse grain reconfigurable architectures into *technology mapping, placement algorithm,* and *routing algorithm.* He summarizes known approaches and shows that some designers of coarse grain devices use manual placement (e. g. Singh et al., 2000; Miyamori and Olukotun, 1998), while others use heuristic methods like simulated annealing (e. g. Hartenstein and Kress, 1995; Ebeling et al., 1996). Most often, the place and route methods are target specific and require a lot of work put into to adapt to different reconfigurable devices. Seldom, topology abstraction is present.

3. TOPOLOGY ABSTRACTION

We consider coarse-grain reconfigurable architectures that consist of processing elements (PEs) connected in a mesh-like network topology (see Fig. 1). The PEs, which are represented as square boxes, are arranged in an equally spaced 2-D style. The double headed arrows denote data communication links between the PEs. We call this style a *grid* following Bansal et al., 2004.

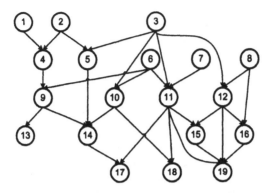

Figure 2.   Data flow graph

In coarse grain reconfigurable systems, often the reconfiguration can be done individually on every node, i. e., reconfiguration can take place partially and during run-time. The temporal assignment of tasks to nodes must be planned with respect to the whole period of this task including the communicating processing elements. Concerning internode communication, direct neighboring communication comprises the lowest costs and thus is most desirable.

We assume that every PE can hold its result as long as there arrive no new results. Thus, the storing of the results is independent of possible reconfigurations of the node. Additional memory for intermediate results is available externally. As the access of this memory is costly, we prefer the local storage. In particular, results stored externally must be saved to the memory bank as well as restored from this bank. We can avoid external storing, if succeeding nodes execute in the neighboring regions. The algorithm introduced below achieves this goal by using the spectral method.

4.   SPECTRAL METHOD

The spectral method as proposed by Hall, 1970 is originally suited for the layout of VLSI chips. Its inherent quadratic objective functions reduces wire lengths significantly. The result of placing elements on a 2-D area using the spectral method can be parameterized by weighting the connections. It is possible to extend the initial 2-D result to a 3-D version in order to introduce the temporal domain. Yet, the adding of a third axis increases the complexity and may lead into results that are difficult to handle. For example, we could derive a placement that is communication optimized and place the nodes referring to these results, while ignoring precedence constraints that would enforce a differ-

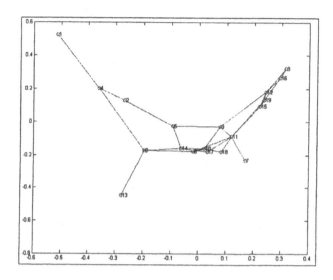

Figure 3.   Spectral placement of the data flow graph of Fig. 2

ent placement. Thus, we realize our placement strategy based on the 2-D version of the spectral method. The temporal domain is introduced by ASAP scheduling (see below). There already exists investigations of the spectral method for fine grained reconfigurable systems targeting temporal placement (Bobda, 2003).

As input for our approach we need a graphical representation G of the algorithm, as displayed in Fig. 2. The vertices V of this graph G represent tasks that can be mapped on one processing element. The edges E denote the connections, i. e., internode dependencies like precedence constraints. The pure communication optimized spectral placement is achieved without referring to additional parameters of the input graphs, i. e., different execution times or precedence constraints can be considered later. Yet, there exist variants to include execution time similarities into the spectral placement (Bobda, 2003). In this work, we use the basic spectral method only.

Fig. 3 shows the results of the spectral placement of the data flow graph G of Fig. 2. If our reconfigurable device is large enough, we can place the whole graph by assigning the top left node to the top left PE and so on. Yet, in most cases, the graph does not fit completely on the device. Thus, the temporal functionality (dynamic reconfiguration) must be used to execute the graph over time. We use this placement of the input graph and derive an appropriate temporal placement method

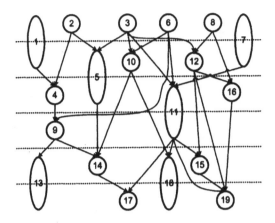

Figure 4. ASAP schedule of the graph.

in the next section. Thereby, the results of the spectral method are valuable information to keep wire lengths short.

The mathematical background comprises the following: We represent the input graph as the Laplacian matrix B, derived from the connection matrix C and the degree matrix D $(B = D - C)$. The spectral method minimizes the sum of squared distances between the nodes $R = X_1^T B X_1 + X_2^T B X_2 + \ldots + X_k^T B X_k$ subject to $X_1^T X_1 = X_2^T X_2 = \ldots = X_k^T X_k = 1$. To solve these equations, we apply the Lagrange multiplier method with the k Lagrange multipliers $\lambda_1, \lambda_2, \ldots, \lambda_k$. The solution are the Eigenvectors associated to the k smallest non zero Eigenvalues. The Eigenvectors place the vertices in space.

5.   TEMPORAL PLACEMENT

We show the concept by referring to the data flow graph of Fig. 2. As processing platform, we assume a coarse grain reconfigurable device consisting of homogenous processing elements. The network topology is as displayed in Fig. 1. Without loss of generality, we reduce the amount of PE to nine in this example.

Fig. 4 shows the data flow graph in some more detail. We have arranged the vertices in ASAP (as soon as possible) style, respecting different execution times, as we want to schedule and place such vertices comprising different execution times. The ASAP scheduling introduces the temporal dimension to the problem by defining execution levels for each node. Due to the precedence constraints and different execution times, we derive six levels in this example.

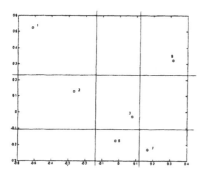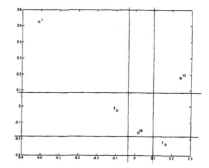

Figure 5.   Spectral placement and pro-   *Figure 6.*   Spectral placement and processing element assignment of level 1.   cessing element assignment of level 2.

In the following, we combine the results of the ASAP scheduling and the spectral placement to efficiently place the nodes on the PE of the reconfigurable device.

We select the vertices and their coordinates of level 1 in the spectral placement of the data flow graph. Their distances respect their closeness in terms of input for later nodes of the graph. Thus, we use this information to assign the vertices to the PEs. The placement is realized by a consecutively assignment. We start with the node comprising the smallest x and largest y values (top-left corner). This node is placed in the top-left corner of the reconfigurable device. We continue with this procedure until the node comprising the largest x and smallest y values is reached. Fig. 5 shows how the vertices of level 1 are assigned to the processing elements.

When scheduling the next level, we have to take care of vertices that have already started with their execution in the previous level. These nodes must not be placed to different processing elements. Additionally, their location acts as an indicator for placing close nodes of the ASAP scheduling in proximity, as far distributed results would foil the intended reduction of communication achieved by the spectral method.

Thus, the procedure is as follows: We extract the corresponding vertices of the level 2 from the communication optimized spectral placement of the data flow graph (refer to Fig. 6). We first lock the already placed vertices to their location (node 1 and 7). Then, we fill the gaps (speaking in terms of free PEs between locked PEs) by assigning the remaining vertices of level 2. The selection of the PE is done as above, i.e., evaluating the x and y location of the vertices. Finally, we achieve a PE assignment that respects the assignment of the previous level and serves

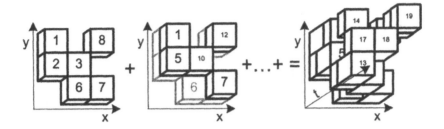

Figure 7.   Combination of micro level placement.

as solid basis for the next level due to the PE assignment referring to
the spectral placement of the whole graph.

If this PE assignment is continued, we achieve an amount of so called
micro levels, which comprise a valid placement each. The dependencies
due to the spectral method guarantees short communication distance
from one to the next level. When combining the placed levels, we derive
a complete schedule as displayed in Fig. 7. Thereby, different execution
times of the nodes result in different heights of the boxes (nodes) in
the final schedule. The results gained are valuable for a configuration
scheduler for the coarse grain device.

Due to using the spectral quadratic wire length optimized placement,
we achieve direct neighbor connections or connections to the same processing element in the next micro level in majority. For the exemplary
data flow graph, Fig. 8 shows the connections. We have mapped all levels into the figure, i.e., all vertices mapped to the same PE are displayed
in the corresponding square box. As an additional result, we derive PEs
that will not be used during execution of the data flow graph.

In this exemplary description, the amount of PEs is in the range of
the amount of vertices each level. In detail, there are always enough
PE to hold all possible nodes of each level and directly derive a valid
schedule. In order to overcome this limitation, we extend our placement
as follows:

If there are always twice as much PEs than vertices per level, we combine two levels to be placed together. This aggregation can be continued
with all integer multiples of the amount of PEs. Thereby, we can often
increase the proximity of vertices comprising internode communication
resulting in more efficient execution.

In order to overcome the opposite limitation, where the amount of
nodes each level is larger than the amount of available PEs, we can split
each level into sub-levels, which each encloses the maximum amount
of nodes. Depending on the individual cases, the intermediate results

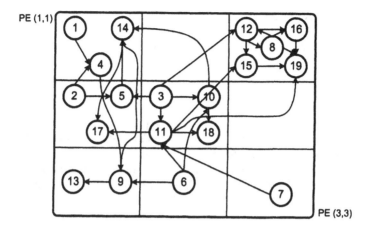

Figure 8.   Internode connection.

might have to be stored externally, increasing the costs. We prefer another option, where we form subproblems, which comprise each a cluster of nodes that are strongly connected. The clusters can be formed independent of the levels by referring to the spectral placement and applying a cluster growth method (Alpert and Kahng, 1994). Then, we start the temporal PE assignment on the nodes of these clusters separately using the method described above.

6.   CONCLUSION

In this paper, we have presented how to use the spectral method for placement on coarse grain reconfigurable systems. The method suits the limited routing capabilities of the devices very well. Using as soon as possible scheduling allows us to effectively introduce the temporal domain into spectral method based placement. The ASAP scheduling thereby enables us to select a sub-amount of the spectral placed vertices. The PE assignment takes place with respect to previously scheduled nodes. Thus, the flexibility, i.e., temporal adaptation of the processing elements of coarse grain reconfigurable devices is achieved with optimized wire length. Finally, we yield a schedule that can reduce the execution time, which otherwise often is negatively impacted by poor routing, i.e., routing that must traverse several processing elements before reaching the data sink.

In the future, we plan to extend the placement in order to reduce waiting cycles due to complicated memory access of coarse grain reconfigurable systems.

Acknowledgements

This work was partly funded by the *Deutsche Forschungsgemeinschaft (SPP 1148)*.

REFERENCES

Alpert, C. J. and Kahng, A. B. (1994). Multi-way partitioning via spacefilling curves and dynamic programming. In *DAC '94: Proceedings of the 31st annual conference on Design automation*, pages 652–657. ACM Press.

Bansal, Nikhil, Gupta, Sumit, Dutt, Nikil, Nicolau, Alex, and Gupta, Rajesh (2004). Network Topology Exploration of Mesh-Based Coarse-Grain Reconfigurable Architectures. In *Proceedings of the DATE*, Paris, France.

Bobda, Christophe (2003). *Synthesis of Dataflow Graphs for Reconfigurable Systems using Temporal Partitioning and Temporal Placement*. PhD thesis, University Paderborn, Heinz Nixdorf Institute.

Ebeling, Carl, Cronquist, Darren C., and Franklin, Paul (1996). RaPiD - Reconfigurable Pipelined Datapath. In *FPL '96: Proceedings of the 6th International Workshop on Field-Programmable Logic, Smart Applications, New Paradigms and Compilers*, pages 126–135. Springer-Verlag.

Hall, Kenneth M. (1970). An r-dimensional Quadratic Placement Algorithm. *Managment Science*, 17(3):219–229.

Hartenstein, Reiner (2001). A Decade of Reconfigurable Computing: a Visionary Retrospective. In *Proceedings of the Conference on Design, Automation and Test in Europe (DATE 01)*.

Hartenstein, Reiner W. (1997). The Microprocessor is no more General Purpose: why Future Reconfigurable Platforms will win. In *Proceedings of the International Conference on Innovative Systems in Silicon, ISIS'97*, Austin, Texas, USA. IEEE Computer Society. Invited Paper.

Hartenstein, Reiner W. and Kress, Rainer (1995). A datapath synthesis system for the reconfigurable datapath architecture. In *Proceedings of the 1995 conference on Asia Pacific design automation (ASP-DAC'95)*, page 77, Makuhari, Chiba, Japan. ACM Press.

Lee, Jong-eun, Choi, Kiyoung, and Dutt, Nikil D. (2003). Compilation Approach for Coarse-Grained Reconfigurable Architectures. *IEEE Design & Test of Computers*, 20(1):26–33.

Miyamori, Takashi and Olukotun, Kunle (1998). REMARC: Reconfigurable Multimedia Array Coprocessor (Abstract). In *FPGA*, page 261.

Nageldinger, Ulrich (2001). *Coarse-Grained Reconfigurable Architecture Design Space Exploration*. PhD thesis, University of Kaiserslautern, CS department (Informatik).

Singh, Hartej, Lee, Ming-Hau, Lu, Guangming, Bagherzadeh, Nader, Kurdahi, Fadi J., and Filho, Eliseu M. Chaves (2000). MorphoSys: An Integrated Reconfigurable System for Data-Parallel and Computation-Intensive Applications. *IEEE Trans. Comput.*, 49(5):465–481.

OFF-LINE PLACEMENT OF TASKS ONTO RECONFIGURABLE HARDWARE CONSIDERING GEOMETRICAL TASK VARIANTS

Klaus Danne[*], Sven Stühmeier
*University of Paderborn, Germany, *funded by DFG Graduate College 776*

Abstract: We consider off-line task placement onto reconfigurable hardware devices (RHDs), which are increasingly used in embedded systems. The tasks are modelled as three dimensional boxes given by their footprint times execution time which results into a three dimensional orthogonal packing problem. Unlike other approaches, we allow several alternative implementation variants for each task, which enables better placements. We apply modified heuristic methods from chip floorplanning to select and place the task variants. Our method computes a set of pareto placement solutions with the objectives to minimize the total execution time and the amount of required RHD area. We have evaluated the placement quality in first simulation experiments.

1. INTRODUCTION

Reconfigurable hardware devices (RHD), such as the prominent field-programmable gate array (FPGA) or coarse grain devises [1], are general-purpose devices that can be (re-)programmed after fabrication. SRAM-based FPGA variants can be reconfigured arbitrarily often, opening up the way to FPGA based computing. For a number of embedded applications, RHDs have been shown to outperform general-purpose processors, and even specialized processors [2]. Often the processing elements of RHDs are arranged as two dimensional arrays which can be reprogrammed (partially) during runtime. Therefore their resources can be reused for differed tasks over time. As modern devices have high densities, several tasks can be mapped onto the device at the same time, enabling true parallel execution. Combined, these features enable multi-tasking in space (e.g. parallel executed tasks) and time (e.g. sequentially executed tasks).

Placement and scheduling of task onto RHDs has attracted wide attention, e.g. in [3–5]. Surprisingly, most authors assume that the tasks

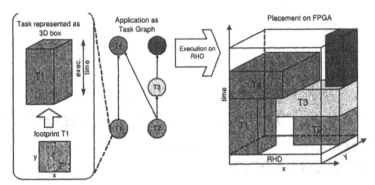

Figure 1.   Placement of a task graph onto a RHD

have a fix rectangular shaped footprint given by *width × length* and an unknown or fix execution time. The problem remains to place the tasks, which are represented by three dimensional objects *footprint × execution time*, into a three dimensional container, given by the RHD array dimensions and the time dimension (see Figure 1).

In contrast to the model with fix tasks, we consider that several implementation variants for each task may exist, differing in the dimensions *width, length* and *execution time*. The problem is now given by selecting a proper variant for each task, assigning an position on the RHD and assigning a start time. The two objectives that should be optimized are the amount of required FPGA area and the total execution time of the task graph. Truly, the option to select variants for each task enlarges the design space, which enables new (potentially better) solutions. Also the problem gets more computational intensive, which makes optimal solving hopeless for a reasonable number of tasks. Therefore, we adopt heuristics form integrated circuit floorplanning. Specifically, we apply a bipartitioning method using slicing trees [6].

In Section 2 we formalize the our placement problem and defines valid solutions. Section 3 describes the applied placement method in detail. In Section 4 we report on first results and conclude the paper in Section 5.

2.   PROBLEM MODELLING

We consider an application modeled as a directed acyclic task graph $G = (V, A)$, which consist of vertices V representing the task set $V = \{T_1, \ldots, T_n\}$ and directed arcs $A \subseteq V \times V$ where an arc $a_{i,k} = (T_i, T_k)$ represents an order constraints between the tasks T_i and T_k. For each task, a set of implementation variants exist $T_i = \{T_{i,1}, T_{i,2} \ldots \}$. Each variant $T_{i,k}$ is characterized by its footprint dimensions $x_{i,k} = x(T_{i,k})$ and $y_{i,k} = y(T_{i,k})$ which it occupies on the RHD when being executed, and by its execution time $t_{i,k} = t(T_{i,k})$. We assume, that the set of variants of each task T_i is a pareto set. I.e. for any given task variant

$T_{i,k} \in T_i$, no other task variant $T_{i,l}$ exists that has less or equal values in all three dimensions x, y and t than $T_{i,k}$.

Problem Definition. For a given task graph G, find a *selection function* $f : V \rightarrow \bigcup_{i=1}^{n} T_i$, which selects a variant for each task, and a *placement function* $p : V \rightarrow \mathbf{N}^3$, which assign an position for each task.

The placement function assigns x, y and t coordinates to each task by $p_x(T_i)$, $p_y(T_i)$ and $p_t(T_i)$. These coordinates define the starting time and the position onto the RHD of the front left vertex of the selected variant $T_{i,f(T_i)}$. Consequently, the placed variant occupies the RHD in x dimension from $p_x(T_i)$ to $p_x(T_i) + x(f(T_i))$, in the y dimension from $p_y(T_i)$ to $p_y(T_i) + y(f(T_i))$ and in the time dimension from $p_t(T_i)$ to $p_t(T_i) + t(f(T_i))$.

Valid solution. A valid solution for a graph G is a selection function f and a placement function p, such that the following predicates hold:

- f selects only existing task variants, i.e. $\forall T_i \in V : f(T_i) \in T_i$

- p places the task variants in such a way, that their three dimensional visualizations do not intersect (see Figure 1). This is the fact, iff all pairs of tasks are in series (non overlapping) either in the x, y or t dimension, which is expressed by equation 1.

$$\forall (T_i, T_k) \in V^2 : T_i \neq T_k \Rightarrow d_{i,k}^x \vee d_{i,k}^y \vee d_{i,k}^t \qquad (1)$$

$$d_{i,k}^x = [p_x(T_i) > p_x(T_k) + x(f(T_k))] \vee [p_x(T_i) + x(f(T_i)) < p_x(T_k)]$$
$$d_{i,k}^y = [p_y(T_i) > p_y(T_k) + y(f(T_k))] \vee [p_y(T_i) + y(f(T_i)) < p_y(T_k)]$$
$$d_{i,k}^t = [p_t(T_i) > p_t(T_k) + t(f(T_k))] \vee [p_t(T_i) + t(f(T_i)) < p_t(T_k)]$$

- no precedence constraints are violated:
$$\forall a_{i,k} \in A : (p_t(T_i) + t(f(T_i)) \leq p_t(T_k)) \qquad (2)$$

3. PLACEMENT METHOD

This section presents the method we use to find a good *selection* and *placement* of task variants of the input graph G. These is done in two phases. In the *partitioning phase*, a placement topology is created. We partition the three dimensional container given by the RHD array dimensions and the time dimension hierarchically into *rooms*, until one room for every task of V exist. This defines the relative position among the tasks, e.g T_1 will be placed left from T_2 in x dimension and in front of T_3 in y dimension. In the *sizing phase*, we compute the possible sizes of every room and finally the possible sizes of the entire container. We

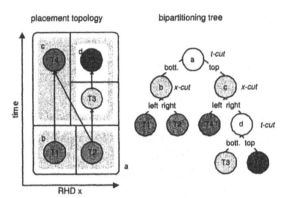

Figure 2.   Placement topology and corresponding bipartitioning tree

chose the container size that minimizes our cost function and derive the variant selection f and the absolute task positions p.

3.1   Placement Topology by Bipartitioning

The partitioning phase creates a placement topology, that defines the relative position of every task. We restrict the placement topologies to topologies, which can be generated by a bipartitioning process. These are called *slicing placement topologies* (in the style of [6]). Figure 2 shows an example of a 2-dimensional slicing placement topology on the left side, and the corresponding bipartitioning tree on the right side. The initial placement is represented by an empty rectangle (room) labeled by a, which has the entire task set assigned $a = V$. The task set of room a is partitioned into two sub-rooms b and c by a horizontal cut and c is defined to be on top of b in the time dimension. Then, room b is cut into two sub-rooms by a vertical cut. This recursive cutting process stops, when an exclusive room for every task exists. The bipartitioning tree on the right side of Figure 2 fully defines the relative placement topology of the left side of Figure 2. Each tree node represents a room and its two direct child nodes represent the sub-rooms created by a cut. The leave nodes represent the final rooms, which hold only one task each. The labels at nodes define the cut *orientation* and the labels at the edges define the cut *order*. The orientation defines along which axis the room is sliced into sub-rooms and can be either vertical *(x-cut)* or horizontal *(t-cut)*. The order of the cut defines the order of the two sub-rooms in the corresponding dimension and is labeled with {*left, right*} for x-cuts or {*top, bottom*} for t-cuts respectively. Since in our placement problem we generally consider 3-dimensional objects, we define additional the *(y-cut)* orientation with the ordering labels {*front, back*}.

When the bipartitioning tree is created to define the relative placement for a given input task graph G, three heuristic decisions have to be made for every cut. 1.) the node's task set has to be partitioned into the two subsets for the two child nodes. 2.) the orientation of the cut has to be defined. 3.) the relative order of the child nodes in the cut dimension has to be defined.

In the circuit layout, the partitioning into two subsets has usually the first goal to place heavily connected circuit blocks close together, while the second goal is generate sub-rooms of about the same size. Up to now, our model does not consider communication cost among the tasks and we only modeled precedence constraints which correspond to some communication. In future work, we will improve our model to consider communication costs and minimize these during the partitioning process. Until then, we make the partitioning only on basis of the size of the tasks in order to keep the sub-rooms of about the same size. Therefore, we define the average size of a task $\bar{S}(T_i)$ as the average over the product of the dimensions of all variants: $\bar{S}(T_i) = \sum_{k=1}^{m=|T_i|} \frac{x_{i,k} \times y_{i,k} \times t_{i,k}}{m}$. When the task set $V(a)$ of a room a should be partitioned into $V(b)$ and $V(c)$, we sort the tasks into a queue in order of decreasing average size. The first task of the queue is assigned to $V(b)$. After that, we keep assigning tasks from the queue to $V(c)$ until the size of $V(c)$ exceeds the size of $V(b)$. Then, we stop assigning tasks to $V(c)$ and start to assign tasks to $V(b)$ until the size of $V(b)$ exceeds the size of $V(c)$ and so on. The procedure terminates when the queue is empty and returns two partitions with about the same size.

The decision concerning the orientation and order of a cut can be made during the partitioning phase when the bipartitioning tree is created or can be made later during the sizing phase. We call that *oriented parti-tioning* and *unoriented partitioning* respectively. When these decisions are made in the fist phase, all nodes and edges of the tree get labeled with orientation and order labels respectively and the tree defines an *oriented ordered placement topology* like in the example in Figure 2. When these decisions are made in the sizing phase, the result of the partition-ing phase is an unlabeled tree which defines an *unoriented placement topology*. Considering the example of Figure 2, an unoriented placement topology would define that e.g. task T_1 and T_2 have a common border, but it is neither defined in which dimension the tasks are side by side nor in which order.

Respecting precedence constraints.   When precedence constrains among tasks have to be respected, the orientation and order of the cuts do matter. Let r_1 be a parent room that gets partitioned into r_2 and r_3. Obviously, an order constraints $a_{i,k} = (T_i, T_k)$ is satisfied, when room r_1 with $T_i, T_k \in r_1$ gets partitioned by a t-cut and r_2 with $T_i \in r_2$ becomes the *bottom* room and r_3 with $T_k \in r_3$ the *top* room. The example in Figure 2 shows, that all dependency arcs among tasks are crossed by an t-cut. The precedence constrains modify our goal of the partitioning process. The first goal remains to slice a parent room r_1 into child rooms r_2, r_3 of about equal size. The second goal is, that their should be either no precedence edge being cut and we let the cut orientation *unoriented* or a maximum of precedence edges should be cut, all in the same direction (e.g from r_2 to r_3), and the cut is defined to be an *t-cut* (e.g. with r_2 being the bottom and r_3 the top room). Currently we use a simple heuristic strategy, where we archive an balanced initial bipartitioning as described above. If precedence edges in both directions have been cut, we modify the partitioning by moving tasks from one side to the other in order to find a partitioning with only edges being cut in one direction. In future work, we plan to use more goal oriented approaches like modified versions of the Kerninghan-Lin [5] and Fiduccia-Mattheyses heuristics that where adapted to directed graphs.

3.2   Sizing of the Placement Topology

The sizing phase takes the relative placement topology in form of bipartitioning tree of the first phase as input and computes an absolute position and size of every room, including the size of the container. Since in general there exist several variants for each task, there exist several variants for every room as well. To be able to compute the variants of a room resulting from the variants of its two sub-rooms, we define (similar to the sizing step functions used in circuit layout [6]) a sizing function for each task and room. In the two dimensional case, the sizing function of a task $s_{T_i} : \mathbf{R} \to \mathbf{R}$ is a monotonically decreasing step function of x, where $s_{T_i}(x)$ is the minimum of the execution times of all task variants that have a width smaller or equal to x (eq. 3). Figure 3(a) shows an example of a sizing function for the 2-dimensional case.

In the 3-dimensional case, $s_{T_i} : \mathbf{R} \times \mathbf{R} \to \mathbf{R}$ is a piecewise constant function, where $s_{T_i}(x,y)$ is the minimum of the execution times of all task variants with dimensions less or equal then x and y (eq. 4).

$$s_{T_i}(x) = \min_{\{T_{i,k} \in T_i | x_{i,k} \leq x\}} t_{i,k} \tag{3}$$

$$s_{T_i}(x,y) = \min_{\{T_{i,k} \in T_i | x_{i,k} \leq x \wedge y_{i,k} \leq y\}} t_{i,k} \tag{4}$$

The sizing functions of any other room can be computed based on the sizing functions of its two child nodes and as consequents the sizing function of the root node can be computed bottom up. The sizing of oriented and unoriented placement topologies have to be distinguished.

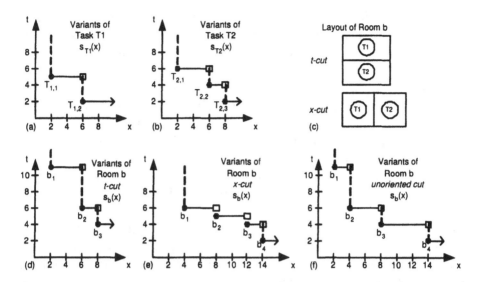

Figure 3. Sizing function tasks T_1 (a) and T_2 (b), possible room layouts (c) and the resulting sizing function s_b of room b for an *t-cut* (d), an *x-cut* (e) and an *unoriented-cut* (f) respectively.

Sizing oriented ordered placement topologies. In the case of oriented ordered placement topologies, the cut orientation of a room in its two sub-rooms is already defined. Let $r1$ be a room that is sliced by a *t-cut* into $r2$ and $r3$, than we obtain the sizing function of r_1 by summing the sizing functions of its child nodes (eq. 5). Figure 3(d) shows the sizing function resulting from adding the sizing function of Figure 3(a) and (b). In case of an *x-cut*, the inverse of the sizing function of $r1$ is the sum of the inverse sizing function of $r2$ and the inverse sizing function of $r3$ (eq. 6). This is illustrated in Figure 3(e).

$$s_{r1} = s_{r2} + s_{r3} \qquad \text{for t-cut} \qquad (5)$$
$$s_{r1}^{-1} = s_{r2}^{-1} + s_{r3}^{-1} \qquad \text{for x-cut} \qquad (6)$$

Note, that in the algorithmic implementation, the sizing function of each task is stored only as its list of variants sorted by x. In the same way the sizing function of any room is stored as a variant list which represents the pareto points of the continuous sizing function. When two sizing functions have to be added as result of a *t-cut*, both lists a processed by a linear scan in x direction and combined to new variants of the parent room. The same is done in t direction in case of an *x-cut* respectively.

In the 3-dimensional case, where the variants are triples, the inverse of a sizing function is not well defined. In case of an *t-cut* we still obtain the sizing function of a room by summing up the sizing functions of the child nodes $(s_{r1}(x,y) = s_{r2}(x,y) + s_{r3}(x,y))$. In case of an *x-cut*, the sizing functions of the child nodes $s_{r2}(x, y)$ and $s_{r2}(x, y)$ are flipped along the $x = t$ plain, summed up and the result is again flipped along the $x = t$ plain to obtain $s_{r1}(x, y)$. The same is done with the $y = t$ plain for an y-cut respectively.

In our algorithmic implementation we store each sizing function as a list of triples $(t_{i,k}, x_{i,k}, y_{i,k})$. Since no total order is defined on the variants in the 3-dimensional case, we combine all variants of the first child with all of the second child. In a second step, we remove all non pareto optimal variants.

The first part of the sizing phase is finished, when the sizing function of the root node of the bipartitioning tree has been computed.

Sizing unoriented placement topologies.   When the orientation of the cuts is left undefined, the placement topology describes a larger set of actual placements then in the oriented case. When combining the variants of two child rooms to the variants of the parent room, we have to consider all possible cut orientations. Therefore, we compute the sizing functions of a room r for a t-cut,x-cut and y-cut as described for the oriented placement topologies. Then, the sizing function of r for the unoriented case $s_r^{unor.-cut}$ is defined as the minimum over its sizing functions for every possible cut orientation (eq. 7). Figure 3(e) shows an example of a sizing function for an unoriented cut in the 2-dimensional case.

$$s_r^{unor.-cut}(x, y) = \min\left(s_r^{t-cut}(x, y), s_r^{x-cut}(x, y), s_r^{y-cut}(x, y)\right) \quad (7)$$

In the algorithmic implementation, we compute the minimum by joining the three variant lists for the different cut orientations of r and remove the non pareto variants. The unoriented placement topology clearly leads to better variants of a room and therefore improves the placement quality. This comes at the cost of computational complexity, since the variant lists for the rooms contain more elements.

3.3   Deriving Selection and Placement Function

When the possible variants of the container have been computed, that is the sizing function of the root node, we select the variant that minimizes our cost function, e.g. the variant with smallest $t \times x$, or $t \times x \times y$ in the 3-dimensional case respectively. This immediately determines the selection of the variants of the two child nodes *child1* and *child2*, since we store which variants of *child1* and *child2* are responsible for which variant of *root* during the recursive sizing process described above. Therefore, when we reach the leafs of the tree in a top down fashion, we obtain the selection function $f(T_i)$ for every task.

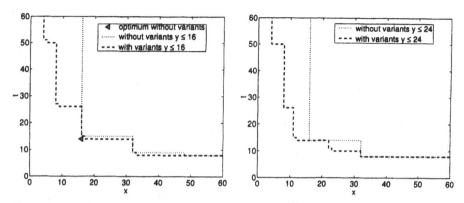

Figure 4. 2-dim. projection of the computed sizing function for the DE benchmark with and without additional task variants.

To complete the solution, the placement function $p(T_i)$ has to be defined. Therefore, we define the position of each room (each node of the tree) in a top down fashion, until the tasks positions are defined. To be able to do so, the bipartitioning tree has to be oriented and ordered. As mentioned before, the cut orientation is defined either during the partitioning phase or in the sizing phase. In our current model, the cut order does not influence the quality of the placement and is chosen randomly.

The position of the container (root node) is initialized to $p_t(root) = 0, p_x(root) = 0, p_y(root) = 0$. The position of each child node with order *bottom*, *left* or *front* is always equal to the position of its parent node and independent of the cut orientation. The position of each *top*, *right* or *back* child node is equal to the position of the parent node, except in the cut dimension: In cut dimension the size of the neighbor node is added to the position of the parent node. E.g. the position of room d of Figure 2 would be $p_t(d) = p_t(c)$ and $p_x(d) = p_x(c) + x(f(T_4))$, since room c is sliced by an x-cut.

4. EXPERIMENTAL RESULTS

As a first test, we applied our method to the DE benchmark application used in [3]. The application is an task graph with 11 nodes consisting of multiply and ALU-operations, which numerically solves a differential equation. In [3], every multiplier was modeled by an 16 times 16 rectangle of FPGA cells using 2 clock cycles ($x_i = 16, y_i = 16, t_i = 2$) and the ALU operations where assumed to occupy $x_k = 16 \times y_k = 1$ cells taking $t_i = 1$ clock cycle. Using the unmodified task graph, our algorithm computed a sizing function consisting of 15 different variants. After introducing 14 different variants for the multiplier tasks as well as for the adder task, our method computed 118 different variants for the overall design. Figure 4 shows both sizing functions as two-dimensional projections, where y is given as parameter for the cases $y \leq 16$ and $y \leq 24$. It can be seen, that the sizing function of the task set with variants introduces more and better design alternatives. The left figure shows also an optimal placement $t = 14, x = y = 16$ taken from [3], which our method came close to, but missed it by one unit in either x or t dimension. We plan to evaluate the quality of the method on a larger set of benchmark applications in future work.

5.   CONCLUSION

In contrast to previous work in the field of RHD task placement, we presented a model that allows several alternative implementations for each task and therefore enables *better* solutions for the placement problem . These variants can be archived by synthesizing the tasks with several footprint constraints and by providing different register transfer level descriptions (e.g. parallel multiplier, bit serial multiplier) for each task. To attack the problem, we adopted algorithms used in floorplanning of integrated circuits, which where extended to the three-dimensional case to consider RHD resource sharing over time. The advantages of our method are, that it 1) considers an enlarged design space, 2) can be applied to task graphs of large size and 3) that not only one solution, but a set of pareto optimal solutions is computed at once. Our first experimental results have shown the applicability of our approach. Improvements and further evaluation on larger benchmarks will be subject of our further work.

REFERENCES

[1] R. Hartenstein. A decade of reconfigurable computing: a visionary retrospective. In *DATE '01: Proceedings of the conference on Design, automation and test in Europe*, pages 642–649. IEEE Press, 2001.

[2] Katherine Compton and Scott Hauck. Reconfigurable computing: a survey of systems and software. *ACM Comput. Surv.*, 34(2):171–210, 2002.

[3] S. P. Fekete, E. Köhler, and J. Teich. Optimale FPGA module placement with temporal precedence constraints. In *Proc. DATE 2001, Design, Automation and Test in Europe*, pages 658–665, Munich, Germany, March 13-16 2001. IEEE Computer Society Press.

[4] K. Bazargan, R. Kastner, and M. Sarrafzadeh. Fast template placement for reconfigurable computing systems. *IEEE Design and Test of Computers*, pages 68–83, March 2000.

[5] Christophe Bobda. *Synthesis of Dataflow Graphs for Reconfigurable Systems using Temporal Partitioning and Temporal Placement*. Dissertation, Universität Paderborn, Heinz Nixdorf Institut, Entwurf Paralleler Systeme, 2003. Euro 35,-, ISBN 3-935433-37-9.

[6] Thomas Lengauer. *Combinatorial Algorithms for Integrated Circuit Layout*. John Wiley, 1990.